중등 필수 영문법 +
객관식·서술형 드릴 및
실전문제 풀이

핵심 영문법 복습 +
서술형 유형별/단계별
집중 훈련

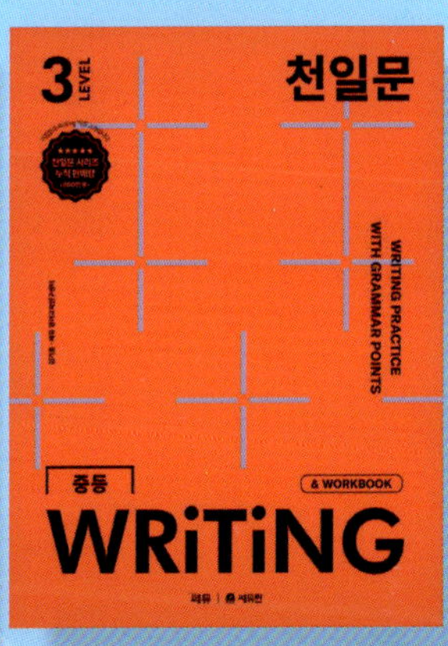

<천일문 중등 WRITING>은 <거침없이 Writing>의 개정 교재입니다.

✳ 연계 학습 예시 *뒷장의 Syllabus를 확인해 보세요.

천일문 중등 GRAMMAR LEVEL 2	POINT
Chapter 01 문장의 주요 형식	
Unit 1 SVC/SVOO	1~2
Unit 2 SVOC – 목적격보어의 종류	3~7
Chapter 02 시제	
Unit 1 현재, 과거, 미래 & 진행형	1~4

천일문 중등 WRITING LEVEL 2	POINT
Chapter 01 문장의 주요 형식	
Unit 1 SVC(2형식)/SVOO(4형식)	1~2
Unit 2 SVOC(5형식)	3~5
Chapter 02 시제	
Unit 1 현재, 과거, 미래 & 진행형	1~2

• 권별 목차가 연계되어 있어 <천일문 중등 GRAMMAR> 학습 후 <천일문 중등 WRITING>으로 서술형 집중 훈련이 가능합니다.
• <천일문 중등 WRITING>은 서술형 내신 기출문제 분석에 초점을 맞춰 내용을 구성하여, <천일문 중등 GRAMMAR> 구성과는 약간의 차이가 있을 수 있습니다.

펴낸이   김기훈 김진희

펴낸곳   ㈜쎄듀/서울시 강남구 논현로 305 (역삼동)

발행일   2024년 11월 1일 초판 1쇄

내용 문의   www.cedubook.com

구입 문의   콘텐츠 마케팅 사업본부

       Tel. 02-6241-2007

       Fax. 02-2058-0209

등록번호   제22-2472호

ISBN   978-89-6806-444-9

       978-89-6806-442-5(SET)

CEDU(쎄듀)는 A **C**omprehensive **E**nglish e**DU**cation(종합적 영어교육)의 약자입니다.

천일문

WRITING PRACTICE
WITH GRAMMAR POINTS

2 LEVEL

중등

WRiTiNG

저자

김기훈

現 ㈜쎄듀 대표이사

現 메가스터디 영어영역 대표강사

前 서울특별시 교육청 외국어 교육정책자문위원회 위원

저서 천일문 〈STARTER·입문편·기본편·핵심편·완성편〉 / 천일문 중등 GRAMMAR
리딩그라피 / 리딩 플랫폼 / 리딩 릴레이 / Reading Q / Listening Q
미리 수능 영어 / 천일문 VOCA / 쓰작 / 잘 풀리는 영문법
어휘끝 / 어법끝 / 첫단추 / 파워업 / ALL쓸 서술형
수능영어 절대유형 시리즈 / 수능실감 등

쎄듀 영어교육연구센터

쎄듀 영어교육연구센터는 영어 콘텐츠에 대한 전문지식과 경험을 바탕으로
최고의 교육 콘텐츠를 만들고자 최선의 노력을 다하는 전문가 집단입니다.

인지영 수석연구원 · **최세림** 선임연구원 · **홍세라** 연구원 · **전진영** 연구원 · **박소민** 연구원

교재 개발에 도움을 주신 분들

김경희 선생님(미카영어)　　**김은정** 선생님(일산 이제이 잉글리쉬)　　**김정미** 선생님(앰버랩영어교습소)
김지연 선생님(송도탑영어학원)　　**박혜선** 선생님(써니잉글리쉬)　　**방성모** 선생님(방성모영어학원)
이동현 선생님(쎔마스터입시학원)　　**이화연** 선생님(써니사이드학원)　　**전혜경** 선생님(JHK영어)
정지안 선생님(쎔영어수학학원)　　**조양희** 선생님(뮤엠영어 신도림동아점)

마케팅　　　콘텐츠 마케팅 사업본부
영업　　　　문병구
제작　　　　정승호
인디자인 편집　올댓에디팅
표지 디자인　모스그래픽
내지 디자인　스튜디오에딩크
일러스트　　박아름
영문교열　　James Clayton Sharp

Foreword

많은 학생이 영문법을 공부한 후 객관식 문항은 순조롭게 풀다가도 서술형만 만나면 멈칫하는 순간을 경험합니다. 감으로 풀거나 답을 찍는 요령이 통하지 않거니와, 문법 단순 암기에서 한 단계 나아가 표현하고자 하는 영어 문장을 자유자재로 써낼 정도로 체득해야 문제없이 쓸 수 있기 때문입니다. 따라서 서술형 문제들은 만점 정복의 가장 결정적인 승부 포인트라 할 수 있으며 그 중요성이 날이 갈수록 강조되고 있습니다.

〈천일문 중등 WRITING〉은 〈거침없이 Writing〉의 개정판으로, 초판 교재의 특장점은 유지함과 동시에 〈천일문 중등 GRAMMAR〉와 브랜드를 통일시켜 목차 연계성을 더 높였습니다. 단순한 쓰기 형태의 문제만 모은 형식적인 대비서가 되는 것을 지양하고, 서술형을 명확한 타깃으로 삼아 최적의 학습 방향과 실질적 효과를 제공하도록 심혈을 기울였습니다.

새로워진 〈천일문 중등 WRITING〉의 특장점을 소개합니다.

+1 최신 개정 교육과정 반영 및 전국 내신 서술형 기출 문제 완벽 분석

새롭게 최신 2022 개정 교육과정을 반영했으며, 총 10,000여 개의 내신 서술형 문제를 수집하여 가장 많이 출제되는 포인트 중심으로 학습하도록 구성했습니다. 학습 포인트 별로 자주 등장하는 서술형 기출 유형까지 포함하여 실전 대비에 최적화된 훈련이 가능합니다.

+2 <천일문 중등 GRAMMAR>와 연계되는 핵심 문법 설명과 단계별 서술형 문항 수록

〈천일문 중등 GRAMMAR〉와 연계 학습이 가능하도록 서술형 대비에 꼭 필요한 핵심 문법 설명을 수록하였으며, 이와 함께 학습한 문법 사항을 쓰기에 적용하는 방법도 제시했습니다. 영작의 가장 기초가 되는 배열과 영작 연습 문제로 충분히 기초를 쌓고, 나아가 실전 응용문제까지 다양하게 접하도록 구성함으로써 서술형을 완벽하게 대비할 수 있습니다.

+3 논술형 수행평가 연습 문제로 장문 영작까지 내신 완벽 대비

기존 내신 서술형 문제는 단문 영작이 주를 이루었지만, 점점 영어 글쓰기의 중요성이 높아짐에 따라 수행평가의 비중도 높아지고 있습니다. 이에 〈천일문 중등 WRITING〉은 실전 글쓰기 실력을 향상할 수 있는 논술형 수행평가 연습문제를 제공합니다. 학습한 문법 사항 중 가장 실용적인 쓰임의 언어형식으로 '예시 글 구성 → 예시 글의 구조 분석 → 학습자 스스로 글의 뼈대 구상 → 개개인의 독창적인 글 완성 → 자세하고 명확한 평가 기준으로 채점'까지 가능하게 하였습니다.

서술형을 어떻게 대비해야 할지 고민하던 학생들도 〈천일문 중등 WRITING〉으로 기본부터 차근차근 학습한다면 어느 순간 서술형에 대해 두려움이 사라지고 정답을 거침없이 써 내려가는 자신 스스로를 발견할 것입니다. 노력이 결실을 맺어 영어의 실력자가 되는 그날까지 여러분을 응원합니다.

저자

Preview

① 본책

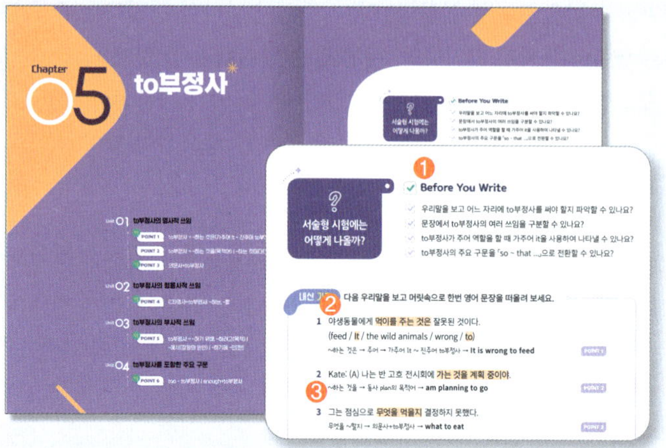

기출 예제로 살펴보는 **Chapter Preview**

❶ 해당 챕터 학습 전 미리 점검하는 주요 영작 포인트
❷ 실제 기출 영작 문제에 제시된 우리말 중 어느 부분이 정답의 단서가 되는지 확인
❸ 정답 도출 과정 제시

효과적인 **POINT별 학습**

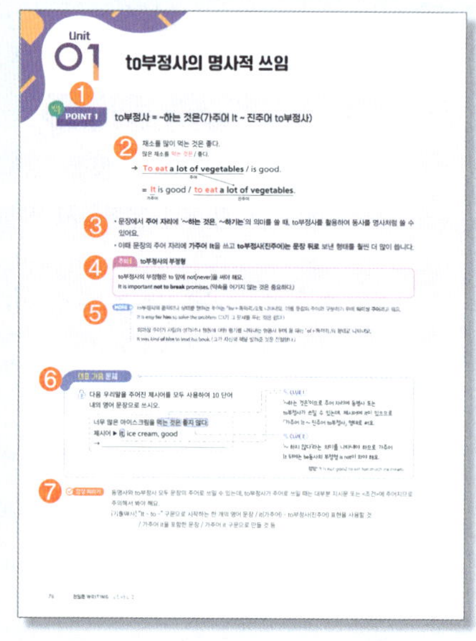

❶ 중요 핵심 문법을 POINT별로 구성 및 내신 기출 빈도수에 따라 빈출 표시
❷ 우리말 어순과 영어의 어순이 비교 가능한 대표 예문
❸ 영작 시 꼭 알아야 하는 주요 문법 사항
❹ 주의 기출에 자주 등장하거나 주의해야 할 문법 사항
❺ MORE+ 실력 향상을 위한 기출 심화 개념
❻ 대표 기출 문제 내신에 자주 출제되는 대표 기출 문제와 그 문제를 푸는 해결 단서 제공
❼ 함정 피하기 서술형 문제를 풀 때 주의해야 할 감점 요인 정리

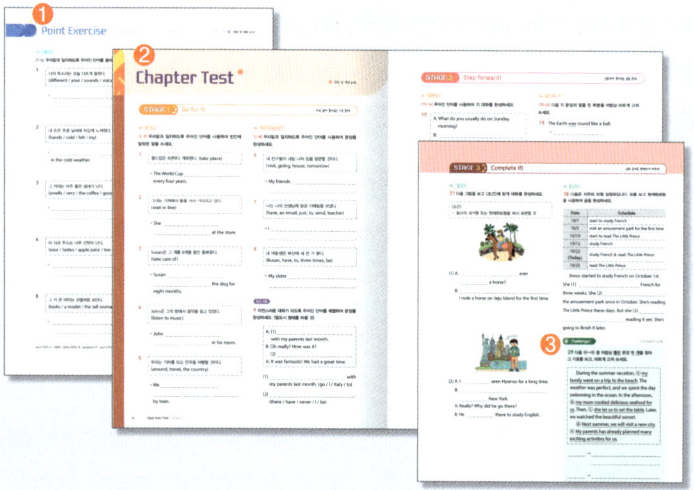

단계적 학습을 위한 **문제 구성**

❶ Point Exercise 학습한 포인트들을 바로 점검하는 연습 문제
❷ Chapter Test 전국 내신 서술형 기출 문제의 출제 유형을 총망라한 단계별 실전 문제

STAGE 1 기본 배열, 영작 문제
STAGE 2 STAGE 1보다 한 단계 높은 응용 문제
STAGE 3 고난도 서술형

❸ Challenge! 앞서 배운 챕터 3개에서 학습한 내용을 점검해보는 누적 문제

중등 내신 대비를 위한 **논술형 수행평가 연습 문제** (총 10회)

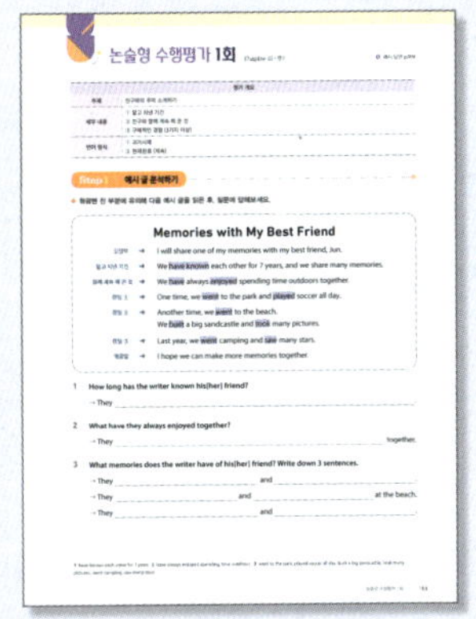   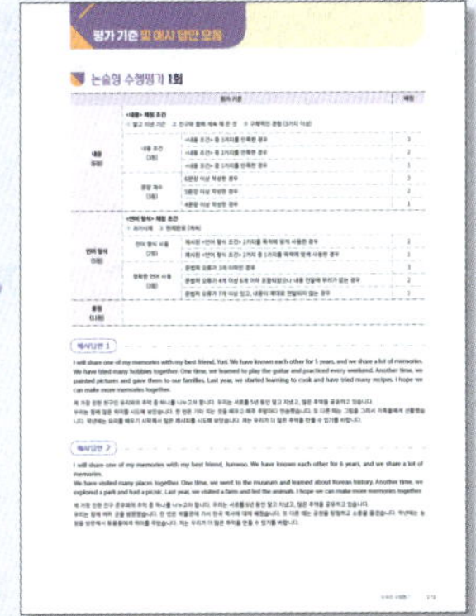

Step 1 예시 글 분석
- 전국 중학교 영어 내신 수행 평가를 분석하여 포맷 구성
- 학습한 여러 언어 형식을 사용하여 기본 영작 연습

Step 2 글의 뼈대 구성
- 스스로 아이디어 구상 및 글의 뼈대 작성
- 주제별 유용한 어휘 및 표현 함께 제공

Step 3 나만의 글 작성
- 제시된 〈조건〉에 맞춰 실전 글쓰기 연습
- Step 2에서 완성한 뼈대에 맞춰 자신만의 글 완성

평가 기준 및 예시 답안
- 누구나 손쉽게 채점 가능한 간결하고 명확한 평가 기준
- 초보 학습자의 부담을 줄여주는 예시 답안 제공

❷ 워크북

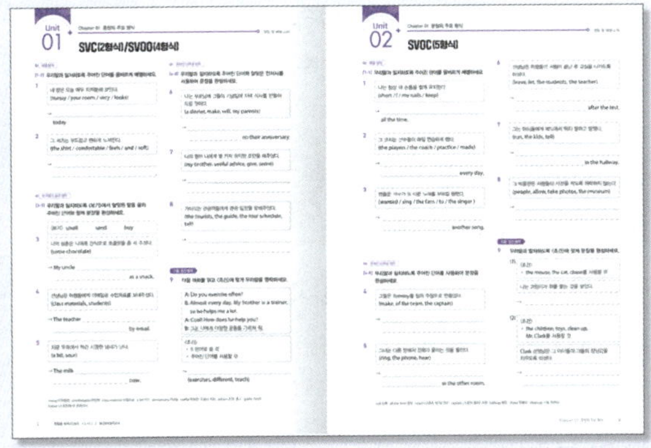 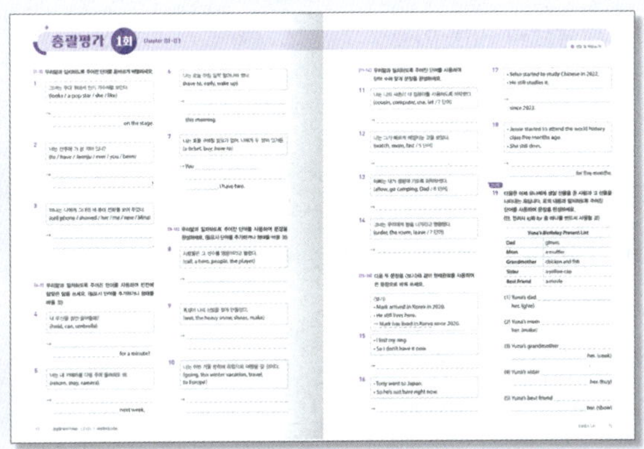

- 완벽 복습 가능한 유닛별 연습 문제
- 각 유닛에서 가장 많이 출제되는 기출 문제 함께 수록

- 총괄평가 3회분 수록 (챕터 3~4개씩 묶어 출제)
- 앞서 익힌 문법 사항의 누적 학습
- 기본 영작, 응용 영작, 고난도 심화 문제로 구성

❸ 부가서비스 (www.cedubook.com)

모든 자료는 www.cedubook.com에서 다운로드 가능합니다.

 1. 어휘리스트 　 2. 어휘테스트

- 교강사 여러분께는 위 부가서비스를 비롯하여, 문제 출제 활용을 위한 한글 파일, 수업용 PDF 파일, 챕터별 추가 문제를 제공해드립니다. (파일 신청 및 문의는 book@ceduenglish.com)

Contents*

Chapter 01

문장의 주요 형식

✓ Before You Write

- ☑ 문장 구조별로 주어/동사/목적어/보어의 어순을 잘 파악하고 있나요?
- ☑ 각 문장 구조의 주요 동사와 그 동사의 의미를 잘 파악하고 있나요?
- ☑ make와 같이 한 동사가 의미에 따라 여러 문장 구조로 쓰일 수 있다는 것을 알고 있나요?
- ☑ 목적격보어 자리에 오는 다양한 형태를 구분해서 사용할 수 있나요?

내신 기출 다음 우리말을 보고 머릿속으로 한번 영어 문장을 떠올려 보세요.

1 (A) 꽃들은 아름답게 보인다.
∼하게 보이다 → 감각동사 look+형용사 → **look beautiful** `POINT 1`

2 엄마는 내게 책 한권을 사 주셨다. (buy, a book)
∼에게 …을 사 주다 → buy+목적어1+목적어2 → **bought me a book** `POINT 2`

3 그들은 특별한 누군가에게 초콜릿을 주었다.
<조건> somebody, to를 모두 사용할 것
∼에게 …을 주다 → give+목적어+to ∼ → **gave the chocolate to somebody** `POINT 2`

4 학생들은 그 선생님을 천재라고 불렀다. (call, genius)
∼을 …라고 부르다 → call+목적어+명사 → **called the teacher a genius** `POINT 3`

5 그 이야기가 우리를 슬프게 만들었다. (make / sad)
∼을 …(상태)로 만들다 → make+목적어+형용사 → **made us sad** `POINT 3`

6 엄마는 내가 집에 일찍 오기를 바라신다.
wants / home / my mom / me / to / come / early
∼가 …하기를 바라다 → want+목적어+to부정사 → **wants me to come** `POINT 4`

7 Tom: Why? What made you stay at home?
Alice: 많은 비가 나를 집에 머물게 했어.
∼가 …하게 하다 → make+목적어+동사원형 → **made me stay** `POINT 5`

정답: **1** The flowers look beautiful. **2** Mom bought me a book. **3** They gave the chocolate to somebody special. **4** Students called the teacher a genius. **5** The story made us sad. **6** My mom wants me to come home early. **7** Heavy rain made me stay at home.

POINT 1　주어+동사+보어

네 책가방은 무거워 보인다.

네 책가방은 / ~하게 보인다 / 무거운.
　　주어　　　　　동사　　　　보어

→ Your backpack / **looks** / **heavy**.

- 감각을 나타내는 동사인 **감각동사(look, sound, taste, smell, feel)** 뒤에 오는 **보어는 반드시 형용사**가 쓰여요. 보어 자리의 형용사는 주어의 상태를 나타내요.

📢 **감각동사＋형용사 보어**

look	～하게 보이다	This place **looks** *amazing*. 이곳은 정말 멋져 보인다.
sound	～하게 들리다	The music **sounded** *great*. 그 음악이 멋지게 들렸다.
taste	～한 맛이 나다	The soup **tastes** *salty*. 그 수프는 짠맛이 난다.
smell	～한 냄새가 나다	These doughnuts **smell** *sweet*. 이 도넛들은 달콤한 냄새가 난다.
feel	～한 느낌이 들다	The fresh air **feels** *good*. 신선한 공기가 좋게 느껴진다.

주의

우리말로 '～하게'라고 해석이 된다고 해서 보어 자리에 부사를 쓰지 않도록 주의하세요.
Your suitcase **looks** *heavily*. (×)　Your suitcase **looks** *heavy*. (○) (네 여행 가방은 무거워 보여.)

대표 기출 문제

🔒 주어진 의미에 맞도록 빈칸을 완성하시오.

(1) 그는 슬퍼 보인다.
→ ___________________

(2) 너는 축구 선수처럼 보인다.
→ ___________________

🔍 **CLUE 1**

'～하게 보이다'는 SVC 문장 형식으로
「주어+look+보어(형용사)」로 써야 해요.

🔍 **CLUE 2**

'(명사)처럼 보이다'는 「주어+look like+보어(명사)」
으로 써야 해요.

정답: (1) He looks sad.　(2) You look like a soccer player.

✓ **함정 피하기**　「감각동사+형용사 보어」와 「감각동사+like(전치사)+명사」는 구분해서 써야 해요.
'～인 것 같다, ～처럼 보이다'라는 의미는 감각동사 뒤에 「like(전치사)+명사」를 붙여 나타내야 해요.
You ~~look~~ (→ look like) a soccer player. (너는 축구 선수처럼 보인다.)
　　　　　　　　　　　　　명사

Point Exercise

정답 및 해설 p.02

[1-5] 우리말과 일치하도록 주어진 단어를 올바르게 배열하세요.

1
너의 목소리는 오늘 다르게 들린다.
(different / your / sounds / voice)

→ _______________________________

_______________________________ today.

2
내 손은 추운 날씨에 차갑게 느껴졌다.
(hands / cold / felt / my)

→ _______________________________

in the cold weather.

3
그 커피는 아주 좋은 냄새가 난다.
(smells / very / the coffee / good)

→ _______________________________

_______________________________ .

4
이 사과 주스는 너무 신맛이 난다.
(sour / tastes / apple juice / too / this)

→ _______________________________

_______________________________ .

5
그 키 큰 여자는 모델처럼 보인다.
(looks / a model / the tall woman / like)

→ _______________________________

_______________________________ .

[6-9] 우리말과 일치하도록 〈보기〉에서 알맞은 말을 골라 주어진 단어와 함께 문장을 완성하세요.

〈보기〉

taste	look	feel	sound

6
그 약은 쓴맛이 났다. (bitter, the medicine)

→ _______________________________

7
너의 방학 계획은 재미있게 들린다.
(vacation plan, fun)

→ _______________________________

8
이 스카프는 정말 부드럽게 느껴진다.
(really, this, soft, scarf)

→ _______________________________

9
Mark는 그의 생일날 행복해 보였다.
(birthday, happy, on)

→ _______________________________

10 다음 대화를 읽고 〈조건〉에 맞게 우리말을 영작하세요.

A: The fresh cookies are here.
B: 이 쿠키들은 맛있어 보여요. 게다가 냄새도 훌륭해요.

〈조건〉
- 알맞은 감각동사를 사용할 것
- these, wonderful, delicious를 사용할 것

→ _______________________________ .

They also _______________________________ .

---

sour (맛이) 신, 시큼한 bitter (맛이) 쓴 medicine 약 scarf 스카프 fresh 갓 구운, 신선한

 주어+동사+간접목적어+직접목적어

우리는 고양이에게 새 장난감을 사 주었다.
우리는 / 사 주었다 / 우리 고양이에게 / 새 장난감을.
　주어　　　동사　　　간접목적어　　　직접목적어

→ We / **bought** / **our cat** / **a new toy**.

우리는 / 사 주었다 / 새 장난감을 / 우리 고양이에게.
　주어　　　동사　　　목적어

→ We / **bought** / a new toy / **for** our cat.

- '~에게 …을 (해)주다'라는 의미를 나타내는 **수여동사**는 뒤에 목적어가 두 개 오는데, '~에게'에 해당하는 **간접목적어**가 먼저 오고, '…을[를]'에 해당하는 **직접목적어**가 이어서 옵니다.
- 「주어+동사+간접목적어+직접목적어」 문장(4형식)은 **직접목적어를 간접목적어 앞으로** 가져와 **목적어가 1개인 문장(3형식)**으로 바꿀 수 있어요. 단, 간접목적어 앞에 전치사 **to**, **for** 중 하나를 써줘야 합니다.
- 다음 동사들은 모두 목적어를 두 개 가지는데, 3형식 문장으로 바꿀 때 동사에 따라 쓰이는 전치사가 달라요.

📢 **간접목적어를 뒤로 보낼 때 to/for를 쓰는 동사**

to	give, send, show, tell, teach, write, lend, bring, pass, pay, read, offer 등
for	buy, make, cook, get, find 등

주의

동사 ask는 ask a question, ask a favor(부탁을 하다)와 같은 표현에 한해 전치사 **of**를 씁니다.
I **asked** my teacher a favor. → I **asked** a favor **of** my teacher. (나는 선생님께 부탁을 드렸다.)

대표 기출 문제

🔒 다음 주어진 단어들을 모두 활용하여 우리말과 같도록 영어 문장을 쓰시오.

그는 내게 케첩을 건네주었다.
(pass, the ketchup)
답: ________________________

CLUE 1
두 개의 목적어, 즉 '~에게'에 해당하는 간접목적어와 '…을'에 해당하는 직접목적어가 등장해요.

CLUE 2
동사 pass 다음에 「간접목적어(~에게)+직접목적어(…을)」 또는 「직접목적어(…을)+to+간접목적어(~에게)」의 순서로 써야 해요.

정답: He passed me the ketchup.
또는 He passed the ketchup to me.

✓ **함정 피하기**

1 '~에게'에 해당하는 목적격 대명사를 문장 뒤쪽에 쓸 때는 대명사 앞에 전치사 to/for/of를 꼭 써야 해요.
Mom **gave** a T-shirt me. (✕) → Mom **gave** a T-shirt **to me**. (○) (엄마가 내게 티셔츠를 주셨다.)

2 어순이 헷갈릴 때는 「수여동사+사람+사물」 또는 「수여동사+사물+to/for/of+사람」으로 기억하세요.
I **made** my best friend strawberry cookies. (나는 내 가장 친한 친구에게 딸기 쿠키를 만들어 주었다.)
　　　　사람　　　　　　사물
I **made** strawberry cookies my best friend.
　　　　사물　　　　　　for　　사람

Point Exercise

배열 영작

[1-2] 우리말과 일치하도록 주어진 단어를 올바르게 배열하세요.

1
> 그녀는 여행에서 그녀의 친구에게 선물을 가져다주었다.
> (a gift / her friend / she / brought)

→ _______________________________

_______________________ from her trip.

2
> 그 요리사는 손님들에게 맛있는 스테이크를 요리해 주었다.
> (the guests / delicious / the chef / steaks / cooked)

→ _______________________________

_______________________________ .

보기에서 골라 영작

[3-5] 우리말과 일치하도록 〈보기〉에서 알맞은 전치사를 골라 주어진 단어와 함께 문장을 완성하세요.

> 〈보기〉
> of   to   for

3 John은 그의 딸에게 영어를 가르쳐주었다.
→ John taught _______________________

_______________________ . (his daughter, English)

4 나는 내 남동생에게 아이스크림을 좀 사 주었다.
→ I bought _______________________

_______________________ .

(some ice cream, my brother)

5 Susan은 그녀의 선생님께 몇 가지 질문을 했다.
→ Susan asked _______________________

_______________________ .

(her teacher, a few questions)

주어진 단어로 영작

[6-7] 우리말과 일치하도록 주어진 단어를 사용하여 같은 의미의 문장 두 개를 완성하세요.
(단, (2)에는 전치사를 사용할 것)

6
> Ben은 우리에게 그의 사진첩을 보여 주었다.
> (show, his photo album)

(1) _______________________

(2) _______________________

7
> 나의 언니는 내게 파스타를 좀 만들어 주었다.
> (make, some pasta, my sister)

(1) _______________________

(2) _______________________

기출: 조건 영작

8 다음 글을 읽고 〈조건〉에 맞게 우리말을 영작하세요.

> Yesterday was my birthday. I got presents from my family. (1) 나의 부모님은 나에게 자전거를 사 주셨다. I'm excited to ride the bike. (2) 나의 오빠는 나에게 책 한 권을 주었다. It was an interesting novel. I'm so happy!

> 〈조건〉
> • 주어진 단어를 사용할 것
> • 반드시 전치사를 포함할 것

(1) _______________________

____

(buy, a bike, parents)

(2) _______________________

____

(give, brother, a book)

guest 손님 chef 주방장, 요리사 novel 소설

POINT 3 명사/형용사 목적격보어

Julia는 그녀의 할아버지를 영웅이라고 부른다.
Julia는 / ~라고 부른다 / 그녀의 할아버지를 / 영웅(이라고).
　주어　　　　동사　　　　　목적어　　　목적격보어(명사)

→ Julia / **calls** / **her grandfather** / **a hero**.

Ted는 항상 그의 방을 깨끗한 상태로 둔다.
Ted는 / 항상 ~하게 둔다 / 그의 방을 / 깨끗한.
　주어　　　　　동사　　　　목적어　목적격보어(형용사)

→ Ted / always **keeps** / **his room** / **clean**.

- 목적어 뒤에 **목적어를 보충 설명해주는 목적격보어**가 등장하는 문장 형식은 자주 출제되므로 잘 알아두어야 해요.
- 목적격보어 자리에 **명사**가 오는 경우, **목적어 = 목적격보어**의 관계입니다.
- 목적격보어 자리에 **형용사**가 오는 경우, 목적격보어는 **목적어의 상태나 성질**을 나타내요.

목적격보어(명사)	목적격보어(형용사)
make＋목적어＋명사: ~을 …로 만들다 **call**＋목적어＋명사: ~을 …라고 부르다 **name**＋목적어＋명사: ~을 …라고 이름 짓다	**make**＋목적어＋형용사: ~을 …(상태)로 만들다 **keep**＋목적어＋형용사: ~을 …(상태)로 두다[유지하다] **find**＋목적어＋형용사: ~을 …하다는 것을 알게 되다 **leave**＋목적어＋형용사: ~을 …한 상태에 두다

대표 기출 문제

주어진 우리말과 일치하도록 괄호 안 단어들을 활용하여 완전한 영어문장으로 완성하시오.

그 냄새는 우리를 배고프게 만들었다.
(The smell, hungry)
→ ________________________

CLUE 1
'~을 …(상태)로 만들다'라는 의미는 목적어 뒤에 목적격보어를 써서 표현해요.

CLUE 2
「make+목적어+목적격보어」에서 목적격보어 자리에는 형용사 hungry가 와야 해요.

정답: The smell made us hungry.

함정 피하기　목적격보어 자리에 쓰인 형용사는 종종 부사처럼 해석이 되지만, 보어 자리에 부사는 쓰일 수 없어요.
The smell made us ~~hungrily~~(→ hungry).

Point Exercise

[1-5] 우리말과 일치하도록 주어진 단어를 올바르게 배열하세요.

1

나의 반 친구들은 Robert를 Rob이라고 부른다.
(Rob / call / my classmates / Robert)

→ ___________________________
___________________________ .

2

그 시험 결과는 나를 초조하게 만들었다.
(me / nervous / made / the test result)

→ ___________________________
___________________________ .

3

그들은 Smith 씨를 리더로 만들었다.
(Mr. Smith / a leader / made / they)

→ ___________________________
___________________________ .

4

그녀는 담요로 그녀의 개를 따뜻하게 해주었다.
(warm / she / with a blanket / her dog / kept)

→ ___________________________
___________________________ .

5

너는 그 수영 수업이 도움이 된다는 것을 알게 될 것이다.
(will / the swimming class / you / helpful / find)

→ ___________________________
___________________________ .

[6-9] 우리말과 일치하도록 주어진 단어를 사용하여 문장을 완성하세요. (필요시 형태를 바꿀 것)

6

그 책은 그를 유명한 작가로 만들었다.
(a famous author, make, the book)

→ ___________________________
____

7

나의 언니와 나는 그 고양이를 Kitty라고 이름 지었다.
(sister, name, and, the cat)

→ ___________________________

8

우리는 도서관에서 우리의 목소리를 낮춰야 한다.
(voices, should, low, keep)

→ ___________________________
in the library.

9

모든 사람이 Jessica가 친절하고 따뜻하다는 것을 알게 되었다. (and, everyone, find, warm, kind)

→ ___________________________

10 우리말과 일치하도록 주어진 단어를 사용하여 다음의 대화를 완성하세요.

A: Look at the baby! Isn't she cute?
B: Yes, she's so lovely. She's smiling at us.
A: <u>아기들의 미소는 우리를 행복하게 해.</u>
B: I totally agree with you.

→ ___________________________
(babies' smiles, happy, make)

---

result 결과 blanket 담요 helpful 도움이 되는, 유용한 author 작가, 저자 totally 완전히, 전적으로 agree with ～에 동의하다

POINT 4 to부정사 목적격보어

한 여성이 나에게 가방을 들어달라고 부탁했다.
한 여성이 / 부탁했다 / 나에게 / 가방을 들어달라고.
　　　주어　　　　동사　　　목적어　　　목적격보어

→ A woman / **asked** / **me** / **to carry** the bag.

- '목적어가 어떤 동작이나 상태가 되도록 ∼하다'라는 의미를 표현하려면 목적어 뒤에 **목적격보어**를 씁니다.
- 이때 want, ask, tell, allow 등의 동사는 목적어의 동작이나 상태를 표현하는 목적격보어로 **to부정사**를 써요.

목적격보어 자리에 to부정사가 오는 동사

want+목적어+to do	∼가 …하기를 원하다[바라다]	**advise**+목적어+to do	∼가 …하도록 조언하다
ask+목적어+to do	∼가 …하기를 요청[부탁]하다	**get**+목적어+to do	∼가 …하도록 시키다
tell+목적어+to do	∼가 …하도록 말하다	**allow**+목적어+to do	∼가 …하도록 허락하다
expect+목적어+to do	∼가 …하기를 기대[예상]하다	**order**+목적어+to do	∼가 …하도록 명령하다

주의

1 to부정사의 부정형은 「not+to부정사」로 나타내요.
Tom은 나에게 문을 **닫지 말아달라고** 부탁했다. → Tom / asked / me / **not to close** the door.

2 to부정사는 '동사'에서 비롯되어 뒤에 보어, 목적어 등이 오므로 to부정사가 이끄는 어구는 알맞은 어순으로 써야 해요.
그는 내가 **그에게 펜을 빌려주기를** 원했다. → He / wanted / me / **to lend him a pen**.
　　　　　　　　　　　　　　　　　　　　　　　　　　동사 간목 직목　(☞ POINT 2)

대표 기출 문제

🔒 대화의 밑줄 친 우리말과 의미가 같도록 <조건>에 맞게 문장을 완성하시오.

> 나는 여러분이 '업사이클링'의 의미를 이해하기 바랍니다.

<조건>
1. 9 단어의 완전한 문장으로 쓸 것
2. 괄호 안의 단어를 반드시 사용할 것
   (want, understand, the meaning of)

→ ________________________________

CLUE 1
동사 want를 활용해 '∼가 …하기를 원하다[바라다]'라는 의미를 써야 해요.

CLUE 2
「want+목적어+목적격보어」에서 목적격보어 자리에는 to부정사를 써야 해요.

정답: I want you to understand the meaning of "upcycling."

Point Exercise

정답 및 해설 p.02

배열 영작

[1-5] 우리말과 일치하도록 주어진 단어를 올바르게 배열하세요.

1
나는 나의 언니에게 우산을 가져와달라고 부탁했다.
(asked / an umbrella / my sister / bring / to / I)

→ ______________________________

______________________________.

2
그 선생님은 학생들에게 꿈을 가지라고 조언하셨다.
(have / advised / the teacher / dreams / students / to)

→ ______________________________

______________________________.

3
우리는 네가 이렇게 빨리 올 거라고 기대하지 않았다.
(so early / to / we / you / expect / didn't / come)

→ ______________________________

______________________________.

4
나의 부모님은 내가 반려동물을 키우는 것을 허락해 주셨다.
(to / my parents / keep / me / a pet / allowed)

→ ______________________________

______________________________.

5
Max는 그의 남동생에게 TV를 끄라고 말했다.
(Max / the TV / his brother / told / turn off / to)

→ ______________________________

______________________________.

주어진 단어로 영작

[6-8] 우리말과 일치하도록 주어진 단어를 사용하여 문장을 완성하세요.

6
그들은 우리에게 조용히 하라고 명령했다.
(order, be, quiet)

→ ______________________________

7
엄마는 나에게 저녁 식사 후에 설거지를 하라고 시키셨다. (get, the dishes, do, Mom)

→ ______________________________ after dinner.

8
그 관광객들은 내가 그들의 사진을 찍어주길 원했다.
(the tourists, pictures, want, of them, take)

→ ______________________________

____

기출: 조건 영작

9 다음 대화를 읽고 Leo가 Jack에게 해 준 조언을 〈조건〉에 맞게 완성하세요.

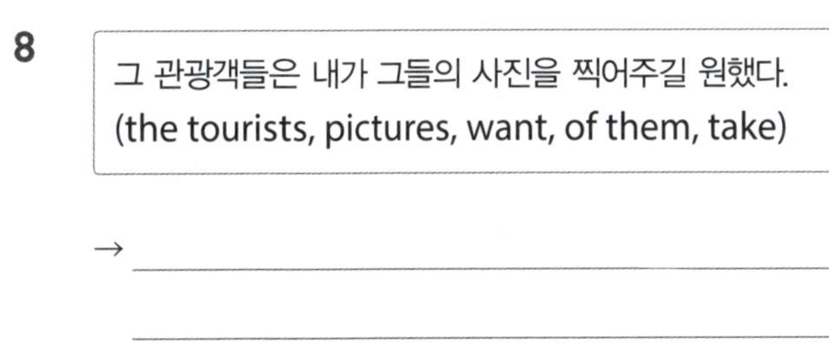

Jack: Leo, did you prepare Sarah's birthday present?
Leo: Yes, I bought warm gloves.
What about you, Jack?
Jack: I should buy something. What does she like?
Leo: She loves eating something sweet.
A cake would be a great choice.

〈조건〉
· 과거시제로 쓸 것
· Jack, a cake, buy, advise를 사용할 것

→ Leo ______________________________.

---

tourist 관광객 prepare 준비하다 choice 선택

POINT 5 동사원형 목적격보어

선생님들은 학생들이 일찍 떠나도록 했다.
선생님들은 / (~하게) 했다 / 학생들이 / 일찍 떠나도록.
　　주어　　　　동사　　　목적어　　　목적격보어

→ Teachers / **let** / **the students** / **leave** early.

- '목적어가 ~을 하게 하다/하도록 시키다'의 의미는 사역동사를 이용하여 씁니다.
- **사역동사 make, have, let** 뒤에는 「목적어+목적격보어(시킨 행동)」가 오며, 이때 **목적격보어로 동사원형**을 쓰는 것이 중요합니다.
- 다만 동사 help는 **목적격보어로 to부정사와 동사원형** 둘 다 쓸 수 있어요.
  I **helped** the old lady **(to) find** her lost bag. 나는 노부인이 잃어버린 가방을 찾는 것을 도와드렸다.

우리는 그 선수가 홈런을 치는 것을 보았다.
우리는 / 보았다 / 그 선수가 / 홈런을 치는 것을.
　주어　　동사　　 목적어　　　　목적격보어

→ We / **saw** / **the player** / **hit** a home run.

- '목적어가 ~하는 것을 보다[듣다, 냄새 맡다, 느끼다]'라는 의미는 **지각동사 see, watch, hear, smell, feel**을 이용해 씁니다. 그 뒤에도 마찬가지로 「목적어+목적격보어」가 오며, **목적격보어로 동사원형**을 씁니다.
- 다만 지각동사는 **동작이 진행 중**이라는 것을 강조하고 싶을 때 **목적격보어 자리에 현재분사(-ing)**도 쓸 수 있어요. (☞ Ch 06 동명사와 분사)
  I **saw** Ben **eating** ice cream. 나는 Ben이 아이스크림 먹고 있는 것을 보았다.

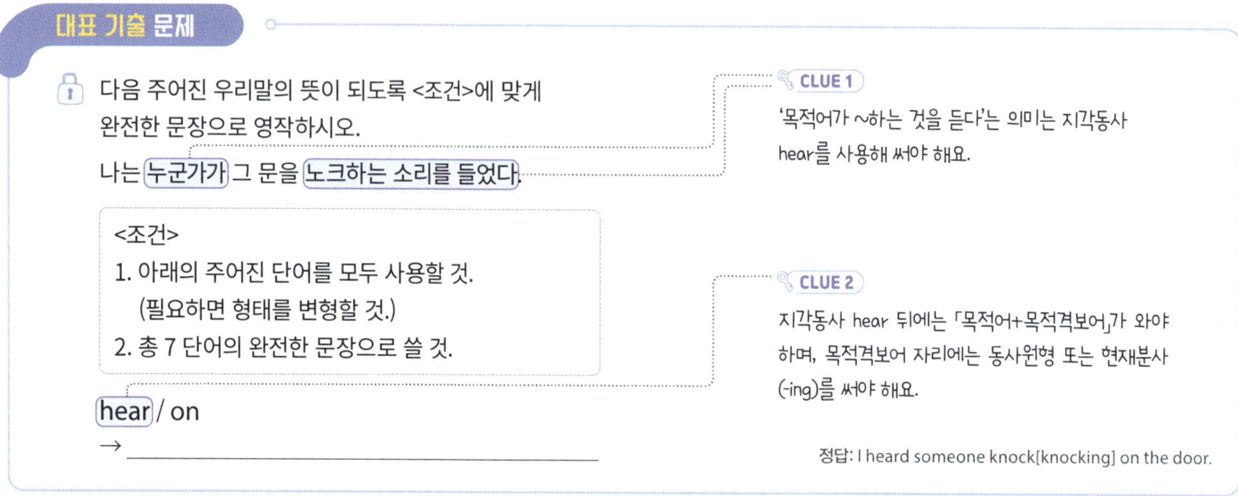

함정 피하기 사역동사나 지각동사가 과거형으로 쓰였다고 해서 목적격보어 자리에도 과거형을 쓰지 않도록 주의하세요.
I heard someone ~~knocked~~(→ knock[knocking]) on the door.

Point Exercise

정답 및 해설 p.02

[1-5] 우리말과 일치하도록 주어진 단어를 올바르게 배열하세요.

1

그 직원은 사람들을 30분 동안 기다리게 만들었다.
(people / made / wait / the staff)

→ ______________________________

______________________ for 30 minutes.

2

Eva는 그녀의 엄마가 주방에서 요리하시는 냄새를 맡았다.
(Eva / mom / smelled / her / cooking)

→ ______________________________

______________________ in the kitchen.

3

그녀는 Daniel이 도서관으로 들어가는 것을 보았다.
(saw / the library / she / Daniel / enter)

→ ______________________________

______________________________ .

4

너는 땅이 흔들리는 걸 느꼈니?
(feel / you / shaking / the ground / did)

→ ______________________________

______________________________ ?

5

그 사서는 아이가 책들을 찾는 것을 도와주었다.
(find / the librarian / the kid / helped / books)

→ ______________________________

______________________________ .

[6-8] 우리말과 일치하도록 주어진 단어를 사용하여 문장을 완성하세요. (필요시 형태를 바꿀 것)

6

Ron은 그의 누나가 바이올린을 연주하는 것을 지켜보았다.
(watch, play, the violin, sister)

→ ______________________________

____

7

나는 그 아이가 내 개를 만지도록 해 주었다.
(dog, touch, let, the child)

→ ______________________________

____

8

그 선생님은 우리에게 교실을 청소하라고 시키셨다.
(have, the teacher, the classroom, clean)

→ ______________________________

____

9 우리말과 일치하도록 〈조건〉에 맞게 문장을 완성하세요.

Anna는 누군가 그녀의 이름을 부르는 것을 들었다.

〈조건〉
- 6 단어로 쓸 것
- hear, name, someone, call를 사용할 것

→ ______________________________

____

shake 흔들리다 librarian (도서관) 사서

Chapter Test [*]

STAGE 1) Go for it!

자신 있게 풀어보는 기초 문제!

배열 영작

[1-4] 우리말과 일치하도록 주어진 단어를 배열하여 문장을 완성하세요.

1
> 전화기 너머로 Jenny의 목소리가 슬프게 들렸다.
> (voice / sad / sounded / Jenny's)

→ ______________________________

______________________________ over the phone.

2
> 규칙적인 운동이 나를 건강하게 했다.
> (healthy / regular / made / exercise / me)

→ ______________________________

______________________________ .

3
> 나의 아빠는 나의 형이 빨래를 개도록 하셨다.
> (my brother / had / the laundry / fold / my dad)

→ ______________________________

______________________________ .

4
> 놀이공원에서 한 여자아이가 나에게 그녀의 부모님을 찾아 달라고 부탁했다.
> (asked / her parents / a girl / find / me / to)

→ ______________________________

______________________________ at the amusement park.

주어진 단어로 영작

[5-7] 우리말과 일치하도록 주어진 단어를 사용하여 문장을 완성하세요. (필요시 형태를 바꿀 것)

5
> 그녀는 그 배우가 무대에서 연기하는 것을 지켜보았다.
> (the actor, watch, perform)

→ ______________________________

______________________________ on stage.

6
> 우리 선생님은 우리에게 새로운 교과서를 주셨다.
> (new, teacher, give, to, textbooks)

→ ______________________________

____

7
> 우리는 이번 주말에 날씨가 맑을 것이라고 예상한다.
> (sunny, the weather, expect, be)

→ ______________________________

______________________________ this weekend.

최신 기출

8 다음 문장을 주어진 〈조건〉에 맞게 완성하세요.

> 〈조건〉
> • call을 사용하고, 필요시 형태를 바꿀 것
> • 주어진 단어를 한 칸에 쓸 것

> She is good at dancing.
> So her friends ______________
>
> ______________ ______________ .
>
> (Dance Master)

◑ 보기에서 골라 영작

[9-15] 다음 빈칸에 들어갈 알맞은 말을 〈보기〉에서 골라 쓰세요. (단, 한 번씩만 사용할 것)

> 〈보기〉
> keep   let   see   name   allow

9 My parents ____________ me to watch TV for an hour a day.

10 Please ____________ the door open. I'll be back in five minutes.

11 Look out the window. You can ____________ snow falling right now.

12 Sophia ____________ her little sister wear her dress.

13 My uncle decided to ____________ his son Andrew.

> 〈보기〉
> to   for

14 The chef cooked beef and chicken ____________ people at the party.

15 Can you show your new bike ____________ me?

◑ 그림 영작

16 다음 그림을 보고 〈보기〉와 같이 주어진 두 문장을 같은 의미의 한 문장으로 바꾸어 쓰세요.

〈보기〉

Something was burning in the kitchen. I smelled it.
→ I smelled something burning in the kitchen.

Two people were flying their kites. I saw them.
→ I ____________ ____________ ____________ ____________ their kites.

최신 기출

17 다음 표를 보고 〈조건〉에 맞게 문장을 완성하세요.

My Christmas Presents		
(1)	from my grandma	new shoes
(2)	from my friend	a baseball cap

> 〈조건〉
> • (1)은 4형식으로, (2)는 3형식으로 쓸 것
> • 주어진 단어를 사용할 것
> • 과거시제로 쓸 것

(1) My grandma ____________ ____________ on Christmas. (send)

(2) My friend ____________ ____________ on Christmas. (get)

[18-22] 우리말과 일치하도록 주어진 단어를 사용하여 단어 수에 맞게 문장을 완성하세요. (필요시 형태를 바꿀 것)

18

> 나의 부모님은 내가 컴퓨터 게임을 하는 것을 허락해 주셨다.
> (let, play, computer games / 7 단어)

→ _______________________________________

____

19

> 나는 이웃집 개가 크게 짖는 것을 들었다.
> (hear, bark, loudly, the neighbor's / 7 단어)

→ _______________________________________

____

20

> 나의 엄마는 내가 내 방을 청소하도록 시키셨다.
> (make, room, clean / 7 단어)

→ _______________________________________

____

21

> 의사는 그녀에게 약을 먹으라고 조언했다.
> (the doctor, advise, medicine, take / 7 단어)

→ _______________________________________

____

22

> 내 친구는 나에게 늦지 말라고 말했다.
> (tell, late, not, be / 8 단어)

→ _______________________________________

____

[23-27] 다음 각 문장에서 어법상 <u>틀린</u> 부분을 찾아 바르게 고쳐 쓰세요.

23 Laura and you look sisters.

_________________ → _________________

24 The pink sweater looks beautifully on you.

_________________ → _________________

25 He bought some snacks to his son at the supermarket.

_________________ → _________________

26 I asked Jamie be quiet in the classroom.

_________________ → _________________

27 Suddenly, Lily felt rain fell down on her head.

_________________ → _________________

28 다음 대화를 읽고 〈조건〉에 맞게 문장을 완성하세요.

> Mom: I'll be late tonight. Chloe, please make dinner for your sister, Emma.
> Chloe: Sure. Don't worry, Mom.
> Mom: And Chloe, Emma, you both need to finish the homework today.
> Chloe, Emma: Got it, Mom.

> 〈조건〉
> • 5형식 문장으로 쓸 것
> • 대화에 쓰인 단어와 주어진 단어를 함께 사용할 것
> • 과거시제로 쓸 것

(1) Mom _______________________________________

_______________________ for her sister. (tell, Chloe)

(2) Mom _______________________________________

_______________________________________.

(get, Chloe and Emma)

○•(도표 영작)

29 다음은 준호의 어머니가 어제 준호가 해야 할 일을 적어 주신 일정표입니다. 표의 내용과 일치하도록 주어진 단어를 사용하여 문장을 완성하세요.

Junho's Schedule

In the morning	throw away the trash
In the afternoon	feed the cat
In the evening	read comic books for an hour

(1) Junho's mother _________________________

____

in the morning. (make, him)

(2) Junho's mother _________________________

____

in the afternoon. (have, him)

(3) Junho's mother _________________________

____

in the evening. (let, him)

○•(조건 영작)

30 다음 대화를 읽고 Dan이 Kate에게 부탁한 내용을 〈조건〉에 맞게 영작하세요.

Kate: Hi, Dan. What are you doing?
Dan: Hi, Kate. We're preparing for Teachers' Day.
Kate: Oh, do you need any help?
Dan: Can you bring a camera tomorrow?
Kate: Sure, I have one.
Dan: Great! Will you take pictures of teachers
       with your camera?
Kate: Trust me. I'm good at taking pictures.

〈조건〉
• 주어진 단어를 사용할 것
• 과거시제로 쓸 것
• 각각 7 단어로 쓸 것

(1) Dan _________________________

_________________________. (ask)

(2) Dan _________________________

_________________________ with her camera. (want)

○•(어법 오류 수정)

31 다음 중 어법상 틀린 문장 <u>두 개</u>를 찾아 그 기호를 쓰고, 문장 전체를 바르게 고쳐 쓰세요.

ⓐ His uncle made him a bookshelf.
ⓑ Eric heard Susie to play the violin.
ⓒ My dad makes dinner for us every weekend.
ⓓ They will buy a new bike their daughter.
ⓔ My brother told me to walk the dog.

_______ → _________________________

____

_______ → _________________________

____

Chapter 02

시제

✔ Before You Write

- ☑ 각 시제의 의미를 알고 동사 형태를 명확하게 쓸 수 있나요?
- ☑ 각 시제별로 함께 자주 쓰이는 시간 표현을 알아볼 수 있나요?
- ☑ 현재완료가 나타내는 여러 의미를 이해하고 있나요?
- ☑ 과거시제와 현재완료를 구분해서 사용할 수 있나요?

내신 기출 다음 우리말을 보고 머릿속으로 한번 영어 문장을 떠올려 보세요.

1 우리는 지난번에 공원을 청소했어.
<보기> last / clean / park / We / up / the / time
과거시제 → 긍정문 → **cleaned up**　　　　　　　　POINT 1

2 A: What are you doing now?
B: I (a) ___________ ___________ to the music. (listen)
A: What were you doing at 9 last night?
B: I (b) ___________ ___________ a book. (read)
현재진행형 → 긍정문 → 1인칭 단수 주어 → **am listening**
과거진행형 → 긍정문 → 1인칭 단수 주어 → **was reading**　　POINT 2

3 It ___________________________ since this morning. (rain a lot)
(1) 현재완료 문장 쓰기: ___________________________
현재완료 → 긍정문 → 3인칭 단수 주어 → **has rained a lot**　　POINT 3

4 우리는 서로를 8년 동안 알고 지내 왔다. (know, each other)
현재완료 (계속) → 긍정문 → 1인칭 복수 주어 → **have known**　　POINT 4

5 (A) 그는 올해 이미 21개의 홈런을 쳤다.
<보기> this / runs / he / 21 / hit / already / home / have / year
현재완료 (완료) → 긍정문 → 3인칭 단수 주어 → **has already hit**　　POINT 5

정답: **1** We cleaned up the park last time. **2** (a) am listening (b) was reading **3** has rained a lot **4** We have[We've] known each other for 8 years.
5 He has[He's] already hit 21 home runs this year.

현재, 과거, 미래 & 진행형

 현재, 과거, 미래

그녀는 / 일한다 / 병원에서 / 현재.
→ She / **works** / at a hospital / **now**.

그녀는 / 일했다 / 병원에서 / 작년에.
→ She / **worked** / at a hospital / **last year**.

그녀는 / 일할 것이다 / 병원에서 / 내년에.
→ She / **will[is going to] work** / at a hospital / **next year**.

📢 현재시제

현재의 사실이나 상태	He **teaches** English at a school. 그는 학교에서 영어를 가르친다.
반복되는 일이나 습관	They **walk** their dog every evening. 그들은 매일 저녁 개를 산책시킨다.
변함없는 일반적인 진리	The Earth **moves** around the Sun. 지구는 태양 주위를 돈다.

📢 과거시제 (☞ p.180 동사 변화형)

과거에 끝난 일이나 상태	I **met** my friend for coffee yesterday. 나는 어제 커피를 마시러 내 친구를 만났다.

*과거시제와 함께 자주 쓰이는 표현: yesterday, last ~, ago, in+과거 연도 등

📢 미래 표현

미래의 일 예측	will+동사원형	They **will arrive** at 5 p.m. 그들은 오후 5시에 도착할 것이다.
	be going to+동사원형	We **are going to have** a picnic today. 우리는 오늘 소풍갈 것이다.

*미래 표현과 함께 자주 쓰이는 표현: tomorrow, next ~, soon, later 등

대표 기출 문제

🔒 다음 대화문의 우리말을 주어진 단어를 활용하여
문장으로 완성하시오.

G: You look worried. What's wrong?
B: 내가 어제 누나의 휴대폰을 잃어버렸어.

→ I ___________________. (lose, cell phone)

CLUE 1
'어제' 잃어버린 것이므로 시제는 과거

CLUE 2
동사 lose(잃어버리다)의 과거형은 lost

정답: lost my sister's cell phone yesterday

Point Exercise

정답 및 해설 p.04

빈칸 완성

[1-6] 우리말과 일치하도록 주어진 단어를 사용하여 빈칸에 알맞은 말을 쓰세요.

1 그는 어제 꽃을 좀 샀다. (some flowers, buy)

→ He ________________ ________________
________________ yesterday.

2 그는 생일 선물을 받았다. (a present, get)

→ He ________________ ________________
________________ for his birthday.

3 나의 아빠가 저녁 식사를 요리하실 것이다. (cook)

→ My dad ________________ ________________
dinner.

4 그녀는 하루에 세 번 이를 닦는다.
(brush, her teeth)

→ She ________________ ________________
________________ three times a day.

5 내 남동생이 주방에서 유리잔을 깼다.
(the glass, break)

→ My brother ________________ ________________
________________ in the kitchen.

6 선생님께서 오늘 우리에게 새로운 학생을 소개해 주실 것이다. (introduce)

→ The teacher ________________ ________________
________________ ________________ a new
student to us today.

주어진 단어로 영작

[7-9] 우리말과 일치하도록 주어진 단어를 사용하여 문장을 완성하세요.

7 그 가수는 매주 새로운 곡을 공연한다.
(perform, the singer, new songs)

→ ________________________________
________________________ every week.

8 나는 내 침대 밑에서 오래된 사진 한 장을 발견했다.
(find, an old photo)

→ ________________________________
________________________ under my bed.

9 Mike는 오늘까지 그의 숙제를 끝낼 것이다.
(finish, homework, going)

→ ________________________________
________________________ by today.

기출 : 조건 영작

10 다음 글을 읽고 〈조건〉에 맞게 우리말을 영작하세요.

Hojun usually goes to school on foot. Today, he got up late in the morning. (1) 그는 학교까지 버스를 탔다. Luckily, he was not late. (2) 그는 오늘밤 일찍 잘 것이다.

〈조건〉
• 주어진 단어를 사용하되 필요시 형태를 바꿀 것

(1) ________________________________
to school. (a bus, take)

(2) ________________________________
________________________ tonight. (early, go to bed)

perform 공연하다, 연주하다 on foot 걸어서 luckily 운 좋게도, 다행히

A: 너는 지금 무엇을 하고 있니?
너는 무엇을 하고 있니 / 지금?

→ A: What **are** you **doing** / now?

B: 나는 책 한 권을 읽고 있어.
나는 / 읽고 있어 / 책 한 권을.

B: I / **am reading** / a book.

나는 네가 전화했을 때 영화를 보고 있었다.
나는 / 보고 있었다 / 영화를 // 네가 전화했을 때.

→ I / **was watching** / a movie // when you called.

📢 현재진행형과 과거진행형의 쓰임과 형태 (☞ p.180 동사 변화형)

현재진행형 (~하고 있다, ~하는 중이다)	지금 진행 중인 일	be동사 현재형(am/are/is)＋동사의 -ing형
과거진행형 (~하고 있었다, ~하는 중이었다)	과거의 특정 시점에 진행되고 있었던 일	be동사의 과거형(was/were)＋동사의 -ing형

주의!   **진행형을 쓸 수 없는 동사**

감정(like, love), 소유(have(가지고 있다)), 인식(know, think), 상태(be, want) 등을 나타내는 동사는 진행형으로 쓰지 않아요.
He **is having** two sisters. (×) → He **has** two sisters. (○) (그는 여동생이 두 명 있다.)

단, 동사가 다른 의미로 쓰여 동작을 나타내거나 일시적인 동작을 의미할 때는 진행형으로 쓸 수 있어요.
He **is having** dinner. (○) (그는 저녁을 먹고 있다.)

MORE ➕   **미래를 나타내는 현재진행형**
현재진행형은 가까운 미래에 예정된 일이나 계획을 나타낼 수도 있어요.
I'm **meeting** my friend tomorrow. (나는 내일 내 친구를 만날 것이다.)

대표 기출 문제

🔒 우리말과 같은 뜻이 되도록 문장을 완성하시오.

When Tom came home yesterday,
________________ for the final exams.
(Tom이 어제 집에 왔을 때, 그녀는 기말고사를 위해
수학을 공부하고 있는 중이었다.)

🔍 **CLUE 1**
'~하는 중이었다'에 사용할 동사의 시제는?
— 과거진행형 「was/were+동사의 -ing형」

🔍 **CLUE 2**
주어가 3인칭 단수인 '그녀(she)'이므로
알맞은 be동사는 was

정답: she was studying math

Point Exercise

[1-3] 우리말과 일치하도록 주어진 단어를 올바르게 배열하세요.

1

> 그들은 지금 교실을 청소하고 있다.
> (the classroom / they /cleaning / are)

→ _______________________________________

_______________________________________ now.

2

> Mia는 그녀의 친구들과 온라인으로 대화하고 있다.
> (is / her friends / Mia / with / chatting)

→ _______________________________________

_______________________________________ online.

3

> 그 소녀들은 그때 뮤지컬을 보고 있었다.
> (were / the girls / the musical / watching)

→ _______________________________________

_______________________________________ then.

[4-7] 우리말과 일치하도록 주어진 단어를 사용하여 문장을 완성하세요.

4

> 나는 소파 위에 누워있다. (lie, on a sofa)

→ _______________________________________

____

5

> 한 남자가 카페에서 그의 노트북 컴퓨터로 일하고 있었다. (a man, laptop, work, with)

→ _______________________________________

_______________________________________ at the cafe.

6

> Lisa는 지금 꽃에 물을 주고 있다.
> (the flowers, water)

→ _______________________________________ now.

7

> 나의 부모님은 함께 그들의 휴가를 계획하고 계셨다.
> (parents, plan, together, vacation)

→ _______________________________________

[8-9] 다음 각 문장의 밑줄 친 부분을 어법상 바르게 고쳐 쓰세요.

8 The students are not <u>follow</u> the rules.

→ _______________________________________

9 Sam and I <u>was jogging</u> in the park this morning.

→ _______________________________________

10 다음 대화를 읽고 〈조건〉에 맞게 우리말을 영작하세요.

> A: Kevin, what are you doing?
> B: (1) <u>나는 내 숙제를 하고 있어.</u> (homework, do)
> A: Didn't you finish it this morning?
> B: No, I didn't. (2) <u>나는 그때 피아노를 연습하고 있었어.</u> (practice, the piano)

> 〈조건〉
> • 주어진 단어를 사용할 것
> • 진행형으로 나타낼 것

(1) _______________________________________

(2) _______________________________________ then.

chat 대화하다, 수다를 떨다 laptop 노트북 water ~에 물을 주다 follow (지시 등을) 따르다; 따라가다 rule 규칙

Unit 02 현재완료의 개념과 형태

POINT 3   현재완료: have[has]+p.p.

그는 이 동네에서 3년 동안 살아 왔다.
그는 / 살아 왔다 / 이 동네에서 / 3년 동안.

→ He / **has lived** / in this town / for three years.

- 과거에 일어난 일이 현재까지 영향을 줄 때는 **현재완료**인 「**have[has]＋과거분사(p.p.)**」 형태로 나타내요.

긍정문	have[has]+p.p. (줄임 표현: 've['s]+p.p.)
부정문	have[has]+부정어(not/never 등)+p.p. (줄임 표현: haven't[hasn't]+p.p.)
의문문	Have[Has]+주어+p.p. ~? — Yes, 주어+have[has]. / No, 주어+haven't[hasn't].

- 과거분사(p.p.)는 과거형과 같은 「**동사원형＋-(e)d**」로 많이 쓰이지만, 불규칙하게 변하는 경우도 많으므로 잘 알아두어야 해요.

📣 동사의 불규칙 과거형·과거분사형(p.p.) (☞ p.180 동사 변화형)

A·A·A형	A·B·B형	A·B·C형
cut-cut-**cut**	buy-bought-**bought**	be-was/were-**been**
put-put-**put**	hear-heard-**heard**	break-broke-**broken**
read[riːd]-read[red]-**read**[red]	have-had-**had**	do-did-**done**
	lose-lost-**lost**	eat-ate-**eaten**
A·B·A형	make-made-**made**	get-got-**got**[ten]
become-became-**become**	send-sent-**sent**	go-went-**gone**
come-came-**come**	teach-taught-**taught**	see-saw-**seen**
run-ran-**run**	meet-met-**met**	take-took-**taken**

- 현재완료는 과거와 연관이 있지만 '현재'의 개념에 더 가깝기 때문에 명백한 과거를 나타내는 부사구 (yesterday, last ~, ago, in＋과거 연도 등)와 함께 쓰지 않아요.
  I ~~have lived~~(→ **lived**) in this town ***three years ago***. 나는 3년 전에 이 동네에서 살았다.

대표 기출 문제

🔒 다음 <보기>와 같이 괄호 안의 동사를 활용하여 현재완료 문장을 완성하시오.

> <보기>
> I want to see a real dragon.
> I have never seen a dragon before. (see)

Daniel ＿＿＿＿＿＿＿＿＿ to Paris before.
This summer will be his first time. (be)

🔍 **CLUE 1**
주어진 동사 see의 현재완료형은 have seen이지만, 문맥상 '본 적이 없다'는 의미의 부정문이 되어야 하므로 — have never seen

🔍 **CLUE 2**
첫 번째 파리 방문이므로 '이전에 가 본 적이 없다'는 의미의 현재완료 부정문이 적절.
— have[has] not[never] p.p.

정답: has not[never] been

Point Exercise

정답 및 해설 p.04

○ 빈칸 완성

[1-6] 주어진 단어를 사용하여 현재완료 문장을 완성하세요.

1 I ____________ ____________ in
the reading club since last year. (be)

2 He ____________ ____________ this book
three times. (read)

3 Emily ____________ ____________ to visit
her grandparents. (go)

4 The tourists ____________ just
____________ at the hotel. (arrive)

5 I ____________ never ____________
a horror movie. (watch)

6 ____________ you ever ____________
a shooting star at night? (see)

○ 주어진 단어로 영작

[7-9] 우리말과 일치하도록 주어진 단어를 사용하여 현재완료
문장을 완성하세요.

7
나는 3년간 수영 수업을 받아왔다.
(swimming lessons, take)

→ ____________________________________
____________________________ for three years.

8
그 요리사는 이미 식사를 준비했다.
(the meal, the cook, prepare)

→ ____________________________________
____________________________ already.

9
그는 지난 월요일 이후로 나에게 전화하지 않았다.
(call)

→ ____________________________________
____________________________ since last Monday.

○ 어법 오류 수정

[10-12] 다음 각 문장의 밑줄 친 부분을 어법상 바르게 고쳐
쓰세요.

10 Jason has never <u>catch</u> a fish.

→ ____________________________________

11 We <u>hasn't eaten</u> dinner yet.

→ ____________________________________

12 She <u>has moved</u> to a new city two years ago.

→ ____________________________________

기출: 조건 영작

13 우리말과 일치하도록 〈조건〉에 맞게 문장을 완성하세요.

〈조건〉
• 주어진 단어를 사용할 것
• 현재완료 문장으로 나타낼 것

(1)
Brown 선생님은 10년 동안 역사를 가르쳐 왔다.
(teach, history, Mr. Brown)

→ ____________________________________
____________________________ for 10 years.

(2)
우리는 아직 콘서트 표를 사지 않았다.
(the concert tickets, buy)

→ ____________________________________
____________________________ yet.

tourist 관광객 shooting star 별똥별 meal 식사 prepare 준비하다

Unit 03 현재완료의 주요 의미

POINT 4　계속, 경험

그녀는 지난주 금요일부터 아팠다.
그녀는 / ~해왔다 / 아픈 / 지난주 금요일부터.

→ She / **has been** / sick / *since* last Friday. <계속>

너는 전에 유명인을 만난 적이 있니?
너는 만난 적이 있니 / 유명인을 / 전에?

→ **Have** you *ever met* / a celebrity / *before*? <경험>

- 현재완료는 여러 의미를 나타낼 수 있는데, '계속'과 '경험'의 의미로 자주 사용돼요.

계속 (지금까지 쭉 ~해오다)	과거부터 현재까지 계속되는 일을 나타내며, 주로 기간을 나타내는 for+기간(~ 동안), since+시점(~ 이후로), how long(얼마나 오래) 등과 함께 쓰여요. I **have known** her *for* 10 years. 나는 그녀를 10년 동안 알고 지내왔다. They **have been** friends *since* childhood. 그들은 어린 시절부터 친구로 지내왔다.
경험 (~한 적이 있다)	과거부터 현재까지의 경험을 나타내며, 주로 before, once, twice, three times, ever(지금까지), never 등과 함께 쓰여요. He **has visited** the U.S. *before*. 그는 전에 미국을 방문한 적이 있다. I **have** *never* **played** the guitar. 나는 기타를 쳐 본 적이 없다. *ever, never는 have[has]와 과거분사(p.p.) 사이에 써요.

대표 기출 문제

🔒 **두 문장의 의미가 포함되도록** 한 문장으로 쓰시오.

Mina moved to Busan 3 years ago.
She still lives there.

→ ________________________________

CLUE 1
과거에 일어난 일(moved)과 현재 '계속'되고 있는 상태(still lives)

CLUE 2
과거에서 현재까지의 의미를 모두 포함할 수 있는 개념은? — 현재완료 「have[has]+p.p.」
3년 전에 이사를 가서 현재 '계속' 살고 있다고 했으므로 기간을 나타내는 말인 「for+기간」을 함께 써야 해요.

정답: Mina has lived in Busan for 3 years.

✓ **함정 피하기** 두 문장을 현재완료를 사용하여 '계속'을 나타내는 한 문장으로 바꿔 쓸 때, 알맞은 부사구로 바꿔 써야 해요.

She began to write the novel *in 2022*. She still writes the novel.
→ She **has written** the novel *since 2022*. (그녀는 2022년 이후로 소설을 써왔다.)

I was sick two days *ago*. I'm still sick now.
→ I **have been** sick *for* two days. (나는 이틀간 아파왔다.)

Point Exercise

[1-3] 우리말과 일치하도록 주어진 단어를 올바르게 배열하세요.

1

그는 스카이다이빙을 해본 적이 없다.
(tried / has / he / skydiving / never)

→ _______________________________ .

2

나의 남동생은 2주째 감기에 걸려 있다.
(has / for / had / my brother / two weeks / a cold)

→ _______________________________
_______________________________ .

3

나는 작년부터 고기를 먹지 않아 왔다.
(last year / not / I / meat / eaten / since / have)

→ _______________________________
_______________________________ .

[4-5] 다음 두 문장을 현재완료를 사용하여 한 문장으로 바꿔 쓸 때 빈칸에 알맞은 말을 쓰세요.

4

It started raining a week ago.
It is still raining.

→ It _______________________ for a week.

5

She started working at this company last year.
She still works at it.

→ She _______________________
_______________________ since last year.

[6-8] 우리말과 일치하도록 주어진 단어를 사용하여 현재완료 문장을 완성하세요.

6

너는 반려동물을 길러본 적이 있니?
(ever, a pet, raise)

→ _______________________________
____

7

그는 2020년 이후로 드럼을 연주해 왔다.
(play, the drums)

→ He _______________________________
_______________________________ .

8

우리는 다른 나라들을 여러 번 가 봤다.
(be, many times, to other countries)

→ _______________________________
____

9 다음 두 문장을 〈조건〉에 맞게 한 문장으로 바꿔 쓰세요.

- Paul began to learn Spanish two years ago.
- He still learns it.

〈조건〉
- 현재완료 문장으로 나타낼 것
- 6 단어로 쓸 것

→ Paul _______________________________
_______________________________ .

skydiving 스카이다이빙 raise 기르다, 키우다 그들은 이미 공항으로 떠났다.
그들은 / 이미 떠났다 / 공항으로.

→ They / **have *already* left** / for the airport. <완료>

나는 방금 충격적인 소식을 들었다.
나는 / 방금 들었다 / 충격적인 소식을.

→ I / **have *just* heard** / the shocking news. <완료>

그는 다리가 부러졌다.
그는 / 부러졌다 / 그의 다리가. (지금도 부러져 있는 상태이다.)

→ He / **has broken** / his leg. <결과>

완료 ((막) ~했다)	과거에 시작한 행동이 현재에 막 끝났음을 나타내며, just(이제 막), already(벌써), recently(최근에), yet(부정문: 아직) 등과 함께 잘 쓰여요. We **haven't received** the package *yet*. 우리는 아직 택배를 받지 않았다. *just, already는 대개 have[has]와 과거분사(p.p.) 사이에, yet은 주로 문장 끝에 씁니다.
결과 (~했다 (그래서 지금 …이다))	과거에 일어난 일의 결과가 현재까지 영향을 미치는 것을 나타내요. We **have lost** the tickets for the concert. 우리는 콘서트 표를 잃어버렸다. (지금도 잃어버린 상태이다.)

주의! have been to(경험) vs. have gone to(결과)

have been to(~에 가 본 적이 있다 (경험))와 have gone to(~에 가버렸다 (결과))는 구별해서 써야 합니다.
She **has been to** Europe. (그녀는 유럽에 가 본 적이 있다.)
She **has gone to** Europe. (그녀는 유럽에 갔다. (지금은 이곳에 없다.))

대표 기출 문제

🔒 다음 주어진 문장을 <예시>와 같이 현재완료를 사용한 문장으로 바꿔 쓰시오.

<예시>
I lost my camera, so I don't have it now.
→ I have lost my camera.

James went to Jeju-do, so he isn't here now.
→ ______________________________

CLUE 1
과거의 일(lost)의 결과가 현재까지 영향을 미치고 있으므로 '결과'를 나타내는 현재완료

CLUE 2
went는 go의 과거형이므로 go를 사용한 알맞은 현재완료 형태는? — have[has] gone

정답: James has gone to Jeju-do.

Point Exercise

배열 영작

[1-3] 우리말과 일치하도록 주어진 단어를 올바르게 배열하세요.

1

나는 이미 내 숙제를 끝냈다.
(have / I / finished / already / homework / my)

→ ________________________________
________________________________ .

2

누군가가 내 휴대전화를 훔쳤다.
(has / cell phone / someone / stolen / my)

→ ________________________________
________________________________ .

3

그들은 아직 해결책을 찾지 못했다.
(not / yet / found / they / a solution / have)

→ ________________________________
________________________________ .

주어진 단어로 영작

[4-8] 우리말과 일치하도록 주어진 단어를 사용하여 현재완료 문장을 완성하세요.

4

Nick은 그의 우산을 잃어버렸다.
(lose, umbrella)

→ ________________________________
____

5

우리는 이미 그 영화를 봤다.
(that movie, see, already)

→ ________________________________
____

6

그 빵집은 방금 모든 빵을 다 팔았다.
(just, the bakery, sell, all of its bread)

→ ________________________________
____

7

나의 반 친구가 실수로 내 안경을 망가뜨렸다.
(break, glasses, classmate)

→ ________________________________
________________________________ by mistake.

8

기차는 아직 역을 떠나지 않았다.
(the station, the train, leave, yet)

→ ________________________________
____

기출: 조건 영작

9 우리말과 일치하도록 〈조건〉에 맞게 문장을 완성하세요.

〈조건〉
• 주어진 단어를 사용할 것
• 현재완료 문장으로 나타낼 것

(1)

그들은 일본 여행에서 방금 돌아왔다.
(just, return, their trip to, from)

→ ________________________________
____

(2)

그녀는 자원봉사하기 위해 아프리카에 갔다.
(to volunteer, go to)

→ ________________________________
____

steal 훔치다 solution 해결책

Chapter Test *

정답 및 해설 p.05

STAGE 1) Go for it!

자신 있게 풀어보는 기초 문제!

빈칸 완성

[1-5] 우리말과 일치하도록 주어진 단어를 사용하여 빈칸에 알맞은 말을 쓰세요.

1
> 월드컵은 4년마다 개최된다. (take place)

→ The World Cup ＿＿＿＿＿ ＿＿＿＿＿ every four years.

2
> 그녀는 가게에서 줄을 서서 기다리고 있다. (wait in line)

→ She ＿＿＿＿＿ ＿＿＿＿＿ ＿＿＿＿＿ ＿＿＿＿＿ at the store.

3
> Susan은 그 개를 8개월 동안 돌봐왔다. (take care of)

→ Susan ＿＿＿＿＿ ＿＿＿＿＿ ＿＿＿＿＿ ＿＿＿＿＿ the dog for eight months.

4
> John은 그의 방에서 음악을 듣고 있었다. (listen to music)

→ John ＿＿＿＿＿ ＿＿＿＿＿ ＿＿＿＿＿ ＿＿＿＿＿ in his room.

5
> 우리는 기차를 타고 전국을 여행할 것이다. (around, travel, the country)

→ We ＿＿＿＿＿ ＿＿＿＿＿ ＿＿＿＿＿ ＿＿＿＿＿ by train.

주어진 단어로 영작

[6-8] 우리말과 일치하도록 주어진 단어를 사용하여 문장을 완성하세요.

6
> 내 친구들이 내일 나의 집을 방문할 것이다. (visit, going, house, tomorrow)

→ My friends ＿＿＿＿＿＿＿＿＿＿ ＿＿＿＿＿＿＿＿＿＿ .

7
> 나는 나의 선생님께 방금 이메일을 보냈다. (have, an email, just, to, send, teacher)

→ I ＿＿＿＿＿＿＿＿＿＿ ＿＿＿＿＿＿＿＿＿＿ .

8
> 내 여동생은 부산에 세 번 가 봤다. (Busan, have, to, three times, be)

→ My sister ＿＿＿＿＿＿＿＿＿＿ ＿＿＿＿＿＿＿＿＿＿ .

최신 기출

9 자연스러운 대화가 되도록 주어진 단어를 배열하여 문장을 완성하세요. (필요시 형태를 바꿀 것)

> A: (1) ＿＿＿＿＿＿＿＿＿＿ with my parents last month.
> B: Oh really? How was it?
> ＿ (2) ＿＿＿＿＿＿＿＿＿＿
> A: It was fantastic! We had a great time.

(1) ＿＿＿＿＿＿＿＿＿＿＿＿＿＿＿ with my parents last month. (go / I / Italy / to)

(2) ＿＿＿＿＿＿＿＿＿＿＿＿＿＿＿ . (there / have / never / I / be)

대화문 완성

[10-14] 주어진 단어를 사용하여 각 대화를 완성하세요.

10
A: What do you usually do on Sunday morning?
B: ___________________________________
_________________ before breakfast.
(a newspaper, read, usually)

11
A: Are you watching TV now?
B: Yes, _______________________________
_______________________________.
(TV show, my, watch, favorite)

12
A: What were you doing at 9 p.m. last night?
B: ___________________________________
_________________ then.
(do, homework, my)

13
A: How long has Mr. Wilson lived in Seoul?
B: He ________________________________
_______________________________.
(Seoul, 2023, live, in)

14
A: _________________________________
Stephen Curry? (hear of)
B: Yes, I have. He is a famous American basketball player.

어법 오류 수정

[15-18] 다음 각 문장의 밑줄 친 부분을 어법상 바르게 고쳐 쓰세요.

15 The Earth was round like a ball.
→ _______________________________

16 They are going starting a new business next year.
→ _______________________________

17 I haven't see my old friend for five years.
→ _______________________________

18 We have lost our room key last night.
→ _______________________________

최신 기출

19 우리말과 일치하도록 주어진 단어를 사용하여 다음의 대화를 완성하세요.

A: Excuse me. I'm looking for my little sister. Can you help me?
B: Sure. What's her name?
A: Her name is Isabel. She's seven years old.
 (1) 그녀는 긴 갈색 머리를 가지고 있어요.
B: What is she wearing today?
A: (2) 그녀는 노란색 티셔츠와 청바지를 입고 있어요.

(1) _______________________________
____
(have, brown hair, long)

(2) _______________________________
____
(a yellow T-shirt, wear, jeans)

[20-24] 다음 두 문장을 〈보기〉와 같이 현재완료를 사용하여 한 문장으로 바꿔 쓰세요.

> 〈보기〉
> Jane started to be sick yesterday.
> She is still sick now.
> → Jane has been sick since yesterday.

20 Jihun started to use the laptop in 2022.
He still uses it.

→ ________________________________

____

21 I started to teach English three years ago.
I still teach it.

→ ________________________________

____

22 My mom lost her wallet.
She doesn't have it now.

→ ________________________________

____

23 He started to work at the school a month ago.
He still works there.

→ ________________________________

____

24 We started the class meeting an hour ago.
We finished it just now.

→ ________________________________

____

25 다음 Oliver와 Chloe의 오늘 일정표를 보고 질문에 알맞은 답을 쓰세요.

Time	Oliver	Chloe
10:00 a.m.	cook some chicken	do yoga
2:00 p.m. (now)	read a magazine	talk on the phone
7:00 p.m.	shop together	

(1) Q: What was Oliver doing at 10 in the morning?

A: He ________________________________.

(2) Q: What is Chloe doing now?

A: She ________________________________.

(3) Q: What are Oliver and Chloe going to do at 7 in the evening?

A: They ________________________________.

26 다음 글을 읽고 〈조건〉에 맞게 우리말을 영작하세요.

> Hannah and I are on the same volleyball team. (1) 우리는 2022년부터 서로를 알고 지내왔다. We always practice together and have great teamwork. (2) 우리는 이전에 많은 경기에서 이겼다.

> 〈조건〉
> • 현재완료 문장으로 나타낼 것
> • 〈보기〉에서 알맞은 단어를 골라 주어진 단어와 함께 사용할 것

> 〈보기〉
> since   for   before   yet

(1) ________________________________

____

(each other, know, 2022)

(2) ________________________________

____

(many games, win)

〔그림 영작〕

27 다음 그림을 보고 〈조건〉에 맞게 대화를 완성하세요.

〈조건〉
• 동사의 과거형 또는 현재완료형을 써서 표현할 것

(1) A: ______________ ______________ ever
   ______________ a horse?

   B: ______________, ______________ ______________.
   I rode a horse on Jeju Island for the first time.

(2) A: I ______________ seen Hyunsu for a long time.

   B: ______________ ______________ ______________
   ______________ New York.

   A: Really? Why did he go there?

   B: He ______________ there to study English.

〔도표 영작〕

28 다음은 지우의 10월 일정표입니다. 표를 보고 현재완료형을 사용하여 글을 완성하세요.

Date	Schedule
10/1	start to study French
10/5	visit an amusement park for the first time
10/10	start to read *The Little Prince*
10/12	study French
10/22 (Today)	study French & read *The Little Prince*
10/25	read *The Little Prince*

Jiwoo started to study French on October 1st. She (1) ______________ French for three weeks. She (2) ______________ the amusement park once in October. She's reading *The Little Prince* these days. But she (3) ______________ ______________ reading it yet. She's going to finish it later.

🎯 **Challenge!** 누적 문제 Ch 01-02

29 다음 ⓐ~ⓔ 중 어법상 틀린 **두 개**를 찾아 그 기호를 쓰고, 바르게 고쳐 쓰세요.

During the summer vacation, ⓐ my family went on a trip to the beach. The weather was perfect, and we spent the day swimming in the ocean. In the afternoon, ⓑ my mom cooked delicious seafood for us. Then, ⓒ she let us to set the table. Later, we watched the beautiful sunset.
　ⓓ Next summer, we will visit a new city. ⓔ My parents has already planned many exciting activities for us.

______ → ______________
____
______ → ______________
____

Chapter 03 조동사

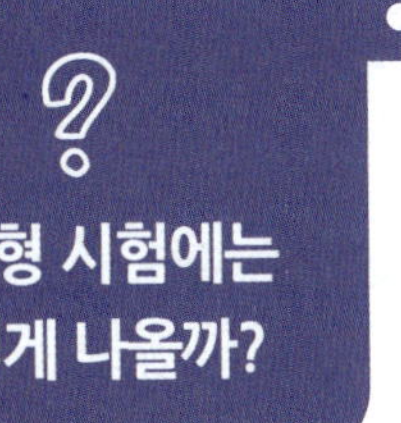

✅ Before You Write

- ✓ 다양한 조동사를 의미에 따라 알맞게 쓸 수 있나요?
- ✓ 조동사 뒤에 오는 동사는 어떤 형태로 써야 할까요?
- ✓ 조동사가 쓰인 문장을 알맞은 어순으로 쓸 수 있나요?
- ✓ be able to/have to는 주어의 인칭과 수, 시제에 따라 어떻게 바꿔 써야 할까요?

내신 기출 다음 우리말을 보고 머릿속으로 한번 영어 문장을 떠올려 보세요.

1 ⓐ Are you able to ride a longboard?

1. 대화문의 밑줄 친 ⓐ의 의미와 같은 문장을 주어진 첫 철자로 영작하시오.

C_______________________________?

be able to = can (능력) → 의문문 → **Can you ride ~?** `POINT 1`

2 (A) 당신은 스마트폰 중독일지도 모른다.

may (추측) → 긍정문 → **may have** `POINT 2`

3 제가 할인받을 수 있나요?

<조건> Can I ~로 시작하는 의문문을 사용할 것

can (허가) → 의문문 → **Can I get ~?** `POINT 3`

4 너는 집에 너무 늦게 오면 안 돼.

<보기> come / shouldn't / you / late / too / home

shouldn't (금지) → **shouldn't come** `POINT 4`

5 너는 초조해 할 필요가 없다.

don't / You / be / have / nervous / to

don't have to (불필요) → **don't have to be** `POINT 5`

6 Joe: Well, 너는 매일 운동을 하는 게 좋겠어.

<보기> better, exercise

had better (충고·권고) → 긍정문 → **had better exercise** `POINT 6`

7 ⓐ 저는 당신의 자원봉사 프로젝트에 참여하고 싶습니다.

(join, I'd like, volunteer project, your, to)

would['d] like to (희망) → **I'd like to join** `POINT 7`

정답: **1** Can you ride a longboard **2** You may have a smartphone addiction. **3** Can I get a discount? **4** You shouldn't come home too late.
5 You don't have to be nervous. **6** you had[you'd] better exercise every day **7** I'd like to join your volunteer project.

can/may/will

 **POINT 1** ~할 수 있다: can(= be able to)

카멜레온은 자신의 색깔을 바꿀 수 있다.
카멜레온은 / 바꿀 수 있다 / 그들의 색깔을.

→ Chameleons / **can change** / their colors.
→ Chameleons / **are able to** change / their colors.

- '~할 수 있다'라고 **능력·가능**을 나타낼 때 조동사 can을 사용하며, 능력의 can은 be able to로
  바꿔 쓸 수 있어요. 이때 be동사를 주어의 인칭과 수, 시제에 알맞게 써야 합니다.
- '~할 수 있었다'라는 **과거의 능력**은 could로 나타내며, was/were able to로 바꿔 쓸 수 있습니다.
  When I was younger, **I could(= was able to)** run very fast. 내가 더 어렸을 때, 아주 빨리 달릴 수 있었다.
- 부정형: cannot[can't] (~할 수 없다) /「am/are/is+not+able to」
  과거 부정형: could not[coudn't] (~할 수 없었다) /「was/were+not+able to」

너는 수영을 잘할 수 있니?
너는 수영할 수 있니 / 잘?

→ **Can** you **swim** / well?
→ **Are** you **able to swim** / well?

- '~할 수 있니?'라는 의미의 의문문은「Can+주어+동사원형 ~?」또는「be동사+주어+able to+동사원형 ~?」의
  형태로 나타낼 수 있어요.

주의 will be able to (~할 수 있을 것이다)

미래의 능력·가능은「will be able to+동사원형」으로 나타냅니다.
조동사는 두 개를 연달아 쓸 수 없으므로 will can으로 쓰지 않도록 주의하세요.
He ~~will can~~(→ **will be able to**) join us for dinner. (그는 저녁 식사에 우리와 함께할 수 있을 것이다.)

대표 기출 문제

🔒 주어진 표현을 이용하여 같은 뜻이 되도록 문장을 완성
하시오.

I [couldn't] speak Chinese.
→ ________________________________
(be able to)

CLUE 1
'~할 수 없었다'라는 불가능은 cannot[can't]의
과거형인 couldn't로 나타내요.

CLUE 2
'~할 수 있다'라는 의미의 be able to의 be동사는
주어의 인칭과 수, 시제에 알맞게 써야 하므로
올바른 be동사의 형태는? — was not[wasn't]

정답: I was not[wasn't] able to speak Chinese.

Point Exercise

배열 영작

[1-4] 우리말과 일치하도록 주어진 단어를 올바르게 배열하세요.

1

그 농구선수는 아주 높이 뛸 수 있다.
(high / can / the basketball player / very / jump)

→ _______________________________

_______________________________ .

2

나는 그 무거운 상자를 혼자 들어 올릴 수 없었다.
(could / I / the heavy box / not / lift)

→ _______________________________

_______________________ by myself.

3

너는 이 수학 문제를 풀 수 있니?
(able / this / you / math / solve / to / are / problem)

→ _______________________________

_______________________________ ?

4

나의 여동생은 9살 때까지 그녀의 신발 끈을 묶을 수 없었다.
(shoes / not / tie / her / was / to / able / my little sister)

→ _______________________________

_______________________ until she was nine.

주어진 단어로 영작

[5-8] 우리말과 일치하도록 주어진 단어를 사용하여 문장을 완성하세요. (필요시 단어를 추가할 것)

5

너는 제시간에 올 수 있니?
(make it, can, on time)

→ _______________________________

6

학생들은 수족관에서 50% 할인을 받을 수 있다.
(a 50% discount, can, students, get)

→ _______________________________

_______________________ at the aquarium.

7

Carl은 그 호수를 헤엄쳐 건널 수 있다.
(across, swim, the lake, able)

→ _______________________________

8

그 소년은 그 퍼즐을 풀 수 없었다.
(the puzzles, the boy, able, solve)

→ _______________________________

____

기출: 조건 영작

9 우리말과 일치하도록 〈조건〉에 맞게 문장을 완성하세요.

모든 아이는 언젠가 그들의 꿈을 찾을 수 있을 것이다.

〈조건〉
• 9 단어로 쓸 것
• every child, dreams, find, their를 사용할 것

→ _______________________________

_______________________ someday.

---

lift 들어 올리다 solve (문제 등을) 풀다. 해결하다 tie 묶다 make it 시간 맞춰 가다 discount 할인 aquarium 수족관

~해도 된다, ~일[할]지도 모른다: may

너는 지금 집에 가도 된다.
너는 / 집에 가도 된다 / 지금.

→ You / **may go** home / now.

- 조동사 may는 '~해도 된다'라는 **허가**의 의미를 나타낼 수 있어요.
- '~하면 안 된다'라고 **금지**를 나타내려면, 「may not+동사원형」으로 나타냅니다.
  You **may not bring** snacks into the library. 도서관에 간식을 가져오면 안 됩니다.
- '~해도 되나요?'라고 **허락**이나 **허가**를 구할 때는 「May+주어+동사원형 ~?」의 어순으로 씁니다.
  May I use the restroom? 화장실을 사용해도 되나요?

그 소문은 사실일지도 모른다.
그 소문은 / 사실일지도 모른다.

→ The rumor / **may** be true.

너는 그것을 믿지 않을지도 모르지만, 그것은 사실이다.
너는 / 믿지 않을지도 모른다 / 그것을, // 하지만 / 그것은 사실이다.

→ You / **may not believe** / it, // but / it's true.

- '~일[할]지도 모른다'라고 불확실한 일에 대한 **추측**을 나타낼 때도 조동사 may를 사용할 수 있어요.
- '~이 아닐지도 모른다, ~하지 않을지도 모른다'라는 의미의 부정형은 「may not+동사원형」의 형태로 씁니다.
- may 대신 might를 쓰기도 하는데, may보다 좀 더 가능성이 적은 일을 추측할 때 쓰여요.
  It **might get** cold tonight, so wear a jacket. 오늘 밤에 추워질지도 모르니, 재킷을 입어라.

대표 기출 문제

🔒 주어진 단어를 배열하여 우리말에 해당하는 영어 문장을 완성하시오.

may / more / need / practice
→ You ________________________.
(너는 더 많은 연습이 필요할지도 모른다.)

🔍 **CLUE 1**
주어진 단어 중 '~할지도 모른다'라고 추측을 나타내는 것은?
— may

🔍 **CLUE 2**
주어진 단어를 배열하여 '더 많은 연습이 필요하다'를 나타내면?
— need more practice

정답: may need more practice

Point Exercise

배열 영작

[1-3] 우리말과 일치하도록 주어진 단어를 올바르게 배열하세요.

1
우리는 다음 주까지 학급 회의를 미룰지도 모른다.
(may / the class meeting / we / put off)

→ _______________________________________
_____________________________ until next week.

2
관광객들은 이 지도와 안내서를 가져가도 된다.
(map / tourists / and / take / a guide book / may / this)

→ _______________________________________
_______________________________________ .

3
내 남동생은 그 장난감들이 더는 필요하지 않을지도 모른다.
(the toys / may / my little brother / need / anymore / not)

→ _______________________________________
_______________________________________ .

주어진 단어로 영작

[4-8] 우리말과 일치하도록 주어진 단어와 may를 사용하여 문장을 완성하세요. (필요시 단어를 추가할 것)

4
당신은 저쪽에 있는 화장실을 사용해도 됩니다.
(the restroom, use, over there)

→ _______________________________________

5
그녀는 그 문제에 대한 답을 알고 있을지도 모른다.
(the question, the answer, know, to)

→ _______________________________________
____

6
우리 팀은 더 많은 연습 없이는 그 경기에서 이기지 못할지도 모른다.
(the match, win, team)

→ _______________________________________
_______________________ without more practice.

7
Sofia와 Tony는 댄스 동아리에 가입할지도 모른다.
(the dance club, and, join)

→ _______________________________________
____

8
이 컴퓨터를 잠시 사용해도 될까요?
(computer, use, for a while, this)

→ _______________________________________

기출: 조건 영작

9 우리말과 일치하도록 <조건>에 맞게 문장을 완성하세요.

그 소녀는 미래에 훌륭한 영화감독이 될지도 모른다.

〈조건〉
• 8 단어로 쓸 것
• excellent, the girl, movie director, become 을 사용할 것

→ _______________________________________
_______________________________ in the future.

---

put off 미루다, 연기하다 tourist 관광객 guide book 안내서 match 경기, 시합 practice 연습; 연습하다 excellent 훌륭한 director 감독

~해도 된다, ~해 주시겠어요?: can
~해 주시겠어요?, ~할 것이다: will

A: 친구네 집에서 자고 와도 되나요?　　B: 그래, 그러렴. / 아니, 안 된단다.
자고 와도 되나요 / 친구네 집에서?

→ A: **Can I** sleep over / at my friend's house?
　 B: Yes, you **can**. / No, you **can't**.

- '~해도 된다'라는 **허락**이나 **허가**의 의미를 나타낼 때, 조동사 may뿐만 아니라 can도 사용할 수 있어요.
  You **can use** my cell phone. 너는 내 휴대 전화를 사용해도 된다.
- '~하면 안 된다'라고 **금지**를 나타내려면, 「cannot[can't]+동사원형」으로 나타냅니다.
  You **cannot touch** the sculptures. 너는 그 조각품들을 만지면 안 된다.
- '~해도 되나요?'라고 **허락**을 구할 때는 「Can+주어+동사원형 ~?」의 어순으로 씁니다.

잠시만 저를 도와주시겠어요?
도와주시겠어요 / 저를 / 잠시만?

→ **Can[Could, Will, Would] you** help / me / for a while?

- 조동사 can과 will은 '~해 줄래요?, ~해 주시겠어요?'와 같은 **요청**의 의미도 나타낼 수 있어요.
  이때 could나 would를 쓰면 좀 더 정중한 표현이 됩니다.
- 조동사 will은 기본적으로 '~할[일] 것이다'라는 의미로 **미래의 일이나 의지**를 나타낼 때도 쓰여요.
  will의 부정형은 will not[won't]으로 씁니다.
  He **won't be** here today. 그는 오늘 여기에 오지 않을 것이다.

대표 기출 문제

🔒 글 (A)의 우리말과 같도록 완전한 영어 문장을 5 단어로 쓰시오. (단, 빈칸에 한 단어씩 쓰시오.)

Andy: How much is it?
Woman: It's 15 dollars.
Andy: That's too expensive for me.
　(A) 제가 할인을 받을 수 있나요?
Woman: No, I'm afraid not.

→ _________ _________ _________ _________
　 _________?

🔍 **CLUE 1**

'~해도 되나요?'라고 허락을 구하는 의문문의
형태는?
— 「Can+주어+동사원형 ~?」

🔍 **CLUE 2**

'할인을 받다'라는 의미의 영어 표현은?
— get a discount

정답: Can I get a discount

Point Exercise

[1-4] 우리말과 일치하도록 주어진 단어를 올바르게 배열하세요.

1
> 너는 네 시험지를 교실 밖으로 가져가도 된다.
> (your / you / exam paper / take / can)

→ ___________________________________
___________________ outside the classroom.

2
> 이 셔츠를 다른 사이즈로 입어 봐도 될까요?
> (this / I / a different size / shirt / can / in / try on)

→ ___________________________________
___________________________________ ?

3
> 이 가방을 잠시 들어주실 수 있나요?
> (hold / for a while / could / this / you / bag)

→ ___________________________________
___________________________________ ?

4
> 저에게 당신의 입장권을 보여주시겠어요?
> (show / your / you / would / ticket / me)

→ ___________________________________
___________________________________ ?

[5-8] 우리말과 일치하도록 can과 will 중 하나를 골라 주어진
단어를 사용하여 문장을 완성하세요.
(필요시 단어를 추가할 것)

5
> 공연 중에 자리를 떠나면 안 됩니다.
> (you, your seat, leave)

→ ___________________________________
during the performance.

6
> 몇 분간 쉬어도 될까요?
> (for a few minutes, a break, take, we)

→ ___________________________________
____

7
> 저희에게 음식 하나를 추천해 주시겠어요?
> (recommend, for us, a dish)

→ ___________________________________
____

8
> 우리 팀은 같은 실수를 반복하지 않을 것이다.
> (the same mistake, team, repeat)

→ ___________________________________

9 우리말과 일치하도록 〈조건〉에 맞게 문장을 완성하세요.

> 휴대 전화 충전기를 잠깐 빌릴 수 있을까요?
>
> 〈조건〉
> • 9 단어로 쓸 것
> • 조동사 can을 사용할 것
> • borrow, for a moment, a phone charger를
>   사용할 것

→ ___________________________________
____

---

try on ~을 입어[신어] 보다 seat 자리, 좌석 performance 공연 recommend 추천하다 dish 음식; 접시 repeat 반복하다 phone charger 휴대 전화 충전기

must/have to/should

POINT 4 ~해야 한다: must, have to, should

승객들은 안전벨트를 매야 한다.
승객들은 / 매야 한다 / 안전벨트를.

→ Passengers / **must** wear / seat belts.
→ Passengers / **have to** wear / seat belts.

- **의무**를 나타내는 조동사 must는 have[has] to로 바꿔 쓸 수 있어요.
  하지만 과거시제일 때 must는 과거형이 없기 때문에 had to(~해야 했다)를 사용해요.
- must는 '~임이 틀림없다'라는 **강한 추측**도 나타낼 수 있어요.
  The game **must be** over. Everyone is leaving the field. 경기가 끝난 것이 틀림없다. 모두가 경기장을 떠나고 있다.

must = have[has] to	~해야 한다 (의무)
	*과거형: had to / 미래형: will have to
must not	~하면 안 된다 (강한 금지)

주의 will have to (~해야 할 것이다)

미래의 의무를 나타낼 때는, 조동사 두 개를 연달아 쓸 수 없으므로 must가 아닌 have to를 사용해야 해요.
We ~~will must~~(→ will have to) leave early to catch the bus. (우리는 버스를 타기 위해 일찍 떠나야 할 것이다.)

너는 수영하기 전에 준비운동을 해야 한다.
너는 / 준비운동을 해야 한다 / 수영하기 전에.

→ You / **should** warm up / before swimming.

- should는 '~해야 한다, ~하는 것이 좋다'라는 의미로 must보다 가벼운 정도의 **의무나 충고**를 나타내요.
- '~하지 말아야 한다'라고 **금지**를 나타낼 때는 should not[shouldn't]으로 씁니다.

대표 기출 문제

다음 우리말에 해당하는 영어 문장을 주어진 단어를 사용
하여 조건에 맞게 쓰시오.

<보기>
- 필요한 경우, 단어의 형태를 어법에 맞게 변형하시오.
- 주어진 단어의 수에 맞게 쓰시오.

그는 그의 숙제를 끝내야만 해. (have, finish)
→ _______________________________ (6 단어)

CLUE 1
주어진 단어 have를 사용해 '~해야 한다'라는
의미를 나타낼 수 있는 말은?
— 「have[has] to+동사원형」

CLUE 2
주어(He)가 3인칭 단수이므로 알맞은 형태는?
— has to finish

정답: He has to finish his homework.

Point Exercise

[1-3] 우리말과 일치하도록 주어진 단어를 올바르게 배열하세요.

1
> 너는 에스컬레이터에서 뛰면 안 된다.
> (not / on / run / the escalator / you / must)

→ ___________________________________
___________________________________.

2
> 수나는 오늘 그녀의 사촌들을 돌봐야 한다.
> (has / cousins / take care of / Suna / her / to)

→ ___________________________________
___________________________________ today.

3
> 너는 그 물건들을 그것들의 원래 위치에 두어야 한다.
> (you / the items / original / in / put / their / place / should)

→ ___________________________________
___________________________________.

[4-9] 우리말과 일치하도록 주어진 단어를 사용하여 문장을 완성하세요. (필요시 형태를 바꿀 것)

4
> 청소년들은 충분한 수면을 취해야 한다.
> (sleep, enough, have, teenagers, get)

→ ___________________________________

5
> 너는 네 ID와 비밀번호를 기억해야 한다.
> (ID, password, remember, and, must)

→ ___________________________________

6
> 그는 그의 여행을 위해 새 여권을 발급받아야 했다.
> (get, have, trip, for, a new passport)

→ ___________________________________
____

7
> 그 가게의 불이 꺼져 있다. 그것은 이제 문을 닫은 것이 틀림없다. (closed, be)

→ The store's lights are off. ___________________
___________________________________ by now.

8
> 학생들은 학교에서 그들의 휴대 전화를 사용하면 안 된다. (cell phones, use, should, students)

→ ___________________________________
___________________________________ in school.

9
> Elly는 학교 행사를 위해 그녀의 연설을 연습해야 한다.
> (practice, have, speech)

→ ___________________________________
for the school event.

10 다음 표지판을 보고 주어진 단어를 사용하여 상황에 맞는 대화를 완성하세요.

A: This place is good for bike riding.
B: Look, there's a sign. You ___________.

→ You ___________________________________
___________________________________ here.

(should, a bike)

escalator 에스컬레이터 original 원래의 teenager 십 대, 청소년 password 비밀번호 passport 여권 speech 연설 event 행사; 사건

POINT 5 ~할 필요가 없다: don't[doesn't] have to

천천히 해라. 서두를 필요가 없다.
천천히 해라. (너는) / 서두를 필요가 없다.

→ Take your time. You / **don't have to** hurry.

그녀는 자신의 점심을 가져올 필요가 없다.
그녀는 / 가져올 필요가 없다 / 그녀 자신의 점심을.

→ She / **doesn't have to** bring / her own lunch.

• must와 have to는 모두 '~해야 한다'라는 의미가 있지만, 부정형의 의미는 서로 다르므로 구분해서 사용해야 합니다.

must not	~하면 안 된다 (강한 금지)
don't[doesn't] have to	~할 필요가 없다, ~하지 않아도 된다 (불필요)
	*과거형: didn't have to

I **didn't have to pay** for the concert ticket. My friend got it for me as a birthday gift.
나는 콘서트 표의 값을 지불할 필요가 없었다. 친구가 나에게 생일 선물로 사 주었다.

대표 기출 문제

🔒 다음 대화의 빈칸에 have to 또는 don't have to 중 알맞은 것을 골라 형태에 맞게 바꿔 문장을 완성하시오.
(주어진 표현을 활용할 것, 완전한 영어 문장을 쓸 것)

> A: What's the weather like today?
> B: It's sunny. _________________.
>   (take an umbrella)

→ _________________________________.

CLUE 1
문맥상 have to(~해야 한다)와 don't have to(~할 필요가 없다) 중 알맞은 의미를 나타내는 것을 골라 써야 해요.

CLUE 2
날씨가 화창하다고 했으므로, '우산을 가져갈 필요가 없다'라는 의미는 don't have to를 사용해 나타내야 해요.

정답: You don't have to take an umbrella

✓ 함정 피하기 우리말이 주어지지 않는 경우, have to를 문맥상 판단하여 알맞은 시제로 바꿔 쓰세요.

My mom **works** Monday through Friday. (나의 엄마는 월요일부터 금요일까지 일하셔.)
She _________________________ on weekends. (그녀는 주말에는 일할 필요가 없으셔.)

→ doesn't have to work

He **had** dinner plans with his friends **last night**. (그는 어젯밤에 친구들과 저녁 약속이 있었다.)
So he _________________________ dinner. (그래서 그는 저녁을 요리할 필요가 없었다.)

→ didn't have to cook

Point Exercise

[1-3] 우리말과 일치하도록 주어진 단어를 올바르게 배열하세요.

1
> 너는 지금 당장 답하지 않아도 된다.
> (right now / have / you / answer / to / don't)

→ ______________________________

______________________________ .

2
> 나는 이번 주말까지 내 숙제를 끝낼 필요가 없다.
> (have / finish / this weekend / by / to / homework / don't / my / I)

→ ______________________________

______________________________ .

3
> 그들은 그 식당에서 줄을 설 필요가 없었다.
> (didn't / in line / to / they / wait / have)

→ ______________________________

______________________________ at the restaurant.

[4-8] 우리말과 일치하도록 주어진 단어와 have to를 사용하여 문장을 완성하세요.

4
> 너는 이 식물에 매일 물을 줄 필요가 없다.
> (plant, water, every day, this)

→ ______________________________

5
> 그는 매주 금요일에는 교복을 입을 필요가 없다.
> (a school uniform, wear)

→ ______________________________

______________________________ on Fridays.

6
> 학부모님들은 그 회의에 참석하시지 않아도 됩니다.
> (attend, parents, the meeting)

→ ______________________________

____

7
> Lily는 통학 버스를 탈 필요가 없다.
> (the school bus, take)

→ ______________________________

____

8
> 우리는 날씨에 대해 걱정할 필요가 없었다.
> (the weather, worry about)

→ ______________________________

____

9 우리말과 일치하도록 〈보기〉에서 알맞은 단어를 골라 have to를 사용하여 문장을 완성하세요.

> 〈보기〉 sign up   pay

> Alex는 대회에 등록해야 하지만, 참가비를 낼 필요는 없다.

→ Alex ______________________________ for

the competition, but he ______________________________

______________________________ a fee.

---

water 물을 주다 attend 참석하다 sign up 신청하다, 등록하다 competition 대회; 경쟁 fee 회비, 입장료; 요금

had better/would like to/used to

POINT 6 ~하는 게 좋다: had better

너는 네 우산을 가져가는 게 좋겠다.
너는 / 가져가는 게 좋겠다 / 네 우산을.

→ You / **had better take** / your umbrella.

너는 정크 푸드를 너무 많이 먹지 않는 게 좋겠다.
너는 / 먹지 않는 게 좋겠다 / 너무 많은 정크 푸드를.

→ You / **had better not eat** / too much junk food.

- had better는 '~하는 게 좋다[낫다]'라는 뜻으로, should보다 더 강한 **충고나 권고**를 나타낼 때 쓰여요.
- 주어가 인칭대명사일 때 줄여서 'd better로 쓰기도 하며, 부정형은 had better not으로 씁니다.
  You'd better not tell anyone about this. 너는 이것에 대해 아무한테도 이야기하지 않는 게 좋겠어.
- had better (not) 뒤에는 항상 동사원형을 쓰는 점에 주의하세요.

대표 기출 문제

공부하면서 스마트폰을 사용하는 친구에게 better를 이용하여 우리말과 같은 의미가 되도록 문장을 완성하시오.

공부하는 동안에는 스마트폰을 사용하지 않는 것이 좋다.

→ ________________________________
  while you are studying.

CLUE 1
'~하지 않는 것이 좋다[낫다]'라고 충고를 나타내는 말이 빈칸에 쓰여야 해요.

CLUE 2
better를 이용하여 충고의 의미를 나타낼 수 있는 영어 표현은?
— had better (not)

정답: You had[You'd] better not use your smartphone

함정 피하기 had better의 부정형을 쓸 때, not의 위치에 주의하세요.
You **had not better** use your smartphone. (×)
→ You **had better not** use your smartphone. (○)

○─ 배열 영작

[1-3] 우리말과 일치하도록 주어진 단어를 올바르게 배열하세요.

1
> 너는 지금 네 약을 먹는 게 좋겠어.
> (your / better / you / medicine / take / had)

→ ___________________________________

___________________________________ now.

2
> 우리는 그 소문을 믿지 않는 게 좋겠다.
> (the rumor / we / not / had / believe / better)

→ ___________________________________

___________________________________ .

3
> 너는 그 콘서트 표를 일찍 사는 게 좋겠다.
> (better / the concert ticket / you / early / buy / had)

→ ___________________________________

___________________________________ .

○─ 주어진 단어로 영작

[4-7] 우리말과 일치하도록 주어진 단어를 사용하여 문장을 완성하세요. (필요시 단어를 추가할 것)

4
> 우리는 마지막 기차를 놓치지 않는 게 좋겠다.
> (the last train, miss, better)

→ ___________________________________

5
> Ted는 그의 실수에 대해 사과하는 게 좋겠다.
> (better, mistake, for, apologize)

→ ___________________________________

____

6
> 너는 그 유리잔을 조심하는 게 좋겠다.
> (careful, that glass, better, be, with)

→ ___________________________________

____

7
> 너는 TV에 너무 가깝게 앉지 않는 게 좋겠다.
> (to the TV, better, too close, sit)

→ ___________________________________

____

기출: 조건 영작

8 다음 대화를 읽고 〈조건〉에 맞게 우리말을 영작하세요.

> A: Andy, I think you eat too many sweets these days.
> B: I know, I just can't stop it.
> A: That's not good for your health.
> <u>너는 과일을 대신 먹는 게 좋겠어.</u>

> 〈조건〉
> • 5 단어로 쓸 것
> • fruit, eat을 사용할 것

→ ___________________________________

___________________________________ instead.

medicine 약 rumor 소문 apologize 사과하다 sweet 단것; 달콤한 health 건강 instead 대신에

~하고 싶다: would like to
(전에는) ~하곤 했다, ~였다[했다]: used to

저는 이 물건을 반품하고 싶어요.
저는 반품하고 싶어요 / 이 물건을.

→ I'**d like to** return / this item.

- would like to는 '~하고 싶다'라는 의미로 공손한 **'희망'**을 나타내며, 주어가 인칭대명사일 때는 줄여서 'd like to로 자주 쓰여요.

우유 한 잔을 드시겠어요?
드시겠어요 / 우유 한 잔을?

→ **Would you like to** drink / a glass of milk?

- Would you like to ~? 의문문은 '~하시겠어요?'라는 의미로 공손한 **'권유·제안'**을 나타내요.

우리 가족은 봄마다 캠핑을 가곤 했다.
우리 가족은 / 캠핑을 가곤 했다 / 봄마다.

→ Our family / **used to** go camping / every spring.

- used to는 '(전에는) ~하곤 했다, (전에는) ~였는데[했는데] (지금은 아니다)'라는 뜻으로 **과거의 습관이나 상태를** 나타내요.
  She **used to have** long hair. 그녀는 긴 머리를 가지고 있었다. (지금은 아니다.)

> **MORE +** '과거의 습관'을 나타내는 used to(~하곤 했다)는 조동사 would로 바꿔 쓸 수 있어요.
> He **used to** eat cereal for breakfast every day. (그는 매일 아침으로 시리얼을 먹곤 했다.)
> = He **would** eat cereal for breakfast every day.

대표 기출 문제

🔒 밑줄 친 ⓐ의 우리말을 주어진 단어를 적절히 배열하여 영어 문장으로 완성하시오.

> ⓐ 나는 내 봉사클럽, Evergreen을 소개하고 싶어.
> (introduce, I'd like, Evergreen, volunteer club, to, my)
>
> → ______________________________________

CLUE 1
'~하고 싶다'라고 희망을 나타내는 말이 빈칸에 쓰여야 해요.

CLUE 2
주어진 단어를 「would['d] like to+동사원형」의 순서로 쓰면 돼요.

정답: I'd like to introduce my volunteer club, Evergreen.

Point Exercise

[1-4] 우리말과 일치하도록 주어진 단어를 올바르게 배열하세요.

1
우리 가족은 매주 금요일 밤에 외식을 하곤 했다.
(eat out / family / used / our / to)

→ ____________________
____________________ every Friday night.

2
그녀는 언젠가 파리를 방문하고 싶다.
(would / Paris / to / she / visit / like)

→ ____________________
____________________ someday.

3
우리 스터디 그룹에 참여하겠니?
(our / would / join / study group / like / to / you)

→ ____________________
____________________ ?

4
나의 남동생은 더 어렸을 때 어둠을 무서워했다.
(my / be afraid of / to / brother / the dark / used)

→ ____________________
____________________ when he was younger.

[5-8] 우리말과 일치하도록 주어진 단어와 would like to 또는 used to를 사용하여 문장을 완성하세요.

5
이 건물은 5년 전에는 도서관이었다.
(be, building, a library, this)

→ ____________________
____________________ 5 years ago.

6
저는 커피 한 잔을 주문하고 싶어요.
(a cup of, order, coffee)

→ ____________________
____

7
나의 아빠와 나는 매주 주말에 낚시를 하러 가곤 했지만 지금은 아니다.
(go fishing, dad, and)

→ ____________________
every weekend, but now we don't.

8
공원에 산책하러 가시겠어요?
(in the park, go for a walk)

→ ____________________
____

9 우리말과 일치하도록 〈조건〉에 맞게 문장을 완성하세요.

우리는 올해 여름에 지역 복지관에서 자원봉사를 하고 싶다.

〈조건〉
• 9 단어로 쓸 것
• at, volunteer, the community center를 사용할 것

→ ____________________
____________________ this summer.

order 주문하다 volunteer 자원봉사를 하다 community center 지역 복지관

Chapter Test *

정답 및 해설 p.07

STAGE 1 Go for it!

자신 있게 풀어보는 기초 문제!

배열 영작

[1-4] 우리말과 일치하도록 주어진 단어를 배열하여 문장을 완성하세요.

1

> 그녀는 다음 주에 치과를 방문해야 한다.
> (has / next week / the dentist / visit / to)

→ She ____________________

____________________ .

2

> 당신의 안전벨트를 매주시겠어요?
> (your / you / would / seat belt / fasten)

→ ____________________

____________________ ?

3

> Sophie는 그녀의 용돈을 낭비해선 안 된다.
> (not / her / waste / should / allowance)

→ Sophie ____________________

____________________ .

4

> 너는 우리의 약속을 또 미뤄선 안 된다.
> (our / may / again / delay / not / appointment)

→ You ____________________

____________________ .

빈칸 완성

[5-7] 우리말과 일치하도록 주어진 단어를 사용하여 빈칸에 알맞은 말을 쓰세요.

5

> 당신은 저에게 이 영화에 대해 설명해 주실 수 있나요?
> (explain, can, movie)

→ ________ ________ ________

________ ________ to me?

6

> 모든 사람은 지금 당장 이 건물을 떠나야 한다.
> (leave, building, must, everyone)

→ ________ ________ ________

________ ________ right now.

7

> 너는 잠시 휴식을 취하는 게 좋겠다.
> (a rest, for a while, take)

→ You ____________________

____

____________________ .

최신 기출

8 다음 밑줄 친 부분과 같은 의미가 되도록 알맞은 조동사를 사용해 문장을 바꿔 쓰세요.

> A: What do you do when you're stressed?
> B: I ride my skateboard when I'm stressed.
>   <u>Are you able to ride a skateboard?</u>
> A: No, I'm not.
> B: Let's go out together! I'll teach you.

→ ____________________ ?

○─ 문장 전환

[9-13] 주어진 문장과 의미가 같도록 괄호 안의 단어를 사용하여 문장 전체를 다시 쓰세요.

9

> Nate must buy a ticket to enter the zoo.
> (have to)

→ _______________________________

____

10

> You cannot play loud music after 10 p.m.
> (may)

→ _______________________________

____

11

> She lived in New York. Now, she doesn't live in New York. (used to)

→ _______________________________

____

12

> Susan couldn't attend the class meeting.
> (be able to)

→ _______________________________

____

13

> We want to adopt a puppy from the shelter.
> (would like to)

→ _______________________________

____

○─ 그림 영작

14 다음은 환경 보호를 위해 해야 할 일을 나타낸 그림입니다. 〈보기〉와 같이 주어진 단어를 사용하여 문장을 완성하세요.

〈보기〉

We <u>should turn off the light</u> when we go out.
(the light, should, turn off)

→ We _______________________________ .

(use, had better, plastic bags)

최신 기출

15 〈보기 A〉와 〈보기 B〉에서 각각 알맞은 말을 골라 상황에 알맞은 문장을 완성하세요. (단, 한 번씩만 쓸 것)

〈보기 A〉		
had better	may	may not

〈보기 B〉	
see a doctor	rain soon
bring food or drinks	

(1) The sky is dark. It _______________________

_______________________ .

(2) You don't look well today. You _______________

_______________________ .

(3) You can eat snacks in the lobby. But you

____

into the library.

[16-19] 〈보기〉에서 알맞은 조동사를 골라 주어진 단어와 함께 배열하여 각 대화를 완성하세요. (단, 한 번씩만 쓸 것)

〈보기〉

may	don't have to
will	had better not

16

A: ______________________________

______________________________ ?

(have / juice / you / more / some)

B: Oh, thanks. But I want some water.

A: Sure. Here you are.

17

A: Tomorrow is Hojin's birthday. I don't know what to buy.

B: I have been to his house before. His room was full of books.

______________________________ .

(like / he / books / reading)

A: I get it. I'll buy him a book then.

18

A: You're eating a hamburger again.

B: I really like hamburgers.

A: But that's not good for your health.

____

______________________________ .

(eat / too / you / hamburgers / often)

19

A: The party starts at 5 o'clock.

B: Okay. What should I bring?

A: ______________________________

______________________________ . (bring / you / anything)

I prepared everything.

[20-23] 다음 각 문장에서 어법상 <u>틀린</u> 부분을 찾아 바르게 고쳐 쓰세요.

20 We'd better went home because it's too late now.

______________ → ______________

21 My sister may is tired because she has just finished her final exams.

______________ → ______________

22 You have not to borrow a pencil. I have two.

______________ → ______________

23 You will must change trains at the next station.

______________ → ______________

24 다음 메모의 내용과 일치하도록 〈조건〉에 맞게 문장을 완성하세요.

Dear Brenda,

Please return the books to the library. Also, you don't need to go to swimming practice today. It's canceled.

From Mom

〈조건〉
- (1), (2) 모두 have to를 사용하되 필요시 형태를 바꿀 것
- 현재시제로 쓸 것

(1) Brenda ______________ ______________

______________ ______________ to the library.

(2) Brenda ______________ ______________

______________ ______________ to swimming practice today.

○─(도표 영작)

25 다음 Henry의 생활 습관 점검표를 보고 〈보기〉와 같이 had better를 사용하여 충고하는 문장을 쓰세요.

Habits	Yes	No
exercise regularly		∨
(1) have a meal three times a day		∨
(2) talk on the phone too long	∨	
(3) buy too many clothes every month	∨	
(4) do laundry every week		∨

〈보기〉
You had better exercise regularly.

(1) ______________________________
____

(2) ______________________________
____

(3) ______________________________
____

(4) ______________________________
____

○─(어법 오류 수정)

26 다음 ⓐ~ⓔ 중 어법상 틀린 두 개를 찾아 그 기호를 쓰고, 바르게 고쳐 쓰세요.

Mike: You look down today. What's the matter, Brian?
Brian: My friend ⓐ will move to Busan. That makes me really sad.
Mike: Come on. You ⓑ can visit him on vacation.
Brian: I know. But I ⓒ can't play soccer with him anymore.
Mike: You will ⓓ can find another friend to play soccer together soon. You ⓔ have to be too sad.
Brian: You're right. Thanks, Mike.

______ → ________________________

______ → ________________________

○ **Challenge!**　　　누적 문제 Ch 01-03

27 다음 중 어법상 틀린 문장 두 개를 찾아 그 기호를 쓰고, 문장 전체를 바르게 고쳐 쓰세요.

ⓐ You must not be late for school.
ⓑ Tom broke his arm last week.
ⓒ We have to being quiet on the subway.
ⓓ I expect my guests to arrive around 7 p.m.
ⓔ Have you ever see the sunrise at the beach?

______ → ________________________

______ → ________________________
____

수동태*

☑ Before You Write

- ☑ 능동태와 수동태의 쓰임 차이를 구분할 수 있나요?
- ☑ 능동태를 수동태로 바꿀 때, 주어 자리에 무엇이 오는지 알고 있나요?
- ☑ 수동태의 「be동사+과거분사(p.p.)」에 적절한 과거분사를 쓸 수 있나요?
- ☑ 수동태 문장에서 시제에 알맞게 be동사의 형태를 바꿀 수 있나요?

내신 기출 다음 우리말을 보고 머릿속으로 한번 영어 문장을 떠올려 보세요.

1 (2) These magazines ___________ at most bookstores. (sell)
(이 잡지들은 대부분의 서점에서 팔린다.)
수동태 → 현재시제 → 긍정문 → **are sold**　　POINT 1

2 그 사진은 Andy에 의해 찍혔다.
정답: The photo __________ __________ __________ Andy.
수동태 → 과거시제 → 긍정문 → **was taken by**　　POINT 2

3 언제 그 차는 도난당했니?
→ __________ __________ __________ __________ __________ ?
수동태 → 과거시제 → 의문사가 있는 의문문 → **When was ~ stolen?**　　POINT 3

4 should / people / protect / the environment
(환경은 사람들에 의해 보호되어야 한다.)
수동태 → 조동사를 포함하는 수동태 → **should be protected**　　POINT 3

5 다음 문장의 밑줄 친 부분을 주어로 하는 수동태 문장을 완성하시오.
My uncle bought me the new backpack.
→ ____
「buy+간접목적어+직접목적어」의 수동태 → 직접목적어가 주어 → **was bought for me**　　POINT 4

6 ⓒ 그것들은 부드러운 초록색 잔디로 뒤덮여 있다.
by 이외의 전치사를 쓰는 수동태 표현 → 현재시제 → 긍정문 → **are covered with**　　POINT 5

정답: **1** are sold **2** was taken by **3** When was the car stolen **4** The environment should be protected by people. **5** The new backpack was bought for me by my uncle. **6** They are[They're] covered with soft green grass.

Unit 01 수동태의 기본 이해

 주어가 동작을 당하는 수동태 = be동사+과거분사(p.p.)

식물들은 매주 아빠에 의해 물이 주어진다.

식물들은 / 물이 주어진다 / 아빠에 의해 / 매주.
　주어　　　　동사　　　　by+행위자

→ 능동태의 목적어를 수동태의 주어로 쓰므로,
목적어가 없는 SV나 SVC 문장은 수동태로 쓸 수 없어요.

My dad / **waters** / the plants / every week. 〈능동태〉

→ The plants / **are watered** / *by* my dad / every week. 〈수동태〉
　　　　　　　be p.p.　　　　　　by+행위자

- 우리가 지금까지 다룬 문장은 주어가 동사의 동작을 하는 능동태(~가 …하다)였어요.
- 하지만, 주어가 동작의 대상이 되면 이를 **수동태**(~가 …하게 되다)라고 하며 「**be동사+과거분사(p.p.)**」의 형태로 나타내요. 그 뒤에는 「**by+행위자**」로 누가 동작을 하는지 밝혀 줘요.
- 이때 be동사는 수동태 문장의 주어의 인칭과 수에 맞게 써야 하며, 과거분사(p.p.)는 특히 불규칙 변화형에 주의해서 써야 해요. (☞ p.180 동사 변화형)
  Some people **speak** French in Canada. 〈능동태〉
  → French **is spoken** by some people in Canada. 〈수동태〉 캐나다에서 불어는 일부 사람들에 의해 쓰인다.

주의!

1 「by+행위자」는 행위자가 일반적인 사람이거나 불분명한 경우, 또는 문맥상 알 수 있는 경우에는 주로 생략해요.
  The mail **is delivered** in the morning. (우편은 아침에 배달된다.)

2 수동태의 행위자가 대명사일 경우, by 뒤는 반드시 목적격으로 써야 해요.
  He manages the restaurant.
  → The restaurant is managed **by he**(→ him). (그 식당은 그에 의해 관리된다.)

대표 기출 문제

🔒 다음 문장을 괄호 안에 지시대로 바꾸시오.

(A) The cat catches the mouse.
(수동태 문장으로 바꾸시오.)

→ _______________________________

CLUE 1
수동태는 능동태의 목적어를 주어로 쓰므로,
문장의 맨 앞에는 먼저 The mouse를 써줍니다.

CLUE 2
수동태의 동사는 「be동사+p.p.」로 나타내며,
be동사는 주어의 수에 맞게 바꿔 써야 해요.
즉, 동사 catches는 is caught로 바꿔 써요. 마지막으로
그 뒤에는 능동태의 주어를 「by+행위자」로 나타내요.

정답: The mouse is caught by the cat.

Point Exercise

[1-4] 우리말과 일치하도록 주어진 단어를 올바르게 배열하세요.

1
> 그 작가의 책은 많은 사람들에 의해 읽힌다.
> (read / lots of / by / is / people)

→ The writer's book _______________

_______________ .

2
> 아이들은 그들의 부모님에 의해 사랑받는다.
> (are / parents / by / loved / their)

→ Children _______________

_______________ .

3
> 그 꽃들은 나의 엄마에 의해 길러진다.
> (mom / the flowers / by / grown / are / my)

→ _______________ .

4
> 그 노인들은 자원봉사자들의 도움을 받는다.
> (volunteers / the old men / helped / are / by)

→ _______________

_______________ .

[5-9] 우리말과 일치하도록 주어진 단어를 사용하여 문장을 완성하세요.

5
> 그 선생님은 학생들에 의해 존경받는다.
> (the teacher, respect, the students)

→ _______________

_______________ .

6
> 저녁 식사가 나의 아빠에 의해 요리된다.
> (cook, dad, dinner)

→ _______________

7
> 몇몇 동물들은 국가에 의해 보호된다.
> (some animals, the country, protect)

→ _______________

____

8
> 많은 돈이 정부에 의해 교육에 쓰인다.
> (education, spend, on, a lot of money)

→ _______________

by the government.

9
> 프랑스는 전 세계 많은 사람들에 의해 방문 된다.
> (many people, France, around the world, visit)

→ _______________

____

10 다음 대화를 읽고 〈조건〉에 맞게 우리말을 영작하세요.

> A: Jina, I want to join your discussion club.
>   What kind of topics do you discuss?
> B: There are a lot of different topics, such as
>   movies, nature, and culture.
>   Every Monday, <u>다른 주제들이 토의 돼.</u>

> 〈조건〉
> • 대화에서 언급된 단어를 사용할 것
> • 4 단어로 쓸 것

→ Every Monday, _______________

_______________ .

volunteer 자원봉사자; 자원봉사를 하다 respect 존경하다; 존중하다 protect 보호하다 education 교육 government 정부 discussion 토론, 논의 topic 주제

POINT 2 수동태의 과거와 미래

내 컴퓨터는 아빠에 의해 고쳐졌다.
내 컴퓨터는 / 고쳐졌다 / 나의 아빠에 의해.
　　주어　　　동사　　　by+행위자

→ My computer / **was fixed** / by my dad.
　(← My dad **fixed** my computer.)

야생 동물들이 소방관들에 의해 구조되었다.
야생 동물들이 / 구조되었다 / 소방관들에 의해.
　　주어　　　　동사　　　by+행위자

→ Wild animals / **were rescued** / by the firefighters.
　(← The firefighters **rescued** wild animals.)

시험은 다음 주 월요일에 모두에 의해 치러질 것이다.
시험은 / 치러질 것이다 / 모두에 의해 / 다음 주 월요일에.
　주어　　　동사　　　by+행위자

→ The quiz / **will be taken** / by everyone / next Monday.
　(← Everyone **will take** the quiz next Monday.)

• 수동태의 시제는 be동사로 나타내며, 능동태 문장을 수동태로 바꿀 때 시제는 바뀌지 않는 것에 주의하세요.

수동태 과거	~되었다	was[were]+과거분사(p.p.)
수동태 미래	~될 것이다	will be+과거분사(p.p.)

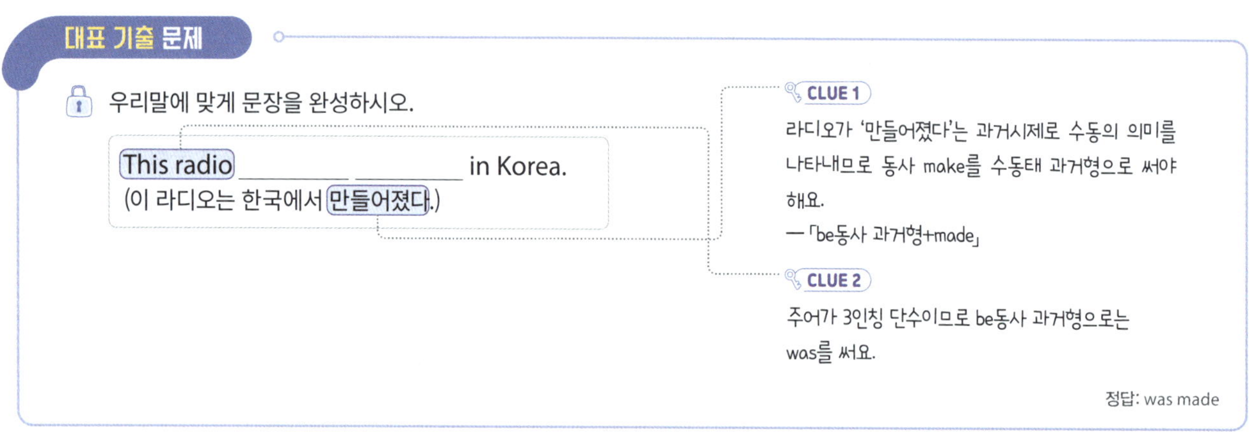

함정 피하기 능동태 문장을 수동태로 바꿀 때 '주어-be동사'의 수일치에 주의하세요.

My sister found the seashell.
→ The seashell was found by my sister. (조개껍질이 내 여동생에 의해 발견되었다.)

I baked these chocolate cookies.
→ These chocolate cookies were baked by me. (이 초콜릿 쿠키들은 나에 의해 구워졌다.)

Point Exercise

○─ **배열 영작**

[1-3] 우리말과 일치하도록 주어진 단어를 올바르게 배열하세요.

1
> 그 편지는 내 가장 친한 친구에 의해 쓰였다.
> (written / best friend / the letter / my / was / by)

→ ____

____.

2
> 한글은 세종대왕에 의해 창제되었다.
> (was / King Sejong / Hangeul / created / by)

→ ____

____.

3
> 모두가 크리스마스 파티에 초대될 것이다.
> (to / be / everyone / the Christmas party / invited / will)

→ ____

____.

○─ **문장 전환**

[4-5] 다음 문장을 수동태로 바꿔 쓰세요.

4
> My grandfather built our new house.

→ ____

____

5
> The teachers will judge this year's talent show.

→ ____

____

○─ **주어진 단어로 영작**

[6-8] 우리말과 일치하도록 주어진 단어를 사용하여 문장을 완성하세요.

6
> 축구 경기가 비 때문에 취소되었다.
> (the soccer match, cancel)

→ ____

________________________________ because of rain.

7
> 그 그림은 침실로 옮겨졌다.
> (to, the picture, the bedroom, move)

→ ____

____

8
> 우승자는 그 심사위원들에 의해 선택될 것이다.
> (choose, the judges, the winner)

→ ____

____

기출: 조건 영작

9 다음 대화를 읽고 질문에 대한 대답을 〈조건〉에 맞게 완성하세요.

> A: These cookies are so sweet. Did you make them yourself?
> B: No, ________________________________.
> (bake, they, my mom)

> 〈조건〉
> • 주어진 단어를 사용할 것
> • 6 단어로 쓸 것

→ No, ____

____.

create 창조하다, 만들다 judge 심사하다; 심사위원

Unit 02 수동태의 여러 가지 형태

 수동태 부정문/의문문, 조동사+수동태

교실은 학생들에 의해 청소되지 않았다.

교실은 / 청소되지 않았다 / 학생들에 의해.
　주어　　　　동사　　　　by+행위자

→ The classroom / **was not cleaned** / by the students.

📢 수동태의 부정문과 의문문

부정문	be동사＋not＋과거분사(p.p.)	The garbage **is not collected** today. 오늘은 쓰레기가 수거되지 않는다.
의문문	(의문사＋)be동사＋주어＋과거분사(p.p.) ~?	**Were** the books **returned** to the library? 그 책들은 도서관에 반납되었니? **When was** the house **built**? 그 집은 언제 지어졌니?

이 약은 식사 후에 복용되어야 한다.

이 약은 / 복용되어야 한다 / 식사 후에.

→ This medicine / **must be taken** / after meals.

📢 조동사를 포함한 수동태

긍정문	조동사＋be p.p.	The package **should be delivered** today. 그 소포는 오늘 배달되어야 한다.
부정문	조동사＋not＋be p.p.	The decision **cannot be changed** now. 그 결정은 이제 바뀔 수 없다.
의문문	조동사＋주어＋be p.p. ~?	**Can** the problem **be fixed** by tomorrow? 그 문제는 내일까지 해결될 수 있나요?

대표 기출 문제

🔒 다음 제시된 우리말과 같은 뜻이 되도록 <조건>에 맞게 한 문장으로 영어로 쓰시오.

돌고래들은 이 지역에서 발견될 수 있다.

<조건>
- 수동태로 표현할 것
- can, dolphins, area를 포함하여 쓸 것

→ ______________________________________

CLUE 1

'~될 수 있다'는 수동의 의미는 조동사 can을 사용해 나타낼 수 있어요.

CLUE 2

조동사를 포함한 수동태는 「조동사+be p.p.」으로 나타내며, p.p. 자리에는 '발견하다'라는 의미의 동사 find를 과거분사 형태로 쓰면 돼요.

정답: Dolphins can be found in this area.

✅ **함정 피하기** 조동사 뒤에는 항상 동사원형이 오므로 항상 be로 써야 해요.

The computer **can is**(→ **be**) **used** by every student. (그 컴퓨터는 모든 학생에 의해 사용될 수 있다.)

Point Exercise

[1-5] 우리말과 일치하도록 주어진 단어를 올바르게 배열하세요.

1
네 방은 내일까지 청소되어야 해.
(be / your / cleaned / room / must)

→ _______________________________
_______________________ by tomorrow.

2
이 호텔에서는 아침식사가 정오 이후에 제공되지 않는다. (not / is / breakfast / served)

→ _______________________________
after noon at this hotel.

3
그 영화는 많은 사람에 의해 관람되었니?
(watched / by / the movie / many people / was)

→ _______________________________
_______________________________?

4
우리의 추억은 영원히 잊히지 않을 것이다.
(be / will / forgotten / our / not / memories)

→ _______________________________
_______________________ forever.

5
그 건물은 전문가들에 의해 설계되지 않았다.
(was / by / designed / not / experts / the building)

→ _______________________________
_______________________________.

[6-9] 우리말과 일치하도록 주어진 단어를 사용하여 문장을 완성하세요.

6
그 상품들은 더 이상 한국에서 만들어지지 않는다.
(those products, make)

→ _______________________________
in Korea anymore.

7
그 원숭이들은 동물원에서 길러지지 않았다.
(in, the monkeys, raise, the zoo)

→ _______________________________
____

8
자유의 여신상은 언제 지어졌니?
(the Statue of Liberty, build)

→ _______________________________

9
그 일은 내일까지 끝나지 않을 것이다.
(the work, finish)

→ _______________________________
by tomorrow.

기출: 조건 영작

10 우리말과 일치하도록 〈조건〉에 맞게 문장을 완성하세요.

〈조건〉
• 수동태를 사용할 것
• 주어진 단어를 사용하되 필요시 형태를 바꿀 것

그 숨겨진 보물은 어디에서 발견되었니?
(find, the hidden treasure)

→ _______________________________
____

serve (음식을) 제공하다 forever 영원히 expert 전문가 product 상품, 제품 raise 기르다 hidden 숨겨진 treasure 보물

SVOO 문형의 수동태

선생님이 주셨다 / 우리에게 / 재미있는 프로젝트를.

The teacher **gave** / us / a fun project .
　　　　　　　　　　　간접목적어　　　직접목적어

우리는 / 주어졌다 / 재미있는 프로젝트가 / 선생님에 의해.

→ We / **were given** / a fun project / by the teacher.

<간접목적어가 주어인 수동태>

재미있는 프로젝트가 / 주어졌다 / 우리에게 / 선생님에 의해.

→ A fun project / **was given** / to us / by the teacher.

<직접목적어가 주어인 수동태>

- SVOO(4형식) 문장은 목적어가 2개이므로, 각 목적어를 주어로 하는 두 가지 형태의 수동태 문장이 가능해요.
- 직접목적어를 주어로 하는 수동태 문장인 경우, 간접목적어 앞에 전치사 to/for/of 중 하나를 써야 해요.
  (☞ Ch 01 문장의 주요 형식)

📢 **직접목적어가 주어인 수동태 문장의 전치사**

be given, be sent, be shown, be taught, be told, be brought 등	+ to
be made, be bought, be cooked 등	+ for
be asked	+ of

My uncle bought me the new backpack.

→ The new backpack **was bought for** me by my uncle. 〈직접목적어가 주어〉

대표 기출 문제

🔒 다음 문장의 밑줄 친 부분을 각각 주어로 하는 수동태 문장을 쓰시오.

Peter gave (1) her (2) some flowers.

(1) _______________________________________

(2) _______________________________________

CLUE 1

동사 gave 뒤에 목적어가 두 개 있으므로, 각 목적어를 주어로 하는 수동태 문장을 두 개 만들 수 있어요.
— (1) her → She was p.p. ~
　(2) some flowers → Some flowers were p.p. ~

CLUE 2

직접목적어(some flowers)를 주어로 하는 수동태 문장에서는 간접목적어 앞에 꼭 전치사를 써야 해요.

정답: (1) She was given some flowers by Peter.
　　　(2) Some flowers were given to her by Peter.

Point Exercise

정답 및 해설 p.09

[1-4] 우리말과 일치하도록 주어진 단어를 올바르게 배열하세요.

1

우리는 이 이야기에 의해 중요한 메시지를 얻었다.
(were / an important message / given / we)

→ _______________________________________

_______________________ by this story.

2

놀라운 사진 한 장이 대중에게 공개되었다.
(the public / a surprising photo / shown /
was / to)

→ _______________________________________

_______________________________________ .

3

나는 나의 할머니에 의해 좋은 이야기들을 들었다.
(my / grandma / was / good stories / told /
I / by)

→ _______________________________________

_______________________________________ .

4

그 신발은 나를 위해서 나의 언니에 의해 구입되었다.
(were / me / bought / the shoes / for)

→ _______________________________________

_______________________ by my sister.

[5-9] 다음 문장의 밑줄 친 부분을 주어로 하는 수동태 문장을 완성하세요.

5 His friends gave <u>him</u> a lot of presents.

→ _______________________________________

by his friends.

6 Dad makes us <u>sandwiches</u> every Sunday morning.

→ _______________________________________

by Dad every Sunday morning.

7 Someone sent me <u>a strange letter</u>.

→ _______________________________________

_______________________ by someone.

8 The chef gives the guests <u>a special dish</u>.

→ _______________________________________

_______________________ by the chef.

9 The waiter brought us <u>the food</u>.

→ _______________________________________

_______________________ by the waiter.

10 다음 문장의 밑줄 친 부분을 각각 주어로 하는 수동태 문장을 완성하세요.

The guide showed (1) <u>the tourists</u>
(2) <u>the palace</u>.

(1) _______________________________________

_______________________ by the guide.

(2) _______________________________________

_______________________ by the guide.

public 대중, 일반 사람들 surprising 놀라운 special 특별한 waiter 종업원, 웨이터 guide 가이드, 안내인 palace 궁전

  by 이외의 전치사를 쓰는 수동태 표현

거리는 눈으로 덮여 있었다.
거리는 / 덮여 있었다 / 눈으로.
　주어　　　동사　　　부사구

→ The streets / **were covered** / **with** snow.

- 수동태에서 행위자는 「by+목적격」의 형태로 쓴다고 앞에서 배웠어요. 하지만, 일부 표현에서는 **by 대신 다른 전치사를 쓰는 경우**가 있어요.
- by 이외의 전치사를 쓰는 수동태 표현은 숙어처럼 한 단위로 외워 두는 것이 좋아요.

by 이외의 전치사를 쓰는 수동태 표현

be covered **with**	~으로 덮여 있다	be known **to**	~에게 알려지다 (대상)
be filled **with**	~으로 가득 차 있다	be known **for**	~으로 유명하다 (이유)
be pleased **with**	~에 기뻐하다	be known **as**	~으로 알려져 있다 (명칭, 별칭 등)
be satisfied **with**	~에 만족하다	be made **of**	~으로 만들어지다
be crowded **with**	~로 붐비다		(재료의 성질이 변하지 않음)
be surprised **at**	~에 놀라다	be made **from**	~으로 만들어지다
be interested **in**	~에 관심[흥미]이 있다		(재료의 성질이 변함)

MORE+ 능동태의 동사가 look after, take care of 등과 같은 구동사(둘 이상의 단어가 합쳐져 하나의 동사 역할을 하는 동사)일 경우, 수동태는 「be p.p.+나머지 부분」으로 바뀝니다. 끝에 붙은 전치사를 빠뜨리지 않도록 주의하세요.
The neighbor **took care of** our dog.
→ Our dog **was taken care of** by the neighbor. (우리 개는 이웃에 의해 돌봐졌다.)

대표 기출 문제

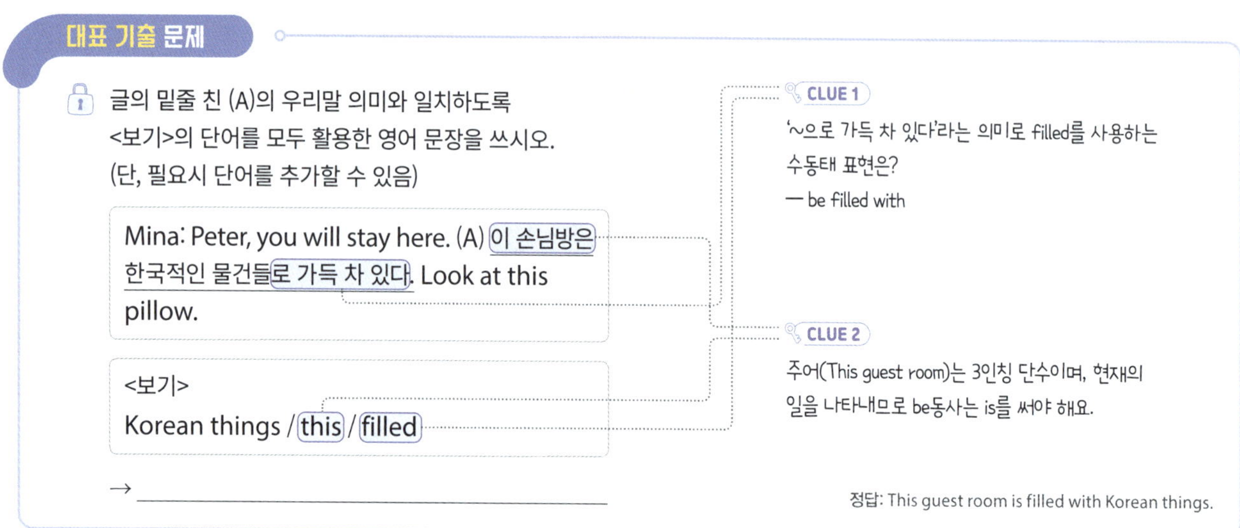

🔒 글의 밑줄 친 (A)의 우리말 의미와 일치하도록 <보기>의 단어를 모두 활용한 영어 문장을 쓰시오.
(단, 필요시 단어를 추가할 수 있음)

Mina: Peter, you will stay here. (A) 이 손님방은 한국적인 물건들로 가득 차 있다. Look at this pillow.

<보기>
Korean things / this / filled

→ _______________________________________

CLUE 1
'~으로 가득 차 있다'라는 의미로 filled를 사용하는 수동태 표현은?
— be filled with

CLUE 2
주어(This guest room)는 3인칭 단수이며, 현재의 일을 나타내므로 be동사는 is를 써야 해요.

정답: This guest room is filled with Korean things.

Point Exercise

배열 영작

[1-5] 우리말과 일치하도록 주어진 단어를 올바르게 배열하세요.

1
> 그 벽은 유리로 만들어졌다.
> (glass / made / was / of)

→ The wall ___________________________ .

2
> 그녀는 그녀의 생일 선물에 기뻐했다.
> (with / birthday gift / pleased / her / was)

→ She ___________________________

___________________________ .

3
> 지하철은 많은 사람들로 붐볐다.
> (people / with / was / a lot of / crowded)

→ The subway ___________________________

___________________________ .

4
> 그 마을은 짙은 안개에 싸여 있었다.
> (covered / thick / was / with / fog)

→ The village ___________________________

___________________________ .

5
> 나의 부모님은 내 결정에 놀라셨다.
> (my / were / at / surprised / decision)

→ My parents ___________________________

___________________________ .

주어진 단어로 영작

[6-9] 우리말과 일치하도록 주어진 단어를 사용하여 문장을 완성하세요.

6
> 나의 언니는 미술에 관심이 있다.
> (sister, interested, art, my)

→ ___________________________

____

7
> 그 양동이는 생선으로 가득 차 있다.
> (the bucket, fill, fish)

→ ___________________________

8
> 우리는 새로운 집에 만족한다.
> (satisfy, new house, our)

→ ___________________________

____

9
> 그 식당은 해산물 요리로 유명하다.
> (its seafood dishes, the restaurant, know)

→ ___________________________

____

기출: 조건 영작

10 우리말과 일치하도록 〈조건〉에 맞게 문장을 완성하세요.

> 그의 다정한 태도는 모두에게 알려져 있다.

> 〈조건〉
> • know를 사용하여 수동태로 쓸 것
> • friendly, manner, everybody를 사용할 것

→ ___________________________

____

thick (안개 등이) 짙은; 두꺼운 fog 안개 village 마을 decision 결정 bucket 양동이, 버킷 manner 태도

Chapter Test *

STAGE 1) Go for it!

자신 있게 풀어보는 기초 문제!

빈칸 완성

[1-5] 우리말과 일치하도록 주어진 단어를 사용하여 빈칸에 알맞은 말을 쓰세요.

1 교복은 학생들에 의해 입어진다. (wear)

→ School uniforms ＿＿＿＿＿＿＿

＿＿＿＿＿＿ ＿＿＿＿＿ students.

2 이 사진은 나의 할아버지에 의해 찍혔다. (take)

→ This picture ＿＿＿＿＿ ＿＿＿＿＿

＿＿＿＿＿ my grandfather.

3 그 병은 커피콩으로 가득 채워져 있다. (fill)

→ The bottle ＿＿＿＿＿＿＿

＿＿＿＿＿ coffee beans.

4 이 안경은 Tommy에 의해 부러졌니? (break)

→ ＿＿＿＿＿ these glasses ＿＿＿＿＿

＿＿＿＿＿ Tommy?

5 무료 와이파이는 그 카페에 의해 제공되지 않는다. (provide)

→ Free wi-fi ＿＿＿＿＿ ＿＿＿＿＿

＿＿＿＿＿ ＿＿＿ the cafe.

배열 영작

[6-8] 우리말과 일치하도록 주어진 단어를 배열하여 문장을 완성하세요. (필요시 형태를 바꿀 것)

6 그 예술가는 많은 단체들에 의해 후원받는다.
(by / be / many / support / organizations)

→ The artist ＿＿＿＿＿＿＿＿＿＿＿

＿＿＿＿＿＿＿＿＿＿＿＿ .

7 축제에서 마술은 많은 아이들에 의해 사랑받았다.
(children / love / be / many / by)

→ The magic tricks ＿＿＿＿＿＿＿＿＿

＿＿＿＿＿＿＿＿＿ at the festival.

8 병과 캔은 환경을 위해 재활용되어야 한다.
(the environment / should / recycle / be / for)

→ Bottles and cans ＿＿＿＿＿＿＿＿＿

＿＿＿＿＿＿＿＿＿ .

최신 기출

9 다음 〈조건〉에 맞게 문장을 완성하세요.

〈조건〉
- 과거시제를 사용할 것
- write, invent, build를 한 번씩만 사용해 수동태로 쓸 것

(1) The light bulb ＿＿＿＿＿＿＿＿＿
by Thomas Edison.

(2) The famous novel ＿＿＿＿＿＿＿＿
by a Korean author.

(3) The pyramids ＿＿＿＿＿＿＿＿＿
by ancient Egyptians.

○━(대화문 완성)

[10-14] 수동태를 사용하여 각 대화를 완성하세요.

10
A: Who found my wallet?
B: Your wallet ＿＿＿＿＿＿ ＿＿＿＿＿＿
＿＿＿＿＿＿ my brother.

11
A: ＿＿＿＿＿＿ Luna ＿＿＿＿＿＿ as
a team leader?
B: Yes, she was. She was elected last week.

12
A: ＿＿＿＿＿＿ those flowers ＿＿＿＿＿＿
by your mom?
B: No, I watered them.

13
A: When did he buy the car?
B: The car ＿＿＿＿＿＿ ＿＿＿＿＿＿
by him 2 years ago.

14
A: ＿＿＿＿＿＿ ＿＿＿＿＿＿ the food
festival ＿＿＿＿＿＿?
B: It was held a week ago.

○━(보기에서 골라 영작)

15 우리말과 일치하도록 〈보기A〉와 〈보기B〉에서 각각 알맞은 말을 골라 문장을 완성하세요.

〈보기 A〉 must	can	may	will

〈보기 B〉 return	plant	buy	send

(1) 그 나무들은 4월 5일에 학교 정원에 심어질 것이다.

→ The trees ＿＿＿＿＿＿＿＿＿
in the school garden on April 5th.

(2) 행사 세부 사항은 이메일로 발송될 수도 있습니다.

→ The event details ＿＿＿＿＿＿＿＿＿
by email.

(3) 그 책들은 도서관에 제시간에 반납되어야 한다.

→ The books ＿＿＿＿＿＿＿＿＿ to
the library on time.

(4) 콘서트 표는 온라인으로 구매될 수 있다.

→ The concert tickets ＿＿＿＿＿＿＿＿
online.

(최신 기출)

16 다음 미술 전시회에 대한 안내문을 읽고, 주어진 단어를 사용해 수동태 문장을 완성하세요.

A famous painting (1) ＿＿＿＿＿＿＿＿＿
＿＿＿＿＿＿＿＿＿ (show) at the Modern
Art Gallery next month.
The title of the painting is *The Starry Night*.
It (2) ＿＿＿＿＿＿＿＿＿ (paint)
Vincent van Gogh in 1889. Don't miss this
amazing artwork!

[17-21] 다음 문장이 능동태면 수동태로, 수동태면 능동태로 바꿔 쓰세요.

17

> The guard closes the park at 10 p.m. every night.

→ ______________________________

______________________________ at 10 p.m. every night.

18

> The first orchestra was organized by the school in September last year.

→ ______________________________

______________________________ in September last year.

19

> This letter was not written by me.

→ ______________________________

____

20

> Jake will be chosen as the Person of the Year by the magazine.

→ ______________________________

____

21

> The city will build an amusement park next year.

→ ______________________________

______________________________ next year.

[22-26] 다음 각 문장에서 어법상 **틀린** 부분을 찾아 바르게 고쳐 쓰세요.

22 Your computer will be fix next week.

______________________ → ______________________

23 The apple juice did not drunk by me.

______________________ → ______________________

24 This cartoon is well known as a lot of children.

______________________ → ______________________

25 The bedrooms will paint by next weekend.

______________________ → ______________________

26 How the telephone was invented?

______________________ → ______________________

27 우리말과 일치하도록 주어진 단어를 사용하여 다음의 대화를 완성하세요.

> A: Sally, what are you doing?
> B: I'm preparing for my presentation about my interests.
> A: What are your interests?
> B: 나는 카메라와 사진에 관심이 있어.
>   (photography, interested, cameras)
>   But I'm nervous about my presentation.
> A: You will do a great job. Don't worry.

→ ______________________________

____

◌━ 도표 영작

28 영화 작품에 관한 표를 보고 다음 글을 완성하세요.

Harry Potter and the Goblet of Fire
「해리 포터와 불의 잔」

(1) Writer	J. K. Rowling
(2) Published	2000
(3) Filmed	2005
(4) Director	Mike Newell

(1) *Harry Potter and the Goblet of Fire*
　　__________________________ J. K. Rowling.

(2) It __________________________ in 2000.

(3) It __________________________ in 2005.

(4) The movie __________________________
　　Mike Newell.

◌━ 어법 오류 수정

29 다음 대화에서 어법상 **틀린** 문장 **두 개**를 찾아 그 기호를 쓰고, 문장 전체를 바르게 고쳐 쓰세요.

> A: Did you hear that? Somi is going to move to another city! ⓐ I was surprised at the news.
> B: Yes, I did. ⓑ A farewell party will be held by Somi. ⓒ All of us will invite to her house.
> A: Really? That sounds great.
> B: ⓓ Invitation cards will be sent to us this weekend. ⓔ They were made from Somi.
> A: OK. I hope to receive mine soon.

__________ → __________________________

　　　　　　__________________________

__________ → __________________________

　　　　　　__________________________

🎯 **Challenge!**　　누적 문제 Ch 02-04

30 다음 중 어법상 **틀린** 문장 **두 개**를 찾아 그 기호를 쓰고, 문장 전체를 바르게 고쳐 쓰세요.

> ⓐ My uncle has worked for his company since 2007.
> ⓑ My car might not repair today.
> ⓒ Jina has to see a doctor tomorrow.
> ⓓ My friend and I have had fun last night.
> ⓔ The airport was crowded with travelers during the holidays.

__________ → __________________________

　　　　　　__________________________

__________ → __________________________

　　　　　　__________________________

to부정사

✅ Before You Write

- ☑ 우리말을 보고 어느 자리에 to부정사를 써야 할지 파악할 수 있나요?
- ☑ 문장에서 to부정사의 여러 쓰임을 구분할 수 있나요?
- ☑ to부정사가 주어 역할을 할 때 가주어 it을 사용하여 나타낼 수 있나요?
- ☑ to부정사의 주요 구문을 「so ~ that ...」으로 전환할 수 있나요?

내신 기출 다음 우리말을 보고 머릿속으로 한번 영어 문장을 떠올려 보세요.

1 야생동물에게 먹이를 주는 것은 잘못된 것이다.
(feed / It / the wild animals / wrong / to)
~하는 것은 → 주어 → 가주어 It ~ 진주어 to부정사 → **It is wrong to feed** `POINT 1`

2 Kate: (A) 나는 반 고흐 전시회에 가는 것을 계획 중이야.
~하는 것을 → 동사 plan의 목적어 → **am planning to go** `POINT 2`

3 그는 점심으로 무엇을 먹을지 결정하지 못했다.
무엇을 ~할지 → 의문사+to부정사 → **what to eat** `POINT 3`

4 (2) 여기에는 먹을 것이 아무것도 없다. (There, here, eat)
~할 → 형용사적 쓰임 → (대)명사+to부정사 → **nothing to eat** `POINT 4`

5 그들은 산책하기 위해 공원에 갔다. (9단어)
~하기 위해 → 목적 → **to take a walk** `POINT 5`

6 그는 오디션에 통과해서 행복했다. (pass / the audition)
~해서 …하다 → 감정의 원인 → **happy to pass** `POINT 5`

7 나는 너무 피곤해서 밖에 나갈 수 없었다. (tired, outside, too)
너무 ~해서 …할 수 없다 → too+형용사/부사+to부정사 → **too tired to go** `POINT 6`

8 그는 그 차를 살 수 있을 정도로 충분히 부유하다.
(rich / buy / enough)
~할 만큼 충분히 …하다 → 형용사/부사+enough+to부정사 → **rich enough to buy** `POINT 6`

정답: **1** It is[It's] wrong to feed the wild animals. **2** I am[I'm] planning to go to the Van Gogh exhibition. **3** He did not[didn't] decide what to eat for lunch. **4** There is nothing to eat here. **5** They went to the park to take a walk. **6** He was happy to pass the audition. **7** I was too tired to go outside. **8** He is[He's] rich enough to buy the car.

to부정사의 명사적 쓰임

POINT 1 to부정사 = ~하는 것은(가주어 It ~ 진주어 to부정사)

채소를 많이 먹는 것은 좋다.
많은 채소를 먹는 것은 / 좋다.

→ **To eat** a lot of vegetables / is good.
　　　　　　　주어

= **It** is good / **to eat** a lot of vegetables.
　가주어　　　　　　　　　진주어

- 문장에서 **주어 자리**에 '~**하는 것은, ~하기는**'의 의미를 쓸 때, to부정사를 활용하여 동사를 명사처럼 쓸 수 있어요.
- 이때 문장의 주어 자리에 **가주어 It**을 쓰고 **to부정사(진주어)는 문장 뒤로** 보낸 형태를 훨씬 더 많이 씁니다.

주의 **to부정사의 부정형**

to부정사의 부정형은 to 앞에 not[never]을 써야 해요.
It is important **not to break** promises. (약속을 어기지 않는 것은 중요하다.)

MORE+ to부정사의 동작이나 상태를 행하는 주어는 「for+목적격」으로 나타내요. 이를 문장의 주어와 구분하기 위해 **의미상 주어**라고 해요.
It is *easy* **for him** to solve the problem. (그가 그 문제를 푸는 것은 쉽다.)

의미상 주어가 사람의 성격이나 행동에 대한 평가를 나타내는 형용사 뒤에 올 때는 「of+목적격」의 형태로 나타내요.
It was *kind* **of him** to lend his book. (그가 자신의 책을 빌려준 것은 친절했다.)

대표 기출 문제

🔒 다음 우리말을 주어진 제시어를 모두 사용하여 10 단어 내의 영어 문장으로 쓰시오.

너무 많은 아이스크림을 먹는 것은 좋지 않다.
제시어 ▶ it, ice cream, good
→ _______________________

CLUE 1
'~하는 것은'이므로 주어 자리에 동명사 또는 to부정사가 쓰일 수 있는데, 제시어에 it이 있으므로 「가주어 It ~ 진주어 to부정사」 형태로 써요.

CLUE 2
'~ 하지 않다'라는 의미를 나타내야 하므로 가주어 It 뒤에는 be동사의 부정형 is not이 와야 해요.

정답: It is not good to eat too much ice cream.

함정 피하기 동명사와 to부정사 모두 문장의 주어로 쓰일 수 있는데, to부정사가 주어로 쓰일 때는 대부분 지시문 또는 <조건>에 주어지므로 주의해서 봐야 해요.
[기출예시] "It ~ to ~" 구문으로 시작하는 한 개의 영어 문장 / it(가주어) ~ to부정사(진주어) 표현을 사용할 것
　　　　　/ 가주어 it을 포함한 문장 / 가주어 it 구문으로 만들 것 등

Point Exercise

○— 배열 영작

[1-4] 우리말과 일치하도록 주어진 단어를 올바르게 배열하세요.

1
일찍 일어나는 것은 쉽지 않다.
(not / get up / to / easy / is / early)

→ ______________________________ .

2
너의 실수로부터 배우는 것은 도움이 된다.
(helpful / it / learn / is / to)

→ ______________________________
from your mistakes.

3
4월에 눈을 보는 것은 놀랍다.
(see / in April / surprising / is / snow / it / to)

→ ______________________________ .

4
다른 사람들의 말을 귀 기울여 듣는 것이 중요하다.
(to / it / listen to / important / is / others)

→ ______________________________
______________________________ carefully.

○— 주어진 단어로 영작

[5-8] 우리말과 일치하도록 주어진 단어와 가주어 It을 사용하여 문장을 완성하세요. (필요시 형태를 바꿀 것)

5
새로운 취미를 발견하는 것은 좋다.
(a new hobby, discover, good)

→ ______________________________

6
여기서 수영하는 것은 위험하다.
(dangerous, here, swim)

→ ______________________________
____

7
물 없이 사는 것은 불가능하다.
(without, impossible, water, live)

→ ______________________________
____

8
밤에 혼자 걷는 것은 안전하지 않다.
(walk, alone, safe, at night)

→ ______________________________
____

기출: 조건 영작

9 다음 대화를 읽고 〈조건〉에 맞게 우리말을 영작하세요.

A: Sam, did you go to the fireworks festival last weekend?
B: Yes, I did. 아름다운 불꽃놀이를 보는 것은 재미있었어.
(the beautiful fireworks, see, exciting)

〈조건〉
• 가주어 It으로 시작할 것
• 주어진 단어를 사용하여 8 단어로 쓸 것

→ ______________________________
____

---

helpful 도움이 되는, 유용한 discover 발견하다 without ~없이 impossible 불가능한 fireworks (복수형) 불꽃놀이

 to부정사 = ~하는 것을(목적어) / ~하는 것이다(보어)

나는 언젠가 런던에 방문하기를 희망한다.
나는 / 희망한다 / 런던에 방문하기를 / 언젠가.
　주어　　동사　　　　목적어

→ I / *hope* / **to visit** London / someday.

- 문장의 **목적어 자리**에 '~하는 것을, ~하기를'의 의미를 쓸 때도 to부정사 형태를 사용할 수 있어요.
- 단, 동사에 따라서 목적어 자리에 동명사가 오는 것도 있으므로 어떤 동사가 to부정사 목적어를 쓰는지를 잘 알아둬야 합니다.
- 다음과 같이 **to부정사를 목적어로 쓰는 동사들**은 주로 **미래**와 관련된 행동이라는 공통점이 있어요.

📢 **to부정사를 목적어로 쓰는 동사들**

want to do	~하는 것을 원하다, ~하고 싶다	promise to do	~하기로 약속하다
decide to do	~하기로 결정[결심]하다	learn to do	~하는 것을 배우다
plan to do	~하는 것을 계획하다	expect to do	~하기를 예상[기대]하다
hope to do	~하는 것을 희망하다[바라다]	agree to do	~하기로 동의하다
wish to do	~하는 것을 바라다	choose to do	~하기로 선택하다
like[love] to do	~하는 것을 (아주) 좋아하다	fail to do	~하는 것을 실패하다
need to do	~할 필요가 있다, ~해야 한다	start[begin] to do	~하는 것을 시작하다

*like, love, start, begin은 목적어로 동명사도 쓸 수 있어요. (☞ Ch 06 동명사와 분사)

내 계획은 올해 돈을 더 많이 저축하는 것이다.
내 계획은 ~이다 / 더 많은 돈을 저축하는 것 / 올해.
　　　　　　　　　　　　보어

→ My plan is / **to save** more money / this year.

- to부정사를 be동사 뒤 **보어 자리**에 쓰면 '~하는 것(이다), ~하기(이다)'의 의미로, 주어가 무엇인지를 설명할 수 있어요.

대표 기출 문제

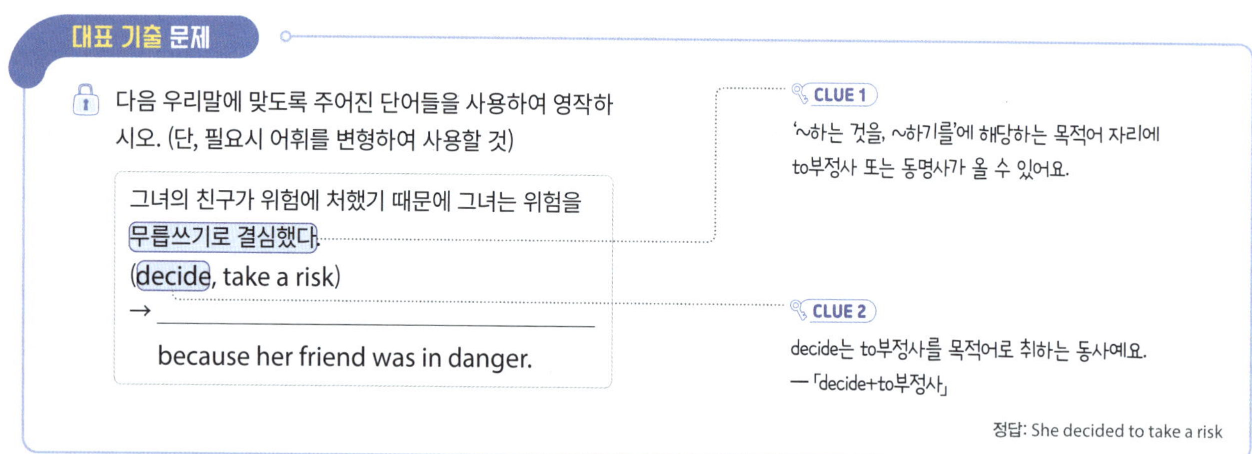

🔒 다음 우리말에 맞도록 주어진 단어들을 사용하여 영작하시오. (단, 필요시 어휘를 변형하여 사용할 것)

그녀의 친구가 위험에 처했기 때문에 그녀는 위험을 무릅쓰기로 결심했다.
(decide, take a risk)

→ ＿＿＿＿＿＿＿＿＿＿＿＿＿＿＿＿＿＿＿
because her friend was in danger.

CLUE 1
'~하는 것을, ~하기를'에 해당하는 목적어 자리에 to부정사 또는 동명사가 올 수 있어요.

CLUE 2
decide는 to부정사를 목적어로 취하는 동사예요.
— 「decide+to부정사」

정답: She decided to take a risk

Point Exercise

정답 및 해설 p.11

[1-3] 우리말과 일치하도록 주어진 단어를 올바르게 배열하세요.

1
우리는 매일 저녁 배드민턴 치는 것을 좋아한다.
(badminton / like / play / to / we)

→ _______________________________
_______________________ every evening.

2
나의 다음 계획은 프랑스어를 배우는 것이다.
(next plan / to / French / is / learn / my)

→ _______________________________
_______________________________ .

3
그들은 내일 그 문제를 다시 논의하기로 동의했다.
(discuss / to / they / the problem / agreed)

→ _______________________________
_______________________ again tomorrow.

[4-8] 우리말과 일치하도록 주어진 단어를 사용하여 문장을 완성하세요.

4
Susan은 영화감독이 되기를 바란다.
(a movie director, hope, be)

→ _______________________________
____

5
그 학생은 수업을 빼먹지 않겠다고 약속했다.
(the student, not, classes, promise, skip)

→ _______________________________
____

6
그는 놀이공원에 가기로 계획했다.
(go, to an amusement park, plan)

→ _______________________________
____

7
나는 내 시간을 더 잘 관리하는 방법을 배웠다.
(manage, learn, better, time)

→ _______________________________
____

8
그들은 주말을 해변에서 보내기로 정했다.
(the weekend, choose, at the beach, spend)

→ _______________________________
____

9 다음 대화를 읽고 〈조건〉에 맞게 우리말을 영작하세요.

A: Jiho, where are you going?
B: I'm going to the gym. (1) <u>나는 운동하기로 결심했어.</u>
A: Are you going to lose weight?
B: No, I'm not. (2) <u>나는 건강을 유지하고 싶어.</u>

〈조건〉
- want, decide, stay healthy, exercise를 사용할 것
- 필요시 형태를 바꿀 것

(1) _______________________________

(2) _______________________________

director 감독, 연출자 skip 빼먹다, 거르다 manage 관리하다 lose weight 살을 빼다, 체중을 줄이다

POINT 3 　의문사+to부정사

너는 이 카메라를 어떻게 사용하는지 아니?

너는 <u>아니</u> / <u>어떻게 사용하는지[사용하는 방법을]</u> / 이 카메라를?
　　　동사　　　　　　　　　목적어

→ Do you know / **how to use** / this camera?

- '무엇을[어떻게/어디에서/언제] ~할지'등의 의미는 다음과 같이 「**의문사+to부정사**」 형태로 나타냅니다.

what to do **how** to make	무엇을 (해야) 할지 어떻게 만들지, 만드는 방법	**where** to go **when** to start	어디에 갈지[가야 할지] 언제 시작할지

- 「의문사+to부정사」는 문장에서 주어/보어/목적어 자리에 모두 쓸 수 있는데, 주로 목적어로 쓰여요.
- 특히 동사 know, decide, learn, tell, ask, teach 등의 목적어 자리에 자주 쓰여요.

  <u>**What to wear** to school</u> bothers me. 〈주어〉 학교에 무엇을 입고 가야 할지는 나를 신경 쓰이게 한다.

  The problem is **how to balance** studying and playing. 〈보어〉

  문제는 어떻게 공부하는 것과 노는 것의 균형을 맞출지이다.

「의문사+to부정사」와 함께 자주 쓰이는 표현

I don't know ~.	I don't know **what to say**. 나는 뭐라고 말해야 할지 모르겠어.
Do you know ~?	Do you know **how to cook** pasta? 너는 파스타 만드는 법을 아니?
Can you tell me ~?	Can you tell me **where to sit**? 어디에 앉아야 할지 제게 알려주시겠어요?
I can't decide ~.	I can't decide **what to eat**. 나는 뭘 먹을지 결정을 못 하겠어.
A taught B ~.	She taught us **how to play** tennis. 그녀는 우리에게 테니스 치는 방법을 가르쳐주었다.

- 「의문사+to부정사」는 「의문사+주어+should+동사원형」으로 바꿔 쓸 수 있습니다.

  I don't know **what to do**. = I don't know **what I should do**.

대표 기출 문제

🔒 다음 빈칸에 들어갈 말을 '의문사+to부정사' 구조를
반드시 활용하여 우리말 의미에 맞게 영어로 쓰시오.

> A: ________________________?
> 　(너는 어디를 여행할지 결정했니?)
> B: Yes, I did. I'm going to travel to London.
> 　(응, 나는 런던으로 여행을 갈 거야.)
>
> → ________________________?

CLUE 1

지시문을 보고 주어진 우리말에서
「의문사+to부정사」를 활용할 수 있는 부분을
확인해요.

CLUE 2

우리말 '어디를 ~할지'를 나타내기 위해서는
의문사 where를 쓰고 뒤에 to부정사를 붙여요.

정답: Did you decide where to travel

Point Exercise

[1-4] 우리말과 일치하도록 주어진 단어를 올바르게 배열하세요.

1
> Tim은 박물관에서 무엇을 먼저 봐야 할지 몰랐다.
> (first / to / know / what / see / didn't)

→ Tim ________________________________

________________________ in the museum.

2
> 우리는 휴가로 어디에 갈지 결정을 못 하겠다.
> (decide / where / can't / go / to / we)

→ ________________________________

________________________ for a vacation.

3
> Ava는 나에게 내일 언제 만날지 물었다.
> (meet / me / when / to / asked / Ava)

→ ________________________________

________________________ tomorrow.

4
> 저에게 공항까지 가는 방법을 알려주시겠어요?
> (tell / get to / how / the airport / to / me)

→ Can you ________________________________

________________________ ?

[5-9] 우리말과 일치하도록 주어진 단어와 to부정사를 사용하여 문장을 완성하세요.

5
> 우리는 뉴욕에서 어디에 머무를지 결정했다.
> (decide, stay, New York, in)

→ ________________________________

6
> 저에게 여행을 위해 무엇을 사야 할지 알려주세요.
> (buy, tell, for the trip)

→ Please ________________________________

________________________ .

7
> 너는 텐트 치는 법을 아니? (set up, know, a tent)

→ ________________________________

____

8
> 나는 Dan에게 뭐라고 말해야 할지 모르겠다.
> (know, say, to Dan)

→ ________________________________

____

9
> 그는 그의 친구에게 자전거 수리하는 법을
> 가르쳐 주었다. (fix, teach, a bike)

→ ________________________________

____

10 다음 대화를 읽고 〈조건〉에 맞게 우리말을 영작하세요.

> A: Lily, can you help me with this camera?
> B: Sure. What's the problem?
> A: 나는 사진을 어떻게 삭제하는지 모르겠어.
> B: You can find the "remove" button here.

〈조건〉
- a photo, delete, know를 사용할 것
- 8 단어로 쓸 것

→ ________________________________

____

set up 세우다, 설치하다 remove 삭제하다, 제거하다 delete 삭제하다

02 to부정사의 형용사적 쓰임

POINT 4   (대)명사+to부정사: ~하는, ~할

나는 하이킹하는 동안 먹을 간식을 좀 가져갈 것이다.
나는 / 가져갈 것이다 / 먹을 약간의 간식을 / 하이킹하는 동안.

→ I / will bring / **some snacks to eat** / during the hike.

- to부정사는 형용사처럼 (대)명사를 뒤에서 수식해, '**~하는, ~할 무엇**'의 의미를 나타낼 수 있어요.
- to부정사가 -thing, -one, -body로 끝나는 대명사를 수식하는 형태도 자주 쓰여요.
  I have **something to tell** you. 네게 말할 것이 있어.

> **주의**
>
> -thing, -one, -body 등으로 끝나는 대명사 뒤에 형용사가 나올 경우, 「-thing, -one, -body+형용사+to부정사」 형태로 씁니다.
> Give me *something* **cold to drink**. (제게 차가운 마실 것을 주세요.)

저에게 쓸 종이를 좀 주세요.
주세요 / 저에게 / 쓸 조금의 종이를.

→ Give / me / **some paper to write on**. (write *on* some paper)

- to부정사의 수식을 받는 명사가 의미적으로 to부정사구 안의 전치사의 목적어일 경우,
  to부정사 뒤에 전치사를 꼭 써야 해요. (Give me some paper **to write**. (×))

「명사+to부정사+전치사」 표현

a chair **to sit on**	(위에) 앉을 의자	someone **to talk to[with]**	(~에게[함께]) 이야기할 누군가
cats **to take care of**	돌볼 고양이들	a hotel **to stay in**	(안에) 머무를 호텔
a pen **to write with**	가지고 쓸 펜	a room **to sleep in**	(안에) 잘 방
paper **to write on**	(위에) 쓸 종이	a house **to live in**	(안에) 살 집
friends **to play with**	함께 놀 친구들	a bed **to sleep on**	(위에) 잘 침대

대표 기출 문제

아래 조건에 맞추어 우리말에 맞게 영작하시오.

- 형용사적 용법을 갖는 to부정사를 사용할 것
- 진행 시제를 사용할 것
- 다음 단어를 사용할 것: sit, for

David는 앉을 의자를 찾고 있었다.

→ _______________________________________

CLUE 1
to부정사가 형용사처럼 앞의 (대)명사를 꾸며주는
'~할, ~하는'의 의미 ─ 「(대)명사+to부정사」

CLUE 2
'(~위에) 앉을 의자'이므로 to sit 뒤에 전치사 on을
써야 해요. ─ a chair to sit on

정답: David was looking for a chair to sit on.

Point Exercise

◑ 배열 영작

[1-5] 우리말과 일치하도록 주어진 단어를 올바르게 배열하세요.

1
> 서울로 떠날 시간이다.
> (time / for / it's / leave / Seoul / to)

→ ______________________________

______________________________ .

2
> 내가 이 상자 드는 것을 도와줄 사람 있어?
> (help / to / is / anyone / me / there)

→ ______________________________

______________________________ with this box?

3
> 우리는 살 집을 찾고 있다.
> (are / live / we / to / in / looking for / a house)

→ ______________________________

______________________________ .

4
> 학생들은 환경을 도울 방법에 대해 논의했다.
> (discussed / to / ways / the environment / help / the students)

→ ______________________________

______________________________ .

5
> 제게 뜨거운 마실 것을 주시겠어요?
> (you / hot / me / drink / can / to / something / give)

→ ______________________________

______________________________ ?

◑ 주어진 단어로 영작

[6-8] 우리말과 일치하도록 주어진 단어를 사용하여 문장을 완성하세요. (필요시 단어를 추가하거나 형태를 바꿀 것)

6
> Kate는 올 겨울에 입을 새 코트가 필요하다.
> (a new coat, wear, need)

→ ______________________________

______________________________ this winter.

7
> 우리는 프랑스에서 방문할 몇몇 장소들을 정했다.
> (places, choose, visit, some)

→ ______________________________

______________________________ in France.

8
> 나는 컴퓨터를 살 돈이 없다.
> (buy, have, money, a computer)

→ ______________________________

____

기출: 조건 영작

9 우리말과 일치하도록 〈조건〉에 맞게 문장을 완성하세요.

> 〈조건〉
> • to부정사를 사용할 것
> • 주어진 단어를 사용할 것

(1) 나는 낭비할 시간이 없어. (waste, no time)

→ ______________________________

____

(2) 그들은 쓸 연필들이 필요하다. (write)

→ ______________________________

environment 환경 waste 낭비하다

Unit 03 to부정사의 부사적 쓰임

POINT 5 to부정사 = ~하기 위해, ~하려고(목적) / ~해서(감정의 원인) / ~하기에 …인[한]

우리는 교통 체증을 피하려고 일찍 출발했다.
우리는 일찍 출발했다 / 교통 체증을 <u>피하기 위해</u>.
<u>행동의 목적</u>

→ We left early / **to avoid** the traffic. (= **To avoid** the traffic, we ~.)

- to부정사는 문장에서 '**~하기 위해, ~하려고**'라는 동작이나 행동의 **목적**을 나타낼 때도 쓰여요.
- to부정사가 가장 많이 나타내는 의미로, 주로 문장의 뒤쪽에 쓰이는데 종종 문장 맨 앞에 쓰이기도 해요.
- '**~하지 않기 위해**'라는 의미는 「not+to부정사」로 나타내요.
  I hurried **not to miss** the train. 나는 기차를 놓치지 않기 위해 서둘렀다.
- '목적'의 의미를 더 확실하게 나타내기 위해 to부정사 앞에 in order를 붙이기도 합니다.
  She went to the library **(in order) to borrow** some books. 그녀는 책을 좀 빌리기 위해 도서관에 갔다.

그는 그 소식을 들어서 기뻤다.
그는 기뻤다 / 그 소식을 <u>들어서</u>.
<u>감정의 원인</u>

→ He was *happy* / **to hear** the news.

- to부정사는 감정을 나타내는 형용사 뒤에 쓰여서 **감정의 원인**을 나타내기도 해요.
  즉, '**~해서(원인) …한 감정을 느낀다**'라는 의미는 「**감정 형용사+to부정사**」의 형태로 씁니다.
- happy, pleased, glad, sad, excited, disappointed 등의 감정 형용사와 함께 자주 쓰여요.

그녀의 글씨체는 읽기 어렵다.
그녀의 글씨체는 / <u>읽기</u> 어렵다.

→ Her handwriting / is *difficult* <u>to read</u>.

- to부정사는 형용사를 뒤에서 수식해, '**~하기에 …인[한]**'이라는 의미를 나타낼 수도 있어요.

대표 기출 문제

🔒 괄호 안의 말을 이용하여 우리말에 맞게 영작하시오.

우리는 <u>건강해지려고</u> 매일 아침을 먹는다.
(<u>be healthy</u>, eat)
→ We ______________________.

CLUE
'~하기 위해, ~하려고'와 같이 목적의 의미를
나타낼 때 to부정사를 씁니다.
— to be healthy

정답: eat breakfast every day to be healthy

Point Exercise

배열 영작

[1-4] 우리말과 일치하도록 주어진 단어를 올바르게 배열하세요.

1
> 버스를 잡기 위해서, 그는 버스 정류장으로 달려갔다.
> (the bus / catch / to)

→ ______________________________ ,

　he ran to the bus stop.

2
> 나는 내 남동생을 깨우기 위해서 방에 들어갔다.
> (wake up / my / to / brother)

→ I entered the room ______________

______________________________ .

3
> Jim은 그의 지갑을 찾기 위해 공원으로 돌아갔다.
> (find / wallet / to / his)

→ Jim went back to the park ____________

______________________________ .

4
> 그들은 그들의 옛 친구들을 만나서 행복했다.
> (were / their / happy / old friends / meet / to)

→ They ______________________________

______________________________ .

주어진 단어로 영작

[5-9] 우리말과 일치하도록 주어진 단어를 사용하여 문장을 완성하세요.

5
> Bill은 사과하기 위해서 나에게 전화했다.
> (call, apologize)

→ Bill ______________________________ .

6
> 그녀는 샐러드를 만들기 위해 약간의 채소를 샀다.
> (vegetables, make, buy, a salad, some)

→ She ______________________________

______________________________ .

7
> 새로운 기술은 사용하기 어려울 수 있다.
> (hard, be, use, technology, can, new)

→ ______________________________

______________________________ .

8
> 나는 전기 자전거를 사기 위해 돈을 저축하는 중이다.
> (save, buy, an e-bike, money)

→ I ______________________________

______________________________ .

9
> 우리 팀은 그 축구 경기에 져서 실망했다.
> (team, disappointed, the soccer game, lose, be)

→ ______________________________

______________________________ .

기출: 문맥에 맞게 영작

10 주어진 문장과 같은 의미가 되도록 to부정사를 사용하여 한 문장으로 쓰세요.

> Sohee came home early because she wanted to take a rest.

→ Sohee came home early ______________

---

apologize 사과하다　technology (과학) 기술　e-bike 전기 자전거　disappointed 실망한　lose 지다; 잃어버리다　take a rest 휴식을 취하다, 쉬다

Unit 04 — to부정사를 포함한 주요 구문

POINT 6   too ~ to부정사 / enough+to부정사

너무 추워서 밖에 나갈 수 없다.
너무 춥다 / 밖에 나가기에는.

→ It is **too** *cold* / **to go** outside.
= It is **so** *cold* // **that** I **can't go** outside.

- 「too+형용사/부사+to부정사」는 '**너무 ~해서 …할 수 없다**'의 의미로 쓰여요.
- 「so+형용사/부사+that+주어+cannot[can't]+동사원형」으로 바꿔 쓸 수 있는데, 이때 과거의 내용을 나타낼 경우에는 couldn't를 써야 해요.
  I got up **too** *late* **to take** the bus. 나는 너무 늦게 일어나서 버스를 탈 수 없었다.
  = I got up **so** *late* **that** I **couldn't take** the bus.

그녀는 맨 위 선반에 닿을 정도로 충분히 키가 크다.
그녀는 / 충분히 키가 크다 / 닿을 정도로 / 맨 위 선반에.

→ She / is *tall* **enough** / **to reach** / the top shelf.
= She is **so** *tall* // **that** she **can reach** / the top shelf.

- 「형용사/부사+enough+to부정사」는 '**~할 만큼 충분히 …하다**'의 의미입니다.
- 「so+형용사/부사+that+주어+can+동사원형」으로 바꿔 쓸 수 있습니다.

대표 기출 문제

🔒 다음 문장을 괄호에 있는 표현을 사용하여 같은 뜻의 문장이 되도록 바꿔 쓰시오.

He was too hungry to get to sleep last night. (so)

→ ___________________________________

CLUE 1
「too+형용사/부사+to부정사」는 '너무 ~해서 …할 수 없다'라는 뜻이에요.

CLUE 2
과거의 내용을 나타내므로 「so+형용사/부사+that+주어+couldn't+동사원형」으로 바꿔 쓸 수 있어요.

정답: He was so hungry that he couldn't get to sleep last night.

✅ **함정 피하기**   「too ~ to부정사」, 「enough+to부정사」 구문을 that절로 바꿔 쓸 때, that절에 주어와 동사의 시제, 인칭, 수를 알맞게 쓰도록 주의하세요.

He **was** too busy **to go** shopping with his kids. (그는 너무 바빠서 그의 아이들과 쇼핑을 갈 수 없었다.)
→ He was so busy **that** he **couldn't go** shopping with his kids.

Point Exercise

[1-3] 우리말과 일치하도록 주어진 단어를 올바르게 배열하세요.

1
> Noah는 너무 어려서 그 이야기를 이해할 수 없었다.
> (to / understand / young / the story / too)

→ Noah was ________________

________________ .

2
> 그 영화는 두 번 볼만큼 충분히 재미있다.
> (watch / interesting / to / twice / enough)

→ The movie is ________________

________________ .

3
> 그 학생은 너무 수줍어서 선생님께 질문하지 못했다.
> (questions / to / too / ask / shy)

→ The student was ________________

________________ to the teacher.

[4-6] 우리말과 일치하도록 주어진 단어와 to부정사를 사용하여 문장을 완성하세요.

4
> 내 신발은 너무 작아서 신을 수 없다.
> (wear, be, small, shoes)

→ ________________

5
> 그녀는 나를 병원에 데려다줄 정도로 충분히 친절했다.
> (kind, be, take, enough)

→ ________________

________________ to the hospital.

6
> 날씨가 산책하러 갈 만큼 충분히 좋다.
> (go, enough, the weather, nice, be)

→ ________________

________________ for a walk.

[7-9] 주어진 문장과 같은 의미가 되도록 빈칸에 알맞은 말을 쓰세요.

7 Julie was too tired to exercise.

→ Julie was ________ ________

________ ________ ________

________ .

8 He is smart enough to teach others.

→ He is ________ ________ ________

________ ________ ________

others.

9 My parents were so busy that they couldn't come home early.

→ My parents were ________ ________

________ ________ home early.

10 우리말과 일치하도록 주어진 단어를 사용하여 단어 수에 맞게 문장을 완성하세요.

> A: You look tired today. Did you sleep well?
> B: Actually, 나는 어젯밤에 너무 걱정이 돼서 잠을 잘 수가 없었어. (worried, sleep, last night)

→ Actually, ________________

________________ . (8 단어)

actually 실은, 사실은

Chapter Test *

정답 및 해설 p.12

STAGE 1) Go for it!

자신 있게 풀어보는 기초 문제!

배열 영작

[1-4] 우리말과 일치하도록 주어진 단어를 배열하여 문장을 완성하세요.

1

> 나는 너에게 할 말이 없어.
> (say / nothing / to / have)

→ I _______________________________

_______________________________ to you.

2

> 지우는 그녀의 이모를 방문하기 위해 런던에 갔다.
> (London / aunt / to / visit / to / went / her)

→ Jiwoo _______________________________

_______________________________ .

3

> 나는 너희 독서 동아리에 가입하게 돼서 기뻐.
> (join / happy / to / book club / your)

→ I'm _______________________________

_______________________________ .

4

> Jim은 그의 차를 어디에 주차해야 할지 몰랐다.
> (where / car / didn't / park / his / to / know)

→ Jim _______________________________

_______________________________ .

주어진 단어로 영작

[5-7] 우리말과 일치하도록 주어진 단어를 사용하여 문장을 완성하세요. (필요시 단어를 추가하거나 형태를 바꿀 것)

5

> 우리는 저녁에 외식하기로 결정했다.
> (eat out, decide, for dinner)

→ We _______________________________

_______________________________ .

6

> 어르신들에게는 새로운 언어를 배우는 것이 쉽지 않다.
> (a new language, learn, easy)

→ It's _______________________________

_______________________________ for elderly people.

7

> 그는 저 의자를 들어 올릴 만큼 충분히 힘이 세다.
> (that, lift, strong, enough, chair)

→ He _______________________________

_______________________________ .

최신 기출

8 〈보기〉와 같이 다음 문장을 가주어 It으로 시작하는 문장으로 다시 쓰세요.

> 〈보기〉
> To follow the rules in class is necessary.
> → It is necessary to follow the rules in class.

To respect others' opinions is important.

→ _______________________________

____

◯ 그림 영작

[9-11] 각 그림의 상황을 나타내는 문장을 〈조건〉에 맞게 완성하세요.

〈보기〉
what   when   how   where

〈조건〉
• 「의문사+to부정사」를 사용할 것
• 〈보기〉에서 알맞은 의문사를 골라 쓸 것
  (단, 중복해서 사용하지 말 것)

9 David doesn't ________________________
____ .
(fix, know, the computer)

10 I can't ________________________________
____ .
(wear, today, decide)

11 Can you ________________________________
______________________________________ ?
(for lunch, decide, meet)

◯ 조건 영작

[12-14] 우리말과 일치하도록 〈조건〉에 맞게 문장을 완성하세요.

〈조건〉
• 가주어 It으로 시작할 것
• 주어진 단어를 사용하되 필요시 단어를 추가할 것

12 진정한 친구들을 갖는 것은 멋지다.
(wonderful, have, true)

→ ____

____

13 반려동물을 잘 돌보는 것은 쉽지 않다.
(a pet, take good care of, easy)

→ ____

____

14 해야 할 일의 목록을 만드는 것은 도움이 되었다.
(make, helpful, a to-do list)

→ ____

____

최신 기출

15 다음 쇼핑 목록을 보고 Sally가 사야 하는 것이 무엇인지 〈조건〉에 맞게 문장을 완성하세요.

<Sally's Shopping List>
☐ a book
☐ three pens

〈조건〉
• to부정사를 사용할 것
• 주어진 단어를 사용할 것

(1) Sally needs to buy ________________________
____ . (read)

(2) Sally needs to buy ________________________
____ . (write)

[16-22] 다음 각 문장에서 어법상 틀린 부분을 찾아 바르게 고쳐 쓰세요.

16 All of us agreed donate some money for poor people.

___________ → ___________

17 In order to making a lot of friends, you need to be a good listener.

___________ → ___________

18 The girl is too shy speak in front of many people.

___________ → ___________

19 Jay wants to find a friend to play now.

___________ → ___________

20 My brother is not enough old to vote.

___________ → ___________

21 Dan was not generous enough forgive his sister.

___________ → ___________

22 She needs some friends to talk.

___________ → ___________

[23-25] 주어진 문장과 같은 의미가 되도록 괄호 안의 지시대로 문장을 바꿔 쓰세요.

23

He was so busy that he couldn't come to the party.
(「too ~ to부정사」 구문을 사용할 것)

→ ___________

24

She is so smart that she can solve the puzzle.
(「enough+to부정사」 구문을 사용할 것)

→ ___________

____

25

I'm too tired to do homework now.
(「so ~ that」 구문을 사용할 것)

→ ___________

___________ now.

26 다음 〈보기〉에서 알맞은 표현을 골라 〈조건〉에 맞게 문장을 완성하세요.

〈보기〉
(A) the market / the park / the theater
(B) walk / watch / buy
(C) my dog / a musical / some vegetables

〈조건〉
• (A), (B), (C)의 각 표현을 한 번씩만 사용할 것
• to부정사를 사용하여 (A)의 각 장소에 간 목적이 드러나도록 쓸 것

(1) I went to ___________

___________.

(2) I went to ___________ ___________

___________.

(3) I went to ___________.

○● 주어진 단어로 영작

27 우리말과 일치하도록 주어진 단어와 to부정사를 사용하여 다음 글을 완성하세요.

> (1) 새로운 기술들을 배우는 것은 좋다. (2) 나는 내 지식을 향상시키기 위해 주로 온라인 강좌를 듣는다. (3) 올해 나는 기타 치는 법을 배우고 싶다. (4) 나는 나를 지도해 주실 좋은 온라인 선생님이 필요하다.

(1) (learn, it, good, skills)

→ __________________________________

____

(2) (improve, take, knowledge, online courses)

→ I usually __________________________

_______________________________ .

(3) (play, learn, want, how)

→ This year, _________________________

_______________________________ .

(4) (a good online teacher, need, guide)

→ __________________________________

____

○● 주어진 단어로 영작

[28-29] 우리말과 일치하도록 주어진 단어를 사용하여 같은 의미의 문장 (1)과 (2)를 완성하세요.

28

> Sara는 좋은 조언을 줄 수 있을 만큼 충분히 현명하다.
> (wise, advice, good, give)

(1) __________________________________

__________________________ (enough, to)

(2) __________________________________

__________________________ (so, that)

29

> 내 남동생은 키가 너무 작아서 롤러코스터를 탈 수 없다.
> (short, the roller coaster, ride)

(1) __________________________________

__________________________ (too, to)

(2) __________________________________

__________________________ (so, that)

🎯 **Challenge!**　　　　　　누적 문제 Ch 03-05

30 다음 중 어법상 <u>틀린</u> 문장 <u>두 개</u>를 찾아 그 기호를 쓰고, 문장 전체를 바르게 고쳐 쓰세요.

> ⓐ It is nice to have friends to talk to.
> ⓑ I don't have to wake up early tomorrow.
> ⓒ New Year's Eve is celebrating worldwide.
> ⓓ She was enough brave to try skydiving.
> ⓔ The jungle was destroyed by a big fire last month.

_______ → __________________________

____

_______ → __________________________

____

동명사와 분사

✅ Before You Write

- [ ] 동명사를 문장의 알맞은 자리에 올바른 형태로 쓸 수 있나요?
- [ ] 동명사를 목적어로 쓰는 동사를 구별하여 영작할 수 있나요?
- [ ] 동명사와 to부정사를 모두 목적어로 쓰는 동사의 경우, 문맥에 따라 알맞은 형태로 영작할 수 있나요?
- [ ] 현재분사나 과거분사를 사용하는 때를 명확히 알고, 올바른 위치에 쓸 수 있나요?

서술형 시험에는 어떻게 나올까?

내신 기출 다음 우리말을 보고 머릿속으로 한번 영어 문장을 떠올려 보세요.

1 좋은 친구가 되는 것은 중요하다.
~하는 것은 → 주어 → **Being a good friend is** POINT 1

2 (3) 나의 취미는 영화 보는 것이다.
~하는 것이다 → 보어 → **is watching movies** POINT 1

3 그들은 이야기하는 것과 사람들과 함께 시간을 보내는 것을 즐긴다.
enjoy → 동명사를 목적어로 쓰는 동사 → **enjoy talking and spending time** POINT 2

4 M: (A) 영수증 가지고 오시는 거 잊지 마세요. (bring / forget)
(미래에) ~할 것을 잊어버리다 → forget+to부정사 → **Don't forget to bring** POINT 3

5 그들은 캠핑 가는 것을 기대하고 있어.
~하는 것을 기대하다 → look forward to -ing → **are looking forward to going** POINT 4

6 (1) 강아지가 울고 있는 아이의 뒤에 달려가고 있었다.
→ A puppy was running after a(n) ___________ child.
~하는, ~하는 중인 → 현재분사 → **a crying child** POINT 5

7 (A) 나는 무섭지만, 경치는 멋지다!
감정을 느낌 → 과거분사 → **I'm scared**
감정을 일으킴 → 현재분사 → **the view is amazing** POINT 6

정답: **1** Being a good friend is important. **2** My hobby is watching movies. **3** They enjoy talking and spending time with people.
4 Don't[Do not] forget to bring the receipt. **5** They are[They're] looking forward to going camping. **6** crying **7** I am[I'm] scared, but the view is amazing!

명사로 쓰이는 동명사

 **POINT 1** 동명사 = ~하는 것은(주어) / ~하는 것이다(보어)

산책하는 것은 좋은 운동이다.
산책하는 것은 / ~이다 / 좋은 운동.
　　주어　　　　동사　　　보어

→ **Taking** a walk / *is* / good exercise.

- 동명사는 동사원형 뒤에 -ing를 붙인 것으로 명사처럼 쓰여요.
- 문장에서 **주어**로 '**~하는 것은, ~하기는**'의 의미를 쓸 때 동명사 형태로 쓸 수 있으며,
  이때 동사는 항상 단수형을 쓴답니다.
- 동명사의 부정형은 「not[never]+동명사」 형태로 나타내요.
  Not sleeping enough is bad for your health. 잠을 충분히 자지 않는 것은 네 건강에 좋지 않다.

나의 취미는 농구를 하는 것이다.
나의 취미는 / ~이다 / 농구를 하는 것.
　　주어　　　　동사　　　보어

→ My hobby / is / **playing** basketball.

- 문장의 보어 자리에 '**~하는 것(이다), ~하기(이다)**'의 의미로도 동명사 형태를 쓸 수 있어요.

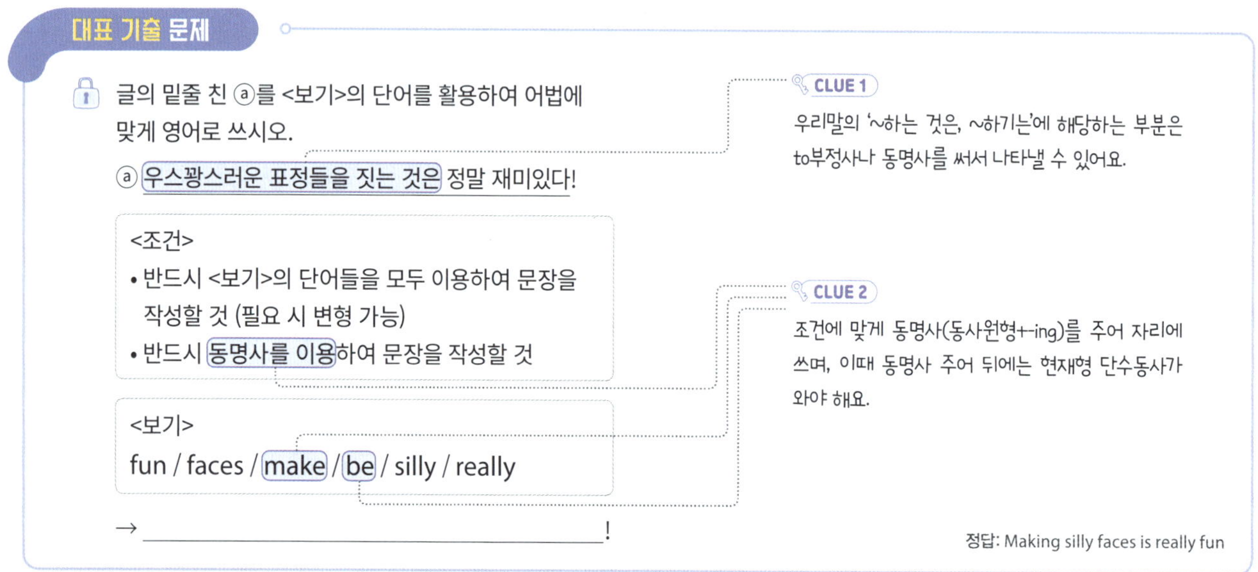

함정 피하기 동명사는 항상 단수 취급하므로, 주어 자리에 쓰인 동명사 뒤에 딸린 명사가 복수형이더라도 단수 동사를 쓴다는 점에
유의하세요.
Making silly faces ~~are~~(→ **is**) really fun.
　　동명사 주어

Point Exercise

[1-3] 우리말과 일치하도록 주어진 단어를 올바르게 배열하세요.

1

많은 물을 마시는 것은 건강에 좋다.
(good / lots of / drinking / water / is)

→ ________________________________

________________________________ for health.

2

나의 언니의 직업은 아이들을 돌보는 것이다.
(job / taking care of / my sister's / children / is)

→ ________________________________

________________________________ .

3

약속을 지키지 않는 것은 네 우정에 상처를 줄 수 있다.
(your friendships / can / keeping / promises / not / hurt)

→ ________________________________

________________________________ .

[4-8] 우리말과 일치하도록 주어진 단어를 사용하여 문장을 완성하세요. (단, 동명사 형태를 쓸 것)

4

그의 좋은 습관은 매일 책을 읽는 것이다.
(a book, be, good habit, read, every day)

→ ________________________________

____

5

사진 찍는 것은 내가 가장 좋아하는 활동이다.
(pictures, be, take, activity, favorite)

→ ________________________________

____

6

다른 사람들의 말을 주의 깊게 듣는 것은 중요하다.
(be, others, important, carefully, listen to)

→ ________________________________

____

7

그림을 그리는 것은 네 창의력을 향상시킬 수 있다.
(pictures, can, draw, creativity, improve)

→ ________________________________

____

8

친구들과 시간을 보내는 것은 나를 행복하게 한다.
(make, spend, happy, friends, with, time)

→ ________________________________

____

9 다음 대화를 읽고 〈조건〉에 맞게 우리말을 영작하세요.

A: What do you want to be when you grow up?
B: I want to be a writer.
A: That's cool! What do you enjoy most about writing?
B: 흥미로운 등장인물들을 만드는 것은 정말 재미있어.

〈조건〉
• 동명사 형태로 쓸 것
• interesting, fun, create, characters를 사용할 것

→ ________________________________

____

---

health 건강 friendship 우정 promise 약속; 약속하다 hurt 상처를 주다, 다치게 하다 creativity 창의력 improve 향상시키다 character 등장인물

많은 사람들은 음악 듣는 것을 즐긴다.

많은 사람들은 / 즐긴다 / 음악 듣는 것을.
　　주어　　　　동사　　　목적어

➔ Many people / **enjoy** / **listening to** music.

- 문장에서 목적어 자리에 '**~하는 것을, ~하기를**'의 의미를 표현할 때 동사에 따라 to부정사 또는 동명사가 쓰여요. 따라서 동사를 잘 확인하고 목적어로 to부정사와 동명사 중 알맞은 형태를 사용해야 해요.
- **to부정사를 목적어로 쓰는 동사들**이 주로 **미래**와 관련된 행동이라면, 다음과 같이 **동명사를 목적어로 쓰는 동사들**은 **과거/현재**와 관련된 행동이에요.

📢 **동명사를 목적어로 쓰는 동사들**

enjoy reading	읽는 것을 즐기다	**finish** cleaning	청소하는 것을 끝내다
keep asking	말하기를 계속하다	**give up** buying	사는 것을 포기하다
practice singing	노래하기를 연습하다	**avoid** meeting	만나는 것을 피하다
consider selling	파는 것을 고려하다	**mind** wasting time	시간 낭비하는 것을 꺼리다
suggest studying	공부하기를 제안하다	**put off** exercising	운동하는 것을 미루다

나는 여가 시간에 추리 소설을 읽는 것을 좋아한다.

나는 / 좋아한다 / 추리 소설을 읽는 것을 / 나의 여가 시간에.
주어　　동사　　　　목적어

➔ I / **like** / **reading[to read]** detective novels / in my free time.

- 다음과 같은 동사들은 목적어로 동명사와 to부정사 둘 다 쓸 수 있어요.

begin running[to run]	달리기 시작하다	**like** swimming[to swim]	수영하는 것을 좋아하다
start cooking[to cook]	요리하기 시작하다	**love** painting[to paint]	그림 그리는 것을 아주 좋아하다
continue walking[to walk]	계속 걷다	**hate** writing[to write]	쓰는 것을 싫어하다

대표 기출 문제

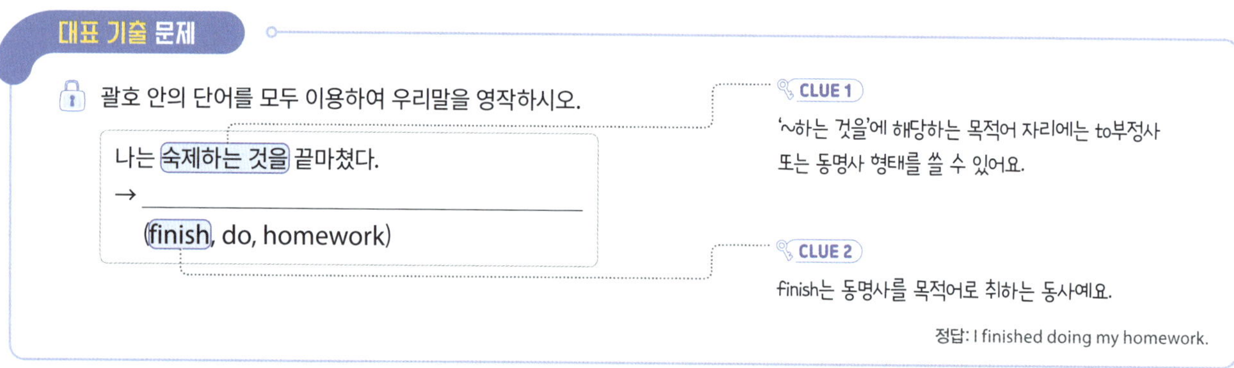

🔒 괄호 안의 단어를 모두 이용하여 우리말을 영작하시오.

나는 숙제하는 것을 끝마쳤다.

➔ ______________________________

(finish, do, homework)

🔖 **CLUE 1**
'~하는 것을'에 해당하는 목적어 자리에는 to부정사 또는 동명사 형태를 쓸 수 있어요.

🔖 **CLUE 2**
finish는 동명사를 목적어로 취하는 동사예요.

정답: I finished doing my homework.

Point Exercise

[1-5] 우리말과 일치하도록 주어진 단어를 올바르게 배열하세요.

1
> 그 아이들은 그리기와 색칠하는 것을 즐겼다.
> (drawing / painting / enjoyed / and)

→ The children _______________________

_______________________________ .

2
> 그 수줍은 소년은 새로운 사람들을 만나는 것을 피했다.
> (new / meeting / avoided / people)

→ The shy boy _______________________

_______________________________ .

3
> 나는 초콜릿 케이크를 먹는 것을 좋아한다.
> (eating / like / I / chocolate cake)

→ _______________________________

_______________________________ .

4
> TV를 꺼도 될까요?
> (the TV / mind / do / turning off / you)

→ _______________________________

_______________________________ ?

5
> 우리는 저녁 식사 전에 집을 청소하는 것을 끝냈다.
> (finished / the house / cleaning / we)

→ _______________________________

_______________________ before dinner.

[6-9] 우리말과 일치하도록 주어진 단어를 사용하여 문장을 완성하세요. (필요시 형태를 바꿀 것)

6
> Ted는 중국어를 배우기 시작했다.
> (learn, start, Chinese)

→ _______________________________

7
> 그들은 학교 축제를 위해 춤추는 것과 노래하는 것을 연습했다. (dance, practice, sing, and)

→ _______________________________

for the school festival.

8
> 나의 부모님은 다른 도시로 이사 갈 것을 고려하셨다.
> (consider, to another city, parents, move)

→ _______________________________

____

9
> 나는 그를 설득하는 것을 포기하지 않을 것이다.
> (will, persuade, give up)

→ _______________________________

____

10 다음 글을 읽고 〈조건〉에 맞게 우리말을 영작하세요.

> Emma had an appointment with Dr. Jones. She arrived at the hospital on time. But he was too busy. <u>그녀는 그를 계속 기다렸다.</u> After 30 minutes, he came to see her.

〈조건〉
· keep, wait for를 사용할 것
· 필요시 단어의 형태를 바꿀 것

→ _______________________________

---

persuade 설득하다 appointment 약속 on time 제때에, 정각에

POINT 3 　동명사/to부정사 목적어 의미가 다른 동사

나는 나갈 때 전등을 껐던 것을 기억한다.
나는 / 기억한다 / 전등을 껐던 것을 // 내가 나갈 때.
주어　　　동사　　　목적어　　　　부사절

→ I / remember / **turning off** the light // when I went out.

너는 나갈 때 전등을 꺼야 하는 것을 기억해야 한다.
너는 / 기억해야 한다 / 전등을 꺼야 하는 것을 // 네가 나갈 때.
주어　　　동사　　　　목적어　　　　부사절

→ You / should **remember** / **to turn off** the light // when you go out.

- **remember, forget, try** 등의 동사들은 목적어 자리에 동명사와 to부정사를 쓰면 각각 뜻이 달라집니다.
- 대개 **동명사 목적어는 과거/현재의 행동**을 나타내고, **to부정사 목적어는 미래에 할 행동**을 의미해요.
  따라서 표현하고자 하는 뜻에 맞게 목적어로 동명사 또는 to부정사 중 알맞은 형태를 써야 해요.

remember+동명사	~했던 것을 기억하다 (과거)	try+동명사	시험 삼아 ~해 보다
remember+to부정사	~할 것을 기억하다 (미래)	try+to부정사	~하려고 노력하다
forget+동명사	~했던 것을 잊어버리다 (과거)	regret+동명사	~한 것을 후회하다
forget+to부정사	~할 것을 잊어버리다 (미래)	regret+to부정사	~하게 되어 유감이다

- 동사 stop은 목적어로 동명사만 취하지만, 그 뒤에 '~하기 위해(목적)'를 나타내는 to부정사가 오기도 해요.
  문맥을 통해 의미를 잘 구분해서 사용해야 돼요.

| stop+동명사 | ~하는 것을 멈추다 |
| stop+to부정사 | ~하기 위해 멈추다 |

I *stopped* **talking** to her. 나는 그녀에게 이야기하는 것을 멈추었다.
　　　　목적어(~하는 것을)

I *stopped* **to talk** to her. 나는 그녀에게 말을 걸기 위해 멈추었다.
　　　'목적'의 to부정사(~하기 위해)

대표 기출 문제

🔒 다음 대화의 빈칸에 들어갈 말을 우리말과 같은 뜻이
되도록 영어로 쓰시오.

> A: What should I bring to the sports day?
> B: Let me see. ______________________.
> 　(물병을 가져오는 거 잊지 마.)

CLUE 1
'~하는 것을'에 해당하는 목적어 자리에
to부정사 또는 동명사 형태를 쓸 수 있어요.

CLUE 2
'(미래에) ~할 것을 잊다'의 의미가 되려면
forget 뒤에 to부정사를 써야 해요.

정답: Don't[Do not] forget to bring a water bottle

Point Exercise

정답 및 해설 p.14

[1-4] 우리말과 일치하도록 주어진 단어를 사용하여 빈칸에 알맞은 말을 쓰세요.

1
> 나는 Ariel과 그 영화를 보았던 것을 기억한다.
> (watch, remember)

→ I ________________________________

    the movie with Ariel.

2
> 그는 일주일에 한 번 그 식물에 물 주는 것을 종종 잊어버린다. (water, forget)

→ He often ________________________

    the plant once a week.

3
> 밤에 컴퓨터 게임 하는 것을 그만둬라.
> (stop, play)

→ ________________________ computer

    games at night.

4
> 내 여동생은 처음으로 파스타를 만들어보았다.
> (try, make)

→ My sister ______________________

    pasta for the first time.

[5-8] 우리말과 일치하도록 주어진 단어를 사용하여 문장을 완성하세요. (필요시 단어를 추가하거나 형태를 바꿀 것)

5
> Larry는 어제 나에게 메시지 보낸 것을 잊어버렸다.
> (forget, a message, send)

→ ________________________________

    ________________________ to me yesterday.

6
> 그 소년은 동전을 줍기 위해 멈췄다.
> (pick up, the coins, stop, the boy)

→ ________________________________

    ____

7
> 너는 네 실내화를 들고 올 것을 기억해야 한다.
> (slippers, remember, bring, should)

→ ________________________________

    ____

8
> 선생님은 우리 이름을 기억하려고 애쓰셨다.
> (names, try, the teacher, remember)

→ ________________________________

    ____

9 다음 대화를 읽고 〈조건〉에 맞게 우리말을 영작하세요.

> A: Hey, tomorrow is the school picnic day.
>   What should I bring?
> B: 네 카메라 가져오는 것을 잊지 마.
>   I'll bring a picnic mat for us.

> 〈조건〉
> • 6 단어로 쓸 것
> • forget, bring, camera를 사용할 것

→ ________________________________

    ____

for the first time 처음으로 pick up ~을 집다. 들어 올리다 slipper 실내화 picnic 소풍

자주 쓰이는 동명사 표현

POINT 4 전치사+동명사, 동명사 주요 표현

우리는 더 많이 재활용함으로써 쓰레기를 줄였다.
우리는 쓰레기를 줄였다 / 더 많이 재활용함으로써.

→ We reduced waste / **by** recycling more.
　　　　　　　　　　동명사(전치사의 목적어)

- 전치사는 주로 「전치사+(대)명사」 형태로 쓰이는데, 전치사 뒤에 오는 (대)명사를 '전치사의 목적어'라고 해요.
- 전치사의 목적어 자리에 동사가 쓰일 때는 동명사 형태로 써야 합니다.

나는 부모님을 위해 저녁을 만드느라 바빴다.
나는 / 바빴다 / 저녁을 만드느라 / 나의 부모님을 위해.

→ I / **was busy** / **making** dinner / for my parents.

- 다음과 같이 동명사가 숙어처럼 사용되는 표현들은 잘 기억하세요.

📢 동명사가 숙어처럼 사용되는 여러 표현

look forward to seeing	보기를 기대하다	be used to using	사용하는 것에 익숙하다
be good at singing	노래하는 것을 잘하다	go swimming	수영하러 가다
spend 시간 playing	노는 데 시간을 보내다	be interested in learning	배우는 것에 관심이 있다
spend 돈 buying	사는 데 돈을 쓰다	How about meeting?	만나는 게 어때?
have trouble solving	해결하는 데 어려움을 겪다	Thank you for coming	와주셔서 고맙습니다
feel like eating	먹고 싶다	be afraid of losing	지는 것을 두려워하다
be busy preparing	준비하느라 바쁘다		

대표 기출 문제

🔒 주어진 단어를 이용하여 우리말과 뜻이 같도록 문장을
완성하시오. (단, 단어의 형태는 필요에 따라 변형 가능)

나는 내일 학교 수학여행을 가는 것을 기대하고 있다.
(go, I'm, on the school trip, to, forward, look)

→ ________________________________ tomorrow.

CLUE 1

'~하는 것을 기대하다'는 의미를 to, forward,
look을 사용해 나타내야 해요. — look forward to

CLUE 2

look forward to 다음에는 동명사를 쓰므로
go를 going으로 써야 해요.

정답: I am[I'm] looking forward to going on the school trip

함정 피하기 look forward to 다음에 동사원형을 쓰지 않도록 유의하세요. 이때 쓰인 to는 전치사이기 때문이에요.
I'm **looking forward to** see(→ seeing) you soon. (나는 너를 곧 보기를 기대하고 있어.)

Point Exercise

정답 및 해설 p.14

배열 영작

[1-5] 우리말과 일치하도록 주어진 단어를 올바르게 배열하세요.

1
점심 식사 후에 산책하는 게 어때?
(about / a walk / taking / how)

→ _________________________________

_________________________ after lunch?

2
수진이는 겨울옷들을 사는 데 돈을 좀 썼다.
(winter clothes / some / buying / money / spent)

→ Sujin _________________________________

_________________________ .

3
민수는 외국인들에게 말하는 것을 두려워한다.
(of / is / to / speaking / afraid / foreigners)

→ Minsu _________________________________

_________________________ .

4
나는 커피 한 잔을 마시고 싶다.
(a cup of / feel / I / coffee / having / like)

→ _________________________________

_________________________ .

5
그는 다른 문화에 대해 배우는 것에 관심이 있다.
(learning / in / is / about / interested / different cultures / he)

→ _________________________________

_________________________ .

foreigner 외국인

주어진 단어로 영작

[6-9] 우리말과 일치하도록 주어진 단어를 사용하여 문장을 완성하세요.

6
저희를 초대해주셔서 감사합니다.
(invite, us, for, you, thank)

→ _________________________________

7
나의 부모님은 요즘 일하느라 바쁘시다.
(busy, work, parents, be)

→ _________________________________

these days.

8
Julie는 작별 인사도 없이 떠났다.
(goodbye, without, say, leave)

→ _________________________________

9
나의 형은 기타 연주하는 것을 잘한다.
(play, brother, the guitar, good, be)

→ _________________________________

기출: 조건 영작

10 다음 편지글을 읽고 〈조건〉에 맞게 우리말을 영작하세요.

Dear Bora,
How's it going? I'm planning to visit Seoul next month. We can spend the days having a lot of fun! 나는 너를 만나기를 기대하고 있어.
With love,
Sophia

〈조건〉
• 6 단어로 쓸 것
• look, meet, forward를 사용할 것

→ _________________________________

POINT 5 명사를 수식하는 분사(~하는, ~된)

Elsa는 우는 아기를 돌봐주었다.
Elsa는 / 돌봐주었다 / 우는 아기를.
　　주어　　　동사　　　목적어

→ Elsa / took care of / the **crying baby**.

이것들은 나의 아빠에 의해 찍힌 사진들이다.
이것들은 / ~이다 / 나의 아빠에 의해 찍힌 사진들.
　주어　　동사　　　　　　보어

→ These / are / *the pictures* taken by my dad.

- 분사는 동사원형에 -ing를 붙인 현재분사(-ing)와 과거분사(p.p.)가 있고 둘 다 형용사처럼 쓰여
명사를 앞이나 뒤에서 수식할 수 있어요. (☞ 동사 변화형 p.180)

현재분사(-ing)	~하는(능동), ~하는 중인(진행)	수식받는 명사가 동작을 **직접** 하거나 하고 있는 것
과거분사(p.p.)	~된(수동, 완료)	수식받는 명사가 동작을 **당하게 되는** 경우

- 분사 뒤에 여러 어구가 딸려 있을 때는 명사 뒤에서 수식해요.
The boy standing at the bus stop is my brother. 버스정류장에 서 있는 소년은 나의 오빠이다.

📢 자주 쓰이는 「분사＋명사」 표현

-ing＋명사	crying baby (우는 아기) boiling water (끓는 물) sleeping child (자는 아이)	smiling girl (웃는 여자아이) running water (흐르는 물) shining star (빛나는 별)	falling leaves (떨어지는 나뭇잎) barking dog (짖는 개) flying bird (날아가는 새)
p.p.＋명사	burnt toast (타버린 토스트) boiled egg (삶은 계란) hidden place (숨겨진 장소) stolen ring (도난당한 반지)	broken window (깨진 창문) baked potato (구운 감자) frozen yogurt (얼린 요구르트) balanced diet (균형 잡힌 식단)	fallen leaves (낙엽) fried chicken (튀긴 치킨) sliced cheese (얇게 썬 치즈)

대표 기출 문제

🔒 우리말에 맞도록 필요시에 제시어를 적절히 변형하여
문장을 완성하시오.

<제시어> write, a, letter

There is a girl ________________________ .
(편지를 쓰는 한 소녀가 있다.)

CLUE 1
우리말에서 '편지를 쓰는'이 형용사처럼
명사 '한 소녀'를 수식해요.

CLUE 2
'~하는'이라는 능동의 의미는 현재분사(-ing)로
나타내며, 뒤에 딸린 어구(a letter)가 있으므로
명사를 뒤에서 수식해야 해요.

정답: writing a letter

Point Exercise

○ **빈칸 완성**

[1-3] 우리말과 일치하도록 주어진 단어를 사용하여 빈칸에 알맞은 말을 쓰세요.

1

그녀는 자고 있는 아기를 조심스럽게 안았다.
(sleep, baby)

→ She held the ______________ ______________
carefully.

2

Luna는 간식으로 구운 감자를 먹었다.
(bake, potatoes)

→ Luna ate ______________ ______________ for
a snack.

3

무대에서 연기하고 있는 그 남자는 내가 가장 좋아하는
배우이다. (act, the man)

→ ______________ ______________ ______________
on the stage is my favorite actor.

○ **주어진 단어로 영작**

[4-8] 우리말과 일치하도록 주어진 단어를 사용하여 문장을 완성하세요.

4

그녀는 파티에서 빛나는 목걸이를 착용했다.
(wear, necklace, the, shine)

→ ______________________________________
______________________________ to the party.

5

Joe와 나는 서울에서 열린 음악 축제에 다녀왔다.
(to, in Seoul, the music festival, go, hold)

→ Joe and I ______________________________
______________________________________ .

6

거리에 많은 떨어진 잎들이 있다.
(in, lots of, fall, be, the street, leaves, there)

→ ______________________________________
____

7

나는 벤치에 앉아 있는 그 소녀를 안다.
(sit, the girl, know, a bench, on)

→ ______________________________________
____

8

나의 삼촌은 독일에서 만들어진 차 한 대를 사셨다.
(uncle, make, a car, in Germany, buy)

→ ______________________________________
____

기출: 한 문장으로 영작

9 다음 두 문장을 우리말과 일치하도록 〈조건〉에 맞게
한 문장으로 바꿔 쓰세요.

The tall woman is my teacher.
She is wearing a red sweater.
(빨간 스웨터를 입고 있는 그 키 큰 여성분은
나의 선생님이시다.)

〈조건〉
• 분사 형태를 사용할 것
• 10 단어로 쓸 것

→ ______________________________________
____

---

hold 들다; (행사를) 열다, 개최하다 snack 간식 act 연기하다; 행동하다 stage 무대 necklace 목걸이 shine 빛나다, 반짝이다 sweater 스웨터

POINT 6 　감정을 나타내는 분사

나는 신나는 액션 영화를 봤다.
나는 / 봤다 / 신나는 액션 영화를.
　주어　　동사　　　　목적어

→ I / saw / an **exciting** *action movie*.

그들은 그 소식을 들어서 정말 신났다.
그들은 / ~했다 / 정말 신난 / 그 소식을 들어서.
　주어　　동사　　보어　　　　부사구

→ **They** / were / **very excited** / to hear the news.

- 감정을 나타내는 단어들은 현재분사나 과거분사 형태로 많이 쓰여요.
- 감정을 나타내는 분사도 형용사처럼 명사를 수식할 수 있고, 동사 뒤에서 주어를 설명하는 보어로도 쓸 수 있어요.
- 사람에게 **어떤 감정을 일으키는 것** 즉, '~하게 하는' 것은 현재분사를,
  어떤 감정을 느끼는 것 즉, '~하게 되는'에는 과거분사를 써요.
  따라서 분사와 관련된 명사가 감정을 일으키는지, 감정을 느끼는지를 잘 판단해야 해요.

감정을 나타내는 빈출 분사

현재분사(-ing)		과거분사(p.p.)	
surprising news	놀라운 뉴스	**surprised** people	놀란 사람들
exciting games	신나는 경기들	**excited** players	신난 선수들
amazing talent	놀라운 재능	**amazed** teachers	놀란 선생님들
interesting classes	재미있는 수업들	**interested** students	재미를 느낀 학생들
boring books	지루한 책들	**bored** readers	지루해하는 독자들
tiring jobs	피곤하게 하는 일들	**tired** workers	피곤한 직원들
shocking stories	충격적인 이야기들	**shocked** listeners	충격을 받은 청중들
touching movies	감동을 주는 영화들	**touched** audiences	감동을 느낀 관객들
pleasing results	기쁘게 하는 결과들	**pleased** family	기쁜 가족
disappointing behavior	실망스러운 행동	**disappointed** parents	실망한 부모
embarrassing situations	당황스러운 상황들	**embarrassed** guests	당황한 손님들

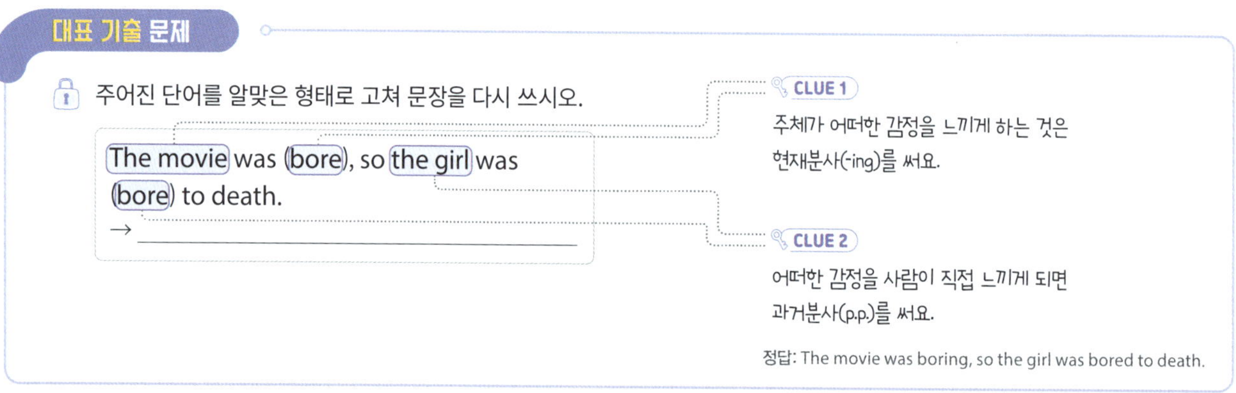

Point Exercise

정답 및 해설 p.14

배열 영작

[1-5] 우리말과 일치하도록 주어진 단어를 올바르게 배열하세요. (필요시 형태를 바꿀 것)

1

학생들은 과학 수업 시간에 지루함을 느꼈다.
(felt / the students / bore)

→ ______________________________
______________________ during the science class.

2

그의 놀라운 이야기는 전혀 사실이 아니었다.
(story / not / was / amaze / true / his)

→ ______________________________
______________________________ at all.

3

나는 그때 당황스러웠던 순간을 기억했다.
(embarrass / remembered / the / moment / I)

→ ______________________________
______________________ at that time.

4

사람들은 고속도로에서 일어났던 사고에 충격을 받았다.
(were / the accident / shock / at / people)

→ ______________________________
______________________ on the highway.

5

그녀는 나에게 판다에 관한 재미있는 사실들을 말해 주었다.
(facts / interest / told / she / me / about pandas)

→ ______________________________
______________________________ .

주어진 단어로 영작

[6-8] 우리말과 일치하도록 주어진 단어를 사용하여 문장을 완성하세요.

6

그 결승전은 매우 신날 거야!
(the final match, will, excite, very, be)

→ ______________________________
____

7

사람들은 그 마술쇼에 놀랐다.
(amaze, the magic show, be, people, at)

→ ______________________________
____

8

나는 그 어려운 질문에 당황했다.
(by, the difficult question, embarrass, be)

→ ______________________________
____

기출: 대화문 완성

9 우리말과 일치하도록 주어진 단어를 사용하여 다음의 대화를 완성하세요.

A: Gwen, how was your weekend?
B: It was great. (1) 나는 수족관에 가서 신났어.
A: Which animal was most impressive?
B: (2) 상어가 놀라웠어! It was very big and scary.

(1) ______________________________
____
(to the aquarium, to go, excite, be)

(2) ______________________________
(amaze, be, the shark)

---

moment 순간; 시기 accident 사고 highway 고속도로 final 마지막의, 최종의 match 경기, 시합 impressive 인상적인, 감명 깊은

Chapter Test [*]

정답 및 해설 p.15

STAGE 1 · Go for it!

자신 있게 풀어보는 기초 문제!

배열 영작

[1-4] 우리말과 일치하도록 주어진 단어를 배열하여 문장을 완성하세요.

1
> 우리는 인터넷으로 쇼핑하는 것을 즐긴다.
> (the Internet / enjoy / on / shopping)

→ We ___________________________

_______________________________ .

2
> 영어로 에세이를 쓰는 것은 어렵다.
> (an essay / is / writing / in English / difficult)

→ _______________________________

_______________________________ .

3
> Aria는 그녀의 친구로부터 편지를 받기를 기대한다.
> (from / receiving / forward / her friend / looks / to / a letter)

→ Aria ___________________________

_______________________________ .

4
> 그 남자는 1950년대에 그려진 그림 한 점을 샀다.
> (painted / a picture / the 1950s / bought / in)

→ The man _________________________

_______________________________ .

주어진 단어로 영작

[5-7] 우리말과 일치하도록 주어진 단어를 사용하여 문장을 완성하세요.

5
> 나는 그 병을 열려고 노력했지만 열 수 없었다.
> (try, the bottle, open)

→ I _______________________________ ,

but I couldn't.

6
> 나는 저 슈퍼마켓에서 과일을 산 것을 기억한다.
> (fruits, buy, that supermarket, remember, at)

→ I _______________________________

_______________________________ .

7
> 수미와 지호는 한마디도 하지 않고 함께 앉아 있었다.
> (sit, be, without, a word, say, together)

→ Sumi and Jiho ___________________

_______________________________ .

최신 기출

8 ⓐ~ⓒ를 알맞은 분사 형태로 바꾸어 다음 글을 완성하세요.

> Today I got my exam paper back. I was very ⓐ <u>disappoint</u> with my score.
> My friend Kevin was ⓑ <u>worry</u> about me and took me to the movies. We watched an ⓒ <u>excite</u> action movie. I felt better after spending time with him.

ⓐ _______________________________

ⓑ _______________________________

ⓒ _______________________________

대화문 완성

[9-13] 주어진 단어를 사용하여 각 대화를 완성하세요.

9

A: Do you like traveling abroad?

B: Yes, I do. _______________________
_______________________ always fun.
(to other countries, traveling, be)

10

A: Sara, _______________________
_______________________ this Saturday?
(how, go shopping, about)
B: That sounds great. I need new shoes.

11

A: The light is on in Tony's room.
B: Oh! He _______________________
_______________________ again.
(the light, forget, turn off)

12

A: Do you know _______________________
_______________________?
(the girl, next to, stand, Tom)
B: Yes, I do. She is Tom's little sister, Nancy.

13

A: How was the novel?
B: The story was very _______________.
(excite) The ending was also
_______________. (amaze)

그림 영작

14 다음 그림을 보고 〈보기〉에서 알맞은 표현을 골라 Wendy를 소개하는 글을 완성하세요. (단, 동명사 형태로 쓸 것)

(1) (2)

〈보기〉

swim   become   visit
art galleries   a swimmer

I'd like to introduce my friend to you. Her name is Wendy. We have been best friends since we first met in 2021.
(1) She loves _______________________
_______________________ in her free time.
(2) She is also good at _______________,
so _______________________ is her dream.

최신 기출

15 다음 학생들의 의견을 읽고, 우리말과 일치하도록 주어진 단어를 사용하여 문장을 완성하세요.

Steve: Selfies are a great way to save
     memories. I love taking them with
     my friends!
Willson: I enjoy taking selfies, but 몇몇 학생들은
     셀카를 찍는 데 너무 많은 시간을 써.
Stella: Filters make my selfies look nice, but
     sometimes they don't really look like
     me.

→ but _______________________
_______________________.
(too much time, them, some students, take,
spend)

[16-19] 다음 두 문장을 〈보기〉와 같이 분사를 사용하여 한 문장으로 연결해 쓰세요.

〈보기〉
I know the girl.
She is wearing a white dress.
→ I know the girl wearing a white dress.

16
There was a bird.
It was singing on the branch.

→ ___________________________

17
I found a book.
It was written in Italian.

→ ___________________________
____

18
Ben saw a picture.
It was taken in the Alps.

→ ___________________________
____

19
The child is my little brother.
He is standing at the bus stop.

→ ___________________________
____

[20-24] 다음 각 문장에서 어법상 틀린 부분을 찾아 바르게 고쳐 쓰세요.

20 Be quiet. There is a slept baby on the bed.

___________ → ___________

21 Joanna loves history. She always keeps to ask questions during history class.

___________ → ___________

22 You should remember cleaning the house this weekend.

___________ → ___________

23 Aron saw his friend on the street. He stopped saying hello to her.

___________ → ___________

24 My family was embarrassing because our dog barked a lot last night.

___________ → ___________

25 다음 (A) 활동에 대하여 자신이 어떻게 생각하는지에 대한 문장을 〈조건〉에 맞게 완성하세요.

(A)
ride a bike   learn a new language
write a poem   travel to new places

(B)
exciting   interesting   boring
fun   easy   difficult

〈조건〉
• 동명사구를 주어로 사용할 것
• 한 문장에 (A)와 (B)의 표현을 하나씩 사용할 것
  (각 표현은 한 번씩만 사용할 것)

〈보기〉 Riding a bike is exciting.

(1) ___________________________
____

(2) ___________________________
____

보기에서 골라 영작

[26-29] 빈칸에 들어갈 알맞은 말을 〈보기〉에서 골라 분사 형태로 바꿔 쓰세요. (단, 한 번씩만 사용할 것)

〈보기〉	
excite	shock
bore	interest

26
> Today was my birthday. My friends surprised me with a cake and gifts. It was a very ________________ day for me.

27
> Yesterday, I watched a documentary film about the South Pole. I became ________________ in animals at the South Pole.

28
> My friend and I went to a movie. I almost fell asleep because the movie was ________________.

29
> My favorite baseball team lost today's game. The result of the game was ________________ because they lost 1-10.

어법 오류 수정

30 다음 글을 읽고 ⓐ~ⓔ 중 어법상 **틀린** 세 개를 찾아 그 기호를 쓰고, 바르게 고쳐 쓰세요.

> Robert ⓐ <u>was very busy prepare for</u> an important project at his company. Because of the stress, he ⓑ <u>started eating</u> more. Actually, he ⓒ <u>likes having</u> a late-night snack as well. As a result, he gained some weight. He decided to exercise at the gym. He couldn't go to the gym often. He often ⓓ <u>forgot exercising</u>. Also, he was too tired after work. He almost ⓔ <u>gave up lose weight</u>. I guess he'll go on a diet again someday.

________ → ________________

________ → ________________

________ → ________________

Challenge!   누적 문제 Ch 04-06

31 다음 중 어법상 **틀린** 문장 **두 개**를 찾아 그 기호를 쓰고, 문장 전체를 바르게 고쳐 쓰세요.

> ⓐ We haven't decided what to eat yet.
> ⓑ She started to cry after hearing the news.
> ⓒ The chickens will fed by my grandfather.
> ⓓ Spilling coffee on the table was embarrassing.
> ⓔ I feel like to travel, but I don't have enough money.

________ → ________________

____

________ → ________________

____

✅ Before You Write

- ✅ 대명사, 형용사, 부사의 각 역할을 잘 이해하고 있나요?
- ✅ 우리말 의미를 보고 알맞은 대명사, 형용사, 부사를 올바른 위치에 쓸 수 있나요?
- ✅ 형용사와 부사의 자리를 혼동하지 않고 잘 구분할 수 있나요?
- ✅ 뒤에 오는 명사에 따라 알맞은 수량 형용사를 사용할 수 있나요?

내신 기출 다음 우리말을 보고 머릿속으로 한번 영어 문장을 떠올려 보세요.

1 There are two balls in the box.
하나는 야구공이고, 다른 하나는 테니스공이다.
one ~, the other ... → 단수 취급 → **One is ~, the other is ...** `POINT 1`

2 각각의 학생들은 서로 다른 재능을 가지고 있다.
<조건> talents, have, student, different, each만 사용할 것
each → 뒤에 단수명사 → 단수 취급 → **Each student has** `POINT 2`

3 At that moment, ⓑ 그는 혼잣말했다.
→ he ____________________.
재귀대명사의 관용 표현 → 과거시제 → **talked to himself** `POINT 3`

4 (1) 주어진 단어를 바르게 배열하시오.
→ Paul ____________________.
(special, ate, something)
-thing으로 끝나는 대명사 → 형용사가 뒤에서 수식 → **something special** `POINT 4`

5 Well, __________ __________ __________ __________.
(우리는 밀가루가 거의 없어.)
명사의 수나 양을 나타내는 형용사 → 셀 수 없는 명사(flour) 앞 → little → **little flour** `POINT 5`

6 A: (A) 나는 자주 내 자전거를 타.
빈도부사 often → 일반동사(ride) 앞 → **often ride** `POINT 6`

정답: **1** One is a baseball, and the other is a tennis ball. **2** Each student has different talents. **3** talked[said] to himself **4** ate something special
5 we have little flour **6** I often ride my bike.

대명사

 **POINT 1** one, another, other(s)를 써야 할 때

두 소녀가 들어왔다. 한 명은 키가 컸다, // 그리고 나머지 한 명은 키가 작았다.

→ [Two] *girls* came in. **One** was tall, // and **the other** was short.

> 절과 절 사이에 콤마를 붙이고, 마지막 절 앞에는 and를 써요.

나는 세 마리의 반려동물들이 있다. 한 마리는 고양이다, // 또 다른 한 마리는 개다, //
그리고 나머지 한 마리는 햄스터이다.

→ I have [three] *pets*.
One is a cat, // **another** is a dog, // and **the other** is a hamster.

· 앞에서 언급된 명사를 대신하지 않고, 그 명사와 같은 종류의 막연한 어떤 것을 가리키는 대명사가 있어요.
이를 **부정대명사**라 하는데, 주로 one, another, other(s)를 사용하여 여러 불특정한 명사를 나열할 수 있어요.

📢 one, another, other를 이용한 여러 가지 표현

one ~, the other …	(둘 중) 하나는 ~, 나머지 하나는 …
one ~, another …, the other ~	(셋 중) 하나는 ~, 또 다른 하나는 …, 나머지 하나는 ~
some ~, others …	(여럿 중) 몇몇은 ~[몇몇 ~은], 다른 몇몇은 …
one ~, the others …	(여럿 중) 하나는 ~, 나머지 모두는 …
some ~, the others …	(여럿 중) 몇몇은 ~[몇몇 ~은], 나머지 모두는 …

주의

1 여럿 중 '나머지 모두'를 가리킬 때는 the others를 써요.
  I got four presents. **One** is from Mom, **another** is from Dad, and **the others** are from my friends.
  (나는 선물을 네 개 받았다. 하나는 엄마에게, 또 다른 하나는 아빠에게, 나머지 모두는 내 친구들에게 받았다.)

2 주어 자리에 another가 오면 단수동사를, (the) others가 오면 복수동사를 써요.
  One is blue, *another* **is** red, and *the others* **are** brown. (하나는 파란색, 다른 하나는 빨간색, 나머지 모두는 갈색이다.)

대표 기출 문제

🔒 우리말과 같은 뜻이 되도록 다음 괄호 안에 주어진 말을
사용하여 문장을 완성하시오.

> There are [two dogs]. (short hair, long hair)
> ([하나는] 털이 짧고, [나머지 하나는] 털이 길다.)
> → ＿＿＿＿＿＿＿＿＿＿ , and ＿＿＿＿＿＿＿＿＿＿ .

CLUE 1
앞에서 언급된 둘(two dogs) 중 '하나'를 가리키는
영어 표현은? — one

CLUE 2
둘 중 '나머지 하나'를 가리키는 영어 표현은?
— the other

정답: One has short hair, the other has long hair

Point Exercise

○ 배열 영작

[1-3] 우리말과 일치하도록 주어진 단어를 올바르게 배열하세요.

1

모자 두 개가 있다. 한 개는 검은색이고, 나머지 한 개는 파란색이다.
(black / is / blue / other / is / one / the)

→ There are two hats. ____________________,

   and ____________________.

2

몇몇 학생은 피자를 좋아하고, 다른 몇몇은 파스타를 좋아한다.
(like / students / some / like / others / pizza / pasta)

→ ____________________,

   and ____________________.

3

민수에게는 삼촌 세 분이 계신다. 한 분은 선생님이시고, 또 다른 한 분은 작가이시며, 나머지 한 분은 요리사이시다.
(a teacher / is / the / is / one / is / a writer / other / another / a cook)

→ Minsu has three uncles. ____________________

   ____________________, ____________________,

   and ____________________.

○ 주어진 단어로 영작

[4-7] 우리말과 일치하도록 주어진 단어를 사용하여 문장을 완성하세요.

4

그는 책 두 권을 읽었다. 한 권은 소설이었고, 나머지 한 권은 만화책이었다.
(a novel, a comic book, was)

→ He read two books. ____________________

   ____

5

Laura는 올해 세 나라를 여행할 것이다. 한 곳은 영국이고, 또 다른 한 곳은 프랑스이며, 나머지 한 곳은 스페인이다. (is, England, Spain, France)

→ Laura will travel to three countries this year.

   ____

   ____

6

많은 사람이 카페에 있다. 몇몇은 커피를 마시고, 다른 몇몇은 오렌지 주스를 마신다.
(coffee, orange juice, drink)

→ Many people are in the cafe. ____________________

   ____

7

나는 쿠키 다섯 개를 샀다. 하나는 내 남동생을 위한 것이고, 또 다른 하나는 나를 위한 것이며, 나머지 모두는 나의 부모님을 위한 것이다.
(is, for, myself, my brother, are, my parents)

→ I bought five cookies. ____________________

   ____

   ____

기출·그림 영작

8 다음 그림과 일치하도록 주어진 단어를 사용하여 문장을 완성하세요.

→ There are two boys in the classroom.

   ____________________ a book, and

   ____________________ a picture.

   (reading, drawing)

England 영국

POINT 2 — each, every, all, both를 써야 할 때

각각의 시험은 열 개의 문제가 있다. 모든 문제는 10점이다.
각각의 시험은 / 가지고 있다 / 열 개의 문제를. 모든 문제는 / ~이다 / 10점의 가치가 있는.

→ **Each test** / *has* / ten questions.
= Each of the tests
   Every question / *is* / worth ten points.

- '각각(의), 각자'라는 뜻의 each는 주로 「**each+단수명사**」 또는 「**each of+복수명사**」의 형태로 쓰여,
  단수 취급합니다. 따라서 그 뒤에 오는 동사도 **항상 단수동사**를 써야 함에 유의하세요.
- '모든'이라는 의미의 every는 형용사로만 쓰이며, 「**every+단수명사**」 형태로 씁니다.
  이때 동사도 **단수동사**를 씁니다.

모든 학생들이 'A'나 'C'를 답했다. 둘 다 틀린 답이었다.
모든 학생들이 / 답했다 / 'A'나 'C'를. 둘 다 / ~이었다 / 틀린 답.

→ **All (of) the students** / answered / "A" or "C."
   Both / *were* / wrong answers.

- '모든 (사람, 것)'이라는 뜻의 all은 보통 「**all (of)+명사**」의 형태로 자주 쓰이며,
  all (of) 뒤에 오는 명사의 수에 동사를 일치시킵니다.
- '둘 다(의), 양쪽(의)'이라는 뜻의 both는 항상 **복수 취급**하며, 「**both (of)+복수명사**」 형태로 자주 쓰여요.

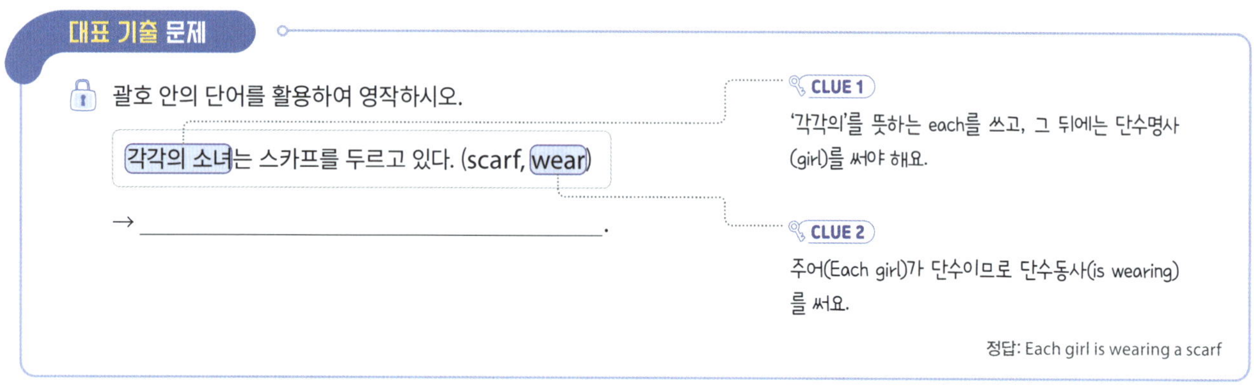

대표 기출 문제

🔒 괄호 안의 단어를 활용하여 영작하시오.

각각의 소녀는 스카프를 두르고 있다. (scarf, wear)

→ ____ .

CLUE 1
'각각의'를 뜻하는 each를 쓰고, 그 뒤에는 단수명사
(girl)를 써야 해요.

CLUE 2
주어(Each girl)가 단수이므로 단수동사(is wearing)
를 써요.

정답: Each girl is wearing a scarf

함정 피하기   each는 항상 단수 취급하므로, 주어와 동사의 수일치에 주의하세요.
Each *girls are* wearing a scarf. (×)
→ **Each *girl is*** wearing a scarf. (○) <Each+단수명사+단수동사>
→ **Each of *the girls is*** wearing a scarf. (○) <Each of+복수명사+단수동사>

Point Exercise

정답 및 해설 p.16

[1-4] 우리말과 일치하도록 주어진 단어를 올바르게 배열하세요.

1 각각의 아이는 다른 꿈을 가지고 있다.
(has / each / a different dream / child)

→ ____

____ .

2 이 건물에는 모든 층에 화장실이 있다.
(a toilet / is / every / on / there / floor)

→ ____

________________________ in this building.

3 내 모든 친구들은 농구 경기를 좋아한다.
(all / like / friends / basketball games / my)

→ ____

____ .

4 그들은 둘 다 과학자가 되고 싶어 한다.
(want / them / be / scientists / both / of / to)

→ ____

____ .

[5-8] 우리말과 일치하도록 주어진 단어를 사용하여 문장을 완성하세요. (필요시 단어를 추가하거나 형태를 바꿀 것)

5 각각의 식당은 특별한 메뉴가 있다.
(the restaurants, a special menu, have, of)

→ ____

____

6 그 놀이공원은 각각의 방문객에게 선물을 줬다.
(a gift, to, the amusement park, visitor, give)

→ ____

____

7 우리 학교에서 모든 학생은 교복을 입어야 한다.
(have to, a uniform, student, wear, every)

→ ____

________________________ in our school.

8 모든 자원봉사자는 아주 부지런했다.
(of, very, diligent, be, the volunteers)

→ ____

____

9 우리말과 일치하도록 〈조건〉에 맞게 문장을 완성하세요.

〈조건〉
- (1)은 6 단어, (2)는 5 단어로 쓸 것
- 주어진 단어를 사용하되 필요시 형태를 바꿀 것

(1) 각각의 경기가 9시에 시작한다.
(start, game, at nine o'clock)

→ ____

(2) 각각의 학생이 다른 장점을 갖고 있다.
(student, different, have, strengths)

→ ____

toilet 화장실 uniform 교복, 유니폼 diligent 부지런한, 근면한 volunteer 자원봉사자; 자원봉사를 하다 strength 장점; 힘

-self[-selves]를 써야 할 때

그는 그 실수에 대해 자신을 탓한다.
그는 / 탓한다 / 그 자신을 / 그 실수에 대해.
주어   동사   목적어

→ **He** / blames / **himself** / for the mistake.

- 문장의 목적어가 '(~들) 자신'이라는 의미로 주어와 같은 대상을 가리킬 때, 목적어 자리에 '-self[-selves]' 형태의 **재귀대명사**를 씁니다. 이때, 문장에서 목적어를 생략할 수 없듯이 재귀대명사도 생략할 수 없어요.

나는 저녁 식사를 혼자 힘으로 만들었다.
나는 / 만들었다 / 저녁 식사를 / 혼자 힘으로.

→ I / made / dinner / **by myself**.

- 목적어 자리에 쓰인 재귀대명사가 '(~들) 자신'으로 해석되지 않거나, 재귀대명사를 포함하여 의미가 달라지는 다음과 같은 표현들은 잘 알아두어야 해요.

📢 재귀대명사의 관용 표현

by oneself	혼자서; 혼자 힘으로	make oneself at home	(집에 있는 것처럼) 편히 쉬다
talk[say] to oneself	혼잣말하다	cut oneself	베이다
enjoy oneself	즐거운 시간을 보내다	in itself	그 자체가, 본질적으로
introduce oneself	자기소개를 하다	think to oneself	속으로 생각하다
help oneself (to)	(~을) 마음껏 먹다	between ourselves	우리끼리 얘긴데

- 재귀대명사는 '직접, 스스로, 자체'라는 의미로 문장의 주어나 목적어를 강조할 때도 쓰여요.
- 이때, 재귀대명사는 강조하는 말(주어, 목적어) 바로 뒤나 문장 맨 뒤에 쓰이며, 덧붙인 말이므로 생략할 수 있어요.

/ **myself** finished painting the fence. 〈주어 강조〉 나는 울타리를 칠하는 것을 직접 끝냈다.

(= I finished painting the fence **myself**.)

She liked *the song* **itself**. 〈목적어 강조〉 그녀는 그 노래 자체를 좋아했다.

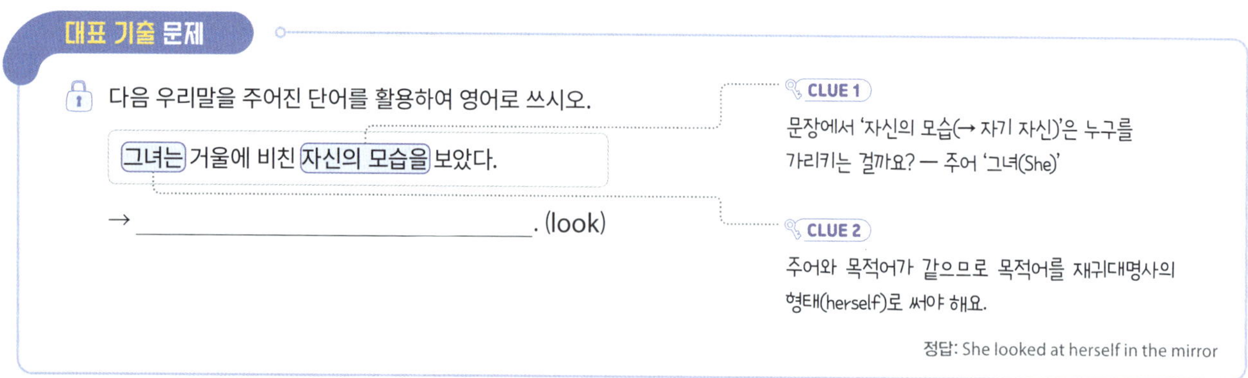

Point Exercise

○ 배열 영작

[1-4] 우리말과 일치하도록 주어진 단어를 올바르게 배열하세요.

1
너는 너 자신을 자랑스러워해야 한다.
(to / yourself / you / be proud of / have)

→ ____________________________________

____________________________________ .

2
그들은 그들 자신을 위해 케이크 하나를 샀다.
(a cake / they / themselves / bought / for)

→ ____________________________________

____________________________________ .

3
나의 엄마는 어제 칼에 베이셨다.
(herself / my / cut / with a knife / mom)

→ ____________________________________

____________________________ yesterday.

4
가끔, 나는 집에서 혼잣말을 한다.
(myself / to / I / at home / talk)

→ Sometimes, ____________________________

____________________________________ .

○ 주어진 단어로 영작

**[5-9] 우리말과 일치하도록 주어진 단어를 사용하여 문장을
완성하세요. (필요시 단어를 추가하거나 형태를 바꿀 것)**

5
준호는 자기 자신에 대한 이야기를 쓰고 있다.
(a story, be, about, writing)

→ Junho ____________________________

____________________________________ .

6
나의 언니는 자기 자신을 아주 많이 사랑한다.
(sister, very much, love)

→ ____________________________________

____

7
Dave와 나는 음악 축제에서 즐거운 시간을 보냈다.
(enjoy, and)

→ ____________________________________

____________________________ at the music festival.

8
간식을 마음껏 먹으렴. 너는 탁자 위에서 그것들을
찾을 수 있단다. (the snacks, help, to)

→ ____________________________________

You can find them on the table.

9
그 아이들은 매일 직접 아침 식사를 준비한다.
(prepare, the children, breakfast)

→ ____________________________________

____________________________ every day.

○ 기출: 조건 영작

10 우리말과 일치하도록 〈조건〉에 맞게 문장을 완성하세요.

그는 휴대 전화로 자기 자신을 사진 찍고 있다.

〈조건〉
• 재귀대명사를 사용할 것
• 7 단어로 쓸 것
• take a picture of를 사용할 것

→ ____________________________________

____________________________ with the cell phone.

be proud of ~을 자랑스러워하다 snack 간식

02 형용사와 부사

 **POINT 4** 명사를 꾸미거나 주어, 목적어를 보충 설명할 때

그들은 어젯밤에 흥미로운 경기를 보았다.
그들은 / 보았다 / 흥미로운 경기를 / 어젯밤에.

→ They / watched / an **exciting** *game* / last night.

이 액션 영화는 흥미진진해 보인다.
이 액션 영화는 / ~해 보인다 / 흥미진진한.
　　주어(명사)　　　동사　　　보어(형용사)

→ **This action movie** / looks / **exciting**.

우리는 이 액션 영화가 흥미진진하다고 생각한다.
우리는 / ~하다고 생각한다 / 이 액션 영화가 / 흥미진진한.
　주어　　　　동사　　　　목적어(명사)　　보어(형용사)

→ We / think / **this action movie** / **exciting**.

📣 형용사의 역할과 어순

(대)명사 수식	형용사+명사 -thing, -body, -one+형용사 Let's do *something* **fun** this weekend. 이번 주말에 재미있는 거 하자.
보어 역할	주어+동사+**형용사** (주어 보충 설명) 주어+동사+목적어+**형용사** (목적어 보충 설명)

대표 기출 문제

🔒 다음 우리말에 맞게 주어진 단어를 모두 활용하여 어순에 맞게 영어로 쓰시오.

우리는 흥미로운 무언가를 경험할 수 있다.
(can, something, experience, interesting, we)

→ ______________________________

CLUE 1
우리말의 '흥미로운 무언가'는 주어진 단어 중 어느 것을 사용해 써야 할까요?
— something, interesting

CLUE 2
something과 같이 -thing으로 끝나는 말은 형용사가 뒤에서 꾸며줘야 해요.

정답: We can experience something interesting.

Point Exercise

[1-4] 우리말과 일치하도록 주어진 단어를 올바르게 배열하세요.

1
> 그 수프는 매우 짠 맛이 난다.
> (tastes / the soup / salty / very)

→ ______________________________

______________________________.

2
> Mia는 복통 때문에 매운 것을 먹지 않을 것이다.
> (eat / spicy / not / anything / will)

→ Mia ______________________________

______________________ because of stomachaches.

3
> 나는 내 새 책상을 위한 편안한 의자가 필요하다.
> (a / I / chair / need / comfortable)

→ ______________________________

______________________ for my new desk.

4
> 나의 개가 밖에서 이상한 무언가를 발견했다.
> (found / strange / dog / something / my)

→ ______________________________

______________________ outside.

[5-8] 우리말과 일치하도록 주어진 단어를 사용하여 문장을 완성하세요.

5
> 그녀는 하이킹과 같은 활동적인 취미들을 즐긴다.
> (hobbies, enjoy, active)

→ ______________________________

______________________ like hiking.

6
> 우리는 안개 사이로 선명한 무언가를 볼 수 없었다.
> (couldn't, clear, see)

→ ______________________________

______________________ through the fog.

7
> 나의 남동생과 나는 어젯밤에 시끄러운 무언가를 들었다.
> (and, brother, loud, hear)

→ ______________________________

______________________ last night.

8
> 이 영화는 사람들을 행복하게 만들었다.
> (make, movie, people, this)

→ ______________________________

____

9 우리말과 일치하도록 〈조건〉에 맞게 문장을 완성하세요.

> 〈조건〉
> • something과 anything을 각각 한 번씩 사용할 것
> • 주어진 단어를 사용할 것

(1) 내가 오늘 네게 맛있는 무언가를 만들어 줄게.

→ ______________________________

______________________ for you today.

(will, delicious, make)

(2) 그는 생일 선물로 비싼 것을 원하지 않는다.

→ ______________________________

______________________ for his birthday present.

(expensive, want)

stomachache 복통 strange 이상한, 낯선 active 활동적인 fog 안개 loud 시끄러운

many, much, (a) few, (a) little을 써야 할 때

많은 관광객들이 매년 이탈리아를 방문한다.
많은 관광객들이 / 방문한다 / 이탈리아를 / 매년.
many+셀 수 있는 명사의 복수형

➜ **Many** *tourists* / visit / Italy / every year.

몇 명의 사람들이 그 강연에 참석했다.
몇 명의 사람들이 / 참석했다 / 그 강연에.
a few+셀 수 있는 명사의 복수형

➜ **A few** *people* / attended / the lecture.

나는 지금 시간이 조금 필요해.
나는 필요해 / 조금의 시간이 / 지금.
a little+셀 수 없는 명사

➜ I need / **a little** *time* / now.

- 명사의 수나 양을 나타내는 형용사는 그것이 꾸미고 있는 명사가 **셀 수 있는 명사**인지, **셀 수 없는 명사**인지를 구분하여 알맞은 것을 사용해야 해요.
- 또한, few와 little은 부정의 의미를 가지므로 a few, a little과 구별하여 사용해야 합니다.

📢 수량을 나타내는 형용사

	셀 수 있는 명사의 복수형 앞	셀 수 없는 명사 앞
많은	**many** friends	**much** time
	a lot of[lots of], plenty of friends/time	
조금 있는	**a few** friends	**a little** time
거의 없는	**few** friends	**little** time

대표 기출 문제

🔒 우리말 뜻에 맞도록 빈칸에 들어갈 알맞은 말을 쓰시오.

너는 크림과 우유를 조금 사용하게 될 거야.

→ You will use ___________ cream and milk.

CLUE 1
'cream'과 'milk'는 셀 수 없는 명사예요.

CLUE 2
'조금'이라는 의미로 셀 수 없는 명사(cream and milk) 앞에 쓸 수 있는 형용사는? — a little

정답: a little

Point Exercise

배열 영작

[1-4] 우리말과 일치하도록 주어진 단어를 올바르게 배열하세요.
(필요시 형태를 바꿀 것)

1
길에 차가 거의 없다.
(few / there / on the road / cars / are)

→ _______________________________________ .

2
많은 소년들과 소녀들이 안경을 쓰고 있다.
(boys / glasses / are / lot / girls / wearing / and / of / a)

→ _______________________________________
_______________________________________ .

3
며칠 동안 매우 추웠다.
(was / for / days / very / cold / few)

→ It _______________________________________ .

4
수프에 약간의 소금과 후추를 넣어라.
(and / salt / into the soup / put / pepper / little)

→ _______________________________________ .

보기에서 골라 영작

[5-8] 우리말과 일치하도록 〈보기〉에서 알맞은 말을 골라 주어진
단어를 사용하여 문장을 완성하세요. (단, 한 번씩만 쓸 것)

〈보기〉 many   much   a few   little

5
많은 책들이 우리에게 유용한 지식을 준다.
(knowledge, give, books, useful)

→ _______________________________________
to us.

6
Ben과 나는 시간이 거의 없다. 우리는 지금 기차를
타야한다. (time, have, and)

→ _______________________________________
We should take the train now.

7
몇 명의 남자들이 지하철을 기다리고 있다.
(be, men, waiting for, the subway)

→ _______________________________________
____

8
너는 쇼핑몰에서 많은 돈을 낭비하면 안 된다.
(waste, money, shouldn't)

→ _______________________________________
_______________________________________ at the mall.

기출: 조건 영작

9 다음 대화를 읽고 〈조건〉에 맞게 우리말을 영작하세요.

A: Elisha, where are you going?
B: I'm going to the Han River Park.
A: 그 공원에는 이미 사람들이 많이 있어.
   How about going to the park nearby
   instead?
B: Yeah, that sounds great.

〈조건〉
• 5 단어로 쓸 것
• there, be, people을 사용할 것

→ _______________________________________
_______________________________ in the park already.

---

pepper 후추 knowledge 지식 waste 낭비하다; 낭비 instead 대신에

나는 주말에 자주 영화를 보러 간다.
나는 / 자주 영화를 보러 간다 / 주말에.

→ I / **often go** to a movie / on weekends.
　　　　빈도부사+일반동사

지하철은 아침에 항상 붐빈다.
지하철은 / 항상 붐빈다 / 아침에.

→ The subways / **are always** crowded / in the morning.
　　　　　　be동사+빈도부사

그녀는 많은 사람들 앞에서 거의 말을 못 해. 그녀는 수줍음이 매우 많아.
그녀는 / 거의 말을 못 해 / 많은 사람들 앞에서. 그녀는 수줍음이 매우 많아.

→ She / **can hardly** speak / in front of many people. She's very shy.
　　　　조동사+빈도부사

- 어떤 일이 얼마나 자주 일어나는지를 나타내는 **빈도부사**는 문장에 쓰인 동사의 종류에 따라 정해진 위치에 써야 해요.
- 일반동사가 쓰인 문장에서는 **일반동사 앞**에, be동사나 조동사가 쓰인 문장에서는 **be동사/조동사 뒤**에 써야 합니다.

📢 **빈도부사의 종류와 의미**

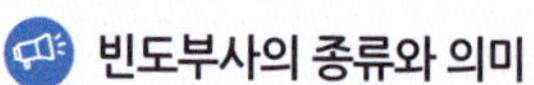

대표 기출 문제

🔒 다음 질문에 대한 대답을 제시된 의미의 문장으로 완성하시오.

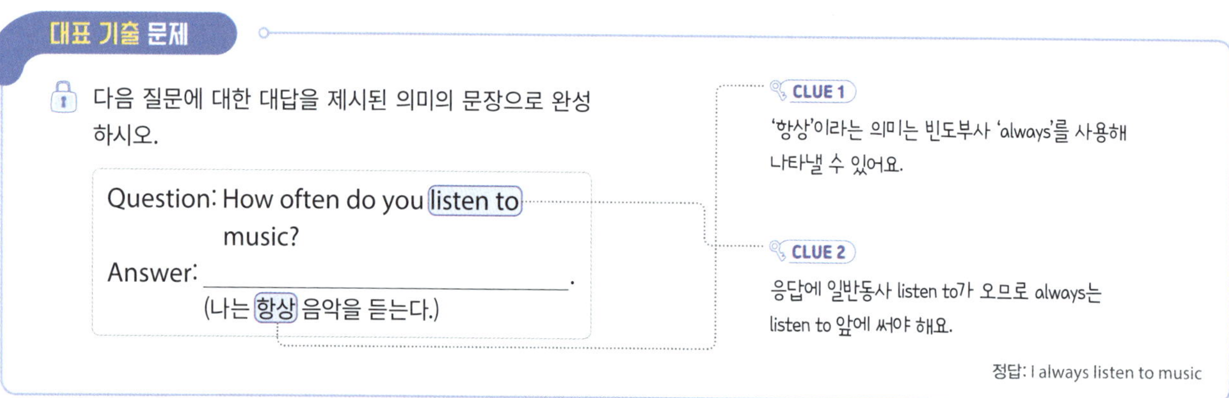

Point Exercise

정답 및 해설 p.17

[1-4] 우리말과 일치하도록 주어진 단어를 올바르게 배열하세요.

1

나의 오빠는 오후에 보통 도서관에 있다.
(is / the library / usually / in)

→ My brother ________________________

________________________ in the afternoon.

2

유진이는 주말에 거의 운동을 하지 않는다.
(exercises / the weekend / rarely / on)

→ Yujin ________________________

________________________ .

3

그들은 항상 버스를 타고 학교에 간다.
(school / go / by bus / they / always / to)

→ ________________________

________________________ .

4

나는 아침에 거의 일찍 일어나지 못한다.
(early / wake up / I / in the morning / hardly / can)

→ ________________________

________________________ .

[5-8] 우리말과 일치하도록 주어진 단어를 사용하여 문장을 완성하세요.

5

우리는 시험에서 때때로 실수를 한다.
(mistakes, make)

→ ________________________

________________________ on tests.

6

그녀는 그녀의 개와 산책을 자주 하지 않는다.
(take a walk, doesn't)

→ ________________________

________________________ with her dog.

7

Brian은 밤에 컴퓨터 게임을 절대 하지 않는다.
(computer games, play)

→ ________________________

________________________ at night.

8

우리 선생님은 모두에게 항상 친절하시다.
(kind, teacher, be)

→ ________________________

________________________ to everyone.

9 다음 Austin과 Emily의 일과표를 보고 〈보기〉에서 알맞은 말을 골라 문장을 완성하세요.

	Austin	Emily
(1) go to the gym	never	every day
(2) be at home after school	five times a week	once a week

〈보기〉	
never	seldom

(1) Austin ________________________

________________________ .

(2) Emily ________________________

________________________ .

Chapter Test *

정답 및 해설 p.17

STAGE 1) Go for it!

자신 있게 풀어보는 기초 문제!

배열 영작

[1-4] 우리말과 일치하도록 주어진 단어를 배열하여 문장을 완성하세요.

1
> Ted의 가방 안에는 몇 권의 책들이 있다.
> (books / there / a few / in / Ted's bag / are)

→ _______________________________

_______________________________ .

2
> 우리는 후식으로 단 것이 필요하다.
> (sweet / we / something / for dessert / need)

→ _______________________________

_______________________________ .

3
> 나는 강한 바람에 내 눈을 거의 뜰 수 없었다.
> (eyes / I / hardly / could / open / my)

→ _______________________________

_______________________________ in the strong wind.

4
> Kevin은 혼자 힘으로 그의 반려동물을 돌본다.
> (takes care of / by / his / Kevin / himself / pet)

→ _______________________________

_______________________________ .

주어진 단어로 영작

[5-7] 우리말과 일치하도록 주어진 단어를 사용하여 문장을 완성하세요.

5
> 나는 학교 첫날에 자기소개를 했다. (introduced)

→ _______________________________

on the first day of school.

6
> 나무 위에 두 마리의 동물이 있다. 한 마리는 다람쥐이고, 나머지 한 마리는 새이다.
> (a squirrel, is, a bird)

→ There are two animals on the tree.

_______________________________ ,

and _______________________________ .

7
> 몇몇은 여름을 좋아하고, 다른 몇몇은 겨울을 좋아한다. (like, winter, summer)

→ _______________________________ ,

and _______________________________ .

최신 기출

8 우리말과 일치하도록 주어진 단어를 배열하여 다음의 대화를 완성하세요. (필요시 형태를 바꿀 것)

> A: I lost my dog. Can you help me?
> B: Sure. How does she or he look?
> A: She has black and white fur.
> B: 그녀에 관해 특별한 점이 있니?
>   (anything / be / about / there / her / special)
> A: She has a short, white tail.

→ _______________________________

_______________________________ ?

○─ 대화문 완성

[9-12] 주어진 단어를 사용하여 〈보기〉와 같이 질문에 대한 대답을 완성하세요. (단, 완전한 문장으로 쓸 것)

〈보기〉
A: How often do you eat out?
B: I hardly eat out. (hardly)

9
A: How often are you late for school?
B: I ________________________ .
  (never)

10
A: How often does Cathy watch TV after work?
B: She ________________________ .
  (rarely)

11
A: How often do you and Fred read books in the library?
B: We ________________________ .
  (often)

12
A: How often can you see stars at night in your city?
B: We ________________________
  in our city. (sometimes)

○─ 그림 영작

[13-14] 〈보기〉와 같이 그림을 보고 주어진 단어와 알맞은 부정대명사를 사용하여 문장을 완성하세요.

〈보기〉

There are five fruits. One is a banana, another is a lemon, and the others are apples. (a banana, a lemon, apples)

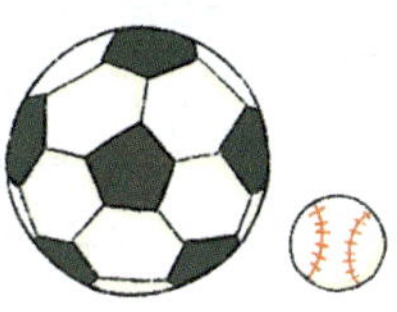

13 I have two balls. ________________________

____

(a soccer ball, a baseball)

14 My family is going to visit three countries this vacation. ________________________

____

(Japan, the United States, Canada)

최신 기출

15 다음 Sue의 일정표를 보고 〈보기〉에서 알맞은 말을 골라, 각 질문에 알맞은 대답을 완성하세요.

	Mon	Tue	Wed	Thu	Fri
do yoga	○	○		○	○
study math		○		○	

〈보기〉
sometimes   often   always

(1) Q: How often does Sue do yoga?
  A: Sue ________________________

  ________________________ .

(2) Q: How often does Sue study math?
  A: Sue ________________________

  ________________________ .

[16-21] 우리말과 일치하도록 〈보기〉에서 알맞은 말을 골라 주어진 단어를 사용하여 문장을 완성하세요.
(단, 한 번씩만 쓸 것)

〈보기〉

a few	few	a little
little	many	plenty of

16 Sally는 어제 공원에서 몇 마리의 토끼들을 보았다. (rabbit)

→ Sally saw ___________________
at the park yesterday.

17 서두르지 마. 연극 시간이 많이 남아 있어. (time)

→ Don't hurry.
We have ___________________
for the play.

18 나는 내 새로운 학교에 대한 정보가 거의 없다. (information)

→ I have ___________________
about my new school.

19 나의 언니는 그녀의 친구들에게 많은 선물들을 받았다. (present)

→ My sister got ___________________
from her friends.

20 Tony는 시험에서 실수를 거의 하지 않았다. (mistake)

→ Tony made ___________________
on the exams.

21 나의 오빠와 나는 엄마의 생신을 위해 돈을 좀 모았다. (money)

→ My brother and I have saved
___________________ for my mom's
birthday.

[22-26] 다음 각 문장의 밑줄 친 부분을 어법상 바르게 고쳐 쓰세요.

22 Linda, take off your shoes and make <u>you</u>
at home.

____

23 Sally <u>runs sometimes</u> with her dog
along the river.

____

24 Both of us <u>takes</u> a bus to school every day.

____

25 Each <u>flowers have</u> its own smell.

____

26 You'd better not drink too <u>many waters</u>
before bed.

____

27 우리말과 일치하도록 〈보기〉에서 알맞은 말을 골라 주어진 단어와 함께 문장을 완성하세요.

A: What do you want for lunch?
B: How about making sandwiches?
A: That sounds great. What do we need for sandwiches?
B: (1) 우리는 달걀이 좀 필요해.
A: (2) Oh, 우리는 빵이 거의 없어.
I'll go buy some now.

〈보기〉

a few	few	a little	little

(1) ___________________
(egg, need)

(2) Oh, ___________________.
(bread, have)

[28-31] 다음 각 빈칸에 들어갈 말을 〈보기〉에서 골라 쓰세요.
(단, 한 번씩만 사용할 것)

〈보기〉
few　　　　a few　　　　much　　　　little

28 ________________ years ago, Kate went to summer camp with her friends.

29 There was ________________ money in my pocket. So, I couldn't buy some snacks.

30 Last Saturday, I had so ________________ fun with my family at the beach.

31 Your writing is very good because it has ________________ errors.

32 다음 글을 읽고 ⓐ~ⓒ에 들어갈 알맞은 재귀대명사를 쓰세요.

Sarah and her brother went to the park. Sarah brought a book and read it by ____ⓐ____ . Her brother played on the swings and enjoyed ____ⓑ____ . At the end of the day, they were proud of ____ⓒ____ for having a great time.

ⓐ ________________

ⓑ ________________

ⓒ ________________

33 다음 글을 읽고 ⓐ~ⓒ 중 어법상 **틀린** 문장을 찾아 그 기호를 쓰고, 문장 전체를 바르게 고쳐 쓰세요.

ⓐ Some people enjoy movies, but others prefer books. ⓑ For example, one of my friends likes to draw, and another likes to dance. ⓒ Everyone finds fun something to do in their own way.

________ → ________________

____

Challenge!　　　　　누적 문제 Ch 05-07

34 다음 중 어법상 **틀린** 문장 **두 개**를 찾아 그 기호를 쓰고, 문장 전체를 바르게 고쳐 쓰세요.

ⓐ Every student wear a seat belt in the school bus.
ⓑ Irene often visits her uncle's house.
ⓒ Dr. Green went to Africa to take care of the sick.
ⓓ She added a little sugar to her coffee.
ⓔ Many teenagers are very interested in play computer games.

________ → ________________

____

________ → ________________

____

비교 표현

✅ Before You Write

- ☑ 원급, 비교급, 최상급 표현은 영어로 어떻게 나타낼까요?
- ☑ 형용사/부사를 비교급과 최상급으로 나타내려면 형태를 어떻게 바꿔야 할까요?
- ☑ '훨씬 더'라는 의미를 나타내려면 비교급 앞에 어떤 부사를 써야 할까요?
- ☑ 원급과 비교급을 이용한 관용 표현을 알고 알맞게 쓸 수 있나요?

내신 기출 다음 우리말을 보고 머릿속으로 한번 영어 문장을 떠올려 보세요.

1 그들은 우리가 하는 것만큼 열심히 일한다. (as, hard)

정답: _______________________________________

~만큼 …하게 → 원급 비교 → as+부사+as → **as hard as**   POINT 1

2 외모는 인성만큼 중요하지 않다.

(character, not, as, appearance, is, as, important)

~만큼 …하지 않은 → 원급 비교 → not as+형용사+as → **is not as important as**   POINT 1

3 나는 내 남동생보다 훨씬 더 키가 크다.

→ _______________________________ (I, my brother)

~보다 훨씬 더 …한 → 강조 부사+비교급+than → **much taller than**   POINT 2

4 (2) 영어는 나에게 가장 흥미로운 과목이다. (interesting, subject)

가장 …한 → the+형용사의 최상급+명사 → **the most interesting subject**   POINT 3

5 그 자동차는 이 자전거보다 약 열 배만큼 비싸다.

(be, ten, as, as, this, the, time, expensive, about, bike, car)

…보다 몇 배 더 ~한 → 배수사 as ~ as → **ten times as expensive as**   POINT 4

6 당신이 더 많이 배울수록, 당신은 더 현명해진다.

<보기> the / learn / you / wiser / the / more / you / become

→ _______________________________

더 ~할수록, 더 …하다 → The 비교급 ~, the 비교급 … → **The more ~, the wiser...**   POINT 5

정답: **1** They work as hard as we do. **2** Appearance is not[isn't] as important as character. **3** I am[I'm] much[still, far, a lot, even 등] taller than my brother. **4** English is the most interesting subject to me. **5** The car is about ten times as expensive as this bike. **6** The more you learn, the wiser you become.

Unit 01 원급, 비교급, 최상급

POINT 1   as+형용사[부사]의 원급+as: ~만큼 …한[하게]

한국에서 야구는 축구만큼 인기 있다.
야구는 / 인기 있다 / 축구만큼 / 한국에서.

→ Baseball / is **as popular** / **as** soccer / in Korea.

- 서로 정도가 비슷하거나 같은 두 대상을 비교할 때는 형용사나 부사의 원래 형태인 원급을 사용해요.
- 원급 비교는 「**as**+형용사[부사]의 원급+**as**」로 표현하며, '**~만큼 …한[하게]**'라는 의미를 나타냅니다.

한강은 나일 강만큼 길지 않다.
한강은 / 길지 않다 / 나일 강만큼.

→ The Han River / is **not as[so] long** / **as** the Nile River.

- 서로 정도가 같지 않음을 나타낼 때는 「**not as[so]**+형용사[부사]의 원급+**as**」로 표현하고,
  '**~만큼 …하지 않은[하지 않게]**'이라고 해석해요.

주의

동사를 수식하는 부사의 원급으로는 many가 아니라 much를 써야 해요.
You can rest as **many**(→ **much**) as you need. (필요한 만큼 쉬어도 돼.)

MORE+ 원급 비교의 두 번째 as 뒤에는 「주어+동사」가 오는 것이 원칙이지만, 구어에서는 목적어 형태를 사용하는 경우가 많아요.
She is as popular as **he is**. (그녀는 그만큼 인기 있다.)
= him

대표 기출 문제

🔒 우리말과 같도록 비교하는 문장을 쓰시오.

John은 Tom만큼 빨리 달린다.

→ ______________________________

CLUE 1
우리말에 '~만큼 …한[하게]'이라는 의미가 쓰였으므로
「as+형용사[부사]의 원급+as」를 떠올려야 해요.
'John은 달린다 / 빨리 / Tom만큼.'의 어순으로
씁니다.

CLUE 2
'달리다'라는 의미의 동사 runs를 수식하려면 '빨리'
라는 의미의 부사 fast를 써야 해요.
as fast as 뒤에는 비교 대상인 Tom이 와야 해요.

정답: John runs as fast as Tom (does).

Point Exercise

[1-4] 우리말과 일치하도록 주어진 단어를 올바르게 배열하세요.

1

> 고양이는 강아지만큼 영리하다.
> (as / a dog / as / is / smart)

→ A cat ____________________

____________________ .

2

> 그 담요는 깃털만큼 푹신하다.
> (a feather / as / as / soft / is)

→ The blanket ____________________

____________________ .

3

> 내 남동생은 나만큼 키가 크다.
> (tall / I / is / as / as / am)

→ My brother ____________________

____________________ .

4

> 오늘은 어제만큼 춥지 않다.
> (cold / yesterday / as / not / is /as)

→ Today ____________________

____________________ .

[5-7] 우리말과 일치하도록 주어진 단어를 사용하여 빈칸에 알맞은 말을 쓰세요.

5

> 그녀의 책상은 거울처럼 깨끗하다. (clean)

→ Her desk ____________ ____________

____________ ____________ a mirror.

6

> 그 변호사는 영화배우만큼이나 유명했다. (famous)

→ The lawyer ____________ ____________

____________ ____________ a movie

star.

7

> 이 자동차는 스포츠카만큼 빠르지 않다. (fast)

→ This car ____________ ____________

____________ ____________ the sports

car.

8 다음 각 문장의 밑줄 친 부분을 어법상 바르게 고쳐 쓰세요.

(1) This summer is <u>as hotter as</u> last summer.

→ ____________________

(2) I don't like the movie <u>as many as</u> you do.

→ ____________________

9 다음 두 문장을 주어진 단어와 원급 비교를 사용하여 한 문장으로 바꿔 쓰세요.

(1)

> An apple pie is $15.
> A lemon pie is $15.

→ An apple pie ____________________

a lemon pie. (cheap)

(2)

> Mt. Kilimanjaro is 5,895 meters high.
> Mt. Everest is 8,849 meters high.

→ Mt. Kilimanjaro ____________________

____________________ Mt. Everest. (high)

feather (새의) 깃털 blanket 담요 mirror 거울 lawyer 변호사

   비교급+than ~: ~보다 더 …한[하게]

나는 내 남동생보다 키가 더 크다.
나는 / 키가 더 크다 / 내 남동생보다.

→ I / am **taller** / **than** my brother.

- 두 대상을 비교해서 차이가 나는 것을 '**~보다 더 …한[하게]**'라고 말할 때, 「**형용사[부사]의 비교급+than ~**」의 형태를 사용해요.

비교급의 형태

대부분의 형용사/부사	+-er	fast – fast**er**
-e로 끝나는 형용사/부사	+-r	nice – nic**er**
「자음+y」로 끝나는 형용사/부사	y를 i로 고치고 +-er	easy – eas**ier**
「모음 1개+자음 1개」로 끝나는 형용사/부사	마지막 자음을 한 번 더 쓰고 +-er	fat – fat**ter**
2음절 이상의 형용사/부사	more +	beautiful – **more** beautiful
불규칙하게 변하는 형용사/부사	good/well – **better** many/much – **more** far (거리가 먼) – **farther/further** far (정도가 더한) – **further**	bad – **worse** little – **less**

박쥐는 사람보다 훨씬 더 잘 들을 수 있다.
박쥐들은 / 훨씬 더 잘 들을 수 있다 / 사람들보다.

→ Bats / can hear **much better** / **than** humans.

- 비교급을 강조하거나 수식할 때는 **비교급 앞에** '훨씬'이라는 의미의 **much, still, even, far, a lot** 등을 쓸 수 있어요.
- very나 too는 원급을 강조하는 부사로, 비교급 앞에 쓸 수 없어요.
  I am **very** *taller* than my brother. (×)

대표 기출 문제

다음 표를 보고 주어진 낱말을 이용하여 Sara와 Ted를 비교하는 문장을 영어로 완성하시오.

	Sara	**Ted**
Height	170 cm	165 cm
Age	15 years	13 years

(1) Sara ___________________________ . (tall)
(2) Ted ___________________________ . (young)

CLUE 1
두 대상을 비교하고 있으므로 비교급 표현인 「형용사[부사]의 비교급+than」으로 나타낼 수 있어요.

CLUE 2
형용사 tall은 키를 비교, young은 나이를 비교할 때 쓰이므로, 표의 내용에 따라 각각 taller than, younger than으로 씁니다. than 뒤에는 비교 대상이 꼭 와야 해요.

정답: (1) is taller than Ted (2) is younger than Sara

Point Exercise

배열 영작

[1-3] 우리말과 일치하도록 주어진 단어를 올바르게 배열하세요.

1
빛은 소리보다 더 빠르게 이동한다.
(than / light / faster / sound / travels)

→ ________________________________

________________________________.

2
나의 오빠는 나보다 더 늦게 잔다.
(do / later / my brother / than / goes to bed / I)

→ ________________________________

________________________________.

3
나에게 현재는 과거보다 훨씬 더 중요하다.
(more / than / the past / the present / important / is / much)

→ ________________________________

________________________ to me.

주어진 단어로 영작

[4-8] 우리말과 일치하도록 주어진 단어를 사용하여 문장을 완성하세요.

4
오늘 날씨가 어제보다 더 안 좋다.
(yesterday, bad)

→ Today's weather ________________

________________________________.

5
그 가수의 새 노래는 그의 예전 노래보다 더 인기가 있다. (popular, his last one)

→ The singer's new song ________________

________________________________.

6
이 의자는 저 소파보다 덜 편하다.
(little, that sofa, comfortable)

→ This chair ________________________

________________________________.

7
Milo는 Justin보다 중국어를 더 잘 한다.
(speak, well, Chinese)

→ Milo ________________________

________________________________.

8
검은 운동화가 파란 운동화보다 훨씬 더 저렴했다.
(even, cheap, the blue sneakers)

→ The black sneakers ________________

________________________________.

기출: 도표 영작

9 다음 표를 보고 〈조건〉에 맞게 문장을 완성하세요.

Seoul to Busan

	Price	Time
Taking a train	₩58,000	2 hours and 50 minutes
Taking an express bus	₩34,000	4 hours and 15 minutes

〈조건〉
• (1), (2) 모두 '기차를 타는 것'을 주어로 사용할 것
• 주어진 단어를 사용해 현재시제로 쓸 것

(1) ________________________________

____

(much, expensive)

(2) ________________________________

____

(even, fast)

past 과거 present 현재; 선물 comfortable 편안한 sneakers 운동화 price 가격, 값 express bus 고속버스 expensive 비싼, 돈이 많이 드는

the+최상급(+명사)+in[of] ~: ~ 중에서 가장 …한[하게]

그 방은 이 집에서 가장 큰 방이다.
그 방은 / 가장 큰 방이다 / 이 집에서.

→ The room / is **the biggest** one / **in** this house.

- 「**the+형용사[부사]의 최상급**」은 '가장 …한[하게]'라는 의미로, 셋 이상을 비교해서 하나가 다른 것들보다 정도가 가장 심하거나 가장 덜함을 나타내요.
- 최상급은 범위를 나타내는 말인 in[of] 등과 함께 「**the+최상급(+명사)+in[of] ~**」 형태로 쓰일 수 있어요. '~중에서 가장 …한[하게]'라는 의미를 나타내요.
  Lisa is **the smartest of** all my friends. Lisa는 내 모든 친구들 중에서 가장 똑똑하다.

📢 **최상급의 형태**

대부분의 형용사/부사	+-est	slow – slow**est**
-e로 끝나는 형용사/부사	+-st	nice – nice**st**
「자음+y」로 끝나는 형용사/부사	y를 i로 고치고 +-est	heavy – heav**iest**
「모음 1개+자음 1개」로 끝나는 형용사/부사	마지막 자음을 한 번 더 쓰고 +-est	big – big**gest**
2음절 이상의 형용사/부사	most +	amazing – **most** amazing
불규칙하게 변하는 형용사/부사	good/well – **best** many/much – **most** far (거리가 먼) – **farthest/furthest** far (정도가 더한) – **furthest**	bad – **worst** little – **least**

MORE+ 최상급 앞에 the를 써야 하는 것에 주의하세요. 단, 부사의 최상급 앞 the는 생략할 수 있어요.
I *get up* **(the) earliest** in my family. (나는 나의 가족 중 가장 일찍 일어난다.)

- 최상급을 이용한 표현으로는 「**one of the+최상급+복수명사**」가 있어요. '가장 ~한 … 중 하나'라는 의미예요.
  The Mona Lisa is **one of the most famous paintings** in history.
  모나리자는 역사상 가장 유명한 그림 중 하나이다.

대표 기출 문제

🔒 위 글의 밑줄 친 (A)를 주어진 <조건>에 맞게 영작하시오.

(A) 이곳은 세계에서 가장 건조한 사막이다.

<조건>
- 최상급 표현을 사용할 것
- 'It'으로 시작하여 the world로 끝나는 문장으로 쓸 것
- 총 8개의 단어로 문장을 완성할 것

→ ____________________

CLUE 1
'가장 ~한 명사'라는 의미는 「the+최상급+명사」를 사용해 나타낼 수 있어요. 형용사 dry(건조한)를 사용해 최상급으로 나타내면? — the driest desert

CLUE 2
'~(중)에서'라는 범위를 나타내는 말이 필요하므로, 전치사 in과 주어진 단어를 사용해 in the world로 나타내요.

정답: It is the driest desert in the world.

Point Exercise

배열 영작

[1-3] 우리말과 일치하도록 주어진 단어를 올바르게 배열하세요. (필요시 형태를 바꿀 것)

1
> 브라질은 남아메리카에서 가장 큰 나라이다.
> (the / Brazil / is / South America / large / country / in)

→ ________________________________

________________________________ .

2
> 2월은 일 년 중 가장 짧은 달이다.
> (a year / short / February / the / month / is / in)

→ ________________________________

________________________________ .

3
> 그는 우리 반에서 가장 곱슬곱슬한 머리를 가지고 있다.
> (our class / he / the / has / curly / in / hair)

→ ________________________________

________________________________ .

주어진 단어로 영작

[4-8] 우리말과 일치하도록 주어진 단어를 사용하여 문장을 완성하세요.

4
> 이 건물은 우리나라에서 가장 높다.
> (high, our country, in)

→ This building ________________________ .

5
> 루트 사막은 세계에서 가장 더운 곳이다.
> (hot, in, place, the world)

→ The Lut Desert ________________________

________________________________ .

6
> 한강은 벚꽃을 보기에 가장 좋은 장소 중 하나이다.
> (spot, good)

→ The Han River ________________________ to see cherry blossoms.

7
> Becky는 내 친구들 중에서 가장 너그럽다.
> (friends, generous, of)

→ ________________________________

____

8
> 나는 우리 반에서 Andy가 가장 창의적인 학생이라고 생각한다. (class, creative, in, student)

→ I think that ________________________

________________________________ .

기출: 도표 영작

9 다음 표를 보고 〈조건〉에 맞게 문장을 완성하세요.

Name	Age	Height	Weight
Terry	15	165 cm	53 kg
Jim	14	160 cm	55 kg
Nicky	16	154 cm	56 kg

〈조건〉
- (1)은 Age, (2)는 Height, (3)은 Weight의 내용을 보고 현재시제로 쓸 것
- 형용사 tall, heavy, young의 최상급을 사용할 것

(1) Jim ________________________ student of the three.

(2) Terry ________________________ student of the three.

(3) Nicky ________________________ student of the three.

curly 곱슬곱슬한 desert 사막 spot 장소 cherry blossoms 벚꽃 generous 관대한, 너그러운 creative 창의적인 height 키, 높이

원급, 비교급을 이용한 표현

POINT 4 배수사 as ~ as / as ~ as possible

그 러닝화는 다른 신발들보다 두 배 더 비싸다.
그 러닝화는 / 두 배 더 비싸다 / 다른 신발들의.

→ The running shoes / are **twice as expensive** / **as** other shoes.

📢 원급을 포함하는 주요 관용 표현

배수사(twice[two times], three times 등)+as+원급+as	…의 몇 배 더 ~한[하게]
as+원급+as possible (= as+원급+as+주어+can[could])	가능한 한 ~한[하게]

Please come **as soon as possible**. 가능한 한 빨리 와주세요. (= Please come **as soon as you can**.)

POINT 5 The 비교급 ~, the 비교급 … / 비교급 and 비교급

더 많이 웃을수록, 더 행복해진다.
더 많이 / 당신이 웃을수록, // 더 행복한 / 당신은 ~해지다.

→ **The more** / you laugh, // **the happier** / you become.

📢 비교급을 포함하는 주요 관용 표현

The+비교급 (주어+동사 ~), the+비교급 (주어+동사 …)	더 ~할수록, 더 …하다
비교급 and 비교급	점점 더 ~한[하게]

• 두 번째 관용 표현(비교급 and 비교급)의 비교급이 「**more+원급**」 형태인 경우에는
「**more and more+원급**」으로 써야 해요.
This game is getting **more and more popular**. 이 게임이 점점 더 인기를 끌고 있다.

대표 기출 문제

🔒 다음 우리말을 주어진 단어를 이용하여 영작하시오.

날씨가 더 따뜻할수록 나는 기분이 더 좋아진다.
(warm, good 사용)

→ ___________ the weather is, ___________
I feel.

CLUE 1
'더 ~할수록 더 …하다'라는 우리말을 보고
「the+비교급 (주어+동사 ~),
the+비교급 (주어+동사 …)」 표현을 떠올려야 해요.

CLUE 2
형용사 warm(따뜻한)과 good(좋은)의 비교급은?
— warmer, better

정답: The warmer, the better

Point Exercise

정답 및 해설 p.19

[1-5] 우리말과 일치하도록 주어진 단어를 사용하여 빈칸에 알맞은 말을 쓰세요. (필요시 형태를 바꿀 것)

1
David는 가능한 한 일찍 학교에 간다.
(as, possible, early)

→ David goes to school ＿＿＿＿＿＿＿

＿＿＿＿＿＿＿ ＿＿＿＿＿＿＿

＿＿＿＿＿＿＿.

2
시험이 더 가까워질수록, Alice는 더 긴장했다.
(close, nervous)

→ ＿＿＿＿＿＿＿＿＿＿＿ the test

came, ＿＿＿＿＿＿＿ ＿＿＿＿＿＿＿

＿＿＿＿＿＿ Alice got.

3
이번 주에 날씨가 점점 더 추워지고 있다. (cold, and)

→ The weather is getting ＿＿＿＿＿＿

＿＿＿＿＿＿＿＿＿＿ this week.

4
새로운 경기장은 이전 것의 세 배만큼 더 크다.
(big, three times)

→ The new stadium is ＿＿＿＿＿＿

＿＿＿＿＿＿＿ ＿＿＿＿＿＿

＿＿＿＿＿＿＿ the old one.

5
우리가 더 많이 연습할수록, 우리의 공연은 더 좋아질 것이다. (more, good)

→ ＿＿＿＿＿＿ ＿＿＿＿＿＿ we practice,

＿＿＿＿＿＿ ＿＿＿＿＿＿ our

performance will be.

[6-7] 우리말과 일치하도록 주어진 단어를 올바르게 배열하세요.

6
그 노트북 컴퓨터는 데스크톱 컴퓨터의 두 배 더 가볍다.
(as / is / the laptop / light / twice / as / the desktop computer)

→ ＿＿＿＿＿＿＿＿＿＿＿＿＿

＿＿＿＿＿＿＿＿＿＿＿＿＿.

7
네가 더 많이 영어를 연습할수록, 너는 더 유창하게 말할 수 있다.
(more / you / fluently / the / you / practice / more / speak / can / the / English)

→ ＿＿＿＿＿＿＿＿＿＿＿＿＿,

＿＿＿＿＿＿＿＿＿＿＿＿＿.

8 다음 글을 읽고 〈조건〉에 맞게 우리말을 영작하세요.

Plastic straws are a problem for the environment. Many restaurants and cafes aren't allowed to use them. But 종이 빨대는 플라스틱 빨대의 약 세 배만큼 더 비싸다.

So people are trying to find better options instead of using paper straws.

〈조건〉
• as ~ as 표현을 사용할 것
• 주어진 단어를 사용할 것

→ But paper straws are about ＿＿＿＿＿

＿＿＿＿＿＿＿＿＿＿＿＿＿.

(times, plastic straws)

stadium 경기장, 스타디움 fluently 유창하게 straw 빨대 environment 환경 allow 허용하다, 허락하다 option 선택권, 옵션 instead of ~ 대신에 about 약, ~쯤

Chapter Test *

정답 및 해설 p.19

STAGE 1 ▶ Go for it!

자신 있게 풀어보는 기초 문제!

배열 영작

[1-4] 우리말과 일치하도록 주어진 단어를 배열하여 문장을 완성하세요.

1
> 이 영화관은 우리나라에서 가장 크다.
> (largest / the / our / in / is / country)

→ This cinema _______________

_________________________ .

2
> Tim은 그의 남동생보다 컴퓨터 게임을 덜 자주 한다.
> (often / does / less / his / than / brother)

→ Tim plays computer games _______________

_________________________ .

3
> 달은 지구보다 훨씬 더 작다.
> (far / smaller / the Earth / than / is)

→ The Moon _______________

_________________________ .

4
> 겨울이 다가오자 해가 점점 더 빨리 진다.
> (and / earlier / sets / earlier / the Sun)

→ When winter comes, _______________

_________________________ .

빈칸 완성

[5-7] 우리말과 일치하도록 주어진 단어를 사용하여 빈칸에 알맞은 말을 쓰세요.

5
> Jay는 나보다 농구를 더 잘한다.
> (play, well, basketball)

→ Jay _______________ _______________

_______________ _______________ I do.

6
> 네가 더 높이 올라갈수록, 너는 더 멀리 볼 수 있다.
> (high, far)

→ _______________ _______________ you go up,

_______________ _______________ you can see.

7
> 이것은 이 식당에서 가장 비싼 요리이다.
> (restaurant, dish, expensive, in)

→ This is _______________ _______________

_______________ _______________

_______________ _______________ .

최신 기출

8 우리말과 일치하도록 주어진 단어를 배열하여 다음의 대화를 완성하세요.

> A: How was your science test?
> B: It was okay.
> <u>그 시험은 내가 예상했던 것만큼 어렵지 않았어.</u>
> (difficult / the test / was / I / as / not / as / expected)
> A: That's great. I'm sure you did well.

→ _________________________

_________________________ .

그림 영작

[9-11] 다음 그림을 보고 〈조건〉에 맞게 문장을 완성하세요.

〈조건〉
• 비교 표현을 사용할 것
• 주어진 단어를 사용하되 필요시 단어를 추가하거나 형태를 바꿀 것

9 ________________________________,
________________________________.
(exercise, the, will become, healthy, much, you)

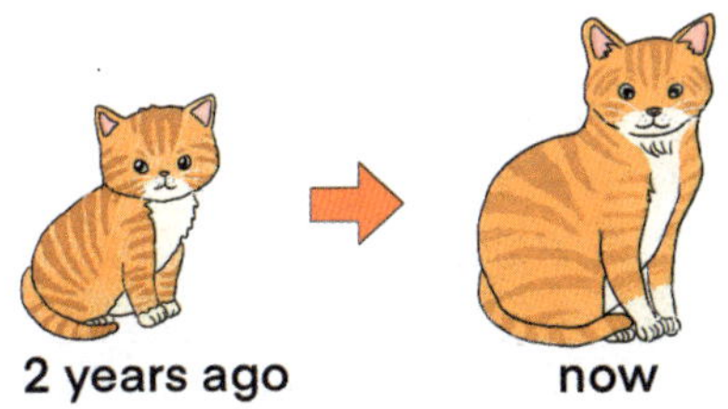

10 As time goes on, ________________________
________________________.
(big, and, my cat, getting, be)

11 ________________________ your soup,
________________________.
(the, much, season, will taste, spicy, it, you)

어법 오류 수정

[12-16] 다음 각 문장에서 어법상 <u>틀린</u> 부분을 찾아 바르게 고쳐 쓰세요.

12 The English exam was as not difficult as the math exam.

________________ → ________________

13 The South Pole is more cold than the North Pole.

________________ → ________________

14 My family loves our dog as many as I do.

________________ → ________________

15 Becky's hands are very bigger than her mother's.

________________ → ________________

16 Singapore is one of the cleanest country in the world.

________________ → ________________

최신 기출

17 다음 대화를 읽고 〈조건〉에 맞게 우리말을 영작하세요.

A: Which is more tiring, a long flight or a long drive?
B: Normally, <u>긴 비행이 긴 운전보다 훨씬 더 피곤해.</u>

〈조건〉
• 대화에서 쓰인 단어를 사용하되 필요시 단어를 추가할 것
• 11 단어로 쓸 것

→ Normally, ________________________
________________________.

[18-20] 다음은 수학여행지에 대한 학생들의 선호도 조사 결과를 정리한 그래프입니다. 주어진 단어와 비교 표현을 사용하여 문장을 완성하세요.

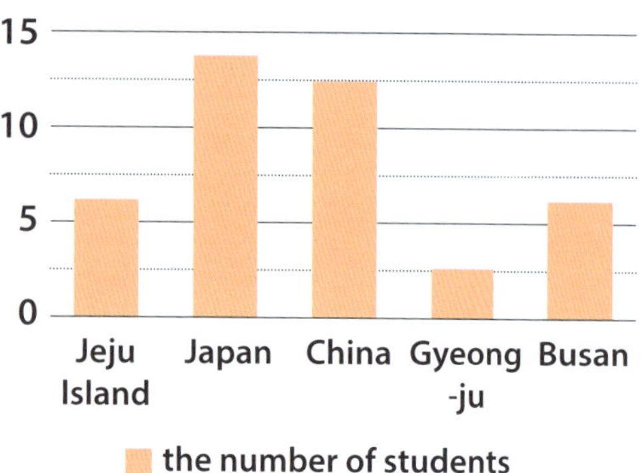

18

Japan __________________

China among the students. (popular, is)

19

The students like Jeju Island __________

__________________ Busan. (much)

20

Gyeongju __________________

__________________ among all places.

(popular, little, is, place)

21 주어진 단어를 사용하여 다음의 대화를 완성하세요.

Kevin: Hi, Tim. Where are your glasses?

Tim: Oh, I'm wearing contact lenses today.

Kevin: How do they feel?

Tim: They are pretty comfortable.

Kevin: Aren't they more expensive than glasses?

Tim: Not really. Contact lenses

(1) __________________

eyeglasses. (as, cheap)

Kevin: That's nice. Isn't it hard to put them in?

Tim: It can take a few minutes at first.

But, (2) __________________

you wear them, __________________

__________ it gets. (often, easy, the)

Kevin: That's interesting. I should try wearing contact lenses, too.

22 다음 세 명의 수영 선수들을 비교하는 표를 보고 〈조건〉에 맞게 문장을 완성하세요.

	Peter	Harry	Brian
(1) **Age**	12	16	14
(2) **Height**	160 cm	173 cm	166 cm
(3) **200 m Record**	2:10	1:58	1:58

〈조건〉
- (1)은 Age, (2)는 Height, (3)은 200 m Record의 내용을 보고 쓸 것
- 각 주어진 단어를 사용해 현재시제로 쓸 것

(1) Peter __________________

__________________ the three. (young)

(2) Harry __________________ Peter.
(tall)

(3) Brian __________________ Harry.
(fast)

○● 주어진 단어로 영작

23 James의 일기를 읽고 우리말과 일치하도록 주어진 단어를 사용하여 문장을 완성하세요.

> I learned about global warming today. My teacher said that (1) 지구가 점점 더 더워지고 있다. These days, (2) 기온은 예전과 같지 않다. For example, (3) 이번 여름은 지난여름보다 훨씬 더 덥다. My teacher told us some ways to protect the environment. (4) 우리가 환경에 대해서 더 많이 관심을 가질수록, 그것은 더 좋아지게 될 것이다.
>
> *global warming: 지구 온난화

(1) _______________________________________

_______________________________________ .

(hot, getting, the Earth, and)

(2) the temperature _____________________

_______________________________________ .

(the same, it used to be, as)

(3) this summer ________________________

_______________________________________ .

(hot, a lot, last summer)

(4) _______________________________________

____

(much, care about, good, will, the environment, be)

○● 어법 오류 수정

24 다음 ⓐ~ⓔ 중 어법상 틀린 세 개를 찾아 그 기호를 쓰고, 바르게 고쳐 쓰세요.

> ⓐ She solved the puzzle <u>as easy as</u> her brother.
> ⓑ Baseball is <u>one of the most popular sports</u> in Korea.
> ⓒ Nancy studies <u>as hard as</u> her twin sister.
> ⓓ The science test was <u>more even difficult than</u> the math test.
> ⓔ My math score is <u>more worse than</u> my art score.

_______ → _______________________________

_______ → _______________________________

_______ → _______________________________

🎯 **Challenge!**　　　　　누적 문제 Ch 06-08

25 다음 중 어법상 틀린 문장 두 개를 찾아 그 기호를 쓰고, 문장 전체를 바르게 고쳐 쓰세요.

> ⓐ The baby cried louder and louder.
> ⓑ Everyone was surprised at the news.
> ⓒ They feel nervously about starting a new school.
> ⓓ Don't forget to set the alarm before bed.
> ⓔ The desert is the bigger of the four deserts.

_______ → _______________________________

____

_______ → _______________________________

____

Chapter 09 접속사

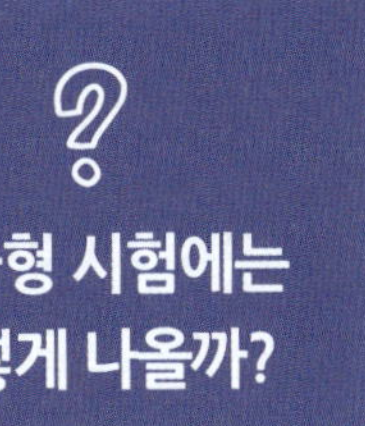

✅ Before You Write

- ☑ and, but, or와 각각 짝을 이루는 접속사를 올바르게 사용할 수 있나요?
- ☑ 시간/이유/조건 등 각 문장의 의미에 따라 어떤 접속사를 사용해야 할까요?
- ☑ 문장에서 어느 부분을 접속사 that을 사용해서 나타낼 수 있을까요?
- ☑ 의문사 의문문이 문장의 일부가 된다면 어떤 어순으로 써야 할까요?

내신 기출 다음 우리말을 보고 머릿속으로 한번 영어 문장을 떠올려 보세요.

1 그는 그렇다고**도**, 아니라고**도 말하지 않았다**. (yes / nor / say)
A도 B도 둘 다 하지 않았다 → neither A nor B → **said neither yes nor no**   `POINT 1`

2 Michael과 Emma는 오늘 **둘 다** 늦었다.
A와 B 둘 다 → both A and B 주어 → 항상 복수 취급
→ **Both Michael and Emma were**   `POINT 2`

3 **조용히 해라, 그렇지 않으면** 그 아기가 깰 것이다.
절과 절 연결 → ~해라, 그렇지 않으면 ~ → **Be quiet, or ~**   `POINT 3`

4 그는 **점심을 먹은 후에** 양치했다.
절과 절 연결 → 시간 → ~한 후에 → **after he ate lunch**   `POINT 4`

5 (2) 음식이 **너무 매워서 나는** 많은 물을 **마셨다**.
절과 절 연결 → 이유와 결과 → 너무 ~해서 …하다 → **so spicy that I drank**   `POINT 5`

6 A: What will you do this weekend?
B: **비가 오면**, 나는 영화를 볼 거야.
절과 절 연결 → 조건 → 만약 ~라면 → **If it is rainy**   `POINT 6`

7 **나는** Ted가 친절**하다고 생각해**.
~하다고 생각하다 → 접속사 that으로 연결 → think의 목적어 역할 → **I think that**   `POINT 7`

8 (2) Where did they meet yesterday?
→ **나는** 그들이 어제 **어디에서** 만났는**지 궁금하다**.
어디에서 ~하는지 → 의문사절 연결 → wonder의 목적어 역할 → **I wonder where**   `POINT 8`

정답: **1** He said neither yes nor no. **2** Both Michael and Emma were late today. **3** Be quiet, or the baby will wake up. **4** He brushed his teeth after he ate lunch[After he ate lunch, he brushed his teeth]. **5** The dish was so spicy that I drank much water. **6** If it is[it's] rainy, I will[I'll] watch a movie. **7** I think (that) Ted is kind. **8** I wonder where they met yesterday.

and, but, or의 쓰임

 **POINT 1** 짝을 이루는 and, but, or

우리는 저녁을 요리하거나 포장 음식을 주문할 수 있어.

우리는 / 저녁을 요리하거나 / 포장 음식을 주문할 수 있어.

either A ~ or B

→ We / **can** either cook dinner / **or** order takeout.

or 뒤에 조동사 can은 생략할 수 있으므로 동사원형을 쓰면 돼요.

그는 매일 운동할 뿐만 아니라 건강식도 먹는다.

그는 / 매일 운동할 뿐만 아니라 / 건강식도 먹는다.

not only A ~ but (also) B

→ He / not only exercises daily / but (also) eats healthy meals.

(= He eats healthy meals **as well as** exercises daily.)

- 접속사 and, but, or는 단어와 단어, 구와 구, 절과 절을 대등하게 연결해 주는 역할을 합니다.
  그런데 이러한 접속사가 다음과 같이 다른 단어와 짝을 이루어 하나의 접속사 역할을 하는 경우가 있어요.

📢 **짝을 이루는 and, but, or (상관접속사)**

both A and B	A와 B 둘 다
either A or B	A와 B 둘 중 하나
neither A nor B	A와 B 둘 다 아닌
not only A but (also) B = B as well as A	A뿐만 아니라 B도

주의❗

접속사 and, but, or와 마찬가지로 짝을 이루는 접속사 표현들 역시 연결되는 말은 문법적으로 같은 성격이어야 해요.
Jina is good at both swimming and ~~plays~~(→ playing) soccer. (지나는 수영과 축구를 둘 다 잘한다.)

대표 기출 문제

🔒 다음 주어진 우리말을 괄호 안의 단어를 반드시 사용하여
영작하시오.

Minsu는 수학과 음악을 둘 다 좋아한다.
(math, music, both)

→ ______________________

CLUE 1

'A와 B 둘 다'라는 의미는 both를 사용해
「both A and B」 형태로 나타내요.

CLUE 2

접속사 and로 연결되는 두 어구는 성격이 같아야
하므로 A와 B 자리에는 각각 math, music을 쓰면
돼요.

정답: Minsu likes both math and music.

Point Exercise

정답 및 해설 p.21

[1-3] 우리말과 일치하도록 주어진 단어를 올바르게 배열하세요.

1
> 그는 어제 전화하지도 메시지를 보내지도 않았다.
> (neither / a message / he / sent / called / nor)

→ ____

________________________________ yesterday.

2
> Jake뿐만 아니라 그의 친구들도 축구하는 것을 좋아한다.
> (playing / but also / his friends / Jake / like / not only / soccer)

→ ____

________________________________ .

3
> 우리는 반려동물로 개와 고양이 중 하나를 키우고 싶다.
> (a cat / or / to have / we / a dog / either / want)

→ ____

________________________________ as a pet.

[4-8] 우리말과 일치하도록 주어진 단어를 사용하여 문장을 완성하세요. (필요시 단어를 추가하거나 형태를 바꿀 것)

4
> 그들의 여행 동안 날씨는 비도 오고 추웠다.
> (rainy, be, the weather, both, cold)

→ ____

________________________________ during their trip.

5
> 그는 저녁에 체육관에 가거나 집에서 쉴 것이다.
> (rest, the gym, go to, at home, will, either)

→ ____

________________________________ in the evening.

6
> 그 식당에서 음식은 신선하지도 맛있지도 않았다.
> (tasty, fresh, the food, nor, be)

→ ____

________________________________ at the restaurant.

7
> 그녀는 어제 수영을 했을 뿐만 아니라 테니스도 쳤다.
> (but also, swim, play, tennis)

→ ____

________________________________ yesterday.

8
> Lisa는 피아노를 치는 것과 음악 듣는 것 둘 다 즐긴다.
> (play the piano, listen to music, enjoy, both)

→ ____

____

9 주어진 문장과 같은 의미의 문장이 되도록 〈조건〉에 맞게 바꿔 쓰세요.

> She is not only a good team player but also a great leader.

> 〈조건〉
> • as well as를 사용할 것
> • 12 단어로 쓸 것

→ ____

____

tasty (풍미가 강하고) 맛있는

POINT 2 상관접속사의 수일치

미술과 음악 둘 다 내가 가장 좋아하는 과목들이다.
미술과 음악 둘 다 / 내가 가장 좋아하는 과목들이다.
　　　　both A and B

→ **Both** art **and** music / **are** my favorite subjects.
　　　　　　주어　　　　　　　동사

- and, but, or와 짝을 이룬 표현이 주어로 쓰일 때, **동사는 주로 동사와 가까운 B의 인칭과 수에 일치**시킵니다.
- 단, 「**both A and B**」가 주어로 쓰일 때는 항상 복수동사를 써요.

  Either Jane **or** *William is* from Canada. Jane과 William 둘 중 한 명이 캐나다 출신이다.

  Neither my sister **nor** *I like* shopping. 나의 누나와 나는 둘 다 쇼핑을 좋아하지 않는다.

  Not only the teacher **but also** *the students* **are** excited. 선생님뿐만 아니라 학생들도 신이 나 있다.

  (= *The students* **as well as** the teacher **are** excited.)

POINT 3 명령문, and[or]+주어+동사

침착해라, 그렇지 않으면 너는 또 같은 실수를 할 것이다.
침착해라, // 그렇지 않으면 너는 할 것이다 / 같은 실수를 / 또.
　명령문　　　　　or　　　주어　동사　　목적어　　부사

→ Stay calm, // [or] you'll make / the same mistakes / again.

- 접속사 and와 or는 명령문 뒤에 쓰여 다음과 같은 의미로 쓰일 수 있어요.
  이때 앞뒤 내용의 논리 관계를 잘 따져 and와 or 중 알맞은 접속사를 사용해야 합니다.

명령문, **and**+주어+동사 ~	~해라, **그러면** ~할 것이다
명령문, **or**+주어+동사 ~	~해라, **그렇지 않으면** ~할 것이다

  Hurry up, [and] you'll catch the bus. 서둘러라, **그러면** 너는 버스를 잡아탈 수 있을 것이다.

  Hurry up, [or] you'll miss the train. 서둘러라, **그렇지 않으면** 너는 기차를 놓칠 것이다.

대표 기출 문제

🔒 주어진 단어를 포함하여 영작하시오.

사람들에게 친절해라, 그러면 너는 많은 친구들을
사귈 수 있다.

→ ________________________________ . (make)

CLUE 1
'~해라'라고 명령하는 문장은 동사원형(Be)으로
시작해요.

CLUE 2
명령문 뒤에 '그러면 ~'이라는 의미의 문장을
덧붙일 때는 「and+주어+동사 ~」로 나타내요.

정답: Be kind to people, and you can make many friends

Point Exercise

[1-3] 우리말과 일치하도록 주어진 단어를 올바르게 배열하세요.

1
집에 일찍 가라, 그렇지 않으면 너희 부모님이 화를 내실 것이다.
(be / home / your parents / go / will / or / angry / early)

→ ________________________, ________________

__________________________________.

2
심호흡해 봐, 그러면 너는 기분이 좀 나아질 거야.
(you / take / feel / and / will / a deep breath / better)

→ ________________________, ________________

__________________________________.

3
그와 그의 여동생 둘 다 수영을 잘한다.
(and / swimming / both / at / are / he / good / his sister)

→ ________________________________

__________________________________.

[4-7] 우리말과 일치하도록 주어진 단어를 사용하여 문장을 완성하세요.

4
Daniel과 나 둘 중 한 명이 매일 아침에 교실 준비하는 것을 돕는다.
(either, to set up, help, the classroom)

→ ________________________________

__________________________ every morning.

5
자신감을 가져라, 그러면 너는 영어를 잘 말할 수 있다.
(confident, speak, be, can, well)

→ ________________________________

____

6
내 고양이와 개 둘 다 목욕하는 것을 싫어한다.
(take a bath, cat, dog, nor, like)

→ ________________________________

____

7
Ryan과 Sophie 둘 다 동물 보호소에서 자원봉사를 한다. (volunteer, both, at the animal shelter)

→ ________________________________

____

8 다음 그림을 보고 남자아이에게 해 줄 충고의 말을 〈조건〉에 맞게 완성하세요.

〈조건〉
- 6 단어로 쓸 것
- a stomachache, have, will을 사용할 것

→ Don't eat too many snacks, ____________

__________________________________.

breath 숨, 호흡 set up 준비하다; 설치하다 confident 자신감 있는 animal shelter 동물 보호소 stomachache 복통

부사절을 이끄는 접속사

POINT 4 시간을 나타내는 접속사

네가 어젯밤에 나에게 전화했을 때, 나는 TV를 보고 있었다.
네가 나에게 전화했을 때 / 어젯밤에, // 나는 / 보고 있었다 / TV를.
　　　　　　부사절　　　　　　　　　주어　　동사　　목적어

→ **When** you called me / last night, // I / was watching / TV.

- 시간, 이유, 결과, 조건, 양보 등 '부사'에 해당하는 의미를 나타내는 접속사가 이끄는 절을 **부사절**이라고 해요. 부사절은 문장 앞이나 뒤에 쓰는데, 문장 앞에 올 때는 반드시 부사절 뒤에 콤마(,)를 써야 합니다.
- 다음과 같이 **시간**을 나타내는 접속사는 다양하므로, 문맥에 따라 알맞은 접속사를 쓸 줄 알아야 합니다.

📢 시간을 나타내는 접속사

when	~할 때	until[till]	~할 때까지
while	~하는 동안에	before/after	~하기 전에/~한 후에

우리는 비가 그칠 때까지 여기에서 기다릴 것이다.
우리는 기다릴 것이다 / 여기에서 // 비가 그칠 때까지.
　주어　　　동사　　　　　　　　　　부사절

→ We **will wait** / here // **until** the rain stops.

- 시간을 나타내는 부사절에서는 그 내용이 미래를 나타내더라도 미래시제를 쓰지 않고 현재시제를 써야 해요.
  When I ~~will get~~(→ **get**) home, I will call you. 내가 집에 도착하면 너에게 전화할게.

대표 기출 문제

🔒 다음 조건과 일치하도록 우리말에 맞게 괄호 안에 주어진 단어를 활용하여 문장을 완성하시오.

<조건>
- 접속사 after 또는 while 을 이용할 것

네가 숙제를 끝낸 후에 사탕을 얻게 될 거야.

→ You'll get candies ____________________ .
　(your homework)

CLUE 1
시간을 나타내는 부사절 중 '~한 후에'라는 의미는 접속사 after를 사용해서 나타내요.

CLUE 2
'끝낸 후에'는 미래에 일어날 일이지만, 시간을 나타내는 접속사(after)가 이끄는 절에서는 현재시제를 써야 하는 점에 주의하세요.

정답: after you finish your homework

Point Exercise

배열 영작

[1-4] 우리말과 일치하도록 주어진 단어를 올바르게 배열하세요.

1
> 비가 그친 후, 우리는 밖에 놀러 나갔다.
> (the rain / after / stopped)

→ ______________________________,
we went outside to play.

2
> 내가 교실에 도착했을 때, 아무도 없었다.
> (I / arrived / the classroom / when / at)

→ ______________________________,
there was nobody.

3
> 오빠는 그의 숙제를 끝낸 뒤에 컴퓨터 게임을 할 것이다.
> (his homework / finishes / after / he)

→ My brother will play a computer game
______________________________.

4
> Amy는 기차를 기다리는 동안에 점심을 먹었다.
> (the train / was / waiting for / she / while)

→ Amy had lunch ______________________________
______________________________.

주어진 단어로 영작

[5-8] 우리말과 일치하도록 주어진 단어를 사용하여 문장을
완성하세요. (필요시 단어를 추가하거나 형태를 바꿀 것)

5
> 그녀는 운동할 때 항상 흥겨운 음악을 듣는다.
> (work out)

→ She always listens to joyful music __________
______________________________.

6
> 네가 방을 나서기 전에 창문을 닫아라.
> (the room, leave)

→ Close the window ______________________________
______________________________.

7
> 그는 TV를 보는 동안, 잠이 들었다.
> (watch, be, TV)

→ ______________________________
______________________________, he fell asleep.

8
> 그녀는 그녀의 목표에 도달할 때까지 포기하지 않을
> 것이다. (goal, reach)

→ ______________________________
______________________________, she won't give up.

기출: 조건 영작

9 주어진 문장을 보고 〈조건〉에 맞게 문장을 완성하세요.

> **〈조건〉**
> • 〈보기〉에서 알맞은 접속사를 골라 한 번씩 사용할 것
> • 주어진 단어를 사용하되 필요시 형태를 바꿀 것

> **〈보기〉**
> until   while   after

(1) ______________________________,
we took a taxi home. (end, the concert)

(2) The restaurant won't open ______________
______________________________.
(from his vacation, the chef, return)

(3) ______________________________,
my brother took a nap.
(a movie, watching, I, be)

---

work out 운동하다 joyful 흥겨운, 기쁨을 주는 reach ~에 이르다, 도달하다 give up 포기하다

POINT 5   이유[원인], 결과를 나타내는 접속사

비가 와서 경기가 취소되었다.
경기가 취소되었다 // 비가 왔기 때문에.
　　결과　　　　　　　이유[원인]

→ **The game was canceled // because it rained.**

- '~하기 때문에, ~해서'라고 **이유나 원인**을 나타내는 접속사에는 because, since, as 등이 있어요.
- 이러한 접속사는 문장을 이루는 절과 절의 의미 관계를 잘 파악하여 알맞은 위치에 써야 해요.

주의!

1 because는 접속사이므로 뒤에 「주어+동사」를 쓰고, because of는 전치사이므로 뒤에 명사(구)를 써야 해요.
I didn't go out **because** it snowed heavily. (눈이 많이 왔기 때문에 나는 밖에 나가지 않았다.)
I didn't go out **because of** heavy snow. (폭설 때문에 나는 밖에 나가지 않았다.)

2 as, since 등과 같은 접속사는 여러 의미로 쓰일 수 있으므로, 문맥을 통해 의미를 잘 파악해야 해요.

as	~할 때, ~하면서 (시간)	**As** she opened the door, the cat ran out.
	~하기 때문에 (이유) (= because[since])	**As** the traffic was heavy, we were late.
	~처럼, ~대로	**As** you know, the library closes early on Fridays.
since	~한 이후로 (시간)	He has lost some weight **since** he began his diet.
	~하기 때문에 (이유) (= because[as])	They ordered a pizza **since** they were hungry.

비가 너무 많이 와서 경기가 취소되었다.
비가 너무 많이 와서 // 경기가 취소되었다.
　　이유[원인]　　　　　　결과

→ **It rained so *much* // that the game was canceled.**

- '너무[매우] ~해서 …하다'라고 **이유[원인]와 결과**를 나타낼 때는 「so+형용사/부사+that+주어+동사」의 형태로 쓸 수 있어요. 이때 접속사 that 뒤에는 결과를 나타내는 절을 씁니다.

MORE+ 목적을 나타내는 so (that)
so (that)은 '~하기 위해'라는 뜻의 목적을 나타내는 접속사예요. (☞ Level 3 Ch 08 접속사)
I bought a ticket early **so (that)** I could get a good seat. (나는 좋은 자리를 얻기 위해 표를 일찍 샀다.)

대표 기출 문제

🔒 다음 문장을 주어진 단어를 이용하여 영어로 완성하시오.

나는 이 차가 너무 뜨거워서 마실 수가 없다.
(so, that)

→ _______________________________

CLUE 1
'너무 ~해서 …하다'라고 원인과 결과를 나타내고
있어요.

CLUE 2
주어진 단어를 사용하여 「so+형용사/부사+that+
주어+동사」의 형태로 '너무 ~해서 …하다'라는
의미를 나타낼 수 있어요.

정답: This tea is so hot that I can't[cannot] drink it.

배열 영작

[1-4] 우리말과 일치하도록 주어진 단어를 올바르게 배열하세요.

1
> James는 너무 바빠서 나의 문자 메시지를 보지 못했다.
> (too / he / because / was / busy)

→ James didn't see my text message __________
____________________________________ .

2
> 길이 매우 미끄러워서 나는 넘어졌다.
> (so / I / that / slippery / fell down)

→ The road was __________________________
____________________________ .

3
> Jason은 나의 가장 친한 친구이기 때문에 나의
> 부모님은 그를 알고 계신다.
> (is / my / friend / as / best / he)

→ My parents know Jason ________________
____________________________ .

4
> 그 성은 매우 아름다워서 매년 많은 사람이 그곳을
> 방문한다. (visit / lots of / that / people / so /
> there / beautiful)

→ The castle is ______________________
____________________________ every year.

주어진 단어로 영작

**[5-8] 우리말과 일치하도록 주어진 단어를 사용하여 문장을
완성하세요. (필요시 단어를 추가하거나 형태를 바꿀 것)**

5
> 그녀는 지루해서 파티를 일찍 떠났다.
> (bored, the party, be, because, left, early)

→ ____________________________________ ,
____________________________________ .

6
> 그 신발이 너무 낡아서 그는 새로운 것을 살 것이다.
> (the shoes, be, buy, that, will, new ones, old)

→ ____________________________________
____

7
> Daisy는 배가 매우 고팠기 때문에 빵집으로 갔다.
> (be, go, hungry, because, to the bakery,
> very)

→ Daisy ______________________________
____________________________________ .

8
> 내 여동생은 너무 어려서 이 책을 이해할 수 없다.
> (this book, little sister, that, can, understand,
> be, young)

→ ____________________________________
____

기출: 한 문장으로 영작

9 주어진 두 문장을 so ~ that ...을 사용하여 한 문장으로
바꿔 쓰세요.

(1)
> The weather was very hot.
> We ordered ice cream.

→ ____________________________________
____

(2)
> The restaurant is very popular.
> You should wait for an hour.

→ ____________________________________
____

slippery 미끄러운 fall down 넘어지다 castle 성 order 주문하다

POINT 6 조건, 양보를 나타내는 접속사

만약 네가 코트를 입지 않는다면, 너는 추울 것이다.
만약 네가 코트를 입지 않는다면, // 너는 추울 것이다

→ **If** you *don't wear* a coat, // you'll feel cold.
= **Unless** you *wear* a coat, // you'll feel cold.

- '만약 ~한다면[라면]'이라고 **조건**을 나타낼 때는 접속사 if를 사용해서 나타내요.
- '만약 ~하지 않는다면'이라고 나타낼 때는 if ~ not의 형태로 쓰거나, 접속사 unless를 사용해서 나타낼 수 있어요.
- 조건을 나타내는 부사절에서도 문장의 내용이 미래를 나타내더라도 현재시제를 써야 합니다.
  If the weather ~~will be~~(→ **is**) good tomorrow, we will have a barbecue.
  만약 내일 날씨가 좋다면, 우리는 바비큐 파티를 할 것이다.

비록 그들은 쌍둥이긴 하지만, 서로 닮지 않았다.
비록 그들은 쌍둥이긴 하지만, // 그들은 닮지 않았다 / 서로.

→ **Although** they're twins, // they don't look like / each other.

- '비록 ~이긴 하지만'이라는 **양보**의 의미를 나타낼 때는 접속사 though, although를 사용해요.
  이때 양보란 기대되는 상황과 반대되는 상황을 나타내는 것을 의미해요.

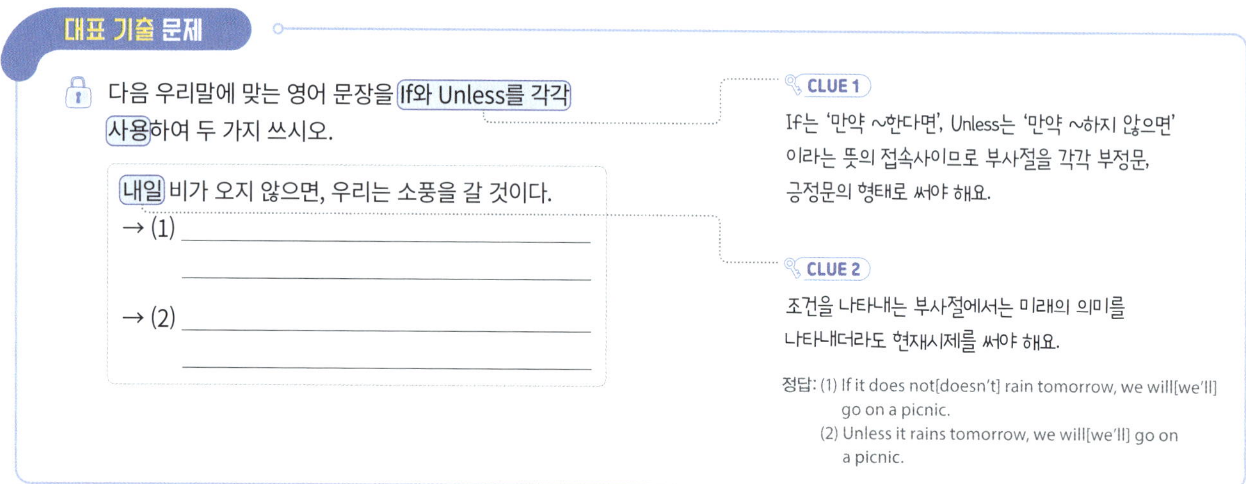

함정 피하기 unless는 부정의 의미(if ~ not)를 나타내므로, if절을 unless를 사용해 바꿔 쓸 때 부정문으로 쓰지 않도록 주의하세요.
Unless it ~~doesn't rain~~(→ **rains**) tomorrow, we will go on a picnic.

Point Exercise

[1-4] 우리말과 일치하도록 주어진 단어를 올바르게 배열하세요.

1

> 만약 네가 답을 안다면, 나에게 알려 줘.
> (the answer / know / if / you)

→ _______________________________

_______________________________, let me know.

2

> 그가 진실을 말하지 않는다면, 나미는 그를 용서하지 않을 것이다.
> (he / the truth / tells / unless)

→ Nami won't forgive him _______________________________

_______________________________.

3

> 비록 나의 할아버지는 일흔 살이셨지만, 마라톤을 완주하셨다.
> (although / years / was / my grandfather / old / seventy)

→ _______________________________

_______________________________, he finished the marathon.

4

> 비록 지난번 시험은 매우 어려웠지만, 나는 좋은 점수를 받았다.
> (difficult / the last exam / though / was / very)

→ _______________________________

_______________________________, I got a good score.

[5-7] 우리말과 일치하도록 주어진 단어와 if, unless, although 중 하나를 사용하여 문장을 완성하세요. (단, 한 번씩만 쓸 것)

5

> 만약 네가 후식을 좀 원한다면, 내가 네게 쿠키를 줄게.
> (some dessert, want)

→ _______________________________,

I will give you cookies.

6

> 비록 우리는 최선을 다했지만, 경기에서 졌다.
> (do, our best)

→ _______________________________,

we lost the game.

7

> 만약 Tim이 버스를 놓치지 않는다면, 제시간에 공항에 도착할 것이다. (miss, the bus)

→ Tim will arrive at the airport on time

_______________________________.

8 우리말과 일치하도록 〈조건〉에 맞게 문장을 완성하세요.

> 만약 네가 여름에 우유를 차갑게 보관하지 않는다면, 그것은 쉽게 상할 것이다.

〈조건〉
- 주어진 접속사로 시작할 것
- (1), (2) 모두 keep, go bad, milk, cold, easily, in summer를 사용할 것

(1) _______________________________

_______________________________ (if)

(2) _______________________________

_______________________________ (unless)

truth 진실 forgive 용서하다

명사절을 이끄는 접속사

 접속사 that

나는 네가 여동생이 한 명 있다는 것을 몰랐다.
나는 몰랐다 // 네가 여동생이 한 명 있다는 것을.
주어　　동사　　　　　　　　목적어

→ I didn't know // **(that)** you had a sister.
　　　　　　　　　　　　명사절 ←

> 문장에서 주어, 목적어, 보어와 같은 명사 역할을
> 하는 절을 의미해요.

- 주어와 동사를 포함한 절이 접속사 that과 함께 「that+주어+동사 ~」 형태로 쓰이면,
  문장에서 주어, 보어, 목적어와 같은 **명사 역할**을 할 수 있어요.
- 그중 문장에서 목적어 역할을 하는 that절이 가장 많이 쓰이는데, 이때 that은 생략할 수 있어요.
  따라서, 동사 뒤에 「주어+동사」가 연이어서 나오는 형태가 되기도 해요.
  I **believe** he is telling the truth. 나는 그가 진실을 말하고 있다고 믿는다.

📢 **that절을 목적어로 취하는 동사**

I **think** that	나는 ~하다고 생각하다	I **hear** that	나는 ~하다고 듣다
I **know** that	나는 ~하다는 것을 알고 있다	I **mean** that	나는 ~하다는 것을 의미하다
I **say** that	나는 ~하다고 말하다	I **promise** that	나는 ~할 것을 약속하다
I **believe** that	나는 ~하다고 믿다	I **imagine** that	나는 ~하다고 상상하다
I **hope** that	나는 ~하길 바라다	I **am sure** that	나는 ~하다고 확신하다
I **realize** that	나는 ~하다는 것을 깨닫다	I **guess** that	나는 ~하다고 추측하다

- 접속사 that이 이끄는 절은 문장에서 주어나 보어 역할을 하기도 해요. that절이 주어 역할을 할 때는 주어가
  너무 길어지기 때문에 주로 주어 자리에는 가주어 It을 쓰고, 진짜 주어인 that절은 문장 뒤로 보내요.

주어	**That** the child is a genius is true. 그 아이가 천재라는 것은 사실이다. = **It** is true **that** the child is a genius. 　가주어　　　　　　진주어
보어	The problem is **that** we don't have much time. 문제는 우리가 시간이 별로 없다는 것이다.

대표 기출 문제

🔒 우리말에 알맞게 영문을 완성하시오. (주어진 단어는
반드시 사용하고 필요한 단어를 추가하여 문장을
완성할 것)

나는 비가 올 거라고 생각하지 않는다.
→ I ______________________________ rain.
　(think, that, it, will)

🔍 **CLUE 1**

우리말에서 문장의 목적어에 해당하는 부분은?
— 비가 올 거라고(it will rain)

🔍 **CLUE 2**

목적어 자리에 명사(구)가 아닌 절(it will rain)을
쓰려면 절 앞에 접속사 that을 붙이면 돼요.

정답: do not[don't] think that it will[it'll]

Point Exercise

정답 및 해설 p.21

[1-3] 우리말과 일치하도록 주어진 단어를 올바르게 배열하세요.

1
> Jake는 그가 농구하는 것을 아주 좋아한다고 말했다.
> (that / playing / Jake / loved / said / basketball / he)

→ _______________________________________

_______________________________________.

2
> 그녀가 약속을 어겼다는 것은 매우 놀라웠다.
> (surprising / she / that / the promise / broke / was / very / it)

→ _______________________________________

_______________________________________.

3
> 우리는 선생님의 생신이 다가오고 있다고 들었다.
> (our teacher's / was / heard / we / birthday / coming)

→ _______________________________________

_______________________________________.

5
> 모든 부모가 그들의 아이들이 건강하길 바란다.
> (children, parent, healthy, will, be, every)

→ _______________________________________

____

6
> 그는 그의 숙제를 집에 두고 온 것을 깨달았다.
> (left, at home, homework)

→ _______________________________________

____

7
> 소라는 그 애플파이가 매우 맛있다고 생각했다.
> (tasty, was, so, the apple pie, Sora)

→ _______________________________________

____

[4-7] 우리말과 일치하도록 〈보기〉에서 알맞은 말을 골라 주어진 단어와 함께 문장을 완성하세요.

> 〈보기〉
> thought   realized   hopes   believe

4
> 나는 모든 사람이 평등하다고 믿는다.
> (everyone, equal, is)

→ _______________________________________

____

8 우리말과 일치하도록 〈조건〉에 맞게 문장을 완성하세요.

> 나는 로봇들이 미래에 많은 일을 할 거라고 상상한다.
>
> 〈조건〉
> • do, imagine, many, will, jobs를 사용할 것
> • 접속사를 생략하지 말고 사용할 것

→ _______________________________________

_______________________________ in the future.

surprising 놀라운 promise 약속; 약속하다 equal 평등한

POINT 8 간접의문문

너는 그의 이름이 무엇인지 아니?
너는 아니 // 무엇이 그의 이름인지?
　　주어　동사　　　목적어

→ Do you know // **what** his name is?
　　　　　　　　　의문사　주어　동사

(← Do you know? + what is his name?)

- 의문문이 절의 형태로 다른 문장의 일부로 쓰이는 경우가 있는데, 이러한 문장을 **간접의문문**이라고 합니다.
- 간접의문문에서 의문사가 이끄는 절은 「**의문사＋주어＋동사 ～**」의 어순으로 써야 하며,
  의문사가 주어일 때는 「**의문사(주어)＋동사 ～**」의 순서로 쓰이므로 주의하세요.
  Can you tell me **what** *happened* yesterday? 어제 무슨 일이 있었는지 내게 말해줄 수 있니?

> **주의**
>
> 의문사가 이끄는 절이 think, believe, guess, suppose, imagine과 같이 생각이나 추측을 나타내는 동사의 목적어로 쓰일 때는
> 의문사를 문장 맨 앞에 써야 해요.
> Do you *think*? + **What is the answer**?
> → **What** do you *think* **the answer is**? (○), Do you *think* **what the answer is**? (×)

나는 그가 영화표를 샀는지 모른다.
나는 알지 못한다 // 그가 영화표를 샀는지?
　주어　　동사　　　　　목적어

→ I don't know // **if[whether]** he **bought** the tickets for the movie.
　　　　　　　　　　if[whether]　주어　동사　　　　목적어

(← I don't know. + Did he buy the tickets for the movie?)

- 의문사를 포함하지 않는 의문문이 간접의문문으로 쓰이는 경우, '～인지 (아닌지)'라는 의미의
  접속사 if[whether]를 사용해 「**if[whether]＋주어＋동사 ～**」로 나타냅니다.

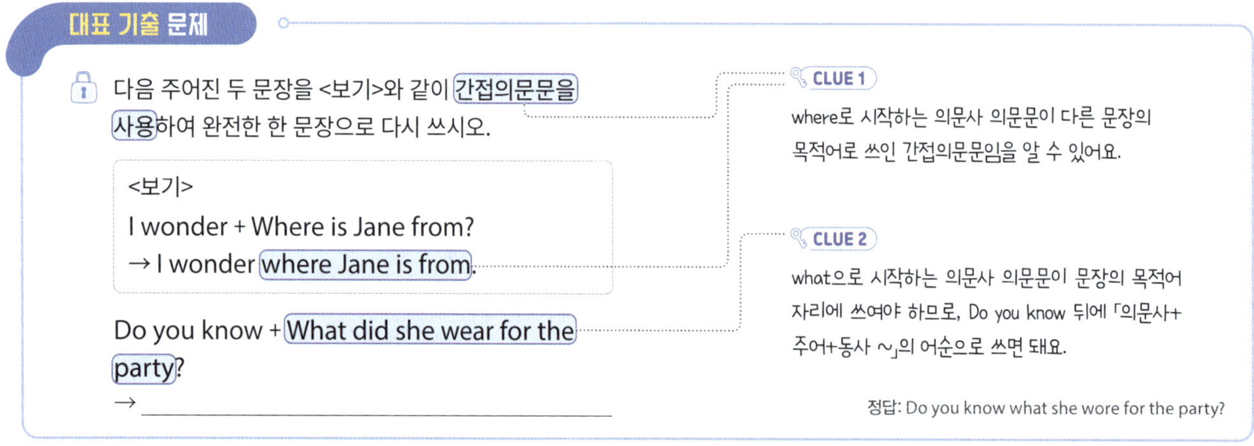

대표 기출 문제

🔒 다음 주어진 두 문장을 <보기>와 같이 간접의문문을
사용하여 완전한 한 문장으로 다시 쓰시오.

<보기>
I wonder + Where is Jane from?
→ I wonder where Jane is from.

Do you know + What did she wear for the party?
→ ___________________________________

CLUE 1
where로 시작하는 의문사 의문문이 다른 문장의
목적어로 쓰인 간접의문문임을 알 수 있어요.

CLUE 2
what으로 시작하는 의문사 의문문이 문장의 목적어
자리에 쓰여야 하므로, Do you know 뒤에 「의문사＋
주어＋동사 ～」의 어순으로 쓰면 돼요.

정답: Do you know what she wore for the party?

✓ **함정 피하기** 과거시제로 쓰인 의문문의 경우, 간접의문문으로 쓸 때 동사의 시제에 유의하세요.
Do you know + What **did** she *wear* for the party?
→ Do you know what she ~~wear~~(→ wore) for the party?

Point Exercise

배열 영작

[1-3] 우리말과 일치하도록 주어진 단어를 올바르게 배열하세요.

1
> 너는 오늘 우리가 숙제가 있는지 아니?
> (we / have / today / if / homework)

→ Do you know ________________

________________ ?

2
> 당신이 어떻게 이 아이디어를 생각해냈는지 말씀해 주시겠어요?
> (this / came up with / how / you / idea)

→ Could you tell me ________________

________________ ?

3
> 너는 우주가 어떻게 만들어졌다고 생각하니?
> (the universe / think / created / you / how / was / do)

→ ________________

________________ ?

배열 영작: 주어진 단어로 영작

[4-8] 우리말과 일치하도록 주어진 단어를 사용하여 문장을 완성하세요.

4
> 나는 그 항공편이 지연되었는지 잘 모르겠다.
> (delayed, the flight, is)

→ I'm not sure ________________

________________ .

5
> 너는 그녀가 어제 우리에게 뭐라고 말했는지 기억하니?
> (told, remember, yesterday)

→ Do you ________________

________________ ?

6
> 제게 당신이 하루에 TV를 몇 시간 보는지 알려주세요.
> (know, TV, watch, many hours)

→ Please let me ________________

________________ a day.

7
> 너는 그 버스가 언제 도착할지 아니?
> (the bus, arrive, will, know)

→ ________________

____

8
> 그녀는 어젯밤에 누가 그녀에게 전화를 했는지 궁금했다.
> (her, called, wondered, last night)

→ ________________

____

기출: 한 문장으로 영작

9 주어진 두 문장을 〈보기〉와 같이 한 문장으로 바꿔 쓰세요.

> 〈보기〉
> Can you tell me? + Why were you late?
> → Can you tell me why you were late?

> Did you hear? + Where did Jina leave for?

→ ________________

____

---

universe 우주 create 만들다 delay 지연시키다, 연기하다 flight 항공편; 비행 wonder 궁금해하다

Chapter Test [*]

STAGE 1 Go for it!

자신 있게 풀어보는 기초 문제!

배열 영작

[1-4] 우리말과 일치하도록 주어진 단어를 배열하여 문장을 완성하세요.

1
> 비록 Ben은 너무 피곤했지만, 그는 방을 청소했다.
> (Ben / though / tired / was / too)

→ _______________________________________

_______________________, he cleaned up his room.

2
> 날씨가 너무 더워서 그는 그의 재킷을 벗었다.
> (hot / took off / so / he / jacket / that / his)

→ It was _______________________________

_______________________________________.

3
> 나는 햄버거뿐만 아니라 밀크셰이크도 주문했다.
> (as / a hamburger / as / a milkshake / well)

→ I ordered _____________________________

_______________________________________.

4
> 너는 이 단어가 무슨 뜻인지 아니?
> (you / what / do / word / know / this / means)

→ _______________________________________

_____________________________________?

주어진 단어로 영작

[5-7] 우리말과 일치하도록 주어진 단어를 사용하여 문장을 완성하세요.

5
> 만약 네가 배고프다면, 나는 네게 샌드위치를 만들어 줄 수 있어.
> (if, hungry, be)

→ _______________________________________

_______________________, I can make you a sandwich.

6
> Liam은 그가 어렸을 때 태권도를 배웠다.
> (when, be, young)

→ Liam learned Taekwondo ________________

_______________________________________.

7
> 엄마는 내가 창문을 깨뜨려서 화가 나셨다.
> (the window, be, because, break, angry)

→ Mom ___________________________________

_______________________________________.

최신 기출

8 다음 주어진 문장을 〈조건〉에 맞게 바꿔 쓰세요.

> If you pay attention in class, you will understand the lesson better.

〈조건〉
- 명령문과 접속사 and를 사용해 쓸 것
- 11 단어로 쓸 것

→ _______________________________________

____

보기에서 골라 영작

[9-16] 빈칸에 들어갈 알맞은 접속사를 〈보기〉에서 골라 쓰세요.
(단, 한 번씩만 사용할 것)

> 〈보기〉
> because　　　unless　　　if　　　while

9 _______________ we save energy, we can't protect nature.

10 Jim went to the hospital _______________ he caught a cold.

11 _______________ you don't apologize, she won't forgive you.

12 Someone knocked on the door _______________ I was washing the dishes.

> 〈보기〉
> and　　　but　　　or　　　that

13 Sumi is going to buy either a skirt _______________ pants.

14 I go to the library not only on weekdays _______________ also on Sundays.

15 Henry knew _______________ Susan would come to the concert.

16 This cream can both clean _______________ protect your skin.

그림 영작

17 다음은 과일 가게를 나타낸 그림입니다. 그림을 보고 알맞은 접속사를 사용하여 문장을 완성하세요.

(1) _______________ apples _______________ oranges are two dollars.

(2) _______________ grapes _______________ strawberries are on sale.

(3) Buy three melons, _______________ you can get one free.

최신 기출

18 다음 표를 보고 Eric과 Tom의 공통점을 찾아 〈조건〉에 맞게 문장을 완성하세요.

Do you like ~?	(1) food		(2) sports	
	pasta	salad	tennis	bowling
Eric	○	×	×	×
Tom	○	○	○	×

> 〈조건〉
> • (1)은 both를, (2)는 neither를 사용해서 쓸 것
> • 현재시제를 사용할 것

(1) _______________________________________

(2) _______________________________________

[19-23] 주어진 두 문장을 〈보기〉와 같이 한 문장으로 바꿔 쓰세요.

> 〈보기〉
> I wonder.
> Where is the restroom?
> → I wonder where the restroom is.

19
> Do you know?
> Does Lily live near here?

→ _______________________________________

20
> Can you tell me?
> How long do you sleep on weekends?

→ _______________________________________

21
> Do you think?
> What does Peter want to get on his birthday?

→ _______________________________________

22
> Tell me.
> How did you solve this question?

→ _______________________________________

23
> I'm not sure.
> When will the package be delivered?

→ _______________________________________

[24-28] 다음 각 문장에서 어법상 **틀린** 부분을 찾아 바르게 고쳐 쓰세요.

24 In summer, I enjoy not only surfing but also swim.

_______________ → _______________

25 We didn't go to the beach because of it was very cold.

_______________ → _______________

26 Take this medicine, or you'll feel better.

_______________ → _______________

27 Either you or your brother have to take care of the dog today.

_______________ → _______________

28 You should turn off your phone until the test will be over.

_______________ → _______________

최신 기출

29 다음은 과학박물관의 안내 데스크를 나타낸 그림입니다. 그림에 등장하는 인물들의 질문을 보고 빈칸을 간접의문문으로 완성하세요.

(1) The boy is asking _______________________

____.

(2) The girl is asking _______________________

____.

○━ 문장 전환

[30-34] 주어진 문장과 같은 의미가 되도록 빈칸에 알맞은 말을 쓰세요.

30
> Because the letters in the book were so small, I couldn't read them.

→ The letters in the book were ______________ ______________ ______________ I ______________ ______________ them.

31
> These shoes are not only pretty but also comfortable.

→ These shoes are ______________ ______________ ______________ ______________ ______________.

32
> I don't like rainy days, and I also don't like cloudy days.

→ I like ______________ ______________ ______________ ______________ weather.

33
> If you don't listen to your teacher carefully, you'll miss important things.

→ ______________ ______________ your teacher carefully, ______________ ______________ ______________ important things.

34
> The restaurant serves delicious food, and serves excellent service, as well.

→ The restaurant serves ______________ ______________ ______________ ______________ ______________ ______________.

○━ 조건 영작

35 다음 Megan이 Cathy에게 쓴 편지글을 읽고 〈조건〉에 맞게 우리말을 영작하세요.

> Dear Cathy,
>
> How are you? It's great to hear that you're having a good vacation.
>
> Yesterday, I watched a film about Vincent Van Gogh. (1) <u>비록 그의 재능은 굉장했지만,</u> no one knew about it at the time. I want to read more about him, too. (2) <u>만약 내가 내일 바쁘지 않다면, 난 서점에 갈 거야.</u>
>
> Anyway, take care! I hope to see you soon.
> Love,
> Megan

〈조건〉
- will, busy, a bookstore, go, amazing, talent, not을 사용할 것

(1) ______________________________________ , no one knew about it at the time.

(2) ______________________________________ ______________________________________

◎ **Challenge!**　　　누적 문제 Ch 07-09

36 다음 중 어법상 틀린 문장 **두 개**를 찾아 그 기호를 쓰고, 문장 전체를 바르게 고쳐 쓰세요.

ⓐ Every table has a menu on it.
ⓑ She finished the test a lot more faster than her classmates.
ⓒ He solved the puzzle as easily as his dad.
ⓓ I don't know where is the restaurant.
ⓔ We won't go hiking if it rains tomorrow.

__________ → ______________________________
____

__________ → ______________________________
____

관계대명사

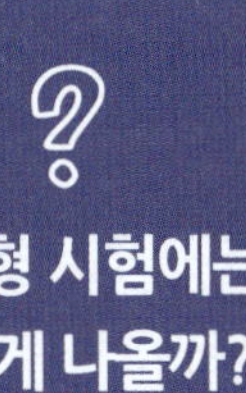

✅ Before You Write

- 관계대명사가 꾸미는 명사(선행사)를 올바르게 파악할 수 있나요?
- 주격/목적격/소유격 관계대명사 중 문장에서의 역할에 따라 알맞은 것을 사용할 수 있나요?
- 선행사의 종류에 따라 알맞은 관계대명사를 사용할 수 있나요?
- 「선행사+관계대명사절」을 올바른 어순으로 쓸 수 있나요?

내신 기출 다음 우리말을 보고 머릿속으로 한번 영어 문장을 떠올려 보세요.

1 Susan은 매우 영리한 아들이 하나 있다. (very smart)
아들 [매우 영리한] → 주어 역할(주격) → 사람 선행사(a son)
→ *a son* [**who** is very smart]   POINT 1

2 그녀는 빨간색 리본들이 있는 그 드레스를 살 것이다.
그 드레스 [빨간색 리본들이 있는] → 주어 역할(주격) → 사물 선행사(the dress)
→ *the dress* [**which** has red ribbons]   POINT 1

3 Daniel은 내가 매우 좋아하는 가수이다.
가수 [내가 매우 좋아하는] → like의 목적어 역할(목적격) → 사람 선행사(a singer)
→ *a singer* [**whom** I like ● very much]   POINT 2

4 (2) 지원이는 Mike가 그녀에게 쓴 편지를 읽고 있다.
편지 [Mike가 그녀에게 쓴] → write의 목적어 역할(목적격) → 사물 선행사(a letter)
→ *a letter* [**which** Mike wrote ● to her]   POINT 2

5 나는 지붕이 노란색인 집을 보았다.
집 [집의 지붕이 노란색인] → a house와 roof는 소유 관계(소유격)
→ *a house* [**whose** roof is yellow]   POINT 3

6 "내가 원하는 것은 너의 건강이다."
~한 것 [내가 원하는] → 선행사를 포함한 관계대명사 what → **What I want**   POINT 4

정답: **1** Susan has a son who[that] is very smart. **2** She will[She'll] buy the dress which[that] has red ribbons. **3** Daniel is a singer who(m)[that] I like very much. **4** Jiwon is reading a letter which[that] Mike wrote to her. **5** I saw a house whose roof is yellow. **6** What I want is your good health.

Unit 01 who, which, that

POINT 1 주격 관계대명사 who, which, that

그녀는 항상 다른 사람들을 돕는 소녀이다.
그녀는 ~이다 / 소녀 [항상 다른 사람들을 돕는].

→ She is / *the girl* [**who** always helps others].
　　　　　선행사　　　　　　　　관계대명사절

(← She is *the girl*. + **She** always helps others.)

- 위와 같이 두 문장을 한 문장으로 표현할 때 who, which, that 등과 같은 관계대명사를 사용할 수 있어요.
- 관계대명사 who는 두 문장을 연결하면서 대명사 She를 대신하므로, 「접속사+대명사」 역할을 합니다.
  이때 선행사 the girl은 who가 이끄는 관계대명사절의 꾸밈을 받게 됩니다.
- 관계대명사 절에서 **관계대명사가 주어**인 경우를 **주격 관계대명사**라고 하며,
  다음과 같이 선행사의 종류에 따라 구별해서 씁니다.

선행사	사람	사물, 동물	모두 가능 (사람+사물, 사람+동물 등)
주격	who	which	that

> **주의** **주격 관계대명사절의 수일치**
>
> 1 주격 관계대명사절 내에서 동사는 선행사의 수에 맞춰 써야 해요.
> He took **my books** [which **was**(→ **were**) on my desk]. (그는 내 책상 위에 있던 책들을 가져갔다.)
>
> 2 또한, 문장의 주어가 선행사로 관계대명사절의 수식을 받아 동사와 멀리 떨어지는 경우, 동사의 수에 주의해야 해요.
> ***The boy*** [who is wearing glasses] **like**(→ **likes**) Hye-na. (안경을 낀 그 소년은 헤나를 좋아한다.)
> 주어(선행사)　　　관계대명사절　　　동사

대표 기출 문제

다음 두 문장을 that을 제외한 적절한 관계대명사를 이용하여 우리말 뜻에 맞는 한 문장으로 만드시오.

The woman is my best friend.
She is dancing on the stage.

무대 위에서 춤추고 있는 그 여자는 나의 제일 친한 친구이다.

→ ___________________________________

CLUE 1
동일한 대상(The woman = She)을 관계대명사로 연결하여 한 문장으로 만들어야 해요.

CLUE 2
주어진 우리말을 '그 여자 [무대 위에서 춤추고 있는]'과 같이 바꿔 봅니다. 선행사(The woman)가 사람이며 관계대명사절 안에서 주어(She)의 역할을 대신하는 것이므로 주격 관계대명사 who를 써요.

정답: The woman who is dancing on the stage is my best friend.

함정 피하기 주격 관계대명사절 안에서 주어는 관계대명사가 대신하고 있으므로 원래 주어를 중복해서 쓰지 않도록 주의하세요.
The woman **who** ~~she~~ is dancing on the stage is my best friend.

Point Exercise

[1-5] 우리말과 일치하도록 주어진 단어를 올바르게 배열하세요.

1
> 나는 유머 감각을 지닌 사람들을 좋아한다.
> (a sense of humor / who / have)

→ I like people ______________________

______________________ .

2
> 우리는 현대 그림 작품들을 전시하는 미술관에 갔다.
> (displays / modern paintings / which)

→ We went to the museum ______________

______________________ .

3
> Chloe는 실크로 만들어진 셔츠를 샀다.
> (made / silk / which / of / is)

→ Chloe bought a shirt ________________

______________________ .

4
> 매일 열심히 훈련한 그 달리기 선수는 경기에서 이겼다.
> (every day / trained / who / hard)

→ The runner ______________________

______________________ won the race.

5
> 창문이 많은 그 건물은 1년 전에 지어졌다.
> (many / windows / has / that)

→ The building ______________________

______________________ was built a year ago.

[6-15] 주어진 두 문장을 〈보기〉와 같이 관계대명사를 사용하여 한 문장으로 바꿔 쓰세요. (단, that은 제외)

> 〈보기〉
> I know the man.
> He lives next door.
> → I know the man who lives next door.

6
> There is a girl.
> She is talking to her friend.

→ There is ______________________

______________________ .

7
> David is wearing shoes.
> They are too big for him.

→ David is wearing ________________

______________________ .

8
> The dog is very cute.
> It has big ears.

→ ______________________

______________________ is very cute.

9
> Do you know that boy?
> He is sitting over there.

→ Do you know ______________________

______________________ ?

10
> I'm looking at this picture.
> It was taken last month.

→ I'm looking at ______________________

______________________ .

a sense of humor 유머 감각 display 전시하다 modern 현대의

11

> Sera helped the man.
> He was looking for a bus stop.

→ Sera helped __________________________

__________________________ .

12

> There is a little cat.
> It is crying alone.

→ There is __________________________

__________________________ .

13

> The restaurant is so popular.
> It is near my house.

→ __________________________

__________________________ is so popular.

14

> The police officer was very kind.
> He helped us.

→ __________________________

__________________________ was very kind.

15

> There are many people.
> They are waiting for the subway.

→ There are __________________________

__________________________ .

[16-18] 다음 그림을 보고 〈조건〉에 맞게 문장을 완성하세요.

〈조건〉
• 주격 관계대명사를 사용할 것 (단, that은 제외)
• 현재진행형을 사용할 것
• 주어진 단어를 사용할 것

16 Look at __________________________

__________________________ .

(smile, us, at, the little boy)

17 There are __________________________

__________________________ .

(climb up, monkeys, the tree, two)

18 __________________________

__________________________ is my sister.

(wear, the girl, a blue cap)

popular 인기 있는

[19-25] 우리말과 일치하도록 주어진 단어와 관계대명사를 사용하여 문장을 완성하세요. (필요시 형태를 바꿀 것)

19
> 그는 4개 국어를 할 줄 아는 한 사람을 안다.
> (can, four, know, a person, speak, languages)

→ _______________________________

____

20
> 펭귄은 날지 못하는 새들 중 하나이다.
> (the penguin, fly, the birds, can, be, one of)

→ _______________________________

____

21
> 이곳은 우리 마을에서 최고의 커피를 파는 카페이다.
> (this, the cafe, sell, be, in, the best coffee, town)

→ _______________________________

____

22
> 의사가 되고 싶어 하는 그 소녀는 내 친구이다.
> (to be, be, the girl, a doctor, want, friend)

→ _______________________________

____

23
> 탁자 위에 있던 그 책은 어디에 있니?
> (the book, on the table, be, where)

→ _______________________________

____

24
> 지붕 위에서 자고 있는 저 고양이는 정말 귀엽다.
> (sleep, cute, the cat, be, on the roof, very)

→ _______________________________

____

25
> 나는 저쪽에서 뛰고 있던 남자아이와 그의 개를 보았다.
> (see, dog, and, over there, the boy, run)

→ _______________________________

____

26 우리말과 일치하도록 〈조건〉에 맞게 문장을 완성하세요.

> 〈조건〉
> - 7 단어로 쓸 것
> - 관계대명사를 사용할 것
> - plan ahead, students, goals, achieve를 사용할 것
>
> 미리 계획하는 학생들이 그들의 목표를 빨리 달성한다.

→ _______________________________

_______________________________ quickly.

---

language 언어 roof 지붕 ahead 미리; 앞쪽에 achieve 달성하다, 성취하다

Unit 02

who(m), which, that

POINT 2　목적격 관계대명사 who(m), which, that

그녀는 모든 사람이 아는 배우이다.
그녀는 ~이다 / 배우 [모든 사람이 아는].

→ She is / *an actress* [**who(m)** everyone knows ●].
(← She is **an actress**. + Everyone knows **her**.)

- **목적격 관계대명사는 관계대명사가 이끄는 절에서 목적어 역할**을 해요. 따라서 위 문장의 관계대명사절에서 who(m)는 knows의 목적어인 her 대신 목적어 역할을 하고 있습니다.
- 목적격 관계대명사도 다음과 같이 선행사의 종류에 따라 구별해서 써야 해요. 선행사가 사람일 때 whom을 쓰지만 말할 때는 보통 who를 씁니다.

선행사	사람	사물, 동물	모두 가능
목적격	who/whom	which	that

- 주격 관계대명사와 달리 목적격 관계대명사는 생략할 수 있어요. 이때 선행사 바로 뒤에 관계대명사절의 「주어＋동사 ~」가 이어지므로 관계대명사절이 어디서부터 어디까지인지 잘 파악해야 해요.

(which[that])
The pizza ˅ [our dad made] tasted good. 우리 아빠가 만들어주신 피자는 맛있었다.

(who(m)[that])
A girl ˅ [I sit next to in class] became my best friend. 수업 시간에 내 옆에 앉는 소녀가 나의 가장 친한 친구가 되었다.

> **주의**
>
> 문장의 주어가 목적격 관계대명사절의 수식을 받는 경우, 주어와 동사의 수일치에 주의하세요.
> ***The cookies*** [she made] **was**(→ **were**) delicious. (그녀가 만든 쿠키들은 맛있었다.)

대표 기출 문제

🔒 다음 두 문장을 관계대명사를 이용하여 한 문장으로 만드시오.

The book was interesting. I read it last week.

→ ___________________________

CLUE 1
주어진 두 문장을 한 문장으로 만들려면, '그 책은 [내가 지난주에 읽은] / 재미있었다.'라는 의미가 되어야 해요.

CLUE 2
사물인 The book을 선행사로 하고, 동사 read의 목적어로 쓰인 대명사 it을 대신해 목적어 역할을 할 수 있는 관계대명사는? — which 또는 that

정답: The book which[that] I read last week was interesting.

✔ **함정 피하기**　목적격 관계대명사절 안에서 목적어는 관계대명사가 대신하고 있으므로 목적어를 중복해서 쓰지 않아야 해요.
The book **which[that]** I read **it** last week was interesting.

Point Exercise

정답 및 해설 p.24

배열 영작

[1-3] 우리말과 일치하도록 주어진 단어를 올바르게 배열하세요.

1
> 그는 모두가 존경하는 선생님이다.
> (the teacher / respects / is / whom / he / everyone)

→ _______________________________________

_______________________________________ .

2
> 그들이 이야기했던 그 주제는 무엇이었니?
> (the subject / they / talked about / that)

→ What was _______________________________

_______________________________________ ?

3
> 그녀가 쓴 소설은 십 대들 사이에서 아주 인기 있다.
> (very popular / wrote / the novel / which / is / she)

→ _______________________________________

_______________________________ among teenagers.

주어진 단어로 영작

[4-7] 우리말과 일치하도록 주어진 단어와 관계대명사를 사용하여 문장을 완성하세요. (단, that은 제외)

4
> 나는 네가 잃어버린 그 카메라를 찾았다.
> (find, lost, the camera)

→ _______________________________________

5
> 우리는 Dean이 추천한 관광 명소를 방문했다.
> (recommended, the tourist attraction, visit)

→ _______________________________________

6
> Gary는 Bella가 캐나다에서 보낸 편지를 받았다.
> (from, a letter, sent, receive, Canada)

→ _______________________________________

____

7
> Sally가 좋아하는 그 배우는 유명하지 않다.
> (the actor, likes, famous, be)

→ _______________________________________

____

기출: 한 문장으로 영작

[8-9] 다음 두 문장을 〈조건〉에 맞게 한 문장으로 바꿔 쓰세요.

8
> I remember the boy.
> We met him at the park.
>
> 〈조건〉
> • 10 단어로 쓸 것
> • 관계대명사 whom을 사용할 것

→ _______________________________________

____

9
> Anna is wearing the blue dress.
> Her sister bought it last weekend.
>
> 〈조건〉
> • 12 단어로 쓸 것
> • 관계대명사를 사용할 것

→ _______________________________________

____

---

respect 존경하다; 존중하다 subject 주제; 과목 recommend 추천하다 tourist attraction 관광 명소 receive 받다

whose, what

소유격 관계대명사 whose

Katie는 털이 매우 긴 개 한 마리를 키운다.
Katie는 키운다 / 개 한 마리를 [털이 매우 긴].

→ Katie raises / *a dog* [**whose** fur is very long].
(← Katie raises ***a dog***. + **Its** fur is very long.)

- **소유격 관계대명사 whose**는 관계대명사가 이끄는 절에서 his, her, its 등의 **소유격 대명사의 역할**을 해요.
- 선행사의 종류에 상관없이 모두 whose로 쓰며, 뒤에는 반드시 소유의 대상이 되는 명사가 와야 해요.

The girl is very sad. + **Her** bike was stolen.
→ *The girl* **whose bike** was stolen is very sad. 자전거가 도난당한 그 여자아이는 매우 슬퍼하고 있다.

I met ***some artists***. + **Their** paintings are popular.
→ I met *some artists* **whose paintings** are popular. 나는 그림들이 인기 있는 몇몇 예술가들을 만났다.

> **주의**
>
> 관계대명사 whose가 이끄는 절 내의 동사는 선행사가 아닌 whose 뒤에 쓰인 명사의 수에 맞춰 써야 해요.
> *The artist* [**whose paintings are** famous] is having an exhibition. (그림이 유명한 그 예술가는 전시회를 열고 있다.)

대표 기출 문제

🔒 다음 주어진 두 문장을 관계대명사를 사용하여
우리말에 맞게 한 문장으로 연결하시오.

I know a boy. His brother is a famous
singer.
→ ___________________________
(나는 그의 형이 유명한 가수인 소년을 알고 있다.)

🔍 **CLUE 1**

두 문장을 연결할 때 앞 문장의 a boy의 소유격
대명사인 His를 대신할 수 있는 관계대명사는?
— 소유격 관계대명사 whose

🔍 **CLUE 2**

주어진 우리말을 '소년 [그의 형이 유명한 가수인]'
으로 바꿔 봅니다. 선행사 a boy 뒤에 His 대신 소유격
관계대명사 whose를 쓰면 돼요. whose 뒤에는 명사
brother가 와야 해요.

정답: I know a boy whose brother is a famous singer.

# Point Exercise

한 문장으로 영작

[1-5] 주어진 두 문장을 〈보기〉와 같이 관계대명사를 사용하여 한 문장으로 바꿔 쓰세요.

〈보기〉
I like the singer.
His songs are great.
→ I like the singer whose songs are great.

1
I have a friend.
Her hobby is swimming.

→ I have ________________________________

________________________________ .

2
This is the house.
Its roof needs repair.

→ This is ________________________________

________________________________ .

3
The boy got presents from his friends.
His birthday is today.

→ ________________________________

________________________________ got presents from his friends.

4
The restaurant is near my house.
Its chef is famous.

→ ________________________________

________________________________ is near my house.

5
Do you know the woman?
Her name is Helen.

→ Do you know ________________________________

________________________________ ?

주어진 단어로 영작

[6-8] 우리말과 일치하도록 주어진 단어와 관계대명사 whose를 사용하여 문장을 완성하세요. (필요시 형태를 바꿀 것)

6
Max의 삼촌은 디자인이 특이한 차를 가지고 있다.
(design, unique, be, a car)

→ Max's uncle has ________________________________

________________________________ .

7
나는 책가방을 잃어버렸던 그 소년을 도와주었다.
(backpack, the boy, be lost)

→ I helped ________________________________

________________________________ .

8
아버지가 요리사인 내 친구는 요리하는 것을 아주 좋아한다. (father, friend, be, a chef)

→ ________________________________

________________________________ loves to cook.

기출: 조건 영작

9 우리말과 일치하도록 〈조건〉에 맞게 문장을 완성하세요.

그녀는 정원이 꽃들로 가득한 집에 산다.

〈조건〉
• 11 단어로 쓸 것
• 관계대명사를 사용할 것
• flowers, a house, be full of, garden을 사용할 것

→ ________________________________

____

---

repair 수리, 보수; 수리하다 be lost (물건 등이) 분실되다, 없어지다 unique 특이한, 독특한 be full of ~로 가득 차다

그가 말한 것이 나를 화나게 했다.
그가 말<u>한 것</u>이 / 나를 화나게 했다.
　　　　주어

→ **What** he said / made me angry.
(= The thing that[which] he said)

- 관계대명사 what은 '~한 것'의 의미로 쓰며, 다른 관계대명사와는 달리 **선행사를 포함한다**는 특징이 있어요. 따라서 위 문장처럼 **what 앞에는 선행사를 따로 쓰지 않으며**, what은 the thing(s) that[which]로 바꿔 쓸 수 있어요.
- what으로 시작하는 명사절은 문장에서 주어, 목적어 역할을 하거나 be동사의 보어 역할을 해요.

주어	**What** James has to do is to clean his room. (= The thing that[which] James has to do) James가 해야 하는 것은 그의 방을 치우는 것이다.
목적어	I can't believe **what** he said. (= the thing that[which] he said) 나는 그가 말한 것을 믿을 수 없다.
보어	The sweater is **what** she made. (= the thing that[which] she made) 그 스웨터는 그녀가 만든 것이다.

대표 기출 문제

🔒 괄호 안에 주어진 단어를 이용하여 주어진 문장을 영작하시오.

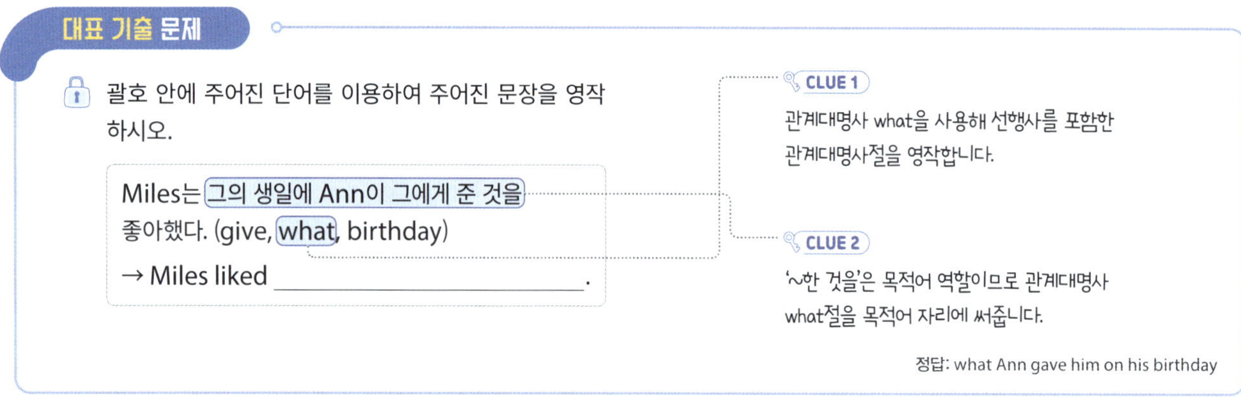

✅ **함정 피하기**

1 what은 선행사를 포함하므로 명사나 대명사 뒤에 사용하지 않아요.

We have everything ~~what~~(→ that) you need. (우리는 당신이 필요로 하는 모든 것을 갖고 있습니다.)

2 what이 관계대명사절 내에서 목적어 역할을 대신할 때, 관계대명사절에 목적어를 중복해서 쓰지 않도록 합니다.

This is *the thing*. I want to eat it for lunch.

→ This is what I want to eat ~~it~~ for lunch. (이것이 내가 점심으로 먹고 싶은 것이다.)

Point Exercise

[1-3] 우리말과 일치하도록 주어진 단어를 올바르게 배열하세요.

1
> 그들은 그녀가 침대 밑에 숨겨 놓은 것을 발견했다.
> (under / the bed / she / what / hid)

→ They found ______________________

______________________ .

2
> 너는 내가 설명한 것을 이해했니?
> (explained / did / what / you / I / understand)

→ ______________________

______________________ ?

3
> 우리를 놀라게 한 것은 Tom의 무례한 태도였다.
> (surprised / was / attitude / what / us / rude / Tom's)

→ ______________________

______________________ .

[4-6] 우리말과 일치하도록 주어진 단어와 관계대명사 what을 사용하여 문장을 완성하세요. (필요시 형태를 바꿀 것)

4
> 우리가 기억하는 것은 그의 이름이다.
> (remember, is, name)

→ ______________________

____

5
> 그녀는 그가 저녁 식사로 요리한 것을 좋아했다.
> (cooked, like, for dinner)

→ ______________________

____

6
> 이 옷들은 내가 주문한 것이 아니다.
> (be, these, ordered, clothes)

→ ______________________ .

____

[7-8] 다음 두 문장을 관계대명사 what을 사용하여 한 문장으로 바꿔 쓰세요.

7
> This is the thing.
> I lost it on the subway.

→ ______________________

____

8
> Tell me the thing.
> You want to do it this summer vacation.

→ ______________________

____

9 다음 대화를 읽고 주어진 단어와 관계대명사 what을 사용하여 우리말에 맞게 영작하세요.

> A: Jimmy, happy birthday! This is for you.
> B: Thank you, Mom. Is this a new cell phone?
> A: Yes, it is. Do you like it?
> B: Of course! 이것은 제가 가지고 싶었던 거예요.
>   (this, want, to have)

→ ______________________

____

hide 감추다 explain 설명하다 surprise 놀라게 하다 attitude 태도 rude 무례한 order 주문하다

Chapter Test *

정답 및 해설 p.25

STAGE 1 Go for it!

자신 있게 풀어보는 기초 문제!

배열 영작

[1-4] 우리말과 일치하도록 주어진 단어를 배열하여 문장을 완성하세요.

1

소민이는 그녀에게 꽃을 준 남자를 모른다.
(gave / some flowers / her / the man / who)

→ Somin doesn't know ___________

___________ .

2

30분 동안 책 읽는 것은 내가 매일 하는 것이다.
(do / every day / what / I)

→ Reading for thirty minutes is ___________

___________ .

3

우리는 맛있는 전통 요리들을 파는 시장에 갔다.
(delicious / which / the market / sold / traditional dishes)

→ We went to ___________

___________ .

4

내가 방문하고 싶었던 박물관은 닫혀 있었다.
(the museum / I / to / that / visit / wanted)

→ ___________

___________ was closed.

빈칸 완성

[5-7] 우리말과 일치하도록 주어진 단어를 사용하여 빈칸에 알맞은 말을 쓰세요. (단, that은 제외)

5

나는 아홉 살인 남동생 한 명이 있다.
(nine, old, years, be)

→ I have a little brother ___________

___________ ___________

___________ .

6

이것은 내가 어제 산 가방이다.
(buy, the bag, yesterday)

→ This is ___________ ___________

___________ ___________

___________ .

7

Josh는 이름이 Matt인 고양이 한 마리가 있다.
(a cat, be, name)

→ Josh has ___________ ___________

___________ ___________

___________ .

최신 기출

8 우리말과 일치하도록 주어진 단어를 배열하여 다음의 대화를 완성하세요. (필요시 형태를 바꿀 것)

A: There are two girls in this photo.
   Which one is your older sister?
B: 풍선들을 들고 있는 사람이 나의 언니야.
   (holding / be / the balloons / who / my older sister / be)

→ The person ___________

___________ .

● 한 문장으로 영작

[9-13] 주어진 두 문장을 관계대명사를 사용하여 한 문장으로 바꿔 쓰세요. (단, that은 제외)

9

> Lisa and Kane are good students.
> They study hard.

→ Lisa and Kane are good students _________

___________________________________ .

10

> The writer was gentle.
> I interviewed him.

→ The writer ___________________________

___________________________________ .

11

> I brought sandwiches and some fruits.
> My mom prepared them.

→ ___________________________________

____

12

> This is the question.
> Its answer isn't clear to me.

→ ___________________________________

____

13

> Amy is reading a book.
> It has over three hundred pages.

→ ___________________________________

____

● 조건 영작

[14-16] 주어진 문장을 〈조건〉에 맞게 완성하세요.

> 〈조건〉
> • 〈보기〉에서 알맞은 관계대명사를 골라 한 번씩 사용할 것
> • 주어진 단어를 사용하되 현재시제로 쓸 것

> 〈보기〉　who　　whom　　which

14 Do you know the person _________________

_________________________? (next door, live)

15 This is the song _____________________

___________________________________ .

(listen to, I, every morning)

16 The artist _________________________

is Vincent Van Gogh. (admire, I, the most)

최신 기출

17 〈A〉와 〈B〉에서 서로 관련 있는 문장을 골라 〈보기〉와 같이 관계대명사를 사용하여 한 문장으로 쓰세요. (단, that은 제외)

> 〈A〉
> • Ellen is a good friend.
> • This is the movie.
> • The park was very peaceful.

> 〈B〉
> • Its ending surprised everyone.
> • She always helps me.
> • We visited it last week.

> 〈보기〉
> Ellen who always helps me is a good friend.

(1) ___________________________________

____

(2) ___________________________________

____

[18-20] 우리말과 일치하도록 각 〈조건〉에 맞게 문장을 완성하세요.

18

> 〈조건〉
> • 관계대명사를 쓸 것
> • 다음 문장을 활용할 것
>   I used the towel last night.

> 나는 어젯밤 내가 사용한 그 수건을 찾을 수 없다.

→ I can't find the towel ___________

___________ .

19

> 〈조건〉
> • 관계대명사를 생략할 것
> • 다음 문장을 활용할 것
>   He spent time with his friends in Seoul.

> Logan은 서울에서 시간을 함께 보낸 그의 친구들을 그리워한다.

→ Logan misses his friends ___________

___________ .

20

> 〈조건〉
> • 관계대명사를 쓸 것
> • 다음 문장을 활용할 것
>   The cafe's garden was very beautiful.

> 나는 정원이 매우 아름다운 카페에 갔다.

→ I went to a cafe ___________

___________ .

[21-25] 다음 각 문장에서 어법상 <u>틀린</u> 부분을 찾아 바르게 고쳐 쓰세요.

21 The hotel whom my family stayed at has good service.

___________ → ___________

22 I met a smart girl that dream is to be a scientist.

___________ → ___________

23 I went to visit a friend whom lives in Japan.

___________ → ___________

24 Mr. Kim is my neighbor who I respect him very much.

___________ → ___________

25 The potatoes that I bought today isn't very fresh.

___________ → ___________

26 다음 ⓐ~ⓔ 중 어법상 <u>틀린</u> <u>두 개</u>를 찾아 그 기호를 쓰고, 바르게 고쳐 쓰세요.

> ⓐ We often visit our cousins <u>which</u> live in Suwon.
> ⓑ The woman <u>whose</u> car was stolen called the police.
> ⓒ I like that dress which <u>have</u> a unique pattern.
> ⓓ The teacher <u>whom</u> many students like is Mr. Johnson.
> ⓔ I can tell you <u>what</u> you want to know.

___________ → ___________

___________ → ___________

● 〔조건 영작〕

27 하준이가 쓴 메모를 보고 질문에 대한 대답을 〈조건〉에 맞게 쓰세요.

> • hope to visit: New York
> • plan to eat: cream pasta
> • want to buy: a bike

> 〈조건〉
> • 관계대명사를 사용할 것
> • 관계대명사절의 주어는 Hajun으로 쓸 것

(1) Q: Where does Hajun hope to visit?

A: The place ______________ ______________

______________ ______________ ______________

______________ New York.

(2) Q: What food does Hajun plan to eat?

A: The food ______________ ______________

______________ ______________ ______________

______________ cream pasta.

(3) Q: What does Hajun want to buy?

A: ______________ ______________ ______________

______________ ______________ is a bike.

● 〔문맥에 맞게 영작〕

28 다음은 Kevin과 Chris의 대화입니다. 대화에 쓰인 단어와 관계대명사를 사용하여 주어진 단어 수에 맞게 문장을 완성하세요. (단, that은 제외)

> Kevin: I'm so excited to see Eva!
> It's been a year since I last saw her. Where is she?
> Chris: She's over there! She's waiting for us.
> Kevin: Is she sitting on the bench?
> Chris: No.
> Kevin: Is she standing in front of the bank?
> Chris: Yes, that's her.

→ Eva is the girl ______________________________

______________________________ . (8 단어)

🎯 **Challenge!**   누적 문제 Ch 08-10

29 다음 중 어법상 **틀린** 문장 <u>두 개</u>를 찾아 그 기호를 쓰고, 문장 전체를 바르게 고쳐 쓰세요.

> ⓐ Be patient, and you'll see results.
> ⓑ I'm reading a book that it has great reviews.
> ⓒ My sister studied far harder than her classmates.
> ⓓ He spoke so quickly that I couldn't understand him.
> ⓔ She either eats apples or drink coffee in the morning.

__________ → __________________________

____

__________ → __________________________

____

동사 변화형

✳ A-B-B형

동사원형	과거형	과거분사형 (p.p.)	현재분사형 (-ing)
bleed (피를 흘리다)	bled	bled	bleeding
bring (가져오다)	brought	brought	bringing
build (짓다)	built	built	building
buy (사다)	bought	bought	buying
catch (잡다)	caught	caught	catching
feed (먹이를 주다)	fed	fed	feeding
feel (느끼다)	felt	felt	feeling
fight (싸우다)	fought	fought	fighting
find (찾다)	found	found	finding
flee (도망치다)	fled	fled	fleeing
get (얻다)	got	got/gotten	getting
have (가지다)	had	had	having
hang (걸다)	hung	hung	hanging
hear (듣다)	heard	heard	hearing
hold (잡다)	held	held	holding
keep (유지하다)	kept	kept	keeping
kneel (무릎을 꿇다)	knelt	knelt	kneeling
lay (눕히다, 놓다)	laid	laid	laying
lead (인도하다)	led	led	leading
learn (배우다)	learned/learnt	learned/learnt	learning
leave (떠나다)	left	left	leaving
lose (잃다)	lost	lost	losing
lend (빌려주다)	lent	lent	lending
make (만들다)	made	made	making
mean (의미하다)	meant	meant	meaning
meet (만나다)	met	met	meeting
pay (지불하다)	paid	paid	paying
say (말하다)	said	said	saying
seek (찾다)	sought	sought	seeking
sell (팔다)	sold	sold	selling
send (보내다)	sent	sent	sending
sleep (잠자다)	slept	slept	sleeping
smell (냄새 맡다)	smelled/smelt	smelled/smelt	smelling
shine (빛나다)	shone	shone	shining
shoot (쏘다)	shot	shot	shooting
sit (앉다)	sat	sat	sitting
spend (소비하다)	spent	spent	spending
spill (엎지르다)	spilled/spilt	spilled/spilt	spilling
stand (서다, 서 있다)	stood	stood	standing
sweep (청소하다)	swept	swept	sweeping
teach (가르치다)	taught	taught	teaching
tell (말하다)	told	told	telling
think (생각하다)	thought	thought	thinking
win (이기다)	won	won	winning

✳ A-B-A형

동사원형	과거형	과거분사형 (p.p.)	현재분사형 (-ing)
become (되다)	became	become	becoming
come (오다)	came	come	coming
run (달리다)	ran	run	running

✳ A-B-C형

동사원형	과거형	과거분사형 (p.p.)	현재분사형 (-ing)
bite (물다)	bit	bitten	biting
blow (불다)	blew	blown	blowing

break (깨뜨리다)	broke	broken	breaking
choose (고르다)	chose	chosen	choosing
do (하다)	did	done	doing
draw (그리다)	drew	drawn	drawing
drink (마시다)	drank	drunk	drinking
drive (운전하다)	drove	driven	driving
eat (먹다)	ate	eaten	eating
fall (떨어지다)	fell	fallen	falling
fly (날다)	flew	flown	flying
forget (잊다)	forgot	forgotten	forgetting
forgive (용서하다)	forgave	forgiven	forgiving
freeze (얼다)	froze	frozen	freezing
give (주다)	gave	given	giving
go (가다)	went	gone	going
grow (자라다)	grew	grown	growing
hide (숨다)	hid	hidden	hiding
know (알다)	knew	known	knowing
lie (눕다)	lay	lain	lying
ride (타다)	rode	ridden	riding
ring (울리다)	rang	rung	ringing
rise (오르다)	rose	risen	rising
see (보다)	saw	seen	seeing
shake (흔들다)	shook	shaken	shaking
show (보여주다)	showed	shown/showed	showing
sing (노래하다)	sang	sung	singing
speak (말하다)	spoke	spoken	speaking
steal (훔치다)	stole	stolen	stealing
swell (부풀다)	swelled	swollen/swelled	swelling
swim (수영하다)	swam	swum	swimming

take (잡다)	took	taken	taking
throw (던지다)	threw	thrown	throwing
wake (잠이 깨다)	woke	woken	waking
wear (입다)	wore	worn	wearing
write (쓰다)	wrote	written	writing

✳ A-A-A형

동사원형	과거형	과거분사형 (p.p.)	현재분사형 (-ing)
cast (던지다)	cast	cast	casting
cost (비용이 들다)	cost	cost	costing
cut (베다)	cut	cut	cutting
hit (치다, 때리다)	hit	hit	hitting
hurt (다치다)	hurt	hurt	hurting
let (~하게 하다)	let	let	letting
put (놓다)	put	put	putting
set (놓다)	set	set	setting
shut (닫다)	shut	shut	shutting
spread (퍼지다)	spread	spread	spreading
read[ri:d] (읽다)	read [red]	read [red]	reading
upset (화나게 하다)	upset	upset	upsetting

✳ A-A-B형

동사원형	과거형	과거분사형 (p.p.)	현재분사형 (-ing)
beat (치다, 때리다)	beat	beaten	beating

논술형 *
수행평가

평가 개요	
주제	친구와의 추억 소개하기
세부 내용	① 알고 지낸 기간 ② 친구와 함께 계속 해 온 것 ③ 구체적인 경험 (3가지 이상)
언어 형식	① 과거시제 ② 현재완료 (계속)

Step 1 | 예시 글 분석하기

➕ 형광펜 친 부분에 유의하여 예시 글을 읽은 후, 각 질문에 답해보세요.

Memories with My Best Friend

도입부	➜	I will share one of my memories with my best friend, Jun.
알고 지낸 기간	➜	We have known each other for 7 years, and we share many memories.
함께 계속 해 온 것	➜	We have always enjoyed spending time outdoors together.
경험 ①	➜	One time, we went to the park and played soccer all day.
경험 ②	➜	Another time, we went to the beach. We built a big sandcastle and took many pictures.
경험 ③	➜	Last year, we went camping and saw many stars.
맺음말	➜	I hope we can make more memories together.

1 How long has the writer known his[her] friend?

→ They ____ .

2 What have they always enjoyed together?

→ They ____ together.

3 What memories does the writer have of his[her] friend? Write down 3 sentences.

→ They _______________________ and _______________________ .

→ They _______________________ and _______________________ at the beach.

→ They _______________________ and _______________________ .

---

1 have known each other for 7 years   **2** have always enjoyed spending time outdoors   **3** went to the park, played soccer all day, built a big sandcastle, took many pictures, went camping, saw many stars

Step 2 | 글의 뼈대 만들기

➕ 나의 친구를 떠올리며, 다음 표의 빈칸을 완성해 보세요.

Memories with My Best Friend

도입부	I will share one of my memories with my best friend, ________________.
알고 지낸 기간	We have known each other for ________________, and we share a lot of memories.
함께 계속 해 온 것	We ________________ together.
경험 ①	One time, ________________. ________________.
경험 ②	Another time, ________________. ________________.
경험 ③	________________.
맺음말	I hope we can make more memories together.

Useful Words & Expressions

경험	**enjoy spending time outdoors** 야외에서 시간 보내는 것을 즐기다	**play soccer in the park** 공원에서 축구하다 **have a picnic by the lake** 호수 근처에서 소풍하다 **ride bikes along the river** 강을 따라 자전거 타다
	try many hobbies 여러 취미를 시도하다	**learn to play the guitar** 기타 치는 것을 배우다 **learn to cook** 요리하는 것을 배우다 **paint pictures** 그림을 그리다
	study hard 열심히 공부하다	**stay late at school** 학교에 늦게까지 남다 **prepare for a science quiz** 과학 퀴즈를 준비하다 **work on a group assignment** 조별 과제를 하다
	visit many places 많은 곳을 가보다	**go to the beach and swim all day** 해변에 가서 종일 수영하다 **visit amusement parks** 놀이공원에 가보다 **explore new neighborhoods** 새로운 동네를 탐험하다

✚ 앞에서 작성한 내용을 바탕으로 다음 〈조건〉에 맞게 글을 완성해 보세요.

〈조건〉
① 6문장 이상 작성할 것
② 다음 언어 형식을 사용해 작성할 것
  • 과거시제
  • 현재완료 (계속)

Memories with My Best Friend

I will share one of my memories with ______________________________________ .

We ____ .

We ____ together.

One time, ____ .

____ .

Another time, ____ .

____ .

____ .

I hope we can make more memories together.

평가 개요	
주제	우리 학교 교칙 소개하기
세부 내용	① 지켜야 할 것 (3가지 이상) ② 하지 말아야 할 것 (2가지 이상)
언어 형식	① 주어+동사+목적어+목적격보어 ② 조동사 must, should, have to

Step 1 | 예시 글 분석하기

➕ 형광펜 친 부분에 유의하여 예시 글을 읽은 후, 표의 빈칸을 완성해 보세요.

Our School Rules

도입부	➔	Our school has some rules to follow.
교칙 ①	➔	First, we **must** arrive on time.
교칙 ②	➔	Second, we **have to** wear the school uniform properly.
교칙 ③	➔	Third, we **shouldn't** use our phones during class.
교칙 ④	➔	Next, we **must keep our desks and classrooms clean**.
교칙 ⑤	➔	Lastly, we **shouldn't** bring food or drinks into the classroom.
맺음말	➔	By following these rules, we can make the school a better place.

교칙 ①	**1**	First, we ____ .
교칙 ②	**2**	Second, we ____________________________________ properly.
교칙 ③	**3**	Third, we ____________________________________ during class.
교칙 ④	**4**	Next, we ____ .
교칙 ⑤	**5**	Lastly, we ____________________________ into the classroom.

1 must arrive on time **2** have to wear the school uniform **3** shouldn't use our phones **4** must keep our desks and classrooms clean **5** shouldn't bring food or drinks

✚ 내가 다니는 학교의 교칙을 떠올리며, 다음 표의 빈칸을 완성해 보세요.

Our School Rules

도입부	Our school has some rules to follow.
교칙 ①	First, we ___________________________________ .
교칙 ②	Second, we ___________________________________ .
교칙 ③	Third, we ___________________________________ .
교칙 ④	Next, we ___________________________________ .
교칙 ⑤	Lastly, we ___________________________________ .
맺음말	By following these rules, we can make the school a better place.

Useful Words & Expressions

지켜야 할 것	**arrive on time** 제시간에 도착하다 **greet our teachers** 선생님들께 인사하다 **listen to the teacher** 선생님 말씀을 듣다 **be kind** 친절하게 하다 **wear indoor shoes** 실내화를 신다 **speak politely** 예의 바르게 말하다 **keep our desk and classroom clean** 책상과 교실을 깨끗하게 유지하다 **wear the school uniform properly** 교복을 올바르게 입다 **raise our hand to ask questions** 질문할 때 손들다 **respect others' opinions** 다른 사람의 의견을 존중하다 **clean the classroom** 교실을 청소하다 **pay attention to** ~에게 집중하다 **complete our homework on time** 숙제를 제시간에 끝내다
하지 말아야 할 것	**use our phones during class** 수업 시간에 휴대 전화를 사용하다 **eat or drink in the classroom** 교실에서 먹거나 마시다 **bring dangerous items to school** 위험한 물건을 학교에 가져오다 **bully other students** 다른 학생들을 괴롭히다 **run in the hallways** 복도에서 뛰다 **do makeup** 화장을 하다 **wear accessories** 액세서리를 하다 **dye our hair** 머리를 염색하다 **perm our hair** 머리를 파마하다

✚ 앞에서 작성한 내용을 바탕으로 다음 〈조건〉에 맞게 글을 완성해 보세요.

〈조건〉
① 5문장 이상 작성할 것
② 다음 언어 형식을 사용해 작성할 것
 • 주어+동사+목적어+목적격보어
 • 조동사 must, should, have to

Our School Rules

Our school has some rules to follow.

First, ____ .

Second, ____ .

Third, ____ .

Next, ____ .

Lastly, ____ .

By following these rules, we can make the school a better place.

평가 개요	
주제	즐거운 주말 계획
세부 내용	① 계획 (3가지 이상) ② 상대방에게 요청한 일 ③ 과거에 반복적으로 일어났던 일
언어 형식	① ask/tell+목적어+to부정사 ② 미래 표현 be going to ③ 과거의 습관 used to

Step 1 | 예시 글 분석하기 ○

➕ 형광펜 친 부분에 유의하여 예시 글을 읽은 후, 각 질문에 답해보세요.

A Fun Weekend Plan

계획	➡	This weekend, I am going to see my cousins.
세부 계획 ①	➡	We are going to visit a park and have a picnic.
세부 계획 ②	➡	I'm going to prepare some snacks and drinks.
요청한 일	➡	I told them to bring some board games.
세부 계획 ③	➡	We are also going to ride our bikes around the park.
과거의 습관	➡	We used to race our bikes when we were younger, but now we don't do that as often.
맺음말	➡	It's going to be a great weekend!

1 What is the writer going to do with his[her] cousins this weekend? Write down 2 sentences.

→ They are going to ___________________________________ .

→ They are going to ___________________________________ .

2 What is the writer going to prepare?

→ He[She] is going to ___________________________________ .

3 What did the writer tell his[her] cousins to do?

→ He[She] told them ___________________________________ .

4 When they were younger, what did they use to do?

→ They ___________________________________ .

---

1 visit a park and have a picnic, ride their bikes around the park   **2** prepare some snacks and drinks   **3** to bring some board games   **4** used to race their bikes

Step 2 | 글의 뼈대 만들기

✚ 이번 주말 계획을 떠올리며, 다음 표의 빈칸을 완성해 보세요.

A Fun Weekend Plan

계획	This weekend, I am going to ____________________.
세부 계획 ①	I/We ____________________.
세부 계획 ②	I/We ____________________.
요청한 일	I ____________________.
세부 계획 ③	I/We ____________ also ____________.
과거의 습관	I/We used to ____________, but now I/we don't do that as often.
맺음말	It's going to be a great weekend!

Useful Words & Expressions

	visit my friend's house 친구의 집에 방문하다	**play computer games** 컴퓨터 게임을 하다 **watch movies** 영화를 보다 **order pizza** 피자를 주문하다 **bring some snacks** 간식을 좀 가져오다
계획	**join a school volunteer event** 학교 자원봉사 행사에 참여하다	**clean up the beach** 해변을 청소하다 **plant trees** 나무를 심다 **bring gloves and sunscreen** 장갑과 선크림을 가져오다
	go to a music festival 음악 페스티벌에 가다	**enjoy the performances** 공연을 즐기다 **have a meal at the food trucks** 푸드트럭에서 식사하다 **bring tickets** 표를 가져오다
	visit my grandparents 조부모님을 방문하다	**cook dinner together** 함께 저녁을 요리하다 **go for a walk** 산책하러 가다 **help them in the garden** 정원에서 일을 도와드리다

2 LEVEL

천일문

| 정답 및 해설 |

중등

WRiTiNG

Chapter 01 | 문장의 주요 형식

Unit 01 SVC(2형식)/SVOO(4형식)

POINT 1 p.11

1 Your voice sounds different
2 My hands felt cold
3 The coffee smells very good
4 This apple juice tastes too sour
5 The tall woman looks like a model
6 The medicine tasted bitter.
7 Your vacation plan sounds fun.
8 This scarf feels really soft.
9 Mark looked happy on his birthday.
10 These cookies look delicious, smell wonderful

10 A: 여기 갓 구운 쿠키들이 있어요.
   B: 이 쿠키들은 맛있어 보여요. 게다가 냄새도 훌륭해요.

POINT 2 p.13

1 She brought her friend a gift
2 The chef cooked the guests delicious steaks
3 English to his daughter
4 some ice cream for my brother
5 a few questions of her teacher
6 (1) Ben showed us his photo album.
   (2) Ben showed his photo album to us.
7 (1) My sister made me some pasta.
   (2) My sister made some pasta for me.
8 (1) My parents bought a bike for me.
   (2) My brother gave a book to me.

8 어제는 나의 생일이었다. 나는 나의 가족들로부터 선물을 받았다. 나의 부모님은 나에게 자전거를 사 주셨다. 나는 자전거를 타게 되어서 신이 난다. 나의 오빠는 나에게 책 한 권을 주었다. 그건 흥미로운 소설이었다. 나는 아주 행복하다!

Unit 02 SVOC(5형식)

POINT 3 p.15

1 My classmates call Robert Rob
2 The test result made me nervous
3 They made Mr. Smith a leader
4 She kept her dog warm with a blanket
5 You will find the swimming class helpful
6 The book made him a famous author.
7 My sister and I named the cat Kitty.
8 We should keep our voices low
9 Everyone found Jessica kind and warm.
10 Babies' smiles make us happy.

10 A: 저 아기를 봐! 귀엽지 않니?
   B: 응. 정말 사랑스러워. 아기가 우리에게 미소를 짓고 있어.
   A: 아기들의 미소는 우리를 행복하게 해.
   B: 네 말에 전적으로 동의해.

POINT 4 p.17

1 I asked my sister to bring an umbrella
2 The teacher advised students to have dreams
3 We didn't expect you to come so early
4 My parents allowed me to keep a pet
5 Max told his brother to turn off the TV
6 They ordered us to be quiet.
7 Mom got me to do the dishes
8 The tourists wanted me to take pictures of them.
9 advised Jack to buy a cake

9 Jack: Leo, 너는 Sarah의 생일 선물을 준비했니?
   Leo: 응. 나는 따뜻한 장갑을 샀어. 너는 어때, Jack?
   Jack: 난 뭔가를 사야 해. 그녀는 무엇을 좋아하니?
   Leo: 그녀는 달콤한 것을 먹는 걸 아주 좋아해. 케이크가 좋은 선택이 될 거야.
   → Leo는 Jack에게 케이크를 사라고 조언했다.

POINT 5 p.19

1 The staff made people wait
2 Eva smelled her mom cooking
3 She saw Daniel enter the library
4 Did you feel the ground shaking
5 The librarian helped the kid find books
6 Ron watched his sister play[playing] the violin.
7 I let the child touch my dog.
8 The teacher had us clean the classroom.
9 Anna heard someone call[calling] her name.

Chapter Test p.20

STAGE 1

1 Jenny's voice sounded sad
2 Regular exercise made me healthy
3 My dad had my brother fold the laundry
4 A girl asked me to find her parents
5 She watched the actor perform[performing]
6 Our teacher gave new textbooks to us.
7 We expect the weather to be sunny
8 call her Dance Master

2 어휘 regular 규칙적인
3 어휘 laundry 세탁, 세탁물 fold 접다, (접어) 개다

5 해설 지각동사 watch의 목적격보어 자리에는 동사원형 또는 현재분사가 올 수 있다.
어휘 perform 공연하다, 연기하다
6 해설 동사 give는 직접목적어 뒤에 간접목적어를 쓸 때 간접목적어 앞에 전치사 to를 쓴다.
7 해설 동사 expect는 목적격보어 자리에 to부정사를 쓴다.
8 그녀는 춤을 잘 춰. 그래서 그녀의 친구들은 그녀를 Dance Master라고 불러.

STAGE 2

9 allow   10 keep
11 see   12 let
13 name   14 for
15 to
16 saw two people flying
17 (1) sent me new shoes
    (2) got a baseball cap for me
18 My parents let me play computer games.
19 I heard the neighbor's dog bark[barking] loudly.
20 My mom made me clean my room.
21 The doctor advised her to take medicine.
22 My friend told me not to be late.
23 look → look like   24 beautifully → beautiful
25 to → for   26 be → to be
27 fell → fall[falling]
28 (1) told Chloe to make dinner
    (2) got Chloe and Emma to finish the homework
       (today)

9 나의 부모님은 내가 하루에 한 시간 동안 TV를 보는 것을 허락하신다.
해설 동사 allow는 목적격보어 자리에 to부정사를 쓴다.
10 그 문을 연 채로 두세요. 저는 5분 안에 돌아올 거예요.
11 창밖을 봐. 너는 지금 눈이 내리는 것을 볼 수 있어.
해설 지각동사 see는 동작이 진행 중인 것을 강조할 때 목적격보어 자리에 현재분사를 쓴다.
12 Sophia는 그녀의 여동생이 그녀의 원피스를 입는 것을 허락해 주었다.
해설 사역동사 let은 목적격보어 자리에 동사원형을 쓴다.
13 나의 삼촌은 그의 아들을 Andrew라고 이름 짓기로 결정하셨다.
14 그 요리사는 파티에 있는 사람들에게 소고기와 닭고기를 요리해 주었다.
해설 동사 cook은 3형식 문장으로 쓸 때 간접목적어 앞에 전치사 for를 쓴다.
15 너는 나에게 네 새 자전거를 보여줄 수 있니?
해설 동사 show는 3형식 문장으로 쓸 때 간접목적어 앞에 전치사 to를 쓴다.
16 〈보기〉 주방에서 무언가가 타고 있었다. 나는 그 냄새를 맡았다.
   → 나는 주방에서 무언가가 타고 있는 냄새를 맡았다.
   두 사람이 그들의 연을 날리고 있었다. 나는 그들을 봤다.
   → 나는 두 사람이 그들의 연을 날리고 있는 것을 봤다.

17

나의 크리스마스 선물들

(1)	나의 할머니로부터	새 신발
(2)	나의 친구로부터	야구모자

(1) 나의 할머니는 크리스마스에 나에게 새 신발을 보내 주셨다.
(2) 나의 친구는 크리스마스에 나에게 야구 모자를 사주었다.
19 해설 지각동사 hear의 목적격보어 자리에는 동사원형 또는 현재분사가 올 수 있다.

어휘 bark (개가) 짖다   loudly 큰 소리로
20 해설 사역동사 make는 목적격보어 자리에 동사원형을 쓴다.
21 해설 동사 advise는 목적격보어 자리에 to부정사를 쓴다.
22 해설 동사 tell이 '～가 …하도록 말하다'의 의미를 나타낼 때는 목적격보어 자리에 to부정사를 쓴다.
23 Laura와 너는 자매처럼 보인다.
해설 '～처럼 보이다'의 의미는 뒤에 명사 보어를 취하므로 look like로 써야 한다.
24 그 분홍색 스웨터는 너에게 아름다워 보인다.
해설 감각동사 look 뒤에는 보어로 형용사를 쓴다.
25 그는 슈퍼마켓에서 그의 아들에게 과자를 좀 사 주었다.
해설 동사 buy는 3형식 문장으로 쓸 때 간접목적어 앞에 전치사 for를 쓴다.
26 나는 Jamie에게 교실에서 조용히 해달라고 부탁했다.
해설 동사 ask는 목적격보어 자리에 to부정사를 쓴다.
27 갑자기, Lily는 그녀의 머리 위에 비가 떨어지는 것을 느꼈다.
해설 지각동사 feel의 목적격보어 자리에는 동사원형이나 동작의 진행을 강조하는 현재분사를 써야 한다.
어휘 suddenly 갑자기
28 엄마: 나는 오늘 밤에 늦을 거야. Chloe, 네 여동생 Emma를 위해 저녁 식사를 만들어주렴.
    Chloe: 물론이에요. 걱정하지 마세요, 엄마.
    엄마: 그리고 Chloe, Emma, 너희 둘은 오늘 숙제를 끝내야 해.
    Chloe, Emma: 알겠어요, 엄마.
    (1) 엄마는 Chloe에게 그녀의 동생을 위해 저녁 식사를 만들어 달라고 말씀하셨다.
    (2) 엄마는 Chloe와 Emma에게 (오늘) 숙제를 끝내도록 시키셨다.
어휘 get it 이해하다, 알아듣다

STAGE 3

29 (1) made him throw away the trash
    (2) had him feed the cat
    (3) let him read comic books for an hour
30 (1) asked Kate[her] to bring a camera tomorrow
    (2) wanted Kate[her] to take pictures of teachers
31 ⓑ → Eric heard Susie play[playing] the violin.
   ⓓ → They will buy their daughter a new bike.
   또는 They will buy a new bike for their daughter.

29

준호의 일정

아침에	쓰레기 버리기
오후에	고양이에게 먹이주기
저녁에	한 시간 동안 만화책 읽기

(1) 준호의 어머니는 그가 아침에 쓰레기를 버리도록 하셨다.
(2) 준호의 어머니는 그가 오후에 고양이에게 먹이를 주게 시키셨다.
(3) 준호의 어머니는 저녁에 그가 한 시간 동안 만화책을 읽는 것을 허락하셨다.
어휘 throw away ～을 버리다   trash 쓰레기   feed 먹이를 주다
30 Kate: 안녕, Dan. 너희들은 뭐 하고 있니?
    Dan: 안녕, Kate. 우리는 스승의 날을 준비하고 있어.
    Kate: 오, 너는 도움이 필요하니?
    Dan: 내일 카메라를 가져와 줄 수 있어?
    Kate: 물론이지, 나는 카메라가 하나 있어.
    Dan: 잘됐다! 네 카메라로 선생님들의 사진을 찍어줄래?
    Kate: 나 믿어봐. 나는 사진을 잘 찍어.
해설 동사 ask, want 뒤에 목적어 Kate[her]를 쓰고 Dan이 Kate에게 부탁한 내용을 to부정사를 사용해 쓴다.
31 ⓐ 그의 삼촌은 그에게 책장을 만들어 주셨다.
   ⓑ Eric은 수지가 바이올린을 연주하는 것을 들었다.
   ⓒ 나의 아빠는 주말마다 우리에게 저녁을 만들어주신다.

ⓓ 그들은 그들의 딸에게 새 자전거를 사줄 것이다.
ⓔ 나의 형은 나에게 개를 산책시켜 달라고 말했다.
[해설] ⓑ 지각동사 hear의 목적격보어 자리에는 동사원형 또는 현재분사가 올 수 있다.

ⓓ 동사 buy는 「주어+buy+간접목적어+직접목적어」의 순서로 쓴다. 또는 「주어+buy+직접목적어+for+간접목적어」의 어순으로 쓸 수 있다.
[어휘] bookshelf 책장, 책꽂이

Chapter 02 | 시제

Unit 01 현재, 과거, 미래 & 진행형

POINT 1 p.27

1 bought some flowers
2 got a present
3 will cook
4 brushes her teeth
5 broke the glass
6 is going to introduce
7 The singer performs new songs
8 I found an old photo
9 Mike is going to finish his homework
10 (1) He took a bus
   (2) He is[He's] going to go to bed early
      또는 He will[He'll] go to bed early

10 호준이는 보통 걸어서 학교에 간다. 오늘, 그는 아침에 늦게 일어났다. 그는 학교까지 버스를 탔다. 운 좋게도, 그는 늦지 않았다. 그는 오늘밤 일찍 잘 것이다.

POINT 2 p.29

1 They are cleaning the classroom
2 Mia is chatting with her friends
3 The girls were watching the musical
4 I am[I'm] lying on a sofa.
5 A man was working with his laptop
6 Lisa is watering the flowers
7 My parents were planning their vacation together.
8 following
9 were jogging[jogged]
10 (1) I am[I'm] doing my homework.
   (2) I was practicing the piano

8 학생들은 규칙을 따르지 않고 있다.
9 Sam과 나는 오늘 아침에 공원에서 조깅을 하고 있었다[했다].
10 A: Kevin, 넌 무엇을 하고 있니?
   B: 나는 내 숙제를 하고 있어.
   A: 너는 오늘 아침에 그것을 끝내지 않았니?
   B: 응, 그렇지 않았어. 나는 그때 피아노를 연습하고 있었어.

Unit 02 현재완료의 개념과 형태

POINT 3 p.31

1 have been
2 has read
3 has gone
4 have, arrived
5 have, watched
6 Have, seen
7 I have[I've] taken swimming lessons
8 The cook has prepared the meal
9 He has not[hasn't] called me
10 caught
11 haven't eaten
12 moved
13 (1) Mr. Brown has taught history
   (2) We have not[haven't] bought the concert tickets

1 나는 작년부터 독서 동아리에 있었다.
2 그는 이 책을 세 번 읽었다.
3 Emily는 그녀의 조부모님을 뵈러 갔다.
4 관광객들이 호텔에 막 도착했다.
5 나는 공포 영화를 본 적이 없다.
6 너는 밤에 별똥별을 본 적이 있니?
10 Jason은 물고기를 잡아본 적이 없다.
   [해설] 현재완료 부정문 형태인 「have[has]+not/never」가 쓰였으므로, 그 뒤에는 catch의 p.p.형태인 caught를 써야 한다.
11 우리는 아직 저녁을 먹지 않았다.
   [해설] 주어 We는 1인칭 복수이므로 hasn't가 아닌 haven't로 고쳐 써야 한다.
12 그녀는 2년 전에 새로운 도시로 이사 갔다.
   [해설] 과거를 나타내는 two years ago는 현재완료와 함께 쓸 수 없으므로 has moved를 과거형인 moved로 고쳐 써야 한다.

Unit 03 현재완료의 주요 의미

POINT 4 p.33

1 He has never tried skydiving
2 My brother has had a cold for two weeks
3 I have not eaten meat since last year
4 has rained
5 has worked at this company

6 Have you ever raised a pet?
7 has played the drums since 2020
8 We have[We've] been to other countries many times.
9 has learned Spanish for two years

4 일주일 전에 비가 내리기 시작했다. 아직 비가 오고 있다.
→ 일주일 동안 비가 내렸다.
5 그녀는 작년에 이 회사에서 일하기 시작했다.
그녀는 아직 거기서 일한다.
→ 그녀는 작년부터 이 회사에서 일해왔다.
9 Paul은 2년 전에 스페인어를 배우기 시작했다.
그는 아직 그것을 배운다.
→ Paul은 2년 동안 스페인어를 배웠다.
해설 2년 전부터 지금까지 스페인어를 배워온 것이므로 현재완료형인 「have[has]+p.p.」로 쓴다. 2년이라는 기간 앞에는 전치사 for를 써야 한다.

POINT 5 p.35

1 I have already finished my homework
2 Someone has stolen my cell phone
3 They have not found a solution yet
4 Nick has lost his umbrella.
5 We have[We've] already seen that movie.
6 The bakery has just sold all of its bread.
7 My classmate has broken my glasses
8 The train has not[hasn't] left the station yet.
9 (1) They have[They've] just returned from their trip to Japan.
(2) She has[She's] gone to Africa to volunteer.

Chapter Test p.36

STAGE 1

1 takes place **2** is waiting in line
3 has taken care of **4** was listening to music
5 will travel around the country
6 are going to visit my house tomorrow
7 have just sent an email to my teacher
8 has been to Busan three times
9 (1) I went to Italy
(2) I have never been there

1 어휘 take place 개최되다, 열리다
2 어휘 wait in line 줄 서서 기다리다
8 해설 '~에 가봤다'는 경험의 의미를 나타낼 때는 have[has] been to를 쓴다.
9 A: 나는 나의 부모님과 함께 지난달에 이탈리아에 갔었어.
B: 오 정말? 어땠니? 나는 그곳에 한 번도 가 본 적이 없어.
A: 환상적이었어! 우리는 아주 즐거운 시간을 보냈어.

STAGE 2

10 I usually read a newspaper
11 I am[I'm] watching my favorite TV show
12 I was doing my homework
13 has lived in Seoul since 2023
14 Have you (ever) heard of
15 is **16** to start
17 haven't seen **18** lost
19 (1) She has long brown hair.
(2) She is[She's] wearing a yellow T-shirt and jeans.
20 Jihun has used the laptop since 2022.
21 I have[I've] taught English for three years.
22 My mom has lost her wallet.
23 He has[He's] worked at the school for a month.
24 We have[We've] (just) finished the class meeting.
25 (1) was cooking some chicken
(2) is talking on the phone
(3) are going to shop together
26 (1) We have[We've] known each other since 2022.
(2) We have[We've] won many games before.

10 A: 너는 일요일 아침에 보통 무엇을 하니?
B: 나는 보통 아침 식사 전에 신문을 읽어.
해설 반복되는 일이나 습관에 대해 말할 땐 현재시제를 쓴다. 빈도부사 usually는 일반동사 앞에 쓴다.
11 A: 너는 지금 TV를 보고 있니?
B: 응, 나는 내가 가장 좋아하는 TV 쇼를 보고 있어.
12 A: 너는 어젯밤 9시에 무엇을 하고 있었니?
B: 나는 그때 나의 숙제를 하고 있었어.
13 A: Wilson 씨는 서울에서 얼마나 오랫동안 살았니?
B: 그는 2023년부터 서울에서 살고 있어.
해설 기간을 나타내는 How long을 사용해서 현재완료로 묻고 있으므로 현재완료로 대답해야 한다.
14 A: 너는 스테판 커리에 대해서 들어 본 적이 있니?
B: 응, 있어. 그는 미국의 유명한 농구 선수야.
어휘 hear of ~에 대해 듣다
15 지구는 공처럼 둥글다.
해설 변함없는 일반적인 진리를 나타낼 때는 현재시제를 써야 한다.
어휘 round 둥근, 원형의
16 그들은 내년에 새로운 사업을 시작할 것이다.
17 나는 내 옛 친구를 5년 동안 보지 못했다.
18 우리는 어젯밤에 우리 방 열쇠를 잃어버렸다.
해설 현재완료 시제는 과거를 나타내는 부사구와 함께 쓰지 않는다.
19 A: 실례합니다. 저는 제 여동생을 찾고 있어요. 저를 도와주실 수 있나요?
B: 물론이죠. 그녀의 이름은 무엇인가요?
A: 그녀의 이름은 Isabel이에요. 그녀는 7살이에요. 그녀는 긴 갈색 머리를 가지고 있어요.
B: 그녀는 오늘 무엇을 입고 있나요?
A: 그녀는 노란색 티셔츠와 청바지를 입고 있어요.
어휘 look for ~을 찾다
[20~24] 〈보기〉 Jane은 어제 아프기 시작했다.
그녀는 지금 여전히 아팠다.
→ Jane은 어제부터 아팠다.
20 지훈이는 2022년에 노트북 컴퓨터를 쓰기 시작했다. 그는 여전히 그것을 쓴다.
→ 지훈이는 2022년부터 노트북 컴퓨터를 써왔다.
21 나는 3년 전에 영어를 가르치기 시작했다. 나는 여전히 그것을 가르친다.
→ 나는 3년 동안 영어를 가르쳐왔다.
22 나의 엄마는 그녀의 지갑을 잃어버리셨다. 그녀는 지금 그것을

가지고 있지 않으시다.
→ 나의 엄마는 그녀의 지갑을 잃어버리셨다.
어휘 wallet 지갑

23 그는 한 달 전에 학교에서 일하기 시작했다. 그는 여전히 그곳에서 일한다.
→ 그는 한 달 동안 학교에서 일해왔다.

24 우리는 한 시간 전에 학급 회의를 시작했다. 우리는 지금 막 그것을 끝마쳤다.
→ 우리는 학급 회의를 (막) 끝마쳤다.
해설 완료를 나타내는 현재완료를 쓴다. 이때, just는 have 뒤에 쓰고, 과거를 나타내는 an hour ago는 현재완료와 함께 쓸 수 없으므로 생략한다.

25

시간	Oliver	Chloe
오전 10시	닭 요리하기	요가하기
오후 2시 (현재)	잡지 읽기	통화하기
오후 7시	함께 쇼핑하기	

(1) Q: Oliver는 아침 10시에 무엇을 하고 있었니?
　　A: 그는 닭을 요리하고 있었어.
(2) Q: Chloe는 현재 무엇을 하고 있니?
　　A: 그녀는 통화를 하고 있는 중이야.
(3) Q: Oliver와 Chloe는 저녁 7시에 무엇을 할 예정이니?
　　A: 그들은 함께 쇼핑을 할 예정이야.

26 Hannah와 나는 같은 배구팀이다. 우리는 2022년부터 서로를 알고 지내왔다. 우리는 항상 함께 연습하고 훌륭한 팀워크를 가지고 있다. 우리는 이전에 많은 경기에서 이겼다.
어휘 volleyball 배구

27 (1) Have you, ridden, Yes, I have
　　(2) haven't, He has gone to, went
28 (1) has studied
　　(2) has visited
　　(3) has not[hasn't] finished

27 (1) A: 너는 말을 타 본 적이 있니?
　　 B: 응, 있어. 나는 제주도에서 처음으로 말을 탔어.
(2) A: 나는 오랫동안 현수를 보지 못했어.
　　 B: 그는 뉴욕에 갔어.
　　 A: 정말? 그는 거기에 왜 갔니?
　　 B: 그는 영어를 공부하기 위해 그곳에 갔어.
해설 현수가 뉴욕에 가서 지금 없는 것이므로 결과를 나타내는 현재완료 has gone to를 써야 한다.

28

날짜	일정
10/1	프랑스어 공부 시작
10/5	처음으로 놀이공원 방문
10/10	*어린 왕자* 읽기 시작
10/12	프랑스어 공부
10/22 (오늘)	프랑스어 공부 & *어린 왕자* 읽기
10/25	*어린 왕자* 읽기

　　지우는 10월 1일에 프랑스어를 공부하기 시작했다. 그녀는 3주 동안 프랑스어를 공부했다. 그녀는 10월에 놀이공원을 한 번 방문했다. 그녀는 요즘 *어린 왕자*를 읽고 있다. 그러나 그녀는 아직 그것을 다 읽지 못했다. 그녀는 그것을 나중에 마칠 예정이다.
어휘 amusement park 놀이공원

29 ⓒ → she let us set the table
　　 ⓔ → My parents have already planned many exciting activities for us

29 　여름 방학 동안, 나의 가족은 해변으로 여행을 갔다. 날씨는 완벽했고, 우리는 바다에서 수영을 하며 시간을 보냈다. 오후에는 엄마가 우리에게 맛있는 해산물을 요리해 주셨다. 그다음 그녀는 우리가 식탁을 차리도록 시키셨다. 나중엔 우리는 아름다운 석양을 감상했다.
　　내년 여름에, 우리는 새로운 도시를 방문할 것이다. 나의 부모님은 이미 우리를 위해 많은 재미있는 활동들을 계획하셨다.
해설 ⓒ 사역동사 let은 목적격보어 자리에 동사원형을 써야 한다.
ⓔ 현재완료는 「have[has]+과거분사(p.p.)」 형태로 쓰며, 이때 주어(My parents)가 3인칭 복수이므로 has는 have로 고쳐 써야 한다.
어휘 ocean 바다, 대양　seafood 해산물　sunset 석양

Chapter 03 | 조동사

Unit 01　can/may/will

p.43

1 The basketball player can jump very high
2 I could not lift the heavy box
3 Are you able to solve this math problem
4 My little sister was not able to tie her shoes
5 Can you make it on time?
6 Students can get a 50% discount
7 Carl is able to swim across the lake.
8 The boy was not[wasn't] able to solve the puzzles.
9 Every child will be able to find their dreams

9 해설 '~할 수 있을 것이다'라는 미래의 능력·가능은 「will be able to+동사원형」으로 나타낸다.

1 We may put off the class meeting
2 Tourists may take this map and a guide book
3 My little brother may not need the toys anymore
4 You may use the restroom over there.
5 She may know the answer to the question.
6 Our team may not win the match
7 Sofia and Tony may join the dance club.
8 May I use this computer for a while?
9 The girl may[might] become an excellent movie director

1 You can take your exam paper
2 Can I try on this shirt in a different size
3 Could you hold this bag for a while
4 Would you show me your ticket
5 You cannot[can't] leave your seat
6 Can we take a break for a few minutes?
7 Can[Will] you recommend a dish for us?
8 Our team will not[won't] repeat the same mistake.
9 Can I borrow a phone charger for a moment?

Unit 02 must/have to/should

1 You must not run on the escalator
2 Suna has to take care of her cousins
3 You should put the items in their original place
4 Teenagers have to get enough sleep.
5 You must remember your ID and password.
6 He had to get a new passport for his trip.
7 It must be closed
8 Students should not[shouldn't] use their cell phones
9 Elly has to practice her speech
10 should not[shouldn't] ride a bike

10 A: 이 장소는 자전거를 타기에 좋아.
B: 봐, 표지판이 있어. 너는 여기서 자전거를 타지 말아야 해.
해설 문맥상 '~하지 말아야 한다'라는 금지를 나타내야 하므로 부정형 should not[shouldn't]를 써야 한다.

1 You don't have to answer right now
2 I don't have to finish my homework by this weekend
3 They didn't have to wait in line
4 You don't[do not] have to water this plant every day.

5 He doesn't[does not] have to wear a school uniform
6 Parents don't[do not] have to attend the meeting.
7 Lily doesn't[does not] have to take the school bus.
8 We didn't[did not] have to worry about the weather.
9 has to sign up, doesn't[does not] have to pay

Unit 03 had better/would like to/used to

1 You had better take your medicine
2 We had better not believe the rumor
3 You had better buy the concert ticket early
4 We had[We'd] better not miss the last train.
5 Ted had better apologize for his mistake.
6 You had[You'd] better be careful with that glass.
7 You had[You'd] better not sit too close to the TV.
8 You had better eat fruit

8 A: Andy, 나는 네가 요즘 단것을 너무 많이 먹는다고 생각해.
B: 맞아, 나는 그것을 멈출 수 없어.
A: 그것은 너의 건강에 좋지 않아. 너는 과일을 대신 먹는 게 좋겠어.

1 Our family used to eat out
2 She would like to visit Paris
3 Would you like to join our study group
4 My brother used to be afraid of the dark
5 This building used to be a library
6 I would[I'd] like to order a cup of coffee.
7 My dad and I used to go fishing
8 Would you like to go for a walk in the park?
9 We would like to volunteer at the community center

Chapter Test   p.56

1 has to visit the dentist next week
2 Would you fasten your seat belt
3 should not waste her allowance
4 may not delay our appointment again
5 Can you explain this movie
6 Everyone must leave this building
7 had better take a rest for a while
8 Can you ride a skateboard

1 어휘 (the) dentist 치과; 치과 의사
2 어휘 seat belt 안전벨트   fasten 매다

3 어휘 waste 낭비하다   allowance 용돈

4 어휘 delay 미루다, 연기하다   appointment 약속

5 어휘 explain 설명하다

7 어휘 take a rest 휴식을 취하다, 쉬다

8 A: 너는 스트레스를 받을 때 무엇을 하니?
B: 나는 스트레스를 받을 때 스케이트보드를 타.
너는 스케이트보드를 탈 수 있니?
A: 아니, 그렇지 않아.
B: 같이 밖에 나가자! 내가 너를 가르쳐줄게.
어휘 stressed 스트레스를 받는

STAGE 2

9 Nate has to buy a ticket to enter the zoo.

10 You may not play loud music after 10 p.m.

11 She used to live in New York.

12 Susan was not[wasn't] able to attend the class meeting.

13 We would[We'd] like to adopt a puppy from the shelter.

14 had better not use plastic bags

15 (1) may rain soon
(2) had better see a doctor
(3) may not bring food or drinks

16 Will you have some more juice

17 He may like reading books

18 You had better not eat hamburgers too often

19 You don't have to bring anything

20 went → go   **21** may is → may be

22 have not to → don't[do not] have to

23 will must → will have to

24 (1) has to return the books
(2) doesn't have to go

9 Nate는 동물원에 들어가기 위해 표를 사야 한다.
해설 주어가 3인칭 단수이므로 has to를 써야 한다.

10 너는 밤 10시 이후에는 시끄러운 음악을 틀면 안 된다.

11 그녀는 뉴욕에 살았다. 지금, 그녀는 뉴욕에 살지 않는다.
→ 그녀는 뉴욕에 살았었다.

12 Susan은 학급 회의에 참석할 수 없었다.
해설 조동사 can은 be able to로 바꿔 쓸 수 있는데, 주어가 3인칭 단수이며 과거시제이므로 was not[wasn't] able to로 써야 한다.
어휘 attend 참석하다

13 우리는 보호소에서 강아지를 입양하고 싶다.
어휘 adopt 입양하다   shelter 보호소

14 〈보기〉 우리는 밖에 나갈 때 불을 꺼야 한다.
우리는 비닐 봉투를 사용하지 않는 게 좋겠다.

15 (1) 하늘이 어둡다. 곧 비가 올지도 모른다.
(2) 너는 오늘 몸이 안 좋아 보여. 너는 병원에 가는 게 좋겠어.
(3) 너는 로비에서 간식을 먹을 수 있다. 하지만 너는 도서관 안으로 음식이나 마실 것을 가져오면 안 된다.
어휘 snack 간식   lobby (건물의) 로비

16 A: 주스를 좀 더 마시겠니?
B: 아, 고마워. 하지만 난 물을 좀 마시고 싶어.
A: 물론이지. 여기 있어.

17 A: 내일은 호진이의 생일이야. 난 무엇을 사야 할지 모르겠어.
B: 나는 전에 그의 집에 가본 적이 있어. 그의 방은 책들로 가득 차 있었어. 그는 책 읽는 것을 좋아할지도 몰라.
A: 알겠어. 나는 그럼 그에게 책을 사 줄게.

18 A: 너 또 햄버거를 먹고 있구나.
B: 나는 햄버거를 정말 좋아해.

A: 하지만 그건 너의 건강에 좋지 않아. 너는 햄버거를 너무 자주 먹지 않는 게 좋겠어.

19 A: 파티는 5시 정각에 시작해.
B: 알겠어. 난 무엇을 가져가야 하니?
A: 너는 아무것도 가져올 필요 없어. 내가 모든 걸 준비했어.
어휘 prepare 준비하다

20 지금 너무 늦었기 때문에 우리는 집에 가는 게 낫겠다.
해설 조동사 had better 뒤에는 동사원형을 써야 한다.

21 나의 언니는 피곤할지도 모른다. 왜냐하면 그녀는 이제 막 기말 시험을 끝냈기 때문이다.
해설 조동사 may 뒤에는 동사원형이 와야 하므로 be를 써야 한다.
어휘 final 마지막의

22 너는 연필을 빌릴 필요가 없어. 내가 두 자루를 갖고 있어.
해설 '~할 필요가 없다'라는 의미를 나타낼 때는 don't[do not] have to를 쓴다.

23 너는 다음 역에서 열차를 갈아타야 할 것이다.
해설 조동사는 두 개를 연달아 쓸 수 없으므로 must는 have to로 고쳐 써야 한다.
어휘 station 역, 정거장

24 Brenda에게,
책들을 도서관에 반납하렴. 게다가, 너는 오늘 수영 연습에 갈 필요 없단다. 그것은 취소되었거든.
엄마가
(1) Brenda는 도서관에 책들을 반납해야 한다.
(2) Brenda는 오늘 수영 연습에 갈 필요가 없다.
어휘 cancel 취소하다

STAGE 3

25 (1) You had better have a meal three times a day.
(2) You had better not talk on the phone too long.
(3) You had better not buy too many clothes every month.
(4) You had better do laundry every week.

26 ⓓ → be able to find
ⓔ → don't[do not] have to be

25

습관	예	아니오
규칙적으로 운동하기		V
(1) 하루에 세 번 식사하기		V
(2) 너무 오래 전화 통화하기	V	
(3) 매달 너무 많은 옷을 사기	V	
(4) 매주 빨래하기		V

〈보기〉 너는 규칙적으로 운동하는 게 좋겠다.
(1) 너는 하루에 세 번 식사를 하는 게 좋겠다.
(2) 너는 너무 오래 전화 통화하지 않는 게 좋겠다.
(3) 너는 매달 너무 많은 옷을 사지 않는 게 좋겠다.
(4) 너는 매주 빨래를 하는 게 좋겠다.
어휘 regularly 규칙적으로   meal 식사   laundry 세탁

26 Mike: 너는 오늘 기분이 좋지 않아 보여. 무슨 일 있니, Brian?
Brian: 나의 친구가 부산으로 이사를 갈 예정이야. 그것은 나를 정말 슬프게 해.
Mike: 힘내. 너는 방학 때 그를 방문할 수 있어.
Brian: 알아. 하지만 난 더 이상 그와 함께 축구를 할 수 없어.
Mike: 너는 함께 축구를 할 또 다른 친구를 곧 찾을 수 있을 거야. 너는 너무 슬퍼할 필요가 없어.
Brian: 네 말이 맞아. 고마워, Mike.
해설 ⓓ 조동사 will이 앞에 있으므로 can을 연달아 쓸 수 없다. '~할 수 있을 것이다'라는 의미는 will be able to로 나타낸다.
ⓔ Mike가 슬퍼하는 Brian을 위로해주는 말이므로 '~할 필요가 없다'라는 의미의 don't[do not] have to를 쓰는 것이 적절하다.

27 ⓒ →We have to be quiet on the subway.
　　ⓔ →Have you ever seen the sunrise at the beach?

27 ⓐ 너는 학교에 지각해서는 안 된다.
　　ⓑ Tom은 지난주에 그의 팔이 부러졌다.
　　ⓒ 우리는 지하철에서 조용히 해야 한다.
　　ⓓ 나는 손님들이 오후 7시쯤 도착할 것으로 예상한다.

ⓔ 너는 해변에서 일출을 본 적이 있니?
해설 ⓒ '~해야 한다'라는 의미의 have to 뒤에는 동사원형을 써야 한다.
ⓔ 현재완료 의문문은 「Have[Has]+주어+p.p. ~?」의 형태이므로 see는 과거분사형인 seen으로 고쳐 써야 한다.
어휘 sunrise 일출, 해돋이

Chapter 04 | 수동태

Unit 01 수동태의 기본 이해

POINT 1　　　　　　　　　　　　　　　　　　　p.63

1 is read by lots of people
2 are loved by their parents
3 The flowers are grown by my mom
4 The old men are helped by volunteers
5 The teacher is respected by the students.
6 Dinner is cooked by my dad.
7 Some animals are protected by the country.
8 A lot of money is spent on education
9 France is visited by many people around the world.
10 different topics are discussed

10 A: 지나야, 나는 너희 토론 동아리에 가입하고 싶어. 너희는 어떤 종류의 주제들을 토론하니?
B: 영화, 자연, 그리고 문화와 같은 많은 다양한 주제들이 있어. 매주 월요일에, 다른 주제들이 토의 돼.

POINT 2　　　　　　　　　　　　　　　　　　　p.65

1 The letter was written by my best friend
2 Hangeul was created by King Sejong
3 Everyone will be invited to the Christmas party
4 Our new house was built by my grandfather.
5 This year's talent show will be judged by the teachers.
6 The soccer match was canceled[cancelled]
7 The picture was moved to the bedroom.
8 The winner will be chosen by the judges.
9 they were baked by my mom

4 나의 할아버지는 우리의 새 집을 지으셨다.
→ 우리의 새 집은 나의 할아버지에 의해 지어졌다.

5 그 선생님들은 올해의 장기자랑을 심사하실 것이다.
→ 올해의 장기자랑은 그 선생님들에 의해 심사될 것이다.
9 A: 이 쿠키들은 아주 달콤해. 네가 그것들을 직접 만들었니?
B: 아니, 그것들은 나의 엄마에 의해 구워졌어.

Unit 02 수동태의 여러 가지 형태

POINT 3　　　　　　　　　　　　　　　　　　　p.67

1 Your room must be cleaned
2 Breakfast is not served
3 Was the movie watched by many people
4 Our memories will not be forgotten
5 The building was not designed by experts
6 Those products are not[aren't] made
7 The monkeys were not[weren't] raised in the zoo.
8 When was the Statue of Liberty built?
9 The work will not[won't] be finished
10 Where was the hidden treasure found?

10 해설 의문사가 있는 수동태의 의문문은 「의문사+be동사+주어+과거분사(p.p) ~?」의 어순으로 쓴다.

POINT 4　　　　　　　　　　　　　　　　　　　p.69

1 We were given an important message
2 A surprising photo was shown to the public
3 I was told good stories by my grandma
4 The shoes were bought for me
5 He was given a lot of presents
6 Sandwiches are made for us
7 A strange letter was sent to me
8 A special dish is given to the guests
9 The food was brought to us
10 (1) The tourists were shown the palace
　　(2) The palace was shown to the tourists

5 그의 친구들은 그에게 많은 선물들을 주었다.

→ 그는 그의 친구들에 의해 많은 선물들을 받았다.

6 아빠는 매주 일요일 아침에 우리에게 샌드위치를 만들어 주신다.

→ 샌드위치는 아빠에 의해 매주 일요일 아침에 우리에게 만들어진다.

7 누군가 나에게 수상한 편지를 보냈다.

→ 수상한 편지가 누군가에 의해 나에게 보내졌다.

8 요리사는 손님들에게 특별한 요리를 제공한다.

→ 특별한 요리는 요리사에 의해 손님들에게 제공된다.

9 웨이터가 우리에게 그 음식을 가져다주었다.

→ 그 음식은 웨이터에 의해 우리에게 전달되었다.

10 가이드는 관광객들에게 궁전을 보여주었다.

(1) 관광객들은 가이드에 의해 그 궁전을 보게 되었다.

(2) 그 궁전은 가이드에 의해 관광객들에게 보여졌다.

[해설] (2) 직접목적어를 주어로 하는 수동태 문장에서는 간접목적어 앞에 전치사를 써야 한다. be shown은 전치사 to와 함께 쓰인다.

POINT 5　　　　　　　　　　p.71

1 was made of glass

2 was pleased with her birthday gift

3 was crowded with a lot of people

4 was covered with thick fog

5 were surprised at my decision

6 My sister is interested in art.

7 The bucket is filled with fish.

8 We are[We're] satisfied with our new house.

9 The restaurant is known for its seafood dishes.

10 His friendly manner is known to everybody.

Chapter Test　　　　　　　　p.72

STAGE 1

1 are worn by　　　　　**2** was taken by

3 is filled with　　　　**4** Were, broken by

5 is not provided by

6 is supported by many organizations

7 were loved by many children

8 should be recycled for the environment

9 (1) was invented　　　(2) was written

(3) were built

1 [어휘] uniform 교복

3 [해설] '~으로 가득 차 있다'는 be filled with를 사용해 나타낸다.

[어휘] bean 콩

4 [해설] 주어(these glasses)가 복수이고 과거시제인 수동태 의문문 이므로 Were these glasses broken ~?으로 써야 한다.

5 [어휘] provide 제공하다

6 [어휘] support 후원하다　organization 단체, 기구

7 [해설] 주어가 The magic tricks로 복수이고 과거시제이므로 were loved로 쓴다.

[어휘] trick 속임수; 재주

8 [해설] 「조동사＋be p.p.」의 형태로 쓴다.

[어휘] environment 환경　recycle 재활용하다

9 (1) 백열전구는 토마스 에디슨에 의해 발명되었다.

(2) 그 유명한 소설은 한국인 작가에 의해 쓰였다.

(3) 피라미드는 고대 이집트인들에 의해 지어졌다.

[어휘] invent 발명하다　light bulb 백열전구　novel 소설 author 작가, 저자　ancient 고대의　Egyptian 이집트 사람

STAGE 2

10 was found by　　　　**11** Was, elected

12 Were, watered　　　**13** was bought

14 When was, held

15 (1) will be planted　　(2) may be sent

(3) must be returned　(4) can be bought

16 (1) will be shown　　(2) was painted by

17 The park is closed by the guard

18 The school organized the first orchestra

19 I did not[didn't] write this letter.

20 The magazine will choose Jake as the Person of the Year.

21 An amusement park will be built by the city

22 fix → fixed　　　　**23** did → was

24 as → to　　　　　**25** paint → be painted

26 the telephone was → was the telephone

27 I am[I'm] interested in cameras and photography.

10 A: 누가 내 지갑을 발견했니?

B: 네 지갑은 나의 형에 의해 발견되었어.

11 A: Luna는 팀 리더로 선출되었니?

B: 응, 그랬어. 그녀는 지난주에 선출되었어.

[해설] be동사 과거형을 사용해 Yes, she was.로 대답하고 있으므로, 과거시제 수동태 의문문인 Was Luna elected ~?로 써야 한다.

[어휘] elect 선출하다

12 A: 저 꽃들은 너희 엄마에 의해 물이 주어졌니?

B: 아니, 그렇지 않아. 내가 그것들에 물을 줬어.

13 A: 그는 언제 그 차를 구매했니?

B: 그 차는 2년 전 그에 의해 구매되었어.

14 A: 음식 축제는 언제 열렸니?

B: 그건 일주일 전에 열렸어.

15 [어휘] plant 심다; 식물　event 행사; 사건　detail 세부 사항

16 유명한 그림이 다음 달 현대 미술관에서 보여질 것입니다. 그림의 제목은 별이 빛나는 밤입니다. 그것은 1889년에 빈센트 반 고흐에 의해 그려졌습니다. 이 놀라운 예술 작품을 놓치지 마세요!

[어휘] title 제목　artwork 예술품, 미술품

17 경비원은 매일 밤 10시에 공원을 닫는다.

→ 공원은 경비원에 의해 매일 밤 10시에 닫힌다.

[어휘] guard 경비원

18 최초의 오케스트라는 작년 9월에 학교에 의해 조직되었다.

→ 학교는 작년 9월에 최초의 오케스트라를 조직했다.

[어휘] organize (집단·팀 등을) 조직하다

19 이 편지는 나에 의해 쓰이지 않았다.

→ 나는 이 편지를 쓰지 않았다.

20 Jake는 그 잡지에 의해 올해의 인물로 선정될 것이다.

→ 그 잡지는 올해의 인물로 Jake를 선정할 것이다.

[어휘] magazine 잡지

21 그 도시는 내년에 놀이공원을 지을 것이다.

→ 놀이공원이 내년에 그 도시에 의해 지어질 것이다.

22 네 컴퓨터는 다음 주에 고쳐질 것이다.

[해설] 미래시제 수동태는 「will be＋p.p.」의 형태로 써야 하므로, fix를 fixed로 고쳐 써야 한다.

23 그 사과 주스는 나에 의해 마셔지지 않았다.

24 이 만화는 많은 어린이들에게 잘 알려져 있다.

[해설] '~에게 알려지다'라는 의미를 나타낼 때는 be known to를 쓴다.

[어휘] cartoon 만화

25 침실은 다음 주 주말까지 페인트칠 될 것이다.

　[해설] 주어인 The bedrooms는 동작 paint의 대상이 되므로 능동이 아닌 수동으로 쓰여야 한다.

26 전화는 어떻게 발명되었나요?

　[해설] 의문사를 포함하는 수동태 의문문이므로 「의문사＋be동사＋주어＋과거분사 ～?」의 어순으로 써야 한다.

27 A: Sally, 뭐하고 있어?

　B: 나는 나의 관심사에 대한 발표를 준비하는 중이야.

　A: 너의 관심사는 무엇이니?

　B: 나는 카메라와 사진에 관심이 있어.

　　하지만 나는 나의 발표 때문에 긴장 돼.

　A: 너는 잘할 거야. 걱정하지 마.

　[어휘] prepare 준비하다　presentation 발표, 프레젠테이션　photography 사진

28 (1) was written by　　(2) was published

　(3) was filmed　　(4) was directed by

29 ⓒ → All of us will be invited to her house.

　ⓔ → They were made by Somi.

28

해리포터와 불의 잔	
(1) 작가	J. K. Rowling
(2) 출간	2000
(3) 영화화	2005
(4) 감독	Mike Newell

(1) 해리포터와 불의 잔은 J. K. Rowling에 의해 쓰였다.

(2) 그것은 2000년에 출간되었다.

(3) 그것은 2005년에 영화화되었다.

(4) 그 영화는 Mike Newell에 의해 감독 되었다.

　[어휘] film 영화화하다; 영화　director (영화 등의) 감독

29 A: 너 그거 들었어? 소미가 다른 도시로 이사 갈 거래! 나는 그 소식에 놀랐어.

　B: 응. 들었어. 소미에 의해 작별 파티가 열릴 거야. 우리 모두 그녀의 집에 초대될 거야.

　A: 정말? 그거 좋겠다.

　B: 초대장이 이번 주말에 우리에게 보내질 거야. 그것들은 소미에 의해 만들어졌어.

　A: 알겠어. 내 것을 얼른 받고 싶다.

　[해설] ⓒ 문맥상 주어인 All of us는 초대되는 것이므로 능동이 아닌 수동인 will be invited가 되어야 한다.

　ⓔ be made from은 '～으로 만들어지다'라는 뜻이므로 행위자 Somi 앞에는 from이 아닌 by를 써야 한다.

　[어휘] farewell 작별　invitation 초대, 초대장　receive 받다, 얻다

30 ⓑ → My car might not be repaired today.

　ⓓ → My friend and I had fun last night.

30 ⓐ 나의 삼촌은 2007년부터 그의 회사에서 일해 오셨다.

　ⓑ 나의 차는 오늘 수리되지 않을지도 모른다.

　ⓒ 지나는 내일 병원에 가야 한다.

　ⓓ 내 친구와 나는 어젯밤에 즐거운 시간을 보냈다.

　ⓔ 휴가 기간 동안 그 공항은 여행객들로 붐볐다.

　[해설] ⓑ 조동사 수동태의 부정문은 「조동사＋not＋be p.p.」의 형태로 써야 한다.

　ⓓ 현재완료는 과거를 나타내는 부사구 last night와 함께 쓸 수 없으므로 현재완료를 과거시제로 고쳐 써야 한다.

　[어휘] repair 수리하다

Chapter 05 | to부정사

Unit 01　to부정사의 명사적 쓰임

POINT 1

p.79

1 To get up early is not easy

2 It is helpful to learn

3 It is surprising to see snow in April

4 It is important to listen to others

5 It is[It's] good to discover a new hobby.

6 It is[It's] dangerous to swim here.

7 It is[It's] impossible to live without water.

8 It is not[It isn't, It's not] safe to walk alone at night.

9 It was exciting to see the beautiful fireworks.

9 A: Sam, 너는 지난 주말에 불꽃 축제에 갔었니?

　B: 응, 그랬어. 아름다운 불꽃놀이를 보는 것은 재미있었어.

POINT 2

p.81

1 We like to play badminton

2 My next plan is to learn French

3 They agreed to discuss the problem

4 Susan hopes to be a movie director.

5 The student promised not to skip classes.

6 He planned to go to an amusement park.

7 I learned to manage my time better.

8 They chose to spend the weekend at the beach.

9 (1) I decided to exercise.

　(2) I want to stay healthy.

9 A: 지호야, 어디 가는 중이니?

　B: 나는 체육관에 가고 있어. 나는 운동하기로 결심했어.

　A: 너는 살을 뺄 거니?

　B: 아니, 그렇지 않아. 나는 건강을 유지하고 싶어.

10 A: Lily, 내가 이 카메라 사용하는 것 좀 도와줄래?
　 B: 물론이지. 뭐가 문제니?
　 A: 나는 사진을 어떻게 삭제하는지 모르겠어.
　 B: 너는 여기 "삭제하기" 버튼을 찾으면 돼.

Unit 02 to부정사의 형용사적 쓰임

Unit 03 to부정사의 부사적 쓰임

10 소희는 쉬고 싶었기 때문에 집에 일찍 왔다.
　 → 소희는 쉬기 위해서 집에 일찍 왔다.

Unit 04 to부정사를 포함한 주요 구문

7 Julie는 너무 피곤해서 운동을 할 수 없었다.
8 그는 다른 사람들을 가르칠 만큼 충분히 똑똑하다.
9 나의 부모님은 너무 바빠서 집에 일찍 오실 수 없었다.
10 A: 너 오늘 피곤해 보인다. 어제 잠은 잘 잤니?
　 B: 사실. 나는 어젯밤에 너무 걱정이 돼서 잠을 잘 수가 없었어.
　 해설 '너무 ～해서 …할 수 없었다'는 의미는 「too+형용사/부사
　 +to부정사」 또는 「so+형용사/부사+that+주어+couldn't」로
　 나타낸다. 8 단어로 써야 하므로 「too+형용사/부사+to부정사」를
　 써야 한다.

Chapter Test p.90

1 해설 to부정사는 대명사를 뒤에서 꾸며 줘야 한다.
3 해설 감정 형용사 happy 뒤에 to부정사를 써서 감정의 원인을
　 나타낸다.
4 해설 '어디에 ～할지'를 나타낼 때는 「where+to부정사」를 쓴다.
　 어휘 park 주차하다
6 어휘 language 언어
7 해설 '～할 만큼 충분히 …하다'는 의미를 나타낼 때는 「형용사/부
　 사+enough+to부정사」의 형태로 쓴다.
　 어휘 lift 들어 올리다
8 〈보기〉 수업 시간에는 규칙을 따르는 것이 필요하다.
　 다른 사람들의 의견을 존중하는 것은 중요하다.
　 어휘 follow 따르다; 따라가다　 rule 규칙, 원칙　 necessary 필요한
　 respect 존중하다　 opinion 의견

STAGE 3

27 해설 (1) '～하는 것은'의 의미를 to부정사를 사용해 나타낼 때는 주로 「가주어 It ~ to부정사 진주어」로 쓴다.
(2) '～하기 위해'라는 목적의 의미를 나타낼 때는 to부정사를 문장의 맨 앞이나 뒤에 쓴다.
(3) '～하고 싶다'는 「want+to부정사」로 나타내며, '～하는 방법'이라는 의미는 「how+to부정사」로 쓴다.
(4) '～하는, ～할'이라는 의미의 형용사적 쓰임의 to부정사는 「(대)명사+to부정사구」로 쓴다.
어휘 improve 향상시키다   knowledge 지식   guide 지도하다; 안내하다

28 해설 「형용사/부사+enough+to부정사」는 '～할 만큼 충분히 …하다'라는 의미로 「so+형용사/부사+that+주어+can」으로 바꿔 쓸 수 있다.
어휘 wise 현명한, 지혜로운   advice 조언, 충고

29 해설 '너무 ～해서 …할 수 없다'는 「too+형용사/부사+to부정사」 또는 「so+형용사/부사+that+주어+can't[cannot]+동사원형」으로 쓸 수 있다.

9 David는 컴퓨터를 어떻게 고쳐야 할지 모른다.
10 나는 오늘 무엇을 입을지 정하지 못하겠다.
11 점심 식사를 하러 어디서 만날지 정해줄래?
14 어휘 to-do list 해야 할 일 목록
15

〈Sally의 쇼핑 목록〉
☐ 책 한 권
☐ 펜 세 자루

(1) Sally는 읽을 책 한 권을 사야 한다.
(2) Sally는 가지고 쓸 펜 세 자루를 사야 한다.
해설 (2) three pens가 의미상 to부정사구의 전치사의 목적어이므로, to부정사(to write) 뒤에는 전치사 with를 써야 한다.

16 우리 모두는 가난한 사람들을 위해 돈을 좀 기부하기로 동의했다.
해설 agree는 to부정사를 목적어로 취하는 동사이다.
어휘 donate 기부하다

17 많은 친구들을 사귀기 위해서, 너는 다른 사람들의 말을 잘 경청하는 사람이 되어야 한다.
해설 목적의 의미를 더 확실히 나타낼 때 「in order+to부정사」의 형태로 쓸 수 있다.

18 그 여자아이는 너무 수줍어서 많은 사람들 앞에서 말할 수 없다.
해설 '너무 ～해서 …할 수 없다'는 의미를 나타낼 때는 「too+형용사/부사+to부정사」를 쓴다.

19 Jay는 지금 함께 놀 친구를 찾고 싶어 한다.
해설 명사 a friend를 to부정사가 뒤에서 수식해 '～와 함께 놀'이라는 의미가 되려면 to play 뒤에 전치사 with가 와야 한다.

20 나의 남동생은 투표할 만큼 충분히 나이가 많지 않다.
어휘 vote 투표하다

21 Dan은 그의 여동생을 용서할 만큼 충분히 너그럽지 않았다.
어휘 generous 너그러운, 관대한   forgive 용서하다

22 그녀는 함께 이야기 나눌 친구들이 좀 필요하다.
해설 '～에게[함께] 이야기 할'이라는 의미가 되려면 to talk to[with]를 써야 한다.

23 그는 너무 바빠서 파티에 올 수 없었다.
24 그녀는 매우 똑똑해서 그 퍼즐을 풀 수 있다.
25 나는 너무 피곤해서 지금 숙제를 할 수 없다.
26 (1) 나는 야채를 좀 사러 시장에 갔다.
(2) 나는 개를 산책시키러 공원에 갔다.
(3) 나는 뮤지컬을 보러 극장에 갔다.

Challenge!

30 ⓐ 대화할 친구가 있는 것은 좋다.
ⓑ 나는 내일 일찍 일어날 필요가 없다.
ⓒ 12월 31일은 전 세계적으로 기념된다.
ⓓ 그녀는 스카이다이빙을 시도할 만큼 충분히 용감했다.
ⓔ 그 정글은 지난달 큰 화재로 인해 파괴되었다.
해설 ⓒ 주어(New Year's Eve)가 동작을 받는 대상이므로 능동이 아닌 수동을 써야 한다. 수동태는 「be동사+과거분사(p.p.)」의 형태로 쓴다.
ⓓ '～할 만큼 충분히 …하다'는 의미를 나타낼 때는 「형용사/부사+enough+to부정사」를 쓴다.
어휘 celebrate 기념하다, 축하하다   worldwide 전 세계적으로   jungle 정글, 밀림   destroy 파괴하다

Chapter 06 | 동명사와 분사

Unit 01 명사로 쓰이는 동명사

POINT 1   p.97

1 Drinking lots of water is good
2 My sister's job is taking care of children
3 Not keeping promises can hurt your friendships
4 His good habit is reading a book every day.
5 Taking pictures is my favorite activity.
6 Listening to others carefully is important.
  또는 Carefully listening to others is important.
7 Drawing pictures can improve your creativity.
8 Spending time with friends makes me happy.
9 Creating interesting characters is really[very] fun.

9 A: 너는 커서 뭐가 되고 싶니?
  B: 나는 작가가 되고 싶어.
  A: 멋지다! 글 쓰는 것에 있어 네가 가장 즐기는 것은 무엇이니?
  B: 흥미로운 등장인물들을 만드는 것은 정말 재미있어.

POINT 2   p.99

1 enjoyed drawing and painting
2 avoided meeting new people
3 I like eating chocolate cake
4 Do you mind turning off the TV
5 We finished cleaning the house
6 Ted started learning[to learn] Chinese.
7 They practiced dancing and singing
8 My parents considered moving to another city.
9 I will not[won't] give up persuading him.
10 She kept waiting for him.

10 Emma는 Jones 의사 선생님과 약속이 있었다. 그녀는 제시간에 병원에 도착했다. 하지만 그는 너무 바빴다. 그녀는 그를 계속 기다렸다. 30분 뒤에, 그는 그녀를 보러 왔다.

POINT 3   p.101

1 remember watching   2 forgets to water
3 Stop playing   4 tried making
5 Larry forgot sending a message
6 The boy stopped to pick up the coins.
7 You should remember to bring your slippers.
8 The teacher tried to remember our names.
9 Don't forget to bring your camera.

9 A: 안녕. 내일은 학교 소풍날이네. 내가 무엇을 가져가야 할까?
  B: 네 카메라 가져오는 것을 잊지 마.
    내가 우리가 쓸 소풍 돗자리를 챙길게.

Unit 02 자주 쓰이는 동명사 표현

POINT 4   p.103

1 How about taking a walk
2 spent some money buying winter clothes
3 is afraid of speaking to foreigners
4 I feel like having a cup of coffee
5 He is interested in learning about different cultures
6 Thank you for inviting us.
7 My parents are busy working
8 Julie left without saying goodbye.
9 My brother is good at playing the guitar.
10 I'm looking forward to meeting you.

10 보라에게.
   잘 지내니? 나는 다음 달에 서울을 방문할 계획이야. 우리는 그날들을 아주 재미있게 보낼 수 있을 거야! 나는 너를 만나기를 기대하고 있어.
   사랑을 담아,
   Sophia

Unit 03 분사

POINT 5   p.105

1 sleeping baby   2 baked potatoes
3 The man acting
4 She wore the shining necklace
5 went to the music festival held in Seoul
6 There are lots of fallen leaves in the street.
7 I know the girl sitting on a bench.
8 My uncle bought a car made in Germany.
9 The tall woman wearing a red sweater is my teacher.

9 그 키 큰 여성분은 나의 선생님이시다. 그녀는 빨간 스웨터를 입고 계신다.

POINT 6   p.107

1 The students felt bored
2 His amazing story was not true
3 I remembered the embarrassing moment
4 People were shocked at the accident
5 She told me interesting facts about pandas
6 The final match will be very exciting!
7 People were amazed at the magic show.
8 I was embarrassed by the difficult question.
9 (1) I was excited to go to the aquarium.
  (2) The shark was amazing!

9 A: Gwen, 주말은 어땠니?
B: 아주 좋았어. 나는 수족관에 가서 신났어.
A: 어떤 동물이 가장 인상적이었니?
B: 상어가 놀라웠어! 그것은 아주 크고 무서웠어.

Chapter Test

p.108

STAGE 1

1 enjoy shopping on the Internet
2 Writing an essay in English is difficult
3 looks forward to receiving a letter from her friend
4 bought a picture painted in the 1950s
5 tried to open the bottle
6 remember buying fruits at that supermarket
7 were sitting together without saying a word
8 ⓐ disappointed ⓑ worried ⓒ exciting

3 어휘 receive 받다
5 해설 '~하려고 노력하다'를 나타낼 때는 「try+to부정사」를 쓴다.
6 해설 과거에 했던 행위를 기억하는 것이므로 「remember+동명사」를 쓴다.
7 해설 전치사 without 뒤에는 동명사를 써야 한다.
8 오늘 나는 시험지를 돌려받았다. 나는 나의 점수에 매우 실망했다. 내 친구 Kevin은 나를 걱정해 나를 영화관에 데려가 주었다. 우리는 신나는 액션 영화를 보았다. 나는 그와 함께 시간을 보내고 난 후 기분이 나아졌다.
해설 ⓐ, ⓑ 각각 주어인 I와 My friend Kevin이 감정을 느끼는 것이므로 과거분사 disappointed와 worried를 써야 한다.
ⓒ 명사 action movie가 감정을 일으키는 것이므로 현재분사 exciting을 써야 한다.
어휘 the movies (복수형) 영화관, 극장

STAGE 2

9 Traveling to other countries is
10 how about going shopping
11 forgot to turn off the light
12 the girl standing next to Tom
13 exciting, amazing
14 (1) visiting art galleries
(2) swimming, becoming a swimmer
15 some students spend too much time taking them
16 There was a bird singing on the branch.
17 I found a book written in Italian.
18 Ben saw a picture taken in the Alps.
19 The child standing at the bus stop is my little brother.
20 slept → sleeping　**21** to ask → asking
22 cleaning → to clean　**23** saying → to say
24 embarrassing → embarrassed
25 (1) Writing a poem is interesting[boring, fun, easy, difficult].
(2) Learning a new language is interesting[fun, easy, difficult 등]. 또는 Traveling to new places is interesting[fun 등].

9 A: 너는 해외로 여행하는 것을 좋아하니?
B: 응, 좋아해. 다른 나라를 여행하는 것은 항상 즐거워.
해설 동명사 주어는 단수 취급한다.
어휘 abroad 해외로
10 A: Sara, 이번 주 토요일에 쇼핑가는 게 어때?
B: 아주 좋아. 나는 새 신발이 필요해.
11 A: Tony의 방에 불이 켜져 있어.
B: 아! 그가 불 끄는 것을 또 잊었네.
해설 해야 할 것을 잊은 것이므로 목적어 자리에 to부정사를 쓴다.
12 A: 너는 Tom 옆에 서 있는 여자아이를 아니?
B: 응, 알아. 그녀는 Tom의 여동생 Nancy야.
13 A: 그 소설은 어땠니?
B: 이야기가 정말 흥미로웠어. 결말도 놀라웠어.
어휘 novel 소설
14 나는 너에게 나의 친구를 소개하고 싶어. 그녀의 이름은 Wendy야. 우리는 2021년에 처음 만난 이후로 가장 친한 친구로 지내왔어.
그녀는 여가 시간에 미술관을 방문하는 것을 아주 좋아해. 그녀는 또한 수영을 잘해서 수영선수가 되는 것이 그녀의 꿈이야.
15 Steve: 셀카는 추억을 남기는 좋은 방법이야. 나는 나의 친구들과 함께 그것들을 찍는 것을 아주 좋아해!
Willson: 나는 셀카 찍는 것을 즐기지만, 몇몇 학생들은 셀카를 찍는 데 너무 많은 시간을 써.
Stella: 필터는 나의 셀카를 멋져보이게 만들지만, 가끔 그것들은 정말 내가 아닌 것처럼 보여.
어휘 selfie 셀카(자신이 스스로 찍는 사진)　filter (사진) 필터
[16~19] 〈보기〉 나는 그 소녀를 안다. 그녀는 하얀 드레스를 입고 있다.
→ 나는 하얀 드레스를 입고 있는 그 소녀를 안다.
16 새 한 마리가 있었다. 그것은 나뭇가지 위에서 지저귀고 있었다.
→ 나뭇가지 위에 지저귀고 있는 새 한 마리가 있었다.
어휘 branch 나뭇가지
17 나는 책 한 권을 발견했다. 그것은 이탈리아어로 쓰여 있었다.
→ 나는 이탈리아어로 쓰인 책 한 권을 발견했다.
18 Ben은 사진을 한 장 보았다. 그것은 알프스에서 찍힌 것이었다.
→ Ben은 알프스에서 찍힌 사진 한 장을 보았다.
19 그 아이는 나의 남동생이다. 그는 버스 정류장에 서 있다.
→ 버스 정류장에 서 있는 그 아이는 나의 남동생이다.
20 조용히 해. 침대에 자고 있는 아기가 있어.
해설 '~하는, ~하는 중인'의 의미로 명사 baby를 수식하는 현재분사 sleeping을 써야 한다.
21 Joanna는 역사를 아주 좋아한다. 그녀는 항상 역사 수업 동안 질문을 계속 한다.
해설 keep은 동명사를 목적어로 취하는 동사이다.
22 너는 이번 주말에 집을 청소할 것을 기억해야 한다.
해설 미래에 할 행동을 나타내므로 remember 뒤에 to부정사가 와야 한다.
23 Aron은 길에서 친구를 봤다. 그는 그녀에게 인사하기 위해 멈췄다.
해설 문맥상 목적을 나타내는 to부정사를 써야 한다. 「stop+-ing」은 '~하는 것을 멈추다'의 의미이다.
24 나의 가족은 어젯밤에 우리 개가 너무 많이 짖어서 당황했다.
해설 주어인 My family가 감정을 느낀 것이므로 과거분사를 써야 한다.
25 〈보기〉 자전거를 타는 것은 신난다.
(1) 시 한 편을 쓰는 것은 흥미롭다[지루하다, 재미있다, 쉽다, 어렵다].
(2) 새로운 언어를 배우는 것은 흥미롭다[재미있다, 쉽다, 어렵다 등]. 또는 새로운 장소를 여행하는 것은 흥미롭다[재미있다 등].
어휘 language 언어　poem (한 편의) 시

26 exciting   **27** interested
28 boring   **29** shocking
30 ⓐ → was very busy preparing for
    ⓓ → forgot to exercise
    ⓔ → gave up losing weight

26 오늘은 내 생일이었다. 나의 친구들은 나를 케이크와 선물들로 놀라게 했다. 나에게 매우 신나는 날이었다.

27 어제, 나는 남극에 관한 다큐멘터리 영화를 봤다. 나는 남극에 사는 동물들에 관심을 가지게 되었다.
[어휘] documentary 다큐멘터리, 기록물   the South Pole 남극

28 나의 친구와 나는 영화를 보러 갔다. 그 영화는 지루해서 나는 거의 잠들 뻔했다.
[어휘] fall asleep 잠들다

29 내가 가장 좋아하는 야구팀이 오늘 게임에서 졌다. 그들이 1대 10으로 졌기 때문에 게임의 결과는 충격적이었다.
[어휘] lose 지다; 잃어버리다   result 결과

30 Robert는 회사에서 중요한 프로젝트를 준비하느라 매우 바빴다. 스트레스 때문에, 그는 더 많이 먹기 시작했다. 사실, 그는 야식 먹는 것을 좋아하기도 한다. 그 결과, 그는 체중이 좀 늘었다. 그는 체육관에서 운동을 하기로 결심했다. 하지만 그는 체육관에 자주 가지 못했다. 그는 운동할 것을 자주 잊어버렸다. 또한, 그는 퇴근 후에는 너무 피곤했다. 그는 살 빼는 것을 거의 포기했다. 나는 그가 언젠가 다이어트를 다시 할 것이라고 생각한다.
[해설] ⓐ '~하느라 바쁘다'는 의미는 「be busy+-ing」로 나타내므로 prepare를 preparing으로 고쳐 써야 한다.
ⓓ 문맥상 미래에 운동을 할 것을 잊어버린 것이므로 to부정사를 써야 한다.
ⓔ give up은 동명사를 목적어로 취하는 동사이다.
[어휘] stress 스트레스   gain weight 체중이 늘다   go on a diet 다이어트를 하다

Challenge!

31 ⓒ → The chickens will be fed by my grandfather.
    ⓔ → I feel like traveling, but I don't have enough money.

31 ⓐ 우리는 아직 무엇을 먹을지 결정하지 않았다.
ⓑ 그녀는 그 소식을 듣고 나서 울기 시작했다.
ⓒ 닭들은 나의 할아버지에 의해 먹여질 것이다.
ⓓ 탁자에 커피를 쏟은 것은 당황스러웠다.
ⓔ 나는 여행을 가고 싶지만, 충분한 돈이 없다.
[해설] ⓒ 의미상 주어(The chickens)가 동사(feed)의 동작을 받는 것이므로 수동태로 써야한다. 미래시제 수동태는 「will be+과거분사(p.p)」로 쓴다.
ⓔ '~하고 싶다'를 나타낼 때는 「feel like+-ing」를 쓴다.
[어휘] spill 쏟다, 엎지르다

Chapter 07 | 대명사, 형용사, 부사

Unit 01 대명사

POINT 1   p.115

1 One is black, the other is blue
2 Some students like pizza, others like pasta
3 One is a teacher, another is a writer, the other is a cook
4 One was a novel, and the other was a comic book.
5 One is England, another is France, and the other is Spain.
6 Some drink coffee, and others drink orange juice.
7 One is for my brother, another is for myself, and the others are for my parents.
8 One is reading, the other is drawing

8 교실에 두 명의 소년들이 있다. 한 명은 책을 읽고 있고, 나머지 한 명은 그림을 그리고 있다.

POINT 2   p.117

1 Each child has a different dream
2 There is a toilet on every floor
3 All my friends like basketball games
4 Both of them want to be scientists
5 Each of the restaurants has a special menu.
6 The amusement park gave a gift to each visitor[each of the visitors].
7 Every student has to wear a uniform
8 All of the volunteers were very diligent.
9 (1) Each game starts at nine o'clock.
     (2) Each student has different strengths.

POINT 3   p.119

1 You have to be proud of yourself
2 They bought a cake for themselves
3 My mom cut herself with a knife
4 I talk to myself at home
5 is writing a story about himself

6 My sister loves herself very much.
7 Dave and I enjoyed ourselves
8 Help yourself to the snacks.
9 The children prepare breakfast themselves
   또는 The children themselves prepare breakfast
10 He is taking a picture of himself

Unit 02 형용사와 부사

1 The soup tastes very salty
2 will not eat anything spicy
3 I need a comfortable chair
4 My dog found something strange
5 She enjoys active hobbies
6 We couldn't see anything clear
7 My brother and I heard something loud
8 This movie made people happy.
9 (1) I will[I'll] make something delicious
   (2) He does not[doesn't] want anything expensive

1 There are few cars on the road
2 A lot of boys and girls are wearing glasses
3 was very cold for a few days
4 Put a little salt and pepper into the soup
5 Many books give useful knowledge
6 Ben and I have little time.
7 A few men are waiting for the subway.
8 You shouldn't waste much money
9 There are lots of[plenty of] people

9 A: Elisha, 너는 어디 가는 중이니?
   B: 나는 한강 공원에 가고 있어.
   A: 그 공원에는 이미 사람들이 많이 있어. 대신 근처에 있는 공원에
      가는 게 어때?
   B: 그래, 그게 좋겠다.

1 is usually in the library
2 rarely exercises on the weekend
3 They always go to school by bus
4 I can hardly wake up early in the morning
5 We sometimes make mistakes
6 She doesn't often take a walk
7 Brian never plays computer games
8 Our teacher is always kind
9 (1) never goes to the gym
   (2) is seldom at home after school

9

	Austin	Emily
(1) 헬스장에 가기	전혀 안 감	매일
(2) 방과 후 집에 있기	일주일에 다섯 번	일주일에 한 번

(1) Austin은 헬스장에 전혀 가지 않는다.
(2) Emily는 방과 후에 집에 거의 없다.

Chapter Test

STAGE 1

1 There are a few books in Ted's bag
2 We need something sweet for dessert
3 I could hardly open my eyes
4 Kevin takes care of his pet by himself
5 I introduced myself
6 One is a squirrel, the other is a bird
7 Some like summer, others like winter
8 Is there anything special about her

5 해설 '자기소개를 하다'는 introduce oneself를 쓴다.
6 해설 '둘 중 하나는 ~, 나머지 하나는 …'을 나타낼 땐 one과 the
   other를 쓴다.
7 해설 '여럿 중 몇몇은 ~, 다른 몇몇은 …'을 나타낼 땐 some과
   others를 쓴다.
8 A: 나는 내 개를 잃어버렸어. 나를 도와줄 수 있니?
   B: 물론이지. 그녀 또는 그는 어떻게 생겼어?
   A: 그녀는 검은색과 흰색 털을 가지고 있어.
   B: 그녀에 관해 특별한 점이 있니?
   A: 그녀는 짧고 하얀 꼬리를 가지고 있어.
   어휘 fur (동물의) 털

STAGE 2

9 am never late for school
10 rarely watches TV after work
11 often read books in the library
12 can sometimes see stars at night
13 One is a soccer ball, and the other is a baseball.
14 One is Japan, another is the United States,
   and the other is Canada.
15 (1) often does yoga
   (2) sometimes studies math
16 a few rabbits　　　17 plenty of time
18 little information　　19 many presents
20 few mistakes　　　21 a little money
22 yourself　　　　　23 sometimes runs
24 take　　　　　　　25 flower has
26 much water
27 (1) We need a few eggs.
   (2) we have little bread

[9~12] 〈보기〉 A: 너는 얼마나 자주 외식을 하니?
　　　　　　 B: 나는 거의 외식을 하지 않아.
9 A: 너는 얼마나 자주 학교에 늦니?
   B: 나는 절대 학교에 늦지 않아.

10 A: Cathy는 퇴근 후에 얼마나 자주 TV를 보니?
   B: 그녀는 퇴근 후에 거의 TV를 보지 않아.
11 A: 너와 Fred는 얼마나 자주 도서관에서 책을 읽니?
   B: 우리는 자주 도서관에서 책을 읽어.
12 A: 너의 도시에서는 밤에 별을 얼마나 자주 볼 수 있니?
   B: 우리 도시에서는 밤에 별을 가끔 볼 수 있어.
   해설 빈도부사는 일반동사 앞, be동사/조동사 뒤에 쓴다.
[13~14] 〈보기〉 다섯 개의 과일이 있다. 하나는 바나나이고, 또 다른
         하나는 레몬이며, 나머지 모두는 사과이다.
13 나는 두 개의 공이 있다. 하나는 축구공이고, 나머지 하나는 야구공
   이다.
14 나의 가족은 이번 휴가에 세 나라를 방문할 예정이다. 한 곳은
   일본이고, 또 다른 한 곳은 미국이며, 나머지 한 곳은 캐나다이다.
   해설 '셋 중 하나는 ~, 또 다른 하나는 …, 나머지 하나는 ~'를
   나타낼 땐 one, another 그리고 the other를 쓴다.

15

	월	화	수	목	금
요가 하기	○	○		○	○
수학공부 하기		○		○	

   (1) Q: Sue는 얼마나 자주 요가를 하니?
       A: Sue는 자주 요가를 해.
   (2) Q: Sue는 얼마나 자주 수학 공부를 하니?
       A: Sue는 가끔 수학 공부를 해.
17 해설 plenty of는 셀 수 있는 명사와 셀 수 없는 명사 앞에 모두
   쓸 수 있다.
22 Linda, 너의 신발을 벗고 편히 쉬렴.
   해설 '편히 쉬다'라는 뜻의 make oneself at home이 되도록 고쳐
   쓴다.
23 Sally는 가끔 강을 따라 그녀의 개와 함께 달린다.
24 우리 둘 다 매일 버스를 타고 학교에 간다.
   해설 both는 항상 복수 취급하므로 복수동사를 써야 한다.
25 각각의 꽃은 고유한 향기를 가지고 있다.
   해설 each는 항상 단수 취급하므로 「each+단수명사+단수동사」
   의 형태로 쓴다.
26 너는 취침 전에 너무 많은 물을 마시지 않는 것이 좋겠다.
   해설 water는 셀 수 없는 명사이므로 복수형으로 쓰지 않으며,
   '많은'이라는 뜻의 수량 형용사는 much를 써야 한다.
27 A: 너는 점심 식사로 무엇을 원하니?
   B: 샌드위치를 만드는 게 어때?
   A: 그거 좋겠다. 우리는 샌드위치에 무엇이 필요하니?
   B: 우리는 달걀이 좀 필요해.
   A: 아, 우리는 빵이 거의 없어. 내가 지금 좀 사러 갈게.

28 A few   29 little
30 much   31 few
32 ⓐ herself ⓑ himself ⓒ themselves
33 ⓒ → Everyone finds something fun to do in their
        own way.

28 몇 년 전에, Kate는 그녀의 친구들과 함께 여름 캠프를 갔다.
29 내 주머니에 돈이 거의 없었다. 그래서 나는 간식을 좀 살 수 없었다.
   어휘 pocket 주머니
30 지난주 토요일에, 나는 해변에서 나의 가족과 함께 정말 즐거운
   시간을 보냈다.
31 네 글은 오류가 거의 없기 때문에 매우 훌륭해.
32 Sarah와 그녀의 남동생은 공원에 갔다. Sarah는 책을 가져가서 혼
   자 읽었다. 그녀의 남동생은 그네에서 놀면서 즐거운 시간을 보냈
   다. 하루가 끝날 때쯤, 그들은 좋은 시간을 보낸 자신들에 대해 자
   랑스러워했다.
33 몇몇 사람들은 영화를 즐기지만, 다른 몇몇은 책을 더 좋아한다. 예
   를 들어, 내 친구 중 한 명은 그림 그리기를 좋아하고, 또 다른 친
   구는 춤추기를 좋아한다. 모든 사람은 그들 자신만의 방식으로 할
   재미있는 무언가를 찾는다.
   해설 ⓒ -thing, -body, -one으로 끝나는 대명사는 형용사가 뒤에
   서 꾸며주므로 something fun으로 고쳐야 한다.
   어휘 prefer 더 좋아하다, 선호하다

Challenge!

34 ⓐ → Every student wears a seat belt in the school
        bus.
   ⓔ → Many teenagers are very interested in
        playing computer games.

34 ⓐ 모든 학생은 통학 버스에서 안전벨트를 착용한다.
   ⓑ Irene은 그녀의 삼촌 댁에 자주 방문한다.
   ⓒ Green 박사는 아픈 사람들을 돌보기 위해 아프리카에 갔다.
   ⓓ 그녀는 그녀의 커피에 약간의 설탕을 넣었다.
   ⓔ 많은 십 대가 컴퓨터 게임을 하는 것에 매우 관심이 있다.
   해설 ⓐ every는 「every+단수명사+단수동사」의 형태로 쓰므로
   wears로 고쳐야 한다.
   ⓔ '~하는 것에 관심이 있다'라는 의미는 「be interested in -ing」의
   형태로 쓴다.
   어휘 seat belt 안전벨트

Chapter 08 | 비교 표현

Unit 01 원급, 비교급, 최상급

POINT 1   p.133

1 is as smart as a dog
2 is as soft as a feather
3 is as tall as I am
4 is not as cold as yesterday
5 is as clean as
6 was as famous as
7 isn't as[so] fast as
8 (1) as hot as   (2) as much as
9 (1) is as cheap as
  (2) is not[isn't] as[so] high as

8 (1) 이번 여름은 지난여름만큼 덥다.

해설 원급 비교는 「as+형용사[부사]의 원급+as」의 형태로 쓰므로 hotter를 hot으로 고쳐 써야 한다.

(2) 나는 네가 그 영화를 좋아하는 것만큼 많이 좋아하지 않는다.

해설 동사 don't like를 수식하는 부사 자리이므로 much를 써야 한다.

9 (1) 사과파이는 15달러이다.
레몬파이는 15달러이다.
→ 사과파이는 레몬파이만큼 저렴하다.

(2) 킬리만자로산은 5,895미터 높이이다.
에베레스트산은 8,849미터 높이이다.
→ 킬리만자로산은 에베레스트산만큼 높지 않다.

POINT 2 p.135

1 Light travels faster than sound
2 My brother goes to bed later than I do
3 The present is much more important than the past
4 is worse than yesterday
5 is more popular than his last one
6 is less comfortable than that sofa
7 speaks Chinese better than Justin
8 were even cheaper than the blue sneakers
9 (1) Taking a train is much more expensive than taking an express bus.
(2) Taking a train is even faster than taking an express bus.

9

서울에서 부산까지

	가격	시간
기차 타기	58,000원	2시간 50분
고속버스 타기	34,000원	4시간 15분

(1) 기차를 타는 것은 고속버스를 타는 것보다 훨씬 더 비싸다.
(2) 기차를 타는 것은 고속버스를 타는 것보다 훨씬 더 빠르다.

POINT 3 p.137

1 Brazil is the largest country in South America
2 February is the shortest month in a year
3 He has the curliest hair in our class
4 is the highest in our country
5 is the hottest place in the world
6 is one of the best spots
7 Becky is the most generous of my friends.
8 Andy is the most creative student in our class
9 (1) is the youngest (2) is the tallest
(3) is the heaviest

9

이름	나이	키	몸무게
Terry	15	165 cm	53 kg
Jim	14	160 cm	55 kg
Nicky	16	154 cm	56 kg

(1) Jim은 셋 중에서 가장 어린 학생이다.
(2) Terry는 셋 중에서 가장 키가 큰 학생이다.
(3) Nicky는 셋 중에서 가장 무거운 학생이다.

Unit 02 원급, 비교급을 이용한 표현

POINT 4, 5 p.139

1 as early as possible
2 The closer, the more nervous
3 colder and colder
4 three times as big as
5 The more, the better
6 The laptop is twice as light as the desktop computer
7 The more you practice English, the more fluently you can speak
8 three times as expensive as plastic straws

8 플라스틱 빨대는 환경에 문제를 일으킨다. 많은 식당들과 카페들은 빨대를 사용하는 것이 허용되지 않는다. 하지만 종이 빨대는 플라스틱 빨대의 약 세 배만큼 더 비싸다.
그래서 사람들은 종이 빨대를 사용하는 대신 더 나은 선택지를 찾으려고 노력하고 있다.

Chapter Test p.140

STAGE 1

1 is the largest in our country
2 less often than his brother does
3 is far smaller than the Earth
4 the Sun sets earlier and earlier
5 plays basketball better than
6 The higher, the farther[further]
7 the most expensive dish in this restaurant
8 The test was not as difficult as I expected

1 어휘 cinema 영화관
4 어휘 set (해, 달이) 지다
6 해설 '더 ~할수록, 더 …하다'는 「The+비교급 (주어+동사 ~), the+비교급 (주어+동사 …)」의 형태로 쓴다.
7 어휘 dish 요리
8 A: 과학 시험은 어땠어?
B: 괜찮았어. 그 시험은 내가 예상했던 것만큼 어렵지 않았어.
A: 잘 됐다. 나는 네가 잘했을 거라고 확신해.
해설 '~만큼 …하지 않은[하지 않게]'이라는 의미는 「not as[so]+형용사[부사]의 원급+as」의 형태로 쓴다.
어휘 expect 예상하다, 기대하다

STAGE 2

9 The more you exercise, the healthier you will become
10 my cat is getting bigger and bigger
11 The more you season, the spicier it will taste
12 as not → not as
13 more cold → colder
14 many → much
15 very → much[still, even, far, a lot 등]

16 country → countries

17 a long flight is much[still, even, far 등] more tiring
than a long drive

18 is more popular than　**19** as much as

20 is the least popular place

21 (1) are as cheap as
(2) the more often, the easier

22 (1) is the youngest (swimmer) of
(2) is taller than　　　(3) is as fast as

9 네가 더 많이 운동할수록, 너는 더 건강해질 것이다.
해설 주어진 그림이 운동을 더 하면 더 건강해지는 것을 표현하고 있으므로, 「The+비교급 (주어+동사 ~), the+비교급 (주어+동사 …)」 형태를 쓴다. much의 비교급을 more로 쓰는 것에 주의한다.

10 시간이 지나면서, 나의 고양이는 점점 더 커지고 있다.
해설 주어진 그림이 시간이 지남에 따라 점점 더 커지는 고양이를 나타내므로, 「비교급 and 비교급」 형태를 사용한다.

11 네가 너의 수프에 양념을 더 많이 넣을수록, 그것은 더 매워질 것이다.
해설 주어진 그림에서 수프에 양념을 더 넣고 매워하고 있으므로, 「The+비교급 (주어+동사 ~), the+비교급 (주어+동사 …)」 형태로 쓴다.
어휘 season 양념을 넣다

12 영어 시험은 수학 시험만큼 어렵지 않았다.
해설 원급 비교는 「not as[so]+형용사[부사]의 원급+as」의 어순으로 써야 하므로 as not이 아닌 not as의 순서로 고쳐야 한다.

13 남극은 북극보다 더 춥다.
해설 뒤에 than이 있고 cold는 1음절이므로 colder로 고친다.
어휘 the South Pole 남극　the North Pole 북극

14 나의 가족은 우리 개를 나만큼 사랑한다.
해설 원급 비교 표현이 쓰였고, 동사 loves를 수식하는 부사 자리이므로 many를 much로 고쳐 써야 한다.

15 Becky의 손은 그녀의 어머니의 손보다 훨씬 더 크다.
해설 very는 원급을 강조하는 부사로, 비교급 앞에는 쓸 수 없다.

16 싱가포르는 세계에서 가장 깨끗한 나라 중 하나이다.

17 A: 어떤 것이 더 피곤하니, 긴 비행 아니면 긴 운전?
B: 보통, 긴 비행이 긴 운전보다 훨씬 더 피곤해.
어휘 normally 보통(은)

18 일본은 학생들 사이에서 중국보다 더 인기가 있다.
해설 학생들이 일본과 중국을 좋아하는 정도에 차이가 있으므로 「형용사[부사]의 비교급+than」의 형태를 사용한다.

19 학생들은 부산만큼 제주도를 좋아한다.
해설 제주도와 부산이 같은 수의 표를 받았으므로 정도가 비슷하거나 같은 대상을 비교하는 「as+형용사[부사]의 원급+as」로 나타낸다.

20 경주는 모든 장소 중 인기가 가장 적은 장소이다.
해설 경주가 가장 적은 표를 받았으므로 「the+형용사[부사]의 최상급」 형태로 나타낸다. little의 최상급을 least로 쓰는 것에 주의한다.

21 Kevin: 안녕, Tim. 네 안경은 어디에 있니?
Tim: 아, 나는 오늘 콘택트렌즈를 끼고 있어.
Kevin: 그것들은 느낌이 어때?
Tim: 꽤 편해.
Kevin: 그것들은 안경보다 더 비싸지 않니?
Tim: 그렇지 않아. 콘택트렌즈는 안경만큼 값이 싸.
Kevin: 좋네. 콘택트렌즈를 끼는 것이 어렵지 않니?
Tim: 처음에는 몇 분이 걸릴 수도 있어. 하지만 네가 더 자주 콘택트렌즈를 낄수록, 그것은 더 쉬워져.
Kevin: 흥미롭다. 나도 콘택트렌즈를 한번 껴봐야겠어.
해설 (1) 문맥상 두 대상을 비교해서 정도가 비슷하거나 같음을 나타내고 있으므로, 「as+형용사[부사]의 원급+as」를 사용한다.
(2) 문맥상 '더 ~할수록, 더 …하다'는 의미를 나타내야 하므로 「The+비교급 (주어+동사 ~), the+비교급 (주어+동사 …)」를 쓴다.

22

	Peter	Harry	Brian
(1) 나이	12	16	14
(2) 키	160 cm	173 cm	166 cm
(3) 200 미터 기록	2:10	1:58	1:58

(1) Peter는 셋 중에서 가장 어리다(어린 수영 선수이다).
(2) Harry는 Peter보다 키가 더 크다.
(3) Brian은 Harry만큼 빠르다.

23 (1) the Earth is getting hotter and hotter
(2) is not[isn't] the same as it used to be
(3) is a lot hotter than last summer
(4) The more we care about the environment,
the better it will[it'll] be.

24 ⓐ → as easily as
ⓓ → even more difficult than
ⓔ → worse than

23　나는 오늘 지구 온난화에 관해 배웠다. 나의 선생님은 지구가 점점 더 더워지고 있다고 말씀하셨다. 오늘날, 기온은 예전과 같지 않다. 예를 들어, 이번 여름은 지난여름보다 훨씬 더 덥다. 나의 선생님은 우리에게 환경을 보호하는 몇 가지 방법들을 말씀해주셨다. 우리가 환경에 대해서 더 많이 관심을 가질수록, 그것은 더 좋아지게 될 것이다.
어휘 protect 보호하다, 지키다　temperature 온도

24 ⓐ 그녀는 그녀의 오빠만큼 그 퍼즐을 쉽게 풀었다.
ⓑ 야구는 한국에서 가장 인기 있는 스포츠 중 하나이다.
ⓒ Nancy는 그녀의 쌍둥이 동생만큼 열심히 공부한다.
ⓓ 과학 시험은 수학 시험보다 훨씬 더 어려웠다.
ⓔ 내 수학 점수는 내 미술 점수보다 훨씬 나쁘다.
해설 ⓐ 동사 solved를 수식하는 부사 자리이므로 easy를 easily로 고쳐 써야 한다.
ⓓ 비교급을 강조하는 부사는 비교급 앞에 써야 한다.
ⓔ bad의 비교급은 worse이므로 more는 함께 쓰지 않는다.

25 ⓒ → They feel nervous about starting a new
school.
ⓔ → The desert is the biggest of the four deserts.

25 ⓐ 그 아기는 점점 더 크게 울었다.
ⓑ 모든 사람은 그 소식에 놀랐다.
ⓒ 그들은 새 학교를 시작하는 것에 대해 긴장감을 느낀다.
ⓓ 자기 전에 알람을 설정하는 것을 잊지 마.
ⓔ 그 사막은 네 개 중에 가장 크다.
해설 ⓒ 감각동사 feel 뒤에는 부사가 아닌 형용사를 써야 하므로 nervously를 nervous로 고쳐 쓴다.
ⓔ '~ 중에서 가장 …한'이라는 의미는 「the+최상급(+명사)+in[of]」로 쓴다.
어휘 loud (소리가) 큰, 시끄러운

Chapter 09 | 접속사

Unit 01 and, but, or의 쓰임

POINT 1 p.147

1 He neither called nor sent a message
2 Not only Jake but also his friends like playing soccer
3 We want to have either a dog or a cat
4 The weather was both rainy and cold
5 He will[He'll] either go to the gym or (will) rest at home
6 The food was neither fresh nor tasty
7 She not only swam but also played tennis
8 Lisa enjoys both playing the piano and listening to music.
9 She is a great leader as well as a good team player.

9 그녀는 좋은 팀원일 뿐만 아니라 멋진 리더이다.

POINT 2, 3 p.149

1 Go home early, or your parents will be angry
2 Take a deep breath, and you will feel better
3 Both he and his sister are good at swimming
4 Either Daniel or I help to set up the classroom
5 Be confident, and you can speak English well.
6 Neither my cat nor (my) dog likes taking[to take] a bath.
7 Both Ryan and Sophie volunteer at the animal shelter.
8 or you will have a stomachache

8 너무 많은 간식을 먹지 마라. 그렇지 않으면 너는 배탈이 날 것이다.

Unit 02 부사절을 이끄는 접속사

POINT 4 p.151

1 After the rain stopped
2 When I arrived at the classroom
3 after he finishes his homework
4 while she was waiting for the train
5 when she works out
6 before you leave the room
7 While he was watching TV
8 Until[Till] she reaches her goal
9 (1) After the concert ended
   (2) until the chef returns from his vacation
   (3) While I was watching a movie

9 (1) 콘서트가 끝난 후, 우리는 택시를 타고 집에 갔다.
   (2) 그 식당은 요리사가 휴가에서 돌아올 때까지 문을 열지 않을 것이다.
   (3) 내가 영화를 보고 있는 동안에 나의 형은 낮잠을 잤다.

POINT 5 p.153

1 because he was too busy
2 so slippery that I fell down
3 as he is my best friend
4 so beautiful that lots of people visit there
5 Because she was bored, she left the party early
6 The shoes are so old that he will[he'll] buy new ones.
7 went to the bakery because she was very hungry
8 My little sister is so young that she can't[cannot] understand this book.
9 (1) The weather was so hot that we ordered ice cream.
   (2) The restaurant is so popular that you should wait for an hour.

9 (1) 날씨가 너무 더워서 우리는 아이스크림을 주문했다.
   (2) 그 식당은 매우 인기 있어서 너는 한 시간 동안 기다려야 한다.

POINT 6 p.155

1 If you know the answer
2 unless he tells the truth
3 Although my grandfather was seventy years old
4 Though the last exam was very difficult
5 If you want some dessert
6 Although we did our best
7 unless he misses the bus
8 (1) If you do not[don't] keep milk cold in summer, it will[it'll] go bad easily.
   (2) Unless you keep milk cold in summer, it will[it'll] go bad easily.

Unit 03 명사절을 이끄는 접속사

POINT 7 p.157

1 Jake said that he loved playing basketball
2 It was very surprising that she broke the promise
3 We heard our teacher's birthday was coming
4 I believe (that) everyone is equal.
5 Every parent hopes (that) their children will be healthy.
6 He realized (that) he left his homework at home.
7 Sora thought (that) the apple pie was so tasty.
8 I imagine that robots will do many jobs

1　if we have homework today
2　how you came up with this idea
3　How do you think the universe was created
4　if[whether] the flight is delayed
5　remember what she told us yesterday
6　know how many hours you watch TV
7　Do you know when the bus will arrive?
8　She wondered who called her last night.
9　Did you hear where Jina left for?

9　〈보기〉 너는 나에게 말해줄 수 있니?＋너는 왜 늦었니?
　　　　　→ 너는 왜 늦었는지 나에게 말해줄 수 있니?
　　너는 들었니?＋지나는 어디로 떠났니?
　　　　　→ 너는 지나가 어디로 떠났는지 들었니?

Chapter Test

STAGE 1

1　Though Ben was too tired
2　so hot that he took off his jacket
3　a milkshake as well as a hamburger
4　Do you know what this word means
5　If you are[you're] hungry
6　when he was young
7　was angry because I broke the window
8　Pay attention in class, and you will understand the lesson better.

3　해설 'A뿐만 아니라 B도'를 나타낼 때는 B as well as A로 쓴다.
4　해설 간접의문문은 「의문사＋주어＋동사 ∼」의 어순으로 쓴다.
8　만약 네가 수업 시간에 집중을 한다면, 너는 수업을 더 잘 이해할 것이다.
　　→ 수업 시간에 집중을 해라, 그러면 너는 수업을 더 잘 이해할 것이다.
　　어휘 pay attention 집중하다, 주의를 기울이다

STAGE 2

9　Unless
10　because
11　If
12　while
13　or
14　but
15　that
16　and
17　(1) Both, and
　　(2) Neither, nor
　　(3) and
18　(1) Both Eric and Tom like pasta.
　　(2) Neither Eric nor Tom likes bowling.
19　Do you know if[whether] Lily lives near here?
20　Can you tell me how long you sleep on weekends?
21　What do you think Peter wants to get on his birthday?
22　Tell me how you solved this question.
23　I'm not sure when the package will be delivered.
24　swim → swimming
25　because of → because

26　or → and
27　have → has
28　will be → is
29　(1) what time the museum closes
　　(2) if[whether] there is a cafeteria inside the museum

9　만약 우리가 에너지를 절약하지 않는다면, 우리는 자연을 보호할 수 없다.
　　어휘 protect 보호하다
10　Jim은 감기에 걸렸기 때문에 병원에 갔다.
11　네가 사과를 하지 않는다면, 그녀는 너를 용서해주지 않을 거야.
　　어휘 forgive 용서하다
12　내가 설거지를 하는 동안 누군가 문을 두드렸다.
　　어휘 knock 두드리다, 노크하다
13　수미는 치마와 바지 둘 중 하나를 살 것이다.
14　나는 평일뿐만 아니라 일요일에도 도서관에 간다.
15　Henry는 Susan이 그 콘서트에 올 거라는 걸 알았다.
16　이 크림은 너의 피부를 깨끗하게 하고 보호할 수도 있다.
17　(1) 사과와 오렌지 둘 다 2달러이다.
　　(2) 포도와 딸기 둘 다 할인하지 않는다.
　　(3) 세 개의 멜론을 사라, 그러면 너는 하나를 공짜로 얻을 수 있다.
　　해설 (2) 'A와 B 둘 다 아닌'을 나타낼 때는 neither A nor B를 쓴다.

18
너는 ∼를 좋아하니?	(1) 음식		(2) 운동	
	파스타	샐러드	테니스	볼링
Eric	○	×	×	×
Tom	○	○	○	×

(1) Eric과 Tom 둘 다 파스타를 좋아한다.
(2) Eric과 Tom 둘 다 볼링을 좋아하지 않는다.
해설 (1) both A and B가 주어로 쓰일 때 동사는 항상 복수형을 쓴다.
(2) neither A nor B가 주어로 쓰일 때 동사는 B의 인칭과 수에 일치시킨다.

[19~23] 〈보기〉 나는 궁금해. 화장실은 어디에 있니?
　　　　　→ 나는 화장실이 어디에 있는지 궁금해.
19　너는 아니? Lily는 이 근처에 사니?
　　→ 너는 Lily가 이 근처에 사는지 아니?
　　해설 의문사를 포함하지 않는 의문문이 목적어 역할을 하므로
　　「if[whether]＋주어＋ 동사」의 어순으로 쓴다.
20　나에게 말해줄 수 있니? 너는 주말에 얼마나 오래 자니?
　　→ 너는 주말에 얼마나 오래 자는지 내게 말해줄 수 있니?
21　너는 생각하니? Peter는 그의 생일에 무엇을 갖고 싶어 하니?
　　→ 너는 Peter가 그의 생일에 무엇을 갖고 싶어 한다고 생각하니?
　　해설 의문사가 이끄는 절이 think와 같이 생각이나 추측을 나타내는
　　동사의 목적어 역할을 할 때는 의문사를 문장 맨 앞에 써야 한다.
22　나에게 말해 줘. 너는 어떻게 이 문제를 풀었니?
　　→ 네가 어떻게 이 문제를 풀었는지 나에게 말해 줘.
23　나는 확실하지 않아. 언제 소포가 배달되니?
　　→ 나는 언제 소포가 배달되는지 확실하지 않아.
　　어휘 package 소포　deliver 배달하다
24　여름에 나는 서핑뿐만 아니라 수영도 즐긴다.
　　해설 접속사로 연결되는 말은 문법적으로 같은 성격이어야 하므로
　　swim은 동명사 swimming으로 고쳐 써야 한다.
25　매우 추웠기 때문에 우리는 해변에 가지 않았다.
　　해설 뒤에 주어와 동사가 있는 완전한 절이 오므로 접속사
　　because를 써야 한다. because of는 전치사로 그 뒤에는 명사(구)
　　가 온다.
26　이 약을 먹어라, 그러면 넌 괜찮아질 것이다.
　　어휘 medicine 약
27　너와 네 오빠 둘 중 한 명은 오늘 그 개를 돌봐야 한다.
　　해설 either A or B가 주어로 쓰일 때는 B에 동사의 수를 일치시킨다.
28　너는 시험이 끝날 때까지 전화기를 꺼둬야 한다.
　　해설 시간을 나타내는 부사절에서는 미래를 나타내더라도 미래시
　　제 대신 현재시제를 써야 한다.

[어휘] be over 끝나다

29 (1) 남자아이는 박물관이 몇 시에 문을 닫는지 묻고 있다.
(2) 여자아이는 박물관 안에 구내식당이 있는지 묻고 있다.
[어휘] cafeteria 카페테리아((셀프 서비스식 식당)), 구내식당

30 so small that, couldn't read
31 comfortable as well as pretty
32 neither rainy nor cloudy
33 Listen to, or you'll miss
34 both delicious food and excellent service
35 (1) Although[Though] his talent was amazing
(2) If I am[I'm] not busy tomorrow, I will[I'll] go to a bookstore.

30 그 책의 글자들은 너무 작아서 나는 그것들을 읽을 수 없었다.
[해설] '너무 ~해서 …하다'라는 의미를 나타낼 때, 「so+형용사/부사+that+주어+동사」로 바꿔 쓸 수 있다.
31 이 신발은 예쁠 뿐만 아니라 편안하다.
[해설] not only A but also B는 B as well as A로 바꿔 쓸 수 있는데, 이때 A와 B의 위치가 바뀌는 것에 유의한다.
32 나는 비 오는 날을 좋아하지 않고, 흐린 날도 좋아하지 않는다.
→ 나는 비 오는 날과 흐린 날 둘 다 좋아하지 않는다.
33 만약 네가 선생님의 말씀을 주의 깊게 듣지 않는다면, 너는 중요한 것들을 놓칠 것이다.
→ 선생님의 말씀을 주의 깊게 들어라, 그렇지 않으면 너는 중요한 것들을 놓칠 것이다.
34 그 식당은 맛있는 음식을 제공하고, 훌륭한 서비스도 제공한다.
→ 그 식당은 맛있는 음식과 훌륭한 서비스 둘 다 제공한다.
[어휘] serve 제공하다
35 Cathy에게,

잘 지내니? 네가 멋진 방학을 보내고 있다는 걸 들으니 좋구나. 어제 나는 빈센트 반 고흐에 관한 영화를 봤어. 비록 그의 재능은 굉장했지만, 그 당시에는 누구도 그것에 대해 알지 못했어. 나는 그에 관해 더 읽고 싶기도 해. 만약 내가 내일 바쁘지 않다면, 난 서점에 갈 거야.
어쨌든, 몸조심해! 나는 널 곧 볼 수 있기를 바라.
사랑을 담아,
Megan
[해설] (2) 조건을 나타내는 부사절에서는 미래를 나타내더라도 현재 시제를 써야 한다.
[어휘] anyway 어쨌든; 그래도   talent 재능

36 ⓑ → She finished the test a lot faster than her classmates.
ⓓ → I don't know where the restaurant is.

36 ⓐ 모든 테이블 위에는 메뉴가 있다.
ⓑ 그녀는 그녀의 반 친구들보다 훨씬 더 빨리 시험을 끝냈다.
ⓒ 그는 그의 아빠만큼 쉽게 퍼즐을 풀었다.
ⓓ 나는 그 식당이 어디에 있는지 모른다.
ⓔ 우리는 내일 비가 오면 도보 여행을 가지 않을 것이다.
[해설] ⓑ fast의 비교급은 faster이므로 more를 삭제해야 한다. a lot은 비교급을 강조해주는 부사이다.
ⓓ 의문사가 있는 간접의문문은 「의문사+주어+동사 ~」의 어순으로 쓴다.

Chapter **10** | 관계대명사

Unit **01**   who, which, that

                    p.167

1 who have a sense of humor
2 which displays modern paintings
3 which is made of silk
4 who trained hard every day
5 that has many windows
6 a girl who is talking to her friend
7 shoes which are too big for him
8 The dog which has big ears
9 that boy who is sitting over there
10 this picture which was taken last month
11 the man who was looking for a bus stop
12 a little cat which is crying alone
13 The restaurant which is near my house
14 The police officer who helped us
15 many people who are waiting for the subway
16 the little boy who is smiling at us
17 two monkeys which are climbing up the tree
18 The girl who is wearing a blue cap
19 He knows a person who[that] can speak four languages.
20 The penguin is one of the birds which[that] can't[cannot] fly.

21 This is the cafe which[that] sells the best coffee in our town.
22 The girl who[that] wants to be a doctor is my friend.
23 Where is the book which[that] was on the table?
24 The cat which[that] is sleeping on the roof is very cute.
25 I saw the boy and his dog that were running over there.
26 Students who[that] plan ahead achieve their goals

[6~15] 〈보기〉 나는 그 남자를 안다. 그는 옆집에 산다.
→ 나는 옆집에 사는 그 남자를 안다.
6 여자아이가 한 명 있다. 그녀는 그녀의 친구에게 이야기를 하고 있다.
→ 그녀의 친구에게 이야기를 하고 있는 여자아이 한 명이 있다.
7 David는 신발을 신고 있다. 그것들은 그에게 너무 크다.
→ David는 그에게 너무 큰 신발을 신고 있다.
8 그 개는 정말 귀엽다. 그것은 큰 귀를 가지고 있다.
→ 큰 귀를 가진 그 개는 정말 귀엽다.
9 너는 저 남자아이를 아니? 그는 저쪽에 앉아 있어.
→ 너는 저쪽에 앉아 있는 저 남자아이를 아니?
10 나는 이 사진을 보고 있다. 그것은 지난달에 찍은 것이다.
→ 나는 지난달에 찍은 이 사진을 보고 있다.
11 Sera는 그 남자를 도와주었다. 그는 버스 정류장을 찾고 있었다.
→ Sera는 버스 정류장을 찾고 있던 그 남자를 도와주었다.
12 작은 고양이 한 마리가 있다. 그것은 혼자 울고 있다.
→ 혼자 울고 있는 작은 고양이 한 마리가 있다.
13 그 식당은 매우 인기 있다. 그것은 우리 집 근처에 있다.
→ 우리 집 근처에 있는 그 식당은 매우 인기 있다.
14 그 경찰관은 매우 친절했다. 그는 우리를 도와주었다.
→ 우리를 도와준 그 경찰관은 매우 친절했다.
15 많은 사람들이 있다. 그들은 지하철을 기다리고 있다.
→ 지하철을 기다리고 있는 많은 사람들이 있다.
16 우리를 보고 웃고 있는 저 어린 남자아이 좀 봐.
해설 선행사(the little boy)가 사람이므로 주격 관계대명사 who를 쓴다. 주격 관계대명사 뒤에 오는 동사는 선행사에 수를 일치시키므로 be동사의 3인칭 단수형 is로 쓴다.
17 나무를 오르고 있는 원숭이 두 마리가 있다.
해설 선행사(two monkeys)가 동물이므로 주격 관계대명사 which를 쓴다. 복수명사이므로 which 뒤에 오는 be동사는 are로 써야 한다.
18 파란 모자를 쓰고 있는 그 소녀는 나의 여동생이다.
해설 선행사(The girl)가 사람이므로 주격 관계대명사 who를 쓴다. 단수명사이므로 who 뒤에는 be동사 is가 와야 한다.
19 해설 '그는 / 안다 / 한 사람을 / 4개 국어를 할 줄 아는.'의 어순이 되어야 하므로 선행사 자리에는 a person이 온다. 선행사가 사람이므로 관계대명사 who 또는 that을 쓴다.
20 해설 '펭귄은 / ~이다 / 새들 중 하나 / 날지 못하는.'의 어순이므로 선행사는 one of the birds가 된다. 선행사가 동물이므로 관계대명사 which 또는 that을 쓴다.
21 해설 '이곳은 / 카페이다 / 최고의 커피를 파는 / 우리 마을에서.'의 어순이 되어야 하므로 선행사 자리에는 the cafe가 온다. 선행사가 사물이므로 관계대명사 which 또는 that을 쓴다.
22 해설 '그 소녀는 / 의사가 되고 싶어 하는 / 내 친구이다.'의 어순이므로 문장의 주어이자 선행사인 The girl 뒤에 관계대명사 who 또는 that을 쓴다.
23 해설 '어디에 / 있니 / 그 책은 / 탁자 위에 있던?'의 어순으로 쓰며, 선행사가 the book이므로 관계대명사는 which 또는 that을 쓴다.
24 해설 '저 고양이는 / 자고 있는 / 지붕 위에서 / 정말 귀엽다.'의 어순이 되어야 하므로 선행사 자리에는 The cat이 온다. 선행사가 동물이므로 관계대명사 which 또는 that을 쓴다.

25 해설 '나는 / 보았다 / 남자아이와 그의 개를 / 저쪽에서 뛰고 있던.'의 어순으로 쓰며, 선행사가 the boy and his dog로 「사람＋동물」이므로 관계대명사 that을 쓴다.

Unit 02 who(m), which, that

1 He is the teacher whom everyone respects
2 the subject that they talked about
3 The novel which she wrote is very popular
4 I found the camera which you lost.
5 We visited the tourist attraction which Dean recommended.
6 Gary received a letter which Bella sent from Canada.
7 The actor who(m) Sally likes is not[isn't] famous.
8 I remember the boy whom we met at the park.
9 Anna is wearing the blue dress which[that] her sister bought last weekend.

8 나는 그 소년을 기억한다. 우리는 그를 공원에서 만났다.
→ 나는 우리가 공원에서 만났던 그 소년을 기억한다.
9 Anna는 파란색 원피스를 입고 있다. 그녀의 언니가 지난 주말에 그것을 샀다.
→ Anna는 그녀의 언니가 지난 주말에 샀던 파란색 원피스를 입고 있다.

Unit 03 whose, what

1 a friend whose hobby is swimming
2 the house whose roof needs repair
3 The boy whose birthday is today
4 The restaurant whose chef is famous
5 the woman whose name is Helen
6 a car whose design is unique
7 the boy whose backpack was lost
8 My friend whose father is a chef
9 She lives in a house whose garden is full of flowers.

[1-5] 〈보기〉 나는 그 가수를 좋아한다. 그의 노래들은 훌륭하다.
→ 나는 노래들이 훌륭한 그 가수를 좋아한다.
1 나는 친구가 한 명 있다. 그녀의 취미는 수영이다.
→ 나는 취미가 수영인 한 친구가 있다.
2 이것은 집이다. 그것의 지붕은 수리가 필요하다.
→ 이것은 지붕이 수리가 필요한 집이다.
3 그 남자아이는 그의 친구들로부터 선물들을 받았다. 그의 생일은 오늘이다.
→ 생일이 오늘인 그 남자아이는 그의 친구들로부터 선물을 받았다.
4 그 레스토랑은 나의 집 근처에 있다. 그곳의 주방장은 유명하다.
→ 주방장이 유명한 그 레스토랑은 나의 집 근처에 있다.
5 너는 그 여자를 아니? 그녀의 이름은 Helen이야.
→ 너는 이름이 Helen인 그 여자를 아니?

6 해설 'Max의 삼촌은 / 가지고 있다 / 차를 / 디자인이 특이한.'의
어순이므로 선행사 a car 뒤에 소유격 관계대명사 whose가 온다.
whose는 a car's를 대신하므로 뒤에 명사 design이 와야 한다.

7 해설 '나는 / 도와주었다 / 그 소년을 / 책가방을 잃어버렸던.'의 어순
이므로 선행사 the boy 뒤에 whose가 온다. whose는 the boy's를
대신하므로 뒤에 명사 backpack이 와야 한다.

8 해설 '내 친구는 / 아버지가 요리사인 / 아주 좋아한다 / 요리하는
것을.'의 어순이므로 선행사 My friend 뒤에 whose가 온다.
whose는 my friend's를 대신하므로 뒤에 명사 father가 와야 한다.

9 해설 '그녀는 / 산다 / 집에 / 정원이 꽃들로 가득한.'의 어순이므로
선행사는 a house가 된다. a house's를 대신할 수 있는 소유격
관계대명사 whose를 써야 한다.

   p.175

1 what she hid under the bed
2 Did you understand what I explained
3 What surprised us was Tom's rude attitude
4 What we remember is his name.
5 She liked what he cooked for dinner.
6 These clothes are not[aren't] what I ordered.
7 This is what I lost on the subway.
8 Tell me what you want to do this summer
   vacation.
9 This is what I wanted to have.

7 이것이 그것이다. 나는 그것을 지하철에서 잃어버렸다.
   → 이것이 내가 지하철에서 잃어버렸던 것이다.
   해설 what이 이끄는 절에 원래의 목적어 it을 쓰지 않도록 주의한다.
8 내게 그것을 말해줘. 너는 이번 여름방학에 그것을 하고 싶어 해.
   → 내게 네가 이번 여름방학에 하고 싶은 것을 말해줘.
9 A: Jimmy, 생일 축하해! 이건 너를 위한 선물이란다.
   B: 고마워요, 엄마. 이거 새 휴대 전화예요?
   A: 응, 맞아. 마음에 드니?
   B: 물론이죠! 이것은 제가 가지고 싶었던 거예요.

Chapter Test   p.176

1 the man who gave her some flowers
2 what I do every day
3 the market which sold delicious traditional dishes
4 The museum that I wanted to visit
5 who is nine years old
6 the bag which I bought yesterday
7 a cat whose name is Matt
8 who is holding the balloons is my older sister

3 어휘 traditional 전통의, 전통적인
5 해설 주격 관계대명사절의 동사는 선행사(a little brother)에 수를
   일치시키므로 be동사는 현재형 단수동사인 is로 쓴다.
7 해설 a cat과 name이 소유 관계이므로 소유격 관계대명사 whose
   를 name 앞에 쓴다.
8 A: 이 사진에는 두 명의 여자아이들이 있어. 어느 쪽이 네 언니야?
   B: 풍선들을 들고 있는 사람이 나의 언니야.
   해설 '사람은 / 풍선들을 들고 있는 / 나의 언니이다.'의 어순이 되
   어야 하고, 문장의 주어가 선행사 The person이므로 관계대명사
   절의 동사는 is holding, 문장의 동사는 is로 써야 한다.

9   who study hard
10 who(m) I interviewed was gentle
11 I brought sandwiches and some fruits which my
    mom prepared.
12 This is the question whose answer isn't clear to
    me.
13 Amy is reading a book which has over three
    hundred pages.
14 who lives next door
15 which I listen to every morning
16 whom I admire the most
17 (1) This is the movie whose ending surprised
       everyone.
    (2) The park which we visited last week was very
       peaceful.
18 which[that] I used last night
19 he spent time with in Seoul
20 whose garden was very beautiful
21 whom → which[that]   22 that → whose
23 whom → who[that]   24 him → 삭제
25 isn't → aren't 또는 potatoes → potato
26 ⓐ → who[that], ⓒ → has

9 Lisa와 Kane은 좋은 학생들이다. 그들은 열심히 공부한다.
   → Lisa와 Kane은 열심히 공부를 하는 좋은 학생들이다.
   해설 주어 They(= Lisa and Kane)를 대신하면서, 사람 선행사
   good students를 받을 수 있는 주격 관계대명사 who를 쓴다.
10 그 작가는 점잖았다. 나는 그를 인터뷰했다.
   → 내가 인터뷰한 그 작가는 점잖았다.
   해설 목적어 him(= The writer)을 대신하면서, 사람 선행사를 받을
   수 있는 목적격 관계대명사 who나 whom을 쓴다.
   어휘 gentle 점잖은   interview 인터뷰하다; 인터뷰
11 나는 샌드위치와 과일을 좀 가져왔다. 나의 엄마가 그것들을 준비
   해 주셨다.
   → 나는 나의 엄마가 준비해 주신 샌드위치와 과일을 좀 가져왔다.
   해설 목적어 them(= sandwiches and some fruits)을 대신하면서,
   사물 선행사를 받을 수 있는 목적격 관계대명사 which를 쓴다.
12 이것은 그 문제이다. 그것의 답이 내게 명확하지 않다.
   → 이것은 내게 답이 명확하지 않은 그 문제이다.
   해설 Its를 대신할 수 있는 소유격 관계대명사 whose를 쓴다.
13 Amy는 책을 읽고 있다. 그것은 300페이지가 넘는다.
   → Amy는 300페이지가 넘는 책을 읽고 있다.
14 너는 옆집에 사는 사람을 아니?
15 이것은 내가 매일 아침에 듣는 노래이다.
16 내가 가장 존경하는 예술가는 빈센트 반 고흐이다.
   어휘 admire 존경하다; 감탄하다
17 〈A〉 Ellen은 좋은 친구이다. 이것은 영화이다.
       그 공원은 매우 평화롭다.
   〈B〉 그것의 결말은 모두를 놀라게 했다. 그녀는 늘 나를 도와준다.
       우리는 지난주에 그곳을 방문했다.
   〈보기〉 늘 나를 도와주는 Ellen은 좋은 친구이다.
   (1) 이것은 결말이 모두를 놀라게 했던 영화이다.
   (2) 우리가 지난주에 방문한 공원은 매우 평화로웠다.
   어휘 peaceful 평화로운
18 해설 목적어 the towel을 대신하는 목적격 관계대명사 which[that]
   을 써야 하므로 목적어 the towel은 중복해서 쓰지 않도록 한다.
   어휘 towel 수건
19 해설 목적격 관계대명사절 안에는 목적어 his friends를 중복해서
   쓰지 않는다.

20 해설 The cafe's garden에서 The cafe's를 대신할 수 있는 소유격 관계대명사 whose를 써야 한다.

21 나의 가족이 머물렀던 그 호텔은 좋은 서비스를 갖추고 있다.

해설 선행사 The hotel은 사람이 아닌 사물이므로 목적격 관계대명사 which 또는 that으로 써야 한다.

22 나는 꿈이 과학자가 되는 것인 한 똑똑한 여자아이를 만났다.

해설 명사 a smart girl과 dream이 소유 관계(a smart girl's dream)이므로 소유격 관계대명사 whose를 쓴다.

23 나는 일본에 사는 한 친구를 방문하러 갔다.

해설 관계대명사 뒤에 동사 lives가 나오고 관계대명사절 안에서 주어 역할을 하고 있으므로 목적격이 아닌 주격 관계대명사가 와야 한다.

24 김 선생님은 내가 아주 많이 존경하는 내 이웃이다.

해설 관계대명사 who가 동사 respect의 목적어 him(= Mr. Kim)을 대신하는 목적격 관계대명사이므로 목적어 him을 중복해서 쓰지 않아야 한다.

어휘 neighbor 이웃

25 오늘 내가 산 감자들은[감자는] 그다지 신선하지 않다.

해설 관계대명사절의 수식을 받는 문장의 주어(The potatoes)가 복수명사이므로 문장의 동사는 aren't로 써야 한다. 또는 동사(isn't)의 수에 맞게 주어를 단수명사 The potato로 고쳐 쓸 수 있다.

26 ⓐ 우리는 수원에 사는 사촌들을 종종 방문한다.

ⓑ 차를 도난당한 여성이 경찰을 불렀다.

ⓒ 나는 독특한 무늬가 있는 저 드레스가 마음에 든다.

ⓓ 많은 학생들이 좋아하는 그 선생님은 Johnson 선생님이다.

ⓔ 나는 네가 알고 싶어 하는 것을 말해 줄 수 있어.

해설 ⓐ 주격 관계대명사의 선행사(our cousins)가 사람이므로 관계대명사 who 또는 that으로 써야 한다.

ⓒ 선행사(that dress)가 단수명사이므로 which 뒤에는 단수동사 has가 와야 한다.

어휘 steal 훔치다　pattern 무늬

ⓒ 나의 언니는 그녀의 같은 반 친구들보다 훨씬 더 열심히 공부했다.

ⓓ 그는 너무 빨리 말해서 나는 그의 말을 이해할 수 없었다.

ⓔ 그녀는 아침에 사과를 먹거나 커피를 마신다.

해설 ⓑ 주격 관계대명사 that이 관계대명사 절 안에서 주어 역할을 하므로 주어 it을 중복해서 쓰지 않도록 삭제해야 한다.

ⓔ 「either A or B」에서 A와 B는 문법적으로 성격이 같아야 한다. 주어(She)가 3인칭 단수이고 eats와 연결되므로 drink를 drinks로 고쳐 써야 한다.

어휘 patient 참을성 있는　review (책, 영화 등에 대한) 리뷰, 논평

27 (1) which[that] Hajun hopes to visit is

(2) which[that] Hajun plans to eat is

(3) What Hajun wants to buy

28 who is standing in front of the bank

27 (1) Q: 하준이는 어디를 방문하길 바라는가?

A: 하준이가 방문하길 바라는 곳은 뉴욕이다.

(2) Q: 하준이는 어떤 음식을 먹을 계획인가?

A: 하준이가 먹기로 계획한 음식은 크림 파스타이다.

(3) Q: 하준이는 무엇을 사고 싶어 하는가?

A: 하준이가 사고 싶어 하는 것은 자전거이다.

28 Kevin: 나는 Eva를 만나게 되어서 정말로 신나! 내가 그녀를 마지막으로 본 지 1년이 되었어. 그녀는 어디에 있니?

Chris: 그녀는 저기에 있어! 그녀는 우리를 기다리고 있어.

Kevin: 그녀는 벤치에 앉아 있니?

Chris: 아니.

Kevin: 그녀는 은행 앞에 서 있니?

Chris: 맞아, 그 사람이 바로 그녀야.

→ Eva는 은행 앞에 서 있는 여자아이이다.

Challenge!

29 ⓑ → I'm reading a book that has great reviews.

ⓔ → She either eats apples or drinks coffee in the morning.

29 ⓐ 인내심을 가져라, 그러면 너는 결과를 보게 될 것이다.

ⓑ 나는 평이 아주 좋은 책 한 권을 읽고 있다.

천일문

2 LEVEL

WORKBOOK

| 정답 및 해설 |

중등

WRiTiNG

Unit 01 SVC(2형식)/SVOO(4형식)　　p.02

1 Your room looks very messy
2 The shirt feels soft and comfortable
3 bought me some chocolate
4 sent students class materials
5 smells a bit sour
6 I will[I'll] make a dinner for my parents
7 My brother gave some useful advice to me.
8 The guide told the tour schedule to the tourists.
9 He teaches me different exercises.

9　A: 너는 운동을 자주 하니?
　　B: 거의 매일 운동해. 나의 형이 트레이너여서 그가 나를 많이 도와줘.
　　A: 멋지다! 그가 너를 어떻게 도와주니?
　　B: 그는 나에게 다양한 운동을 가르쳐 줘.

Unit 02 SVOC(5형식)　　p.03

1 I keep my nails short
2 The coach made the players practice
3 The fans wanted the singer to sing
4 They made Tommy the captain of the team.
5 She heard the phone ring[ringing]
6 The teacher let the students leave
7 He told the kids not to run
8 The museum does not[doesn't] allow people to take photos.
9 (1) I saw[watched] the cat chase[chasing] the mouse.
　(2) Mr. Clark made[had, let] the children clean up their toys.

9　해설 (1) '목적어가 ~하는 것을 보다'는 「see[watch]+목적어+목적격보어」의 순서로 쓴다. 이때 목적격보어 자리에는 동사원형 또는 현재분사를 쓸 수 있다.
　(2) '목적어가 ~을 하게 하다/하도록 시키다'는 「make[have, let]+목적어+목적격보어」의 순서로 쓴다. 이때 목적격보어 자리에는 동사원형을 써야 한다.

Chapter 02 시제

Unit 01 현재, 과거, 미래 & 진행형　　p.04

1 Paul is taking a nap
2 We were waiting for the bus
3 The hairdresser is cutting the boy's hair
4 will study abroad　　5 exercises at the gym
6 got a new job　　7 They won the first prize
8 The girls are shopping for new clothes
9 Are you going to paint the fence
10 (1) I was setting the table
　 (2) I felt thankful for electricity

10 어젯밤에, 아빠는 저녁 식사를 준비하고 계셨다. 나는 그를 돕기 위해 식탁을 차리고 있었다. 갑자기, 전기가 나갔다. 한 시간 후에 불이 다시 켜졌다. 그날, 나는 전기에 감사함을 느꼈다.

Unit 02 현재완료의 개념과 형태　　p.05

1 have broken　　2 has, returned
3 Have, visited　　4 has given
5 I have[I've] met a famous actor
6 They have[They've] been married
7 She has not[hasn't] eaten fast food
8 Has Ian finished packing his bag
9 ridden　　10 have
11 bought
12 (1) Ryan and I have visited that museum
　 (2) I have not[haven't] received your message.

9 나는 이전에 말을 타본 적이 있다.
10 그 아이들은 이 도시에 10년 동안 살고 있다.
11 나의 아빠는 5년 전에 그 차를 사셨다.
　　해설 과거를 나타내는 five years ago는 현재완료와 함께 쓸 수 없으므로 has bought를 bought로 고쳐 써야 한다.

Unit 03 현재완료의 주요 의미　　p.06

1 She has forgotten her email password
2 I have never done scuba diving
3 We have stayed at our uncle's house since last week
4 have practiced yoga
5 has gone to the U.S.
6 Peter has already gone to bed.
7 Have you ever tried Mexican food
8 Our team has just scored a goal
9 (1) I have[I've] lost my favorite pen.
　 (2) My sister has worn these glasses for two years.

4 나는 1년 전에 요가를 시작했다. 나는 여전히 그것을 연습한다.
　　→ 나는 1년 동안 요가를 연습해왔다.
　　해설 과거부터 지금까지 계속 요가를 연습하고 있으므로 현재완료형인 have practiced를 써야 한다.
5 나의 엄마는 일 때문에 미국에 가셨다. 그녀는 지금 여기 안 계신다.
　　→ 나의 엄마는 일 때문에 미국에 가셨다.
　　해설 나의 엄마가 미국에 가셔서 지금 안 계신다는 결과를 나타내므로 현재완료형인 has gone to를 써야 한다.

Unit 01 can/may/will   p.07

1 Jay can memorize his favorite poem
2 Could you lend me your book
3 I wasn't able to find my passport
4 You may not take photos with flash
5 will be able to move into
6 You can't return this
7 Would you give another piece of pizza to me?
8 The clothing store may not be open
9 Guests can[may] check in any time

Unit 02 must/have to/should   p.08

1 All visitors must sign in
2 Everyone has to wear a helmet
3 You should not spend all your money
4 She will have to wake up early
5 Jason must be very tired
6 You don't[do not] have to wait for me.
7 The baby has to take a nap
8 Students should not[shouldn't] be rude to the teachers.
9 has to practice, doesn't[does not] have to memorize

Unit 03 had better/would like to/used to   p.09

1 You had better wear a coat
2 Eddy used to be a dancer
3 I would like to visit the new bakery
4 We had better not miss this bus
5 We had[We'd] better wear sunscreen
6 Would you like to go out for a pizza
7 Tina had better not lose the keys to the locker
8 My grandma used to tell stories to me
9 you had better choose between the two

9 A: 무슨 일이야?
  B: 나는 스트레스를 받고 있어. 나는 이번 주 금요일에 있는 영어 말하기 시험을 준비해야 하지만, 밴드 연습도 가야 해.
  A: 음, 너는 두 가지 중에 선택하는 것이 좋겠어.
  해설 '~하는 게 좋다'라는 충고나 권고의 의미는 had better를 사용해 나타낸다.

1 She looks like a pop star
2 Have you ever been to Jeonju
3 Mina showed me her new cell phone
4 Can you hold my umbrella
5 You may return my camera
6 I had to wake up early
7 don't have to buy a ticket
8 People called the player a hero.
9 The heavy snow made my shoes wet.
10 I am[I'm] going to travel to Europe this winter vacation.
11 I let my cousin use my computer.
12 I watched him swim[swimming] fast.
13 Dad allowed me to go camping.
14 She ordered us to leave the room.
15 I have lost my ring.
16 Tony has gone to Japan.
17 Seho has studied Chinese
18 Jessie has attended the world history class
19 (1) gave gloves to
   (2) made a muffler for
   (3) cooked chicken and fish for
   (4) bought a yellow cap for
   (5) showed a movie to
20 had → has   21 sweetly → sweet
22 has happened → happened
23 have to not → don't[do not] have to
24 (1) you had[you'd] better not eat too fast
   (2) Would you like to have some ice cream for dessert
25 has worked on the science project for
26 has taken violin lessons since

4 어휘 for a minute 잠깐
6 해설 have to의 과거형은 had to로 쓴다.
9 해설 '~을 …(상태)로 만들다'라는 의미를 나타낼 때는 「make+목적어+형용사」의 어순으로 쓴다.
11 해설 사역동사 let의 목적격보어 자리에는 동사원형을 쓴다.
12 해설 지각동사 watch의 목적격보어 자리에는 동사원형 또는 현재분사가 쓰인다.
13 해설 동사 allow는 목적격보어 자리에 to부정사를 쓴다.
14 해설 동사 order는 목적격보어 자리에 to부정사를 쓴다.
[15~18] 〈보기〉 Mark는 2020년에 한국에 도착했다. 그는 여전히 이곳에 산다.
        → Mark는 2020년부터 한국에서 살아왔다.
15 나는 나의 반지를 잃어버렸다. 그래서 나는 지금 그것이 없다.
   → 나는 나의 반지를 잃어버렸다.
16 Tony는 일본에 갔다. 그래서 그는 지금 여기에 없다.
   → Tony는 일본에 가버렸다.
17 세호는 2022년에 중국어를 공부하기 시작했다. 그는 여전히 그것을 공부한다.
   → 세호는 2022년부터 중국어를 공부해왔다.
18 Jessie는 다섯 달 전에 세계사 수업을 듣기 시작했다. 그녀는 여전히 그 수업을 듣는다.
   → Jessie는 다섯 달 동안 세계사 수업을 들었다.
   어휘 attend 출석하다, 참석하다

19

유나의 생일 선물 목록	
아빠	장갑
엄마	목도리
할머니	닭고기와 생선
언니	노란색 모자
가장 친한 친구	영화

(1) 유나의 아빠는 그녀에게 장갑을 주셨다.
(2) 유나의 엄마는 그녀에게 목도리를 만들어 주셨다.
(3) 유나의 할머니는 그녀에게 닭고기와 생선을 요리해 주셨다.
(4) 유나의 언니는 그녀에게 노란색 모자를 사 주었다.
(5) 유나의 가장 친한 친구는 그녀에게 영화를 한 편 보여 주었다.
[어휘] muffler 목도리

20 일 년은 12개월이다.

21 뜨거운 코코아는 매우 달콤한 맛이 났다.
[해설] 감각동사 뒤에는 형용사를 쓴다.

22 그 사고는 3일 전에 일어났다.
[해설] 현재완료 시제는 과거를 나타내는 부사구와 함께 쓰지 않는다.
[어휘] accident 사고

23 너는 식사비를 낼 필요가 없다. 내가 이미 그것을 냈다.
[해설] have to의 부정형은 don't[do not] have to로 쓴다.

24 수미: 엄마, 제가 밥을 더 먹어도 될까요?
엄마: 그래. 하지만 너무 급하게 먹지 않는 게 좋겠다. 천천히 먹지
않으면 체하게 될 거야.
수미: 네. 천천히 먹을게요.
엄마: 디저트로 아이스크림을 먹겠니?
수미: 물론이죠! 저는 아이스크림이 너무 좋아요.
[해설] (1) 문맥상 딸에게 너무 급하게 먹지 말라고 충고하는 문장을
써야 하므로, 주어진 단어 better를 사용해 부정형인 had['d]
better not으로 쓴다.
(2) 문맥상 딸에게 아이스크림을 먹겠냐고 제안하는 문장으로 써야
하므로, 주어진 단어를 사용해 「Would you like to ~?」 문장을 쓰
면 된다.
[어휘] have an upset stomach 체하다, 배탈이 나다

25 A: 요즘 바쁘니, Eric?
B: 응, 맞아. 나는 과학 프로젝트를 하고 있어. 나는 그것을 2주 전
에 시작했어.
A: 언제 그것을 끝낼 거니?
B: 모르겠어. 나는 그것을 몇 주 더 해야 해.
→ Eric은 2주 동안 과학 프로젝트를 해왔다.
[해설] 현재완료 문장에서 기간(two weeks)을 나타내는 말 앞에는
for를 쓴다.

26 A: 세라는 바이올린을 아주 잘 연주하는구나.
B: 나도 동의해. 그녀는 작년 여름 방학에 바이올린 레슨을 받기 시
작했어. 그리고 그녀는 여전히 매주 주말마다 레슨을 받아.
→ 세라는 작년 여름 방학부터 바이올린 레슨을 받아왔다.
[해설] 현재완료 문장에서 시작 시점(last summer vacation) 앞에는
since를 쓴다.

---

4 Our homework is checked by the teacher
5 The gold medal was won by our soccer team
6 The city's park will be cleaned by the volunteers.
7 The school bus is driven by Mr. Johnson.
8 The new songs will be released
9 The comedy movie was watched by a large
audience.
10 The song was written by my favorite musician

4 선생님은 매일 우리의 숙제를 검사하신다.
→ 우리의 숙제는 선생님에 의해 매일 검사된다.
5 우리 축구팀은 올해 금메달을 획득했다.
→ 올해 금메달은 우리 축구팀에 의해 획득되었다.
6 자원봉사자들이 도시의 공원을 청소할 것이다.
→ 도시의 공원은 자원봉사자들에 의해 청소될 것이다.
10 A: 너는 이 노래를 들어본 적 있니?
B: 응. 들어봤어! 그 노래는 내가 가장 좋아하는 음악가인 Taylor에
의해 쓰였어.
A: 정말? 난 몰랐어!
B: 멜로디가 정말 아름다워.
[해설] 주어 The song이 write의 동작을 받는 대상이므로 과거시제
수동태인 was written을 쓴다. 행위자 앞에는 전치사 by를 써야
한다.

Unit 02 수동태의 여러 가지 형태 p.14

1 The plants were not watered
2 When was the fence painted
3 The rules must be followed by everyone
4 This movie should not be watched by kids
5 I was told the secret
6 The answers were shown to us
7 Breakfast was cooked for the guests
8 Your mistake will be forgotten
9 Why was the concert canceled[cancelled]
10 My brother is interested in pet training.
11 This cheese is made from fresh milk

5 나의 가장 친한 친구가 나에게 비밀을 말해주었다.
→ 나는 내 가장 친한 친구에 의해 비밀을 들었다.
6 선생님은 우리에게 정답을 보여주셨다.
→ 정답은 선생님에 의해 우리에게 보여졌다.
7 Miller 씨는 손님들에게 아침 식사를 요리해 주었다.
→ 아침 식사는 Miller 씨에 의해 손님들에게 요리되었다.

Chapter 04 수동태

Unit 01 수동태의 기본 이해 p.13

1 Our family trip was planned by me
2 Maps are provided by the staff
3 The invitation to the school's dance party will be
sent out

Chapter 05 to부정사

Unit 01 to부정사의 명사적 쓰임 p.15

1 She chose to join the debate club
2 It is exciting to explore a new place
3 It is wise not to talk to strangers
4 We don't know where to go for the school trip

5 It is scary to watch
6 decided not to participate in
7 Can you explain how to use this app?
8 I do not[don't] know what to wear for the event.
9 It is not easy to break an old habit.

Unit 02 to부정사의 형용사적 쓰임   p.16

1 I have a vocabulary test to take
2 Mark needs someone to take him
3 Our cat has many toys to play with
4 She is looking for something fun to do
5 Can you recommend a book to read
6 Daniel booked a hotel to stay in
7 I did not[didn't] have a chance to tell
8 Jessica bought a new bed to sleep on.
9 (1) I need a knife to cut the vegetables.
  (2) He needs someone to talk to[with]

Unit 03 to부정사의 부사적 쓰임   p.17

1 to protect the environment
2 is easy to read
3 to improve his health
4 was pleased to hear from her old friend
5 will set an alarm to wake up
6 These clothes are cool to wear
7 I was disappointed to get a low score
8 practiced every day to become a better musician
9 We were excited to meet our favorite author.
10 to research marine life

10 John은 그의 과학 숙제로 해양 생물에 대해 조사하고 싶었기 때문에 도서관에 방문했다.
　→ John은 그의 과학 숙제로 해양 생물에 대해 조사하기 위해 도서관에 방문했다.

Unit 04 to부정사를 포함한 주요 구문   p.18

1 too nervous to perform
2 too busy to have lunch
3 fast enough to win first place
4 He was too angry to talk calmly.
5 My sister is old enough to drive a car.
6 so shocked that she couldn't say
7 so strong that he can carry
8 too sick to attend
9 I was too sleepy to stay awake

6 그 소녀는 너무 충격 받아서 아무 말도 할 수 없었다.
7 그는 그 무거운 상자를 옮길 만큼 충분히 힘이 세다.
8 나는 어제 너무 아파서 그 모임에 참석할 수 없었다.
9 A: 어젯밤에 영화 어땠어?

B: 솔직히, 영화 보는 동안 난 너무 졸려서 깨어 있을 수 없었어.
A: 정말? 그 영화가 그렇게 지루했니?
B: 아니, 내 생각엔 그냥 피곤했던 것 같아.

Chapter 06 동명사와 분사

Unit 01 명사로 쓰이는 동명사   p.19

1 Reading mystery novels is
2 Not wearing a seatbelt is dangerous
3 His job is designing a new website
4 Cathy keeps updating her blog with new posts
5 He put off cleaning his room
6 Writing stories helps to build
7 I began saving[to save] money for a trip
8 We forgot making a reservation
9 Try to focus on one section

9 A: 나는 이 퍼즐을 맞추려고 애쓰는 중이야. 너무 어려워.
B: 한 번에 한 구역에만 집중하려고 노력해 봐. 그 편이 더 쉬울 거야.
해설 '～하려고 노력하다'는 의미를 나타낼 때는 「try+to부정사」로 써야 한다.

Unit 02 자주 쓰이는 동명사 표현   p.20

1 is good at painting landscapes
2 went hiking with his friends
3 Thank you for taking care of my pet dogs
4 made many new friends by joining the drama club
5 My grandparents look forward to seeing us
6 The baker spends hours decorating cakes
7 I left the room without turning off the lights.
8 She has trouble remembering people's names.
9 he is interested in singing

9 Billy와 나는 학교 밴드에서 처음 만났다. 우리는 둘 다 다양한 음악 장르에 관해 이야기하는 것을 즐긴다. 나는 기타를 연주하고, 그는 노래하는 것에 관심이 있다. 우리는 같은 목표를 갖고 있다. 우리는 둘 다 미래에 음악가가 되기를 바란다.
해설 '～에 관심이 있다'는 의미는 「be interested in+-ing」로 쓸 수 있다.

Unit 03 분사   p.21

1 I felt embarrassed about my mistake
2 They found the missing dog
3 The result of the experiment was surprising
4 The letter written by my friend arrived today
5 His disappointing behavior made his parents upset
6 Her speech was very touching.
7 The teacher was amazed by the students' creativity.

8 He moved to the house built near the beach.

9 (1) You seem annoyed.

　(2) The loud music next door is really annoying.

9　A: 너 짜증나 보인다. 무슨 일이야?

　　B: 옆집의 시끄러운 음악이 정말 짜증나.

　　A: 나도 들려.

　　B: 응, 어떤 것도 집중하기 어려워!

　　해설 (1) 주어인 You가 감정을 느끼는 것이므로 과거분사(annoyed)를 써야 한다.

　　(2) 주어인 The loud music이 짜증나는 감정을 일으키는 것이므로 현재분사(annoying)를 써야 한다.

총괄평가 2회 Chapter 04~06　p.22

1 Playing at the amusement park is very fun

2 came home early to do her homework

3 tell me how to get to City Hall

4 spent five thousand won buying a bottle of juice

5 is made of

6 was busy doing housework

7 my package be delivered

8 promised to be honest with each other

9 There is a bench to sit on

10 asked me where to buy the book

11 is big enough to hold all the guests

12 The TV was turned off by my father

13 This book will improve my writing skills

14 The mailman did not[didn't] deliver the invitation

15 Is English spoken by the students

16 was given to his sons by him

17 It is[It's] hard to understand the poem.

18 It is not[It isn't, It's not] good to eat fast food very often.

19 Susan is staying at the hotel located downtown.

20 Look at the old lady watering the flowers.

21 My father was too tired to pick me up after school.

22 Jisu studied hard enough to pass the exam.

23 Nick is so sleepy that he can't[cannot] concentrate on the class.

24 visit → visiting　　**25** for → to

26 to not → not to　　**27** to buy → buying

28 interested　　**29** shocking

30 excited　　**31** touching

32 (1) The visitors were welcomed

　(2) A quiz show was held

　(3) Food and soft drinks were sold

　(4) The school orchestra was conducted

33 ⓑ → remembered having

　ⓓ → excited to see

　ⓔ → is known for

5　해설 '~으로 만들어지다'의 뜻으로 재료의 성질이 변하지 않으므로 be made of를 쓴다.

7　해설 조동사를 포함한 수동태 의문문은 「조동사＋주어＋be＋과거분사(p.p. ~?)」로 쓴다.

　　어휘 deliver 배달하다

11　해설 '~할 만큼 충분히 …하다'를 나타낼 땐 「형용사/부사＋enough＋to부정사」의 순서로 쓴다.

　　어휘 guest 손님, 하객

12 나의 아버지께서 한 시간 전에 TV를 끄셨다.

　　→ TV는 한 시간 전에 나의 아버지에 의해 꺼졌다.

13 나의 글쓰기 실력은 이 책에 의해 개선될 것이다.

　　→ 이 책은 나의 글쓰기 실력을 개선할 것이다.

　　어휘 improve 개선하다, 향상시키다

14 초대장은 어제 우체부에 의해 배달되지 않았다.

　　→ 우체부는 어제 초대장을 배달하지 않았다.

15 그 학생들은 수업 시간 동안 영어를 말하니?

　　→ 영어가 수업 시간 동안 그 학생들에 의해 말해지니?

16 그는 그의 아들들에게 돈을 좀 주었다.

　　→ 약간의 돈이 그에 의해 그의 아들들에게 주어졌다.

17　어휘 poem (한 편의) 시

[19~20] 〈보기〉 아빠는 나에게 자전거를 주셨다. 그것은 이탈리아에서 만들어졌다.

　　　　　　→ 아빠는 나에게 이탈리아에서 만들어진 자전거를 주셨다.

19 Susan은 호텔에 머무르고 있다. 그곳은 시내에 위치해 있다.

　　→ Susan은 시내에 위치한 호텔에 머무르고 있다.

20 저 노부인을 봐. 그녀는 꽃들에 물을 주고 계셔.

　　→ 꽃들에 물을 주고 계시는 저 노부인을 봐.

21 나의 아버지는 너무 피곤하셔서 방과 후에 나를 데리러 오실 수 없었다.

22 지수는 그 시험에 합격할 만큼 충분히 열심히 공부했다.

23 Nick은 너무 졸려서 수업에 집중할 수 없다.

　　어휘 concentrate on ~에 집중하다

24 나는 다음 주에 그 박물관을 다시 방문하는 것을 꺼리지 않는다.

25 이 편지는 나의 할아버지에 의해 나에게 보내졌다.

26 너는 똑같은 실수를 하지 않도록 주의해야 한다.

　　해설 to부정사의 부정형은 not을 to부정사 앞에 쓴다.

27 엄마는 어제 우유 산 것을 잊으셨다. 그녀는 오늘 하나를 더 사셨다.

　　해설 문맥상 과거(어제)에 했던 일을 잊어버린 것이므로 to buy를 buying으로 고쳐야 한다.

28 동민이는 과학에 관심이 있다. 그는 많은 과학책들을 읽는다. 과학자가 되는 것이 그의 꿈이다.

29 아침에 나는 도로에 많은 구급차들을 보았다. 큰 사고가 있었다! 그것은 내게 매우 충격적이었다.

　　어휘 ambulance 구급차　 accident 사고

30 나는 이번 주 금요일을 기다리고 있다. 나의 아버지와 나는 캠핑을 갈 것이다. 나는 그것에 매우 들떠 있다.

31 나는 지난주말에 가족과 함께 영화를 한 편 보았다. 나는 그 영화가 매우 감동적이어서 영화를 보는 동안 울었다.

32

학교 축제	
민희	방문객들 환영하기
수지	퀴즈 쇼 개최하기
동호	음식과 탄산음료 판매하기
나미	학교 오케스트라 지휘하기

(1) 방문객들은 민희에 의해 환영받았다.

(2) 퀴즈 쇼는 수지에 의해 개최되었다.

(3) 음식과 탄산음료는 동호에 의해 판매되었다.

(4) 학교 오케스트라는 나미에 의해 지휘되었다.

　어휘 conduct 지휘하다

33　예나의 가족은 3년 전에 대구로 이사를 갔다. 그들은 그녀의 친척 집에 초대를 받아서 다음 달에 서울을 방문할 것이다.

　　예나는 그곳에서 옛 친구들을 만나는 것을 고려했다. 그녀는 초등학교 때 그들과 좋은 시간을 보냈던 것을 기억했다. 그녀는 그들에게 전화했고 하루를 함께 즐겁게 보내기로 결정했다. 예나는 그들을 다시 만나게 되어 기뻤다. 예나와 그녀의 친구들은 인기 있는 식당을 방문할 것이다. 그곳은 한국식 바비큐로 유명하다.
해설 ⓑ 문맥상 과거에 시간을 보낸 것을 기억하는 것이므로 동명
사 having으로 고쳐 써야 한다.
ⓓ '~해서 …한 감정을 느낀다'라는 의미는 「감정 형용사+to부정
사」의 형태로 쓴다.
ⓔ 식당이 유명한 이유(its Korean barbecue)가 그 뒤에 나오므로
be known for를 써야 한다. be known to는 '~에게 알려지다'라
는 의미로 그 뒤에 알려진 대상이 나온다.
어휘 relative 친척

Chapter 07 대명사, 형용사, 부사

Unit 01 대명사   p.25

1 make yourself at home
2 Some people like coffee, others prefer tea
3 One was soup, another was salad, the other was pasta
4 One lives in Seoul, the other lives in Busan
5 Every question on the exam was difficult.
6 Each of the houses is painted
7 Mr. and Ms. Smith decorated the house themselves.
  또는 Mr. and Ms. Smith themselves decorated the house.
8 (1) Jisu thought to herself
  (2) Each country has its own traditions.

Unit 02 형용사와 부사   p.26

1 We enjoyed a peaceful evening
2 We are looking for someone creative
3 Many students found Mr. Brown's lesson helpful
4 I sometimes visit art galleries
5 Mom is usually tired after work.
6 There was little rain last night.
7 We don't have much information
8 Few students attended the science fair.
9 (1) is always in bed before 10 p.m.
  (2) hardly reads a book before bed

9

	Sam	Hailey
(1) 밤 10시 전에 잠자리에 들기	매일 밤	전혀 안 함
(2) 잠자리에 들기 전에 책 읽기	일주일에 세 번	일주일에 한 번

(1) Sam은 항상 밤 10시 전에 잠자리에 든다.
(2) Hailey는 잠자리에 들기 전에 거의 책을 읽지 않는다.

Chapter 08 비교 표현

Unit 01 원급, 비교급, 최상급   p.27

1 is not as smart as her older sister
2 This novel is thicker than that magazine
3 Today is the hottest day of the year
4 is as cold as ice
5 was a lot easier than the last one
6 finished the race more quickly than his friends
7 has the most beautiful voice in the choir
8 (1) as much as   (2) the fastest animals
9 (1) Tokyo is not[isn't] as[so] cold as
  (2) Taipei is much warmer than

8 (1) 그는 그의 아빠만큼 낚시를 하는 것을 즐긴다.
  (2) 치타는 육지에서 가장 빠른 동물 중 하나이다.
  해설 (2) '가장 ~한 … 중 하나'라는 의미를 나타내는 표현은 「one
  of the+최상급+복수명사」로 쓰므로 animal을 animals로 고쳐
  써야 한다.
9 (1) 도쿄는 오늘 서울만큼 춥지 않다.
  (2) 타이베이는 오늘 서울보다 훨씬 더 따뜻하다.

Unit 02 원급, 비교급을 이용한 표현   p.28

1 as soon as possible   2 busier and busier
3 The earlier, the sooner   4 worse and worse
5 four times as tall as
6 His new house is three times as wide as his old one
7 The city is getting more and more crowded
8 The harder you work, the more you will achieve
9 is twice[two times] as large as the one

9 A: 새로 생긴 쇼핑몰에 갔었니?
  B: 응, 그것은 정말 커! 그것은 중심가에 있는 것보다 두 배만큼 더 커.
  A: 와, 진짜? 나도 확인해봐야겠다.

Chapter 09 접속사

Unit 01 and, but, or의 쓰임   p.29

1 Use sunscreen, or you might get sunburned
2 Both my parents and my friends support my decision
3 He will either buy a new phone or fix the old one
4 Set your goals, and you will[you'll] achieve your dreams.
5 Both Joshua and Mary are going to come to the party.

6 Either the salad or the soup will be served

7 Neither the sweater nor the jacket fits me

8 The cookies as well as the cake were tasty.

9 Not only I but also my sister enjoys cooking.

9 나뿐만 아니라 내 여동생도 요리하기를 즐긴다.

Unit 02 부사절을 이끄는 접속사   p.30

1 While I was waiting for the bus

2 after the teacher gave the instructions

3 because he wanted to avoid the rush hour

4 until she finishes her homework

5 Although she is[she's] allergic to cats

6 (1) The hot chocolate was so hot that I burned my tongue.

  (2) The road was so icy that my mom drove the car carefully.

7 (1) If you do not[don't] have a ticket, you can't[cannot] enter.

  (2) Unless you have a ticket, you can't[cannot] enter.

6 (1) 그 코코아는 매우 뜨거웠다. 나는 혀를 데였다.

  → 그 코코아는 너무 뜨거워서 나는 혀를 데었다.

  (2) 도로는 얼어붙었다. 나의 엄마는 주의해서 차를 운전하셨다.

  → 도로가 너무 얼어붙어서 나의 엄마는 주의해서 차를 운전하셨다.

Unit 03 명사절을 이끄는 접속사   p.31

1 I don't remember if I locked the door

2 I think that everyone should respect each other

3 It is clear that she put a lot of effort

4 I have no idea who left the window open

5 if[whether] Harry will accept my apology

6 when he would arrive at the airport

7 remember where you put your glasses

8 explain why you didn't show up to the meeting

9 He realized (that) his dad's advice was very helpful.

10 I don't know why he canceled[cancelled] the plan.

10 〈보기〉 나는 궁금하다. + 저 기계는 어떻게 작동하니?

  → 나는 저 기계가 어떻게 작동하는지 궁금하다.

  나는 알지 못한다. + 그는 왜 그 계획을 취소했니?

  → 나는 그가 왜 그 계획을 취소했는지 알지 못한다.

Chapter 10 관계대명사

Unit 01 who, which, that   p.32

1 the doctor who saved my life

2 the guide who led the tour

3 his smartphone that is brand new

4 The movie which won the award

5 She raises a cat which has green eyes.

6 The manager who runs the store is friendly.

7 Hazel found a dress which fits her

8 Tourists visited the bridge which connects the two cities.

9 (1) The reporter interviewed the boy who won the competition.

  (2) The lamp which lights the room is broken.

9 (1) 기자는 그 소년을 인터뷰했다. 그는 대회에서 우승을 했다.

  → 기자는 대회에서 우승한 그 소년을 인터뷰했다.

  (2) 그 전등은 고장 났다. 그것은 방을 밝힌다.

  → 방을 밝히는 그 전등은 고장 났다.

Unit 02 who(m), which, that   p.33

1 the singer-songwriter whom I like

2 the movie which I recommended yesterday

3 the student who(m) we elected as school president

4 The shoes which I ordered online

5 I met the person who(m) you mentioned yesterday.

6 The cake which she baked for the party was

7 My brother sold the bike which he does not[doesn't] use anymore.

8 I apologized to the girl who(m)[that] I accidentally pushed.

[3-4] 〈보기〉 나는 책을 잃어버렸다.

  Justin은 지난주에 그것을 빌려주었다.

  → 나는 Justin이 지난주에 빌려준 책을 잃어버렸다.

3 Alice는 학생이다. 우리는 그녀를 학생회장으로 뽑았다.

  → Alice는 우리가 학생회장으로 뽑은 학생이다.

4 그 신발은 마침내 오늘 도착했다. 나는 그것을 온라인으로 주문했다.

  → 내가 온라인으로 주문했던 그 신발은 마침내 오늘 도착했다.

8 나는 그 여자아이에게 사과했다. 나는 실수로 그녀를 밀었다.

  → 나는 실수로 밀친 그 여자아이에게 사과했다.

Unit 03 whose, what   p.34

1 The restaurant whose food is excellent

2 The musician whose performance was fantastic

3 What Gia said surprised everyone

4 I appreciate what my parents did for me

5 What she cooks always tastes delicious.

6 The child whose toy was broken
7 the friend whose birthday is tomorrow
8 This dish is not[isn't] what I ordered.
9 Volunteers helped the people whose houses were damaged.

총괄평가 3회 Chapter 07~10 p.35

1 Jason is looking for something fun
2 Although the weather was cold
3 I couldn't believe that he was very sick
4 the singer whom we like
5 a bike which has four wheels
6 the boy who danced on the street
7 One lives here, and the other lives abroad.
8 Every person has different opinions.
9 one of the most popular clubs
10 so interesting that I read it twice
11 as old as
12 always keep my diary
13 is hardly absent from school
14 a lot more comfortable than
15 Can you tell me if[whether] Sam likes ice cream?
16 Please tell me what time it is in Washington now.
17 What do you think she is talking about?
18 Can you show me how you made these delicious cookies?
19 (1) as[so] early as (2) as large as
   (3) the most popular
20 many → much   21 me → myself
22 watch → watching   23 whom → which[that]
24 her → 삭제   25 will receive → receive
26 because of → because   27 whom → who[that]
28 whose dream is to be a pianist
29 which[that] I planned to visit
30 Sophia wanted to eat
31 so heavy that, couldn't lift
32 not only drawing but also cooking
33 both low prices and great taste
34 (1) who(m)[that] the writer met in a desert
   (2) which[that] he loved a lot
35 (1) more and more popular
   (2) dances better than
   (3) as well as
   (4) the more I practice, the better I can dance

11 A: Jackson과 Brian 중에 누가 더 나이가 많니?
   B: Jackson은 Brian과 나이가 같아. 그들은 쌍둥이거든.
12 A: 너는 얼마나 자주 일기를 쓰니?
   B: 나는 항상 일기를 써.
   어휘 keep a diary 일기를 쓰다
13 A: Jessie는 얼마나 자주 학교에 결석하니?
   B: 그녀는 거의 학교에 결석하지 않아.

어휘 absent 결석한, 부재한
14 A: 너는 어디에 앉고 싶니?
   B: 저 소파에 앉자. 의자보다 훨씬 더 편해 보여.
   A: 알겠어.
[15-18] 〈보기〉 너는 아니? Matt는 지금 왜 저렇게 행복하니?
   → 너는 Matt가 지금 왜 저렇게 행복한지 아니?
15 내게 말해주겠니? Sam은 아이스크림을 좋아하니?
   → Sam이 아이스크림을 좋아하는지 내게 말해주겠니?
   해설 의문사를 포함하지 않는 의문문이 동사 tell의 목적어 자리에 쓰이므로 「if[whether]+주어+동사」의 어순으로 써야 한다.
16 저에게 말해주세요. 지금 워싱턴은 몇 시인가요?
   → 지금 워싱턴은 몇 시인지 저에게 말해주세요.
17 너는 생각하니? 그녀는 무엇에 대해 이야기하고 있니?
   → 너는 그녀가 무엇에 대해 이야기하고 있다고 생각하니?
   해설 의문사가 이끄는 절이 동사 think의 목적어 역할을 하므로 의문사 What을 문장 맨 앞에 써야 한다.
18 나에게 보여줄 수 있니? 너는 어떻게 이 맛있는 쿠키들을 만들었니?
   → 네가 어떻게 이 맛있는 쿠키들을 만들었는지 나에게 보여줄 수 있니?

19

	시작 연도	멤버	팬
A 그룹	2023년	4명	3,000명
B 그룹	2020년	7명	6,000명
C 그룹	2018년	7명	100,000명

(1) A 그룹은 B 그룹만큼 일찍 시작하지 않았다.
(2) B 그룹의 멤버 수는 C 그룹의 멤버 수만큼 많다.
(3) C 그룹은 셋 중에서 가장 인기가 많다.
해설 (1) A 그룹은 2023년에 시작했고, B 그룹은 2020년에 시작했으므로 서로 정도가 같지 않음을 나타내는 「not as[so]+형용사[부사]의 원급+as」로 표현한다.
(2) B 그룹과 C 그룹의 멤버 수가 7명으로 같으므로 원급 비교 「as+형용사[부사]+as」로 나타낸다.
(3) C 그룹 팬의 수가 세 그룹 중 가장 많으므로 최상급 표현으로 나타낸다.
20 나의 엄마는 커피에 너무 많은 설탕을 넣으셨다.
   해설 sugar는 셀 수 없는 명사이므로 many를 much로 고쳐 써야 한다.
21 나는 외국인들에게 영어로 자기소개를 할 수 있다.
   해설 '자기소개를 하다'는 introduce oneself를 쓴다.
22 Tim은 야구하는 것과 야구 경기를 보는 것 둘 다 아주 좋아한다.
   해설 접속사 앞뒤로 연결되는 말은 문법적으로 같은 성격이어야 하므로 watch는 동명사 watching으로 고쳐 쓴다.
23 우리가 어제 봤던 그 영화는 재미있었다.
   해설 선행사 The movie가 사물이므로 목적격 관계대명사 which 또는 that으로 고쳐 써야 한다.
24 나는 부모님께 내가 방과 후에 도와드린 여자에 관해 말씀드렸다.
25 만약 내가 내일 그에게 답장을 받으면 너에게 알려줄게.
   해설 시간을 나타내는 부사절에서는 현재시제가 미래시제를 대신한다.
   어휘 reply 답장; 대답하다
26 민호는 숙제가 너무 많아서 늦게 잤다.
   해설 뒤에 주어와 동사가 있는 완전한 절이 오므로 접속사 because를 써야 한다. because of는 전치사이므로 뒤에 명사(구)가 온다.
27 너는 개를 데리고 걷고 있는 그 남자아이를 아니?
   해설 사람 선행사(the boy)가 관계대명사 절의 주어 역할을 하므로 주격 관계대명사인 who나 that을 써야 한다.
28 해설 소유격 관계대명사로 연결되어야 하므로 The girl's 대신 whose를 쓴다.
29 해설 목적격 관계대명사로 연결되어야 하므로 visit의 목적어 the Art Gallery를 삭제하고 which나 that을 쓴다.
31 그 가구는 너무 무거워서 우리는 그것을 들 수 없었다.
   해설 '너무 ~해서 …하다'라는 의미를 나타낼 때, 「so+형용사/부사+that+주어+동사」로 바꿔 쓸 수 있다.
32 Nancy는 그림을 그리는 것뿐만 아니라 요리도 잘한다.

 B as well as A와 not only A but also B는 서로 바꿔 쓸 수 있
는데, 이때 A와 B의 위치가 바뀌는 것에 유의한다.

33 그 식당은 저렴한 가격으로 유명하다.

그곳은 훌륭한 맛으로도 유명하다.

→ 그 식당은 저렴한 가격과 훌륭한 맛 둘 다로 유명하다.

34 내가 책 어린 왕자를 소개할게. 이것은 어린 남자아이에 관한
이야기야. 작가는 사막에서 그를 만났어. 그 남자아이는 어린 왕자
야. 그는 장미에 대한 이야기를 했어. 그는 그것을 아주 많이 좋아
했지. 그는 또한 자신의 사랑 때문에 변한 여우에 관해서도 이야기
했어. 그 남자아이와 여우는 친구가 되었지.

(1) 이것은 작가가 사막에서 만났던 어린 남자아이에 대한 이야기
이다.

(2) 그는 그가 아주 좋아했던 장미에 대한 이야기를 했다.

35 내 이름은 Amy이다. 나는 쌍둥이 여동생이 있다. 그녀의 이름
은 Tracy이다. 우리는 둘 다 춤을 잘 춘다. 내 친구들은 우리를 좋
아하고 우리와 함께 어울리고 싶어 한다.

그러나, 학교 춤 경연 대회 이후로 상황이 바뀌었다. 내 여동생
이 그 대회에서 우승했고, 그녀는 점점 더 인기가 많아졌다. 그 후
에, 내 모든 친구들은 Tracy가 나보다 춤을 더 잘 춘다고 생각한다.

나는 Tracy만큼 춤을 잘 추고 싶다. 요즘 나는 춤을 열심히 연
습한다. 나는 내가 더 많이 연습할수록, 춤을 더 잘 출 수 있다고
생각한다.

 hang out (with) (~와) 어울리다, 시간을 보내다

Step 3 | 글쓰기

✚ 앞에서 작성한 내용을 바탕으로 다음 〈조건〉에 맞게 글을 완성해 보세요.

〈조건〉
① 6문장 이상 작성할 것
② 다음 언어 형식을 사용해 작성할 것
  · ask/tell+목적어+to부정사
  · 미래 표현 be going to
  · 과거의 습관 used to

A Fun Weekend Plan

This weekend, I am going to ______________________________.

I/We ______________________________.

I/We ______________________________.

I ______________________________.

I/We ______________________________.

I/We used to ______________________________,

but now I/we don't do that as often.

It's going to be a great weekend!

논술형 수행평가 4회 Chapter 04~06

○ 예시 답안 p.216

평가 개요	
주제	박물관 관람
세부 내용	① 관람 내용 (3가지 이상) ② 인상 깊은 점 (2가지 이상) ③ 즐거웠던 점
언어 형식	① 수동태 be동사+p.p. ② by 이외의 전치사를 쓰는 수동태 표현 ③ to부정사의 부사적 쓰임 (감정의 원인) ④ 목적어로 쓰이는 동명사 (enjoy+동명사)

Step 1 | 예시 글 분석하기

✚ 형광펜 친 부분에 유의하여 예시 글을 읽은 후, 표의 빈칸을 완성해 보세요.

A Visit to the Museum

관람 시기 및 전시 주제	➜	Last weekend, I visited a museum exhibiting Egyptian artifacts.
관람 내용 ①	➜	The museum was filled with interesting exhibits.
관람 내용 ②	➜	The history of the items was explained by a guide.
관람 내용 ③	➜	I saw ancient jewelry and tools, and they were beautiful.
인상 깊은 점 ①	➜	I was surprised to see lots of Egyptian mummies.
인상 깊은 점 ②	➜	Especially, I was interested in the Pyramids.
즐거웠던 점	➜	I really enjoyed learning about Egyptian history.

관람 시기 및 전시 주제	1	_____________________, I visited a museum exhibiting _____________________.
관람 내용 ①	2	The museum was filled with _____________________.
관람 내용 ②	3	_____________________ was explained by a guide.
관람 내용 ③	4	I saw _____________________, and they were beautiful.
인상 깊은 점 ①	5	I was surprised to _____________________.
인상 깊은 점 ②	6	Especially, I was _____________________.
즐거웠던 점	7	I really enjoyed _____________________.

1 Last weekend, Egyptian artifacts 2 interesting exhibits 3 The history of the items 4 ancient jewelry and tools 5 to see lots of Egyptian mummies 6 interested in the Pyramids 7 learning about Egyptian history

➕ 박물관을 관람한 경험을 떠올리며, 다음 표의 빈칸을 완성해 보세요.

A Visit to the Museum

관람 시기 및 전시 주제	______________________, I visited a museum exhibiting ______________________.
관람 내용 ①	The museum was filled with ______________________.
관람 내용 ②	______________________ was explained by a guide.
관람 내용 ③	I saw ______________________.
인상 깊은 점 ①	I was surprised to ______________________.
인상 깊은 점 ②	Especially, I was interested in ______________________.
즐거웠던 점	I really enjoyed ______________________.

Useful Words & Expressions

전시 주제	Egyptian artifacts 이집트 유물 the history of the war 전쟁 역사 dinosaurs and fossils 공룡과 화석 traditional Korean pottery 한국 전통 도자기	ancient Greek artifacts 고대 그리스 유물 the history of cars 자동차 역사 space and planets 우주와 행성 insects from around the world 전 세계의 곤충
관람 내용	ancient Egyptian jewelry 고대 이집트 보석 Greek pottery 그리스 도자기 historic battle weapons 역사적인 전쟁 무기 vintage car models 빈티지 자동차 모델 the first electric cars 최초의 전기 자동차 moon rocks 달의 암석 Korean vases 한국 도자기 항아리 butterflies in glass cases 유리 상자 안의 나비	ancient Egyptian mummies 고대 이집트 미라 old war uniforms 옛날 전쟁 군복 vintage car engines and tires 빈티지 자동차 엔진과 타이어 the invention of the first car 최초의 자동차 발명 dinosaur bones 공룡 뼈 models of the planets in the solar system 태양계 행성 모형 fossilized plants 화석화된 식물 astronaut suits 우주비행사 복

✚ 앞에서 작성한 내용을 바탕으로 다음 〈조건〉에 맞게 글을 완성해 보세요.

〈조건〉
① 7문장 이상 작성할 것
② 다음 언어 형식을 사용해 작성할 것
 • 수동태 be동사+p.p.
 • by 이외의 전치사를 쓰는 수동태 표현
 • to부정사의 부사적 쓰임 (감정의 원인)
 • 목적어로 쓰이는 동명사 (enjoy+동명사)

A Visit to the Museum

___________________, ____.

____.

____.

____.

____.

Especially, ____.

I really enjoyed ____.

평가 개요	
주제	꿈의 휴가
세부 내용	① 가고 싶은 여행지 ② 여행 목적 ③ 여행 계획 (3가지 이상) ④ 노력
언어 형식	① to부정사의 명사적 쓰임 (목적어) ② to부정사의 부사적 쓰임 (목적) ③ too ~ to부정사

Step 1 | **예시 글 분석하기**

➕ 형광펜 친 부분에 유의하여 예시 글을 읽은 후, 각 질문에 답해보세요.

My Dream Vacation

여행지	→	My dream vacation is to visit Hawaii.
여행 목적	→	I want to go there to enjoy the beautiful beaches.
여행 계획 ①	→	I plan to try surfing for the first time.
여행 계획 ②	→	Hawaii has many hiking trails, and I want to explore the mountains. The weather in Hawaii is too perfect to stay indoors.
여행 계획 ③	→	I will take many pictures to remember the trip.
노력	→	To make this dream come true, I'll save money and practice swimming.
맺음말	→	I can't wait to visit Hawaii someday!

1 Where is the writer's dream vacation?

→ His[Her] dream vacation is to visit ________________ .

2 Why does the writer want to go there?

→ He[She] wants to go there ________________ .

3 What does the writer want or plan to do there?

→ He[She] plans ________________ .

→ He[She] wants ________________ .

4 What will the writer do to make his[her] dream happen?

→ He[She] will ________________ .

1 Hawaii　2 to enjoy the beautiful beaches　3 to try surfing for the first time, to explore the mountains　4 save money and practice swimming

Step 2 | 글의 뼈대 만들기

➕ 가고 싶은 여행지를 떠올리며, 다음 표의 빈칸을 완성해 보세요.

My Dream Vacation

여행지	My dream vacation is to visit __________________________________.
여행 목적	I want to go there to __________________________________.
여행 계획 ①	I __________________________________.
여행 계획 ②	I __________________________________.
여행 계획 ③	__________________________________.
노력	To make this dream come true, I'll __________________________________.
맺음말	I can't wait to visit __________________________ someday!

Useful Words & Expressions

여행지	Tokyo	**Tokyo Tower** 도쿄 타워 **sushi/soba/ramen/okonomiyaki/takoyaki** 스시/소바/라멘/오코노미야끼/타코야끼	**Disneyland** 디즈니랜드
	London	**Big Ben** 빅 벤 **a soccer stadium** 축구 경기장	**Buckingham Palace** 버킹엄 궁전 **fish and chips** 피시 앤 칩스
	Bangkok	**a floating market** 수상 시장 **pad thai/tom yum soup** 팟타이/똠얌꿍	**visit a temple** 사원에 방문하다
	New York	**Times Square** 타임스퀘어 **the Statue of Liberty** 자유의 여신상 **watch a Broadway musical** 뮤지컬을 보다	**Central Park** 센트럴 파크 **the Empire State Building** 엠파이어 스테이트 빌딩
노력		**save money** 돈을 모으다 **plan a trip in detail** 상세하게 여행계획을 세우다 **make a wish list** 위시리스트를 쓰다 **learn Japanese/Thai/Chinese/Spanish** 일본어/태국어/중국어/스페인어를 배우다 **research a travel destination** 여행지를 조사하다	

✚ 앞에서 작성한 내용을 바탕으로 다음 〈조건〉에 맞게 글을 완성해 보세요.

〈조건〉
① 8문장 이상 작성할 것
② 다음 언어 형식을 사용해 작성할 것
 • to부정사의 명사적 쓰임 (목적어)
 • to부정사의 부사적 쓰임 (목적)
 • too ~ to부정사

My Dream Vacation

My dream vacation is to visit ___________________________________.

___________________________________.

___________________________________.

___________________________________.

___________________________________.

___________________________________.

To make this dream come true, ___________________________________

___________________________________.

I can't wait to ___________________________________!

평가 개요	
주제	새로 배우는 취미 소개하기
세부 내용	① 배우기 시작한 취미 ② 재미있는 점 (2가지 이상) ③ 어려운 점과 더 알고 싶은 부분 ④ 바라는 점
언어 형식	① to부정사의 명사적 쓰임 (주어, 목적어) ② to부정사의 명사적 쓰임 (의문사+to부정사) ③ 주어로 쓰이는 동명사

Step 1 | 예시 글 분석하기

➕ 형광펜 친 부분에 유의하여 예시 글을 읽은 후, 표의 빈칸을 완성해 보세요.

Learning a New Hobby

도입부	→	I feel excited when I learn something new.
배우는 취미	→	I recently started learning how to play the guitar.
재미있는 점 ①	→	It is really enjoyable to practice playing new songs.
재미있는 점 ②	→	Learning new chords is also interesting.
어려운 점	→	Sometimes, it is difficult to remember all the chords.
더 알고 싶은 부분	→	I want to know how to improve my finger movements to play more smoothly.
바라는 점	→	I hope to become a better guitar player soon!

배우는 취미	1	I recently started learning ____________________.
재미있는 점 ①	2	It is really enjoyable ____________________.
재미있는 점 ②	3	____________________ is also interesting.
어려운 점	4	Sometimes, it is difficult ____________________.
더 알고 싶은 부분	5	I want to know ____________________ my finger movements to play more smoothly.
바라는 점	6	I hope ____________________ soon.

1 how to play the guitar 2 to practice playing new songs 3 Learning new chords 4 to remember all the chords 5 how to improve 6 to become a better guitar player

✚ 새로 배우게 된 취미를 떠올리며, 다음 표의 빈칸을 완성해 보세요.

Learning a New Hobby

도입부	I feel excited when I learn something new.
배우는 취미	I recently started learning ________________________________.
재미있는 점 ①	It is really enjoyable to ________________________________.
재미있는 점 ②	________________________________ is also interesting.
어려운 점	Sometimes, it is difficult to ________________________________.
더 알고 싶은 부분	I want to know ________________________________.
바라는 점	I hope to ________________________________!

Useful Words & Expressions

취미 활동	play the piano 피아노를 치다 swim 수영하다 play chess 체스를 두다 take photos 사진을 찍다 write stories 이야기를 쓰다 cook different dishes 다양한 음식을 요리하다 ride a bike 자전거를 타다 paint pictures 그림을 그리다 speak English 영어를 말하다 do magic tricks 마술을 하다
재미있는 점 또는 어려운 점	practice playing new songs 새로운 곡을 연습하다 mix different colors 다양한 색을 섞다 improve swimming speed 수영 속도를 향상시키다 explore different paths 다양한 길을 탐험하다 learn new strategies 새로운 전략들을 배우다 use different filters 다양한 필터를 사용하다 surprise friends with tricks 친구들을 마술로 놀라게 하다 hide the tricks well 마술의 비밀을 잘 숨기다 try new recipes with various ingredients 다양한 재료로 새로운 레시피를 시도하다 measure ingredients correctly 재료를 정확하게 계량하다 learn new chords 새로운 코드를 배우다 draw things realistically 사물을 현실적으로 그리다 hold my breath underwater 물속에서 숨을 참다 turn corners smoothly 코너를 부드럽게 돌다 stay focused for a long time 오랫동안 집중하다 focus the camera properly 카메라 초점을 맞추다

➕ 앞에서 작성한 내용을 바탕으로 다음 〈조건〉에 맞게 글을 완성해 보세요.

〈조건〉
① 6문장 이상 작성할 것
② 다음 언어 형식을 사용해 작성할 것
  • to부정사의 명사적 쓰임 (주어, 목적어)
  • to부정사의 명사적 쓰임 (의문사+to부정사)
  • 주어로 쓰이는 동명사

Learning a New Hobby

I feel excited when I learn something new. ______________________

____.

____.

____.

Sometimes, ____.

____.

I want to know ____________________________________.

____.

I hope to ____!

평가 개요	
주제	나의 롤 모델 소개하기
세부 내용	① 롤 모델 대상 소개 ② 롤 모델이 겪은 역경 ③ 극복 과정 ④ 나의 다짐
언어 형식	① 형용사, 부사 ② not only A but also B ③ 부사절을 이끄는 접속사 (2가지 이상)

Step 1 | 예시 글 분석하기

✚ 형광펜 친 부분에 유의하여 예시 글을 읽은 후, 각 질문에 답해보세요.

My Role Model

롤 모델 → My role model is my grandmother.

본받을 점 ① → She always worked hard to support her family although life was very difficult.

역경 → She faced a lot of problems when my grandfather passed away.

극복 과정 → She not only found a job but also saved money to help her three children go to school.

본받을 점 ② → In addition, she always stayed positive.

Tip in addition(게다가, 또한)은 앞에 나온 내용을 보충하거나 추가 정보를 소개할 때 사용돼요. 보통 문장의 시작 부분에 쓰여요.

다짐 → Like her, I will stay strong when I face challenges.

1 Who is the writer's role model?

→ The writer's role model is _______________________________.

2 What did the writer's grandmother do when life was difficult?

→ She always _______________________________.

3 When did the writer's grandmother face a lot of problems?

→ She faced a lot of problems when the writer's _______________________________.

4 What did the writer's grandmother do to help her children go to school?

→ She not only _________________________ but also _________________________.

1 his[her] grandmother **2** worked hard to support her family **3** grandfather passed away **4** found a job, saved money

Step 2 | 글의 뼈대 만들기

➕ 나의 롤 모델을 떠올리며, 다음 표의 빈칸을 완성해 보세요.

My Role Model

롤 모델	My role model is ____________________.
본받을 점 ①	____________________ ____________________.
역경	____________________ ____________________.
극복 과정	____________________ ____________________.
본받을 점 ②	In addition, ____________________ ____________________.
다짐	Like her[him], I ____________________.

Useful Words & Expressions

롤 모델	**my parents** 나의 부모님　　**my teacher** 니의 선생님　　**my grandparents** 나의 [외]조부모님 **singer** 가수　　**news anchor** 뉴스 진행자　　**dancer** 댄서 **actor** 배우　　**fashion designer** 패션 디자이너　　**rapper** 래퍼 **movie star** 유명 영화배우　　**artist** 예술가　　**athlete** 운동선수
역경	**face a lot of problems[challenges]** 많은 문제[어려움]에 직면하다 **have difficulties in** ～에 어려움을 겪다 **have a hard time -ing** ～하는 데 힘든 시간을 보내다 **suffer from** ～으로 고통받다
극복 과정	**keep a positive attitude** 긍정적인 태도를 유지하다 **work hard/late nights** 열심히/늦은 밤까지 일하다 **train hard** 열심히 훈련하다 **stay positive/strong/focused** 긍정적으로/강하게/집중력을 유지하다 **take risks** 위험을 감수하다 **never give up** 절대 포기하지 않다 **be always with patient with** ～에 항상 인내심을 가지다

Step 3 | **글쓰기**

➕ 앞에서 작성한 내용을 바탕으로 다음 〈조건〉에 맞게 글을 완성해 보세요.

〈조건〉
① 6문장 이상 작성할 것
② 다음 언어 형식을 사용해 작성할 것
  • 형용사, 부사
  • not only A but also B
  • 부사절을 이끄는 접속사 (2가지 이상)

My Role Model

My role model is ____ .

____

____ .

____

____ .

____

____ .

____

____ .

In addition, ____ .

Like her[him], I ____ .

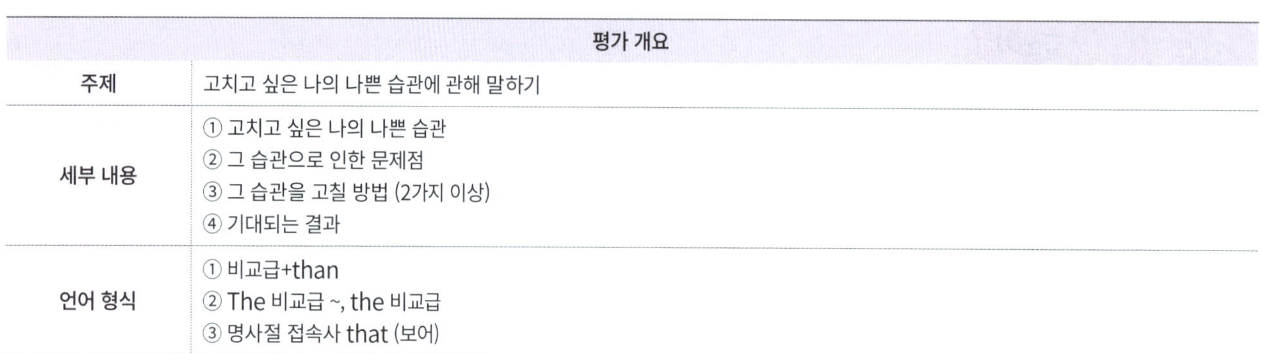

논술형 수행평가 8회 — Chapter 07~10

○ 예시 답안 p.220

평가 개요	
주제	고치고 싶은 나의 나쁜 습관에 관해 말하기
세부 내용	① 고치고 싶은 나의 나쁜 습관 ② 그 습관으로 인한 문제점 ③ 그 습관을 고칠 방법 (2가지 이상) ④ 기대되는 결과
언어 형식	① 비교급+than ② The 비교급 ~, the 비교급 ③ 명사절 접속사 that (보어)

Step 1 | 예시 글 분석하기

➕ 형광펜 친 부분에 유의하여 예시 글을 읽은 후, 각 질문에 답해보세요.

My Bad Habit

나쁜 습관	➡	I eat junk food more often than I should.
문제점	➡	The problem is that I feel less healthy than before.
고칠 방법	➡	To correct this habit, I will use the following methods.
고칠 방법 ①	➡	First, I will try to eat healthier food such as salads and vegetables.
고칠 방법 ②	➡	Second, I will eat junk food only once a month.
기대되는 결과	➡	The less junk food I eat, the healthier I will feel.
맺음말	➡	By changing this habit, I hope to become healthier than before.

1 What is the writer's bad habit?

→ The writer ________________________________ than he[she] should.

2 What's the problem with it?

→ The problem is that he[she] ________________________________ .

3 What will the writer do to correct the habit? Write down 2 sentences.

→ First, he[she] ________________________________ such as salads and vegetables.

→ Second, he[she] ________________________________ .

4 What does the writer expect?

→ The writer expects that ________________ he[she] eats, ________________
he[she] will feel.

1 eats junk food more often 2 feels less healthy than before 3 will try to eat healthier food, will eat junk food only once a month
4 the less junk food, the healthier

✚ 내가 고치고 싶은 나쁜 습관을 떠올리며, 다음 표의 빈칸을 완성해 보세요.

My Bad Habit

나쁜 습관	I ____ .
문제점	The problem is that ________________________ .
고칠 방법	To correct this habit, I will use the following methods.
고칠 방법 ①	First, ____________________________________ ____ .
고칠 방법 ②	Second, __________________________________ ____ .
기대되는 결과	The ____________________________________ , the ____________________________________ .
맺음말	By changing this habit, I hope ________________ ____ .

Useful Words & Expressions

나쁜 습관	문제점	고칠 방법
stay up late 밤늦게까지 깨어있다	feel tired during the day 낮 동안 피곤하다	go to bed earlier 더 일찍 자다
waste my pocket money 용돈을 낭비하다	run out of money quickly 금방 돈이 다 떨어지다	save more money each month 매달 돈을 더 아껴 쓰다
be late for school 학교에 지각하다	miss important lessons 중요한 수업을 놓치다	set an alarm to wake up on time 제때 일어나도록 알람을 맞추다
bite my nails 손톱을 물어뜯다	damage nails and fingers 손톱과 손가락이 상하다	keep hands busy with something else 다른 것으로 손을 바쁘게 하다
be picky about food 편식하다	miss important nutrients 중요한 영양소를 놓치다	try new healthy foods 새로운 건강한 음식을 시도하다
eat junk food too often 정크 푸드를 너무 자주 먹다	gain weight and feel unhealthy 체중이 증가하고 건강이 나빠지다	replace junk food with healthier snacks 정크 푸드를 건강한 간식으로 대체하다
forget my homework 숙제를 잊다	be scolded by my teacher 선생님께 꾸중을 듣다	write down homework in a planner 계획표에 숙제를 적어두다
use my cell phone all day 하루 종일 휴대 전화를 사용하다	lose focus and waste time 집중력을 잃고 시간을 낭비하다	limit phone usage 휴대 전화 사용을 제한하다
play games too much 게임을 너무 많이 하다	forget about schoolwork 학교 공부에 대해 잊어버리다	set time limits for playing games 게임 제한 시간을 설정하다

앞에서 작성한 내용을 바탕으로 다음 〈조건〉에 맞게 글을 완성해 보세요.

〈조건〉
① 6문장 이상 작성할 것
② 다음 언어 형식을 사용해 작성할 것
  · 비교급+than
  · The 비교급 ~, the 비교급
  · 명사절 접속사 that (보어)

My Bad Habit

I ____ .

The problem is that ___________________________ .

To correct this habit, I will use the following methods.

First, ______________________________________

____ .

Second, ____________________________________

____ .

The ____ ,

the ____ .

By changing this habit, I hope __________________

____ .

논술형 수행평가 9회 Chapter 07~10

예시 답안 p.221

평가 개요	
주제	환경 보호를 위해 내가 실천할 방안 설명하기
세부 내용	환경 보호 실천 방안 (4가지 이상)
언어 형식	① 부사절을 이끄는 접속사 ② 간접의문문 ③ 관계대명사

Step 1 │ 예시 글 분석하기

✚ 형광펜 친 부분에 유의하여 예시 글을 읽은 후, 표의 빈칸을 완성해 보세요.

What I Will Do for the Environment

도입부 ➡ It's very important to protect our environment.
Here are some actions I will take to help the environment.

실천 방안 ① ➡ First, I will recycle everything that can be reused,
such as paper, plastic, and glass.

실천 방안 ② ➡ I will also try to reduce the amount of water that I use every day.

실천 방안 ③ ➡ Another way to help is by using public transportation.

실천 방안 ④ ➡ I wonder how I can reduce my energy consumption at home.
I plan to turn off the lights when I'm not using them.

맺음말 ➡ I believe that every small effort can protect our planet.

실천 방안 ①	1	First, I will ________________________________, such as paper, plastic, and glass.
실천 방안 ②	2	I will also try to ________________________ every day.
실천 방안 ③	3	Another way to help is ________________________.
실천 방안 ④	4	I wonder ________________________ at home. I plan to ________________ when I'm not using them.

---

1 recycle everything that can be reused **2** reduce the amount of water that I use **3** by using public transportation **4** how I can reduce my energy consumption, turn off the lights

Step 2 | 글의 뼈대 만들기

✚ 환경을 위해 내가 실천할 방법을 떠올리며, 다음 표의 빈칸을 완성해 보세요.

What I Will Do for the Environment

도입부	It's very important to protect our environment. Here are some actions I will take to help the environment.
실천 방안 ①	First, I will ____ ____ .
실천 방안 ②	I will also try to ______________________________________ ____ .
실천 방안 ③	Another way to help is ___________________________________ ____ .
실천 방안 ④	I wonder ____ . I plan to ____ .
맺음말	I believe that every small effort can protect our planet.

Useful Words & Expressions

실천 방안	use reusable containers 재사용 가능한 용기를 쓰다 use a tumbler 텀블러를 사용하다 use reusable paper 이면지를 사용하다 use paper straws 종이 빨대를 사용하다 use public transportation 대중교통을 이용하다 reduce delivery food 배달 음식을 줄이다 reduce disposable products 일회용품을 줄이다 reduce the use of wet tissues 물티슈 사용을 줄이다 reduce the waste of water 물 낭비를 줄이다 reduce my energy consumption 나의 에너지 소비를 줄이다 stop using unnecessary plastic bags 불필요한 비닐봉지를 사용하는 것을 멈추다 stop wasting paper/tissues/water 종이/휴지/물을 낭비하는 것을 멈추다 turn off the lights 불을 끄다

➕ 앞에서 작성한 내용을 바탕으로 다음 〈조건〉에 맞게 글을 완성해 보세요.

〈조건〉
① 5문장 이상 작성할 것
② 다음 언어 형식을 사용해 작성할 것
  • 부사절을 이끄는 접속사
  • 간접의문문
  • 관계대명사

What I Will Do for the Environment

It's very important to protect our environment. To do this, Here are some actions I will take to help the environment.

First, ____.

____.

____.

____.

____.

____.

I believe that every small effort can protect our planet.

	평가 개요
주제	SNS에 내가 좋아하는 맛집 소개하기
세부 내용	① 방문 날짜, 이름, 위치 ② 간단한 소개 ③ 좋아하는 이유 (3가지 이상)
언어 형식	① not only A but also B ② 주격 관계대명사 ③ 목적격 관계대명사

Step 1 | 예시 글 분석하기

✚ 형광펜 친 부분에 유의하여 예시 글을 읽은 후, 표를 채워 보세요.

My Favorite Restaurant

방문 날짜	→	Date of visit: October 15
이름, 위치	→	My favorite restaurant is Pasta Paradise. It is located in Seoul.
간단한 소개	→	It's a place that offers a variety of Italian dishes like pasta and pizza.
좋아하는 이유	→	I like it for three reasons:
좋아하는 이유 ①	→	First, the Italian food that they serve is not only delicious but also looks great.
좋아하는 이유 ②	→	Second, the soft lighting makes me feel cozy.
좋아하는 이유 ③	→	Third, the staff is always friendly and provides great service.
맺음말	→	You can enjoy a wonderful time here with your friends or family. I highly recommend it!
해시태그(#)	→	#Italianfood #recommendation #musttryfood

> **Tip** 전체 글의 핵심이 되는 내용을 키워드로 뽑아서 해시태그로 쓰면 돼요. 띄어 쓰지 않고 사용해요.

이름, 위치	**1**	My favorite restaurant is ________________. It is located in ________________.
간단한 소개	**2**	It's a place that ________________
좋아하는 이유 ①	**3**	First, the Italian food that they serve is ________________
좋아하는 이유 ②	**4**	Second, ________________
좋아하는 이유 ③	**5**	Third, the staff is ________________

1 Pasta Paradise, Seoul   **2** offers a variety of Italian dishes like pasta and pizza   **3** not only delicious but also looks great   **4** the soft lighting makes me feel cozy
5 always friendly and provides great service

✚ 내가 좋아하는 맛집을 떠올리며, 다음 표의 빈칸을 완성해 보세요.

My Favorite Restaurant

방문 날짜	Date of visit: _______________________
이름, 위치	My favorite restaurant is _______________________ . It is located in _______________________ .
간단한 소개	It's a place that _______________________ .
좋아하는 이유 ①	First, _______________________ _______________________ .
좋아하는 이유 ②	Second, _______________________ _______________________ .
좋아하는 이유 ③	Third, _______________________ _______________________ .
맺음말	You can enjoy a wonderful time here with your friends or family. I highly recommend it!
해시태그	# _____________ # _____________ # _____________

Useful Words & Expressions

좋아하는 이유	clean 깨끗한 friendly 친근한, 정겨운 comfortable 편안한 cozy 아늑한 warm 따뜻한 high-quality 고품질의, 고급의 crispy 바삭한 luxurious 고급스러운	close to ~와 가까운 relaxing 편한 precious 소중한 peaceful 평화로운 eco-friendly 친환경적인 traditional 전통적인 juicy 육즙이 많은 cost-effective 가성비 좋은	calm 차분한 quiet 조용한 simple 간단한 romantic 애정의, 로맨틱한 lovely 사랑스러운 convenient 편리한 chewy 쫄깃쫄깃한 healthy 건강에 좋은

✚ 앞에서 작성한 내용을 바탕으로 다음 〈조건〉에 맞게 글을 완성해 보세요.

〈조건〉
① 6문장 이상 작성할 것
② 다음 언어 형식을 사용해 작성할 것
　· not only A but also B
　· 주격 관계대명사
　· 목적격 관계대명사

My Favorite Restaurant

Date of visit: ＿＿＿＿＿＿＿＿

My favorite restaurant is ＿＿＿＿＿＿＿＿＿＿＿＿.

＿＿＿＿＿＿＿＿＿＿＿＿＿＿.

＿＿＿＿＿＿＿＿＿＿＿＿＿＿.

I like it for three reasons:

First, ＿＿＿＿＿＿＿＿＿＿＿＿＿

＿＿＿＿＿＿＿＿＿＿＿＿＿＿.

Second, ＿＿＿＿＿＿＿＿＿＿＿

＿＿＿＿＿＿＿＿＿＿＿＿＿＿.

Third, ＿＿＿＿＿＿＿＿＿＿＿＿,

＿＿＿＿＿＿＿＿＿＿＿＿＿＿.

You can enjoy a wonderful time here with your friends or family. I highly recommend it!

#＿＿＿＿＿＿＿　　#＿＿＿＿＿＿＿　　#＿＿＿＿＿＿＿

논술형 수행평가 1회

평가 기준			배점
내용 (6점)	**<내용> 채점 조건** ① 알고 지낸 기간 ② 친구와 함께 계속 해 온 것 ③ 구체적인 경험 (3가지 이상)		
	내용 조건 (3점)	<내용 조건> 중 3가지 모두 만족한 경우	3
		<내용 조건> 중 2가지를 만족한 경우	2
		<내용 조건> 중 1가지를 만족한 경우	1
	문장 개수 (3점)	6문장 이상 작성한 경우	3
		5문장 이상 작성한 경우	2
		4문장 이하로 작성한 경우	1
언어 형식 (5점)	**<언어 형식> 채점 조건** ① 과거시제 ② 현재완료 (계속)		
	언어 형식 사용 (2점)	제시된 <언어 형식 조건> 2가지를 목적에 맞게 사용한 경우	2
		제시된 <언어 형식 조건> 2가지 중 1가지를 목적에 맞게 사용한 경우	1
	정확한 언어 사용 (3점)	문법적 오류가 3개 이하인 경우	3
		문법적 오류가 4개 이상 6개 이하 포함되었으나 내용 전달에 무리가 없는 경우	2
		문법적 오류가 7개 이상 있고, 내용이 제대로 전달되지 않는 경우	1
총점 (11점)			

예시 답안 1

I will share one of my memories with my best friend, Yuri. We have known each other for 5 years, and we share a lot of memories. We have tried many hobbies together. One time, we learned to play the guitar and practiced every weekend. Another time, we painted pictures and gave them to our families. Last year, we started learning to cook and have tried many recipes. I hope we can make more memories together.

제 가장 친한 친구인 유리와의 추억 중 하나를 나누고자 합니다. 우리는 서로를 5년 동안 알고 지냈고, 많은 추억을 공유하고 있습니다.
우리는 함께 많은 취미를 시도해 보았습니다. 한 번은 기타 치는 것을 배우고 매주 주말마다 연습했습니다. 또 다른 때는 그림을 그려서 가족들에게 선물했습니다. 작년에는 요리를 배우기 시작해서 많은 레시피를 시도해 보았습니다. 저는 우리가 더 많은 추억을 만들 수 있기를 바랍니다.

예시 답안 2

I will share one of my memories with my best friend, Junwoo. We have known each other for 6 years, and we share a lot of memories.
We have visited many places together. One time, we went to the museum and learned about Korean history. Another time, we explored a park and had a picnic. Last year, we visited a farm and fed the animals. I hope we can make more memories together.

제 가장 친한 친구 준우와의 추억 중 하나를 나누고자 합니다. 우리는 서로를 6년 동안 알고 지냈고, 많은 추억을 공유하고 있습니다.
우리는 함께 여러 곳을 방문했습니다. 한 번은 박물관에 가서 한국 역사에 대해 배웠습니다. 또 다른 때는 공원을 탐험하고 소풍을 즐겼습니다. 작년에는 농장을 방문해서 동물들에게 먹이를 주었습니다. 저는 우리가 더 많은 추억을 만들 수 있기를 바랍니다.

 # 논술형 수행평가 2회

평가 기준			배점
내용 (5점)	**<내용> 채점 조건** ① 지켜야 할 것 (3가지 이상)　② 하지 말아야 할 것 (2가지 이상)		
	내용 조건 (2점)	<내용 조건> 중 2가지 모두 만족한 경우	2
		<내용 조건> 중 1가지를 만족한 경우	1
	문장 개수 (3점)	5문장 이상 작성한 경우	3
		4문장 이상 작성한 경우	2
		3문장 이하로 작성한 경우	1
언어 형식 (5점)	**<언어 형식> 채점 조건** ① 주어+동사+목적어+목적격보어　② 조동사 must, should, have to		
	언어 형식 사용 (2점)	제시된 <언어 형식 조건> 2가지를 목적에 맞게 사용한 경우	2
		제시된 <언어 형식 조건> 2가지 중 1가지를 목적에 맞게 사용한 경우	1
	정확한 언어 사용 (3점)	문법적 오류가 3개 이하인 경우	3
		문법적 오류가 4개 이상 6개 이하 포함되었으나 내용 전달에 무리가 없는 경우	2
		문법적 오류가 7개 이상 있고, 내용이 제대로 전달되지 않는 경우	1
총점 (10점)			

예시 답안 1

Our school has some rules to follow.
First, we must listen to the teacher carefully. Second, we should wear indoor shoes inside the school building.
Third, we must not perm or dye our hair. Next, we have to respect others' opinions.
Lastly, we must not bring dangerous items to school. By following these rules, we can make the school a better place.

우리 학교에는 따라야 할 몇 가지 규칙이 있습니다.
첫째, 우리는 선생님의 말씀을 주의 깊게 들어야 합니다. 둘째, 우리는 학교 건물 안에서 실내화를 착용해야 합니다.
셋째, 우리는 머리를 파마하거나 염색하면 안 됩니다. 그다음, 우리는 다른 사람들의 의견을 존중해야 합니다.
마지막으로, 우리는 위험한 물건을 학교에 가져오면 안 됩니다. 이 규칙들을 지킴으로써 우리는 학교를 더 좋은 곳으로 만들 수 있습니다.

예시 답안 2

Our school has some rules to follow.
First, we must complete our homework on time. Second, we should be kind to our friends.
Third, we must not wear accessories like necklaces or earrings. Next, we have to speak politely to teachers and classmates.
Lastly, we must not run in the hallways. By following these rules, we can make the school a better place.

우리 학교에는 따라야 할 몇 가지 규칙이 있습니다.
첫째, 우리는 숙제를 제시간에 완료해야 합니다. 둘째, 우리는 친구들에게 친절해야 합니다.
셋째, 우리는 목걸이나 귀걸이 같은 액세서리를 착용하면 안 됩니다. 그다음, 우리는 선생님과 친구들에게 예의 바르게 말해야 합니다.
마지막으로, 우리는 복도에서 뛰면 안 됩니다. 이 규칙들을 지킴으로써 우리는 학교를 더 좋은 곳으로 만들 수 있습니다.

논술형 수행평가 3회

평가 기준			배점
내용 (6점)	**<내용> 채점 조건** ① 계획 (3가지 이상)　② 상대방에게 요청한 일　③ 과거에 반복적으로 일어났던 일		
	내용 조건 (3점)	<내용 조건> 중 3가지 모두 만족한 경우	3
		<내용 조건> 중 2가지를 만족한 경우	2
		<내용 조건> 중 1가지를 만족한 경우	1
	문장 개수 (3점)	6문장 이상 작성한 경우	3
		5문장 이상 작성한 경우	2
		4문장 이하로 작성한 경우	1
언어 형식 (6점)	**<언어 형식> 채점 조건** ① ask/tell+목적어+to부정사　② 미래 표현 be going to　③ 과거의 습관 used to		
	언어 형식 사용 (3점)	제시된 <언어 형식 조건> 3가지를 목적에 맞게 사용한 경우	3
		제시된 <언어 형식 조건> 3가지 중 2가지를 목적에 맞게 사용한 경우	2
		제시된 <언어 형식 조건> 3가지 중 1가지를 목적에 맞게 사용한 경우	1
	정확한 언어 사용 (3점)	문법적 오류가 3개 이하인 경우	3
		문법적 오류가 4개 이상 6개 이하 포함되었으나 내용 전달에 무리가 없는 경우	2
		문법적 오류가 7개 이상 있고, 내용이 제대로 전달되지 않는 경우	1
총점 (12점)			

예시 답안 1

This weekend, I am going to visit my friend's house.
We are going to watch movies and do homework. I'm going to bring some snacks.
I told my friend to choose some fun movies. We are also going to order pizza for dinner.
We used to play computer games together, but now we don't do that as often. It's going to be a great weekend!

이번 주말에 저는 친구 집을 방문할 거예요.
우리는 영화를 보고 숙제를 할 예정이에요. 저는 간식을 가져갈 거예요.
저는 친구에게 재미있는 영화를 고르라고 말했어요. 우리는 저녁으로 피자도 주문할 거예요.
우리는 예전에 컴퓨터 게임을 자주 하곤 했지만, 이제는 그렇게 자주 하지 않아요. 멋진 주말이 될 거예요!

예시 답안 2

This weekend, I am going to go to a music festival with my friends.
We are going to enjoy the performances. I'm going to buy some band items.
I told my friends to bring their tickets. We are also going to have a meal at the food trucks.
We used to go to smaller concerts, but now we don't do that as often. It's going to be a great weekend!

이번 주말에 저는 친구들과 함께 음악 페스티벌에 갈 거예요.
우리는 공연을 즐길 예정입니다. 저는 밴드 관련 물품을 살 거예요.
저는 친구들에게 표를 가져오라고 말했어요. 우리는 푸드 트럭에서 식사도 할 거예요.
우리는 예전에 더 작은 콘서트에 가곤 했지만, 이제는 그렇게 자주 하지 않아요. 멋진 주말이 될 거예요!

논술형 수행평가 **4회**

평가 기준			배점
내용 (6점)	**<내용> 채점 조건** ① 관람 내용 (3가지 이상) ② 인상 깊은 점 (2가지 이상) ③ 즐거웠던 점		
	내용 조건 (3점)	<내용 조건> 중 3가지 모두 만족한 경우	3
		<내용 조건> 중 2가지를 만족한 경우	2
		<내용 조건> 중 1가지를 만족한 경우	1
	문장 개수 (3점)	7문장 이상 작성한 경우	3
		6문장 이상 작성한 경우	2
		5문장 이하로 작성한 경우	1
언어 형식 (6점)	**<언어 형식> 채점 조건** ① 수동태 be동사+p.p. ② by 이외의 전치사를 쓰는 수동태 표현 ③ to부정사의 부사적 쓰임 (감정의 원인) ④ 목적어로 쓰이는 동명사 (enjoy+동명사)		
	언어 형식 사용 (3점)	제시된 <언어 형식 조건> 4가지를 목적에 맞게 사용한 경우	3
		제시된 <언어 형식 조건> 4가지 중 3가지를 목적에 맞게 사용한 경우	2
		제시된 <언어 형식 조건> 4가지 중 2가지를 목적에 맞게 사용한 경우	1
	정확한 언어 사용 (3점)	문법적 오류가 3개 이하인 경우	3
		문법적 오류가 4개 이상 6개 이하 포함되었으나 내용 전달에 무리가 없는 경우	2
		문법적 오류가 7개 이상 있고, 내용이 제대로 전달되지 않는 경우	1
총점 (12점)			

예시 답안 1

Last weekend, I visited a museum exhibiting the history of cars.
The museum was filled with old car models. The invention of the first car was explained by a guide.
I saw vintage car engines and tires. I was surprised to see the many changes in cars over time.
Especially, I was interested in the first electric cars. I really enjoyed learning about car history.

지난 주말, 나는 자동차 역사를 전시하는 박물관에 다녀왔다.
그 박물관은 오래된 자동차 모델들로 가득했다. 최초의 자동차 발명이 가이드에 의해 설명되었다.
나는 빈티지 자동차 엔진과 타이어를 보았다. 나는 시간이 지나며 자동차가 많이 변한 것을 보고 놀랐다.
특히, 나는 최초의 전기 자동차에 관심이 있었다. 나는 자동차 역사에 대해 배우는 것이 정말 즐거웠다.

예시 답안 2

Last Saturday, I visited a museum exhibiting insects from around the world.
The museum was filled with preserved insects in glass cases. The life of insects was explained by a guide.
I saw beautiful butterflies and big beetles. I was surprised to see so many different kinds of insects.
Especially, I was interested in the ants and their nests. I really enjoyed watching the live insects.

지난 토요일, 나는 전 세계의 곤충을 전시하는 박물관에 다녀왔다.
그 박물관은 유리 상자에 보존된 곤충들로 가득했다. 곤충의 생애가 가이드에 의해 설명되었다.
나는 아름다운 나비와 큰 딱정벌레들을 보았다. 나는 매우 다양한 종류의 곤충들을 보고 놀랐다.
특히, 나는 개미와 그것들의 집에 관심이 있었다. 나는 살아 있는 곤충들을 관찰하는 것이 정말 즐거웠다.

 ## 논술형 수행평가 5회

평가 기준			배점
내용 (6점)	**<내용> 채점 조건** ① 가고 싶은 여행지　② 여행 목적　③ 여행 계획 (3가지 이상)　④ 노력		
	내용 조건 (3점)	<내용 조건> 중 4가지 모두 만족한 경우	3
		<내용 조건> 중 3가지를 만족한 경우	2
		<내용 조건> 중 2가지를 만족한 경우	1
	문장 개수 (3점)	8문장 이상 작성한 경우	3
		7문장 이상 작성한 경우	2
		6문장 이하로 작성한 경우	1
언어 형식 (6점)	**<언어 형식> 채점 조건** ① to부정사의 명사적 쓰임 (목적어)　② to부정사의 부사적 쓰임 (목적)　③ too ~ to부정사		
	언어 형식 사용 (3점)	제시된 <언어 형식 조건> 3가지를 목적에 맞게 사용한 경우	3
		제시된 <언어 형식 조건> 3가지 중 2가지를 목적에 맞게 사용한 경우	2
		제시된 <언어 형식 조건> 3가지 중 1가지를 목적에 맞게 사용한 경우	1
	정확한 언어 사용 (3점)	문법적 오류가 3개 이하인 경우	3
		문법적 오류가 4개 이상 6개 이하 포함되었으나 내용 전달에 무리가 없는 경우	2
		문법적 오류가 7개 이상 있고, 내용이 제대로 전달되지 않는 경우	1
총점 (12점)			

예시 답안 1

My dream vacation is to visit New York City. I want to go there to see Times Square. I plan to visit Central Park and the Statue of Liberty. New York is full of famous places, and I want to explore many of them. The city is too exciting to spend time resting. I will take many pictures to remember the trip.
To make this dream come true, I'll practice speaking English. I can't wait to visit New York City someday!

제 꿈의 휴가는 뉴욕시에 가는 것입니다. 저는 타임스퀘어를 보기 위해 그 곳에 가고 싶습니다. 저는 센트럴 파크와 자유의 여신상도 방문할 계획입니다. 뉴욕은 유명한 장소들로 가득해서, 그중 많은 곳을 탐험하고 싶습니다. 그 도시는 너무 흥미진진해서 쉬는 데 시간을 보낼 수 없습니다. 저는 여행을 기억하기 위해 많은 사진을 찍을 것입니다. 저는 이 꿈을 이루기 위해 영어 말하기를 연습할 것입니다. 언젠가 뉴욕시에 가는 날이 정말 기대됩니다!

예시 답안 2

My dream vacation is to visit Sydney. I want to go there to see the Sydney Opera House. I plan to spend time at Bondi Beach. Sydney has great hiking spots, and I want to explore the trails. Sydney is too beautiful to stay indoors all day. I will go snorkeling to see the underwater world.
To make this dream come true, I'll save money and get a new swimsuit. I can't wait to visit Sydney someday!

제 꿈의 휴가는 시드니를 방문하는 것입니다. 저는 시드니 오페라 하우스를 보기 위해 그곳에 가고 싶습니다. 저는 본다이 비치에서 시간을 보낼 계획입니다. 시드니에는 멋진 하이킹 코스가 있어서 그 길을 탐험하고 싶습니다. 시드니는 너무 아름다워서 하루 종일 실내에 있을 수 없습니다. 저는 수중 세계를 보기 위해 스노클링을 할 것입니다. 이 꿈을 이루기 위해 돈을 모으고 새 수영복을 살 것입니다. 언젠가 시드니에 가는 날이 정말 기대됩니다!

평가 기준			배점
내용 (6점)	**<내용> 채점 조건** ① 배우기 시작한 취미 ② 재미있는 점 (2가지 이상) ③ 어려운 점과 더 알고 싶은 부분 ④ 바라는 점		
	내용 조건 (3점)	<내용 조건> 중 4가지 모두 만족한 경우	3
		<내용 조건> 중 3가지를 만족한 경우	2
		<내용 조건> 중 2가지를 만족한 경우	1
	문장 개수 (3점)	6문장 이상 작성한 경우	3
		5문장 이상 작성한 경우	2
		4문장 이하로 작성한 경우	1
언어 형식 (6점)	**<언어 형식> 채점 조건** ① to부정사의 명사적 쓰임 (주어, 목적어) ② to부정사의 명사적 쓰임 (의문사+to부정사) ③ 주어로 쓰이는 동명사		
	언어 형식 사용 (3점)	제시된 <언어 형식 조건> 3가지를 목적에 맞게 사용한 경우	3
		제시된 <언어 형식 조건> 3가지 중 2가지를 목적에 맞게 사용한 경우	2
		제시된 <언어 형식 조건> 3가지 중 1가지를 목적에 맞게 사용한 경우	1
	정확한 언어 사용 (3점)	문법적 오류가 3개 이하인 경우	3
		문법적 오류가 4개 이상 6개 이하 포함되었으나 내용 전달에 무리가 없는 경우	2
		문법적 오류가 7개 이상 있고, 내용이 제대로 전달되지 않는 경우	1
총점 (12점)			

예시 답안 1

I feel excited when I learn something new. I recently started learning how to cook different kinds of food.
It is really enjoyable to try new recipes with various ingredients. Cooking for my family is also interesting.
Sometimes, it is difficult to measure the ingredients correctly. I want to know how to make dishes taste better.
I hope to become a great cook in the future!

저는 새로운 것을 배울 때 신이 납니다. 저는 최근에 다양한 종류의 음식을 요리하는 법을 배우기 시작했습니다.
다양한 재료로 새로운 레시피를 시도하는 것이 정말 재미있습니다. 우리 가족을 위해 요리하는 것도 매우 재미있습니다.
가끔은 재료를 정확하게 계량하는 것이 어렵습니다. 저는 요리를 더 맛있게 만드는 방법을 알고 싶습니다.
저는 미래에 훌륭한 요리사가 되고 싶습니다!

예시 답안 2

I feel excited when I learn something new. I recently started learning how to paint.
It is really enjoyable to create different colors and experiment with them. Mixing paints is also interesting.
Sometimes, it is difficult to draw things realistically. I want to know how to improve my brush techniques.
I hope to paint beautiful pictures someday!

저는 새로운 것을 배울 때 신이 납니다. 저는 최근에 그림 그리는 법을 배우기 시작했습니다.
다양한 색을 만들고 그것으로 실험하는 것이 재미있습니다. 물감을 섞는 것도 매우 흥미롭습니다.
가끔은 사물을 현실적으로 그리는 것이 어렵습니다. 저는 붓 사용 기술을 어떻게 향상시킬 수 있을지 알고 싶습니다.
저는 언젠가 아름다운 그림들을 그리고 싶습니다!

 ## 논술형 수행평가 7회

평가 기준			배점
내용 (6점)	**<내용> 채점 조건** ① 롤 모델 대상 소개 ② 롤 모델이 겪은 역경 ③ 극복 과정 ④ 나의 다짐		
	내용 조건 (3점)	<내용 조건> 중 4가지 모두 만족한 경우	3
		<내용 조건> 중 3가지를 만족한 경우	2
		<내용 조건> 중 2가지를 만족한 경우	1
	문장 개수 (3점)	6문장 이상 작성한 경우	3
		5문장 이상 작성한 경우	2
		4문장 이하로 작성한 경우	1
언어 형식 (6점)	**<언어 형식> 채점 조건** ① 형용사, 부사 ② not only A but also B ③ 부사절을 이끄는 접속사 (2가지 이상)		
	언어 형식 사용 (3점)	제시된 <언어 형식 조건> 3가지를 목적에 맞게 사용한 경우	3
		제시된 <언어 형식 조건> 3가지 중 2가지를 목적에 맞게 사용한 경우	2
		제시된 <언어 형식 조건> 3가지 중 1가지를 목적에 맞게 사용한 경우	1
	정확한 언어 사용 (3점)	문법적 오류가 3개 이하인 경우	3
		문법적 오류가 4개 이상 6개 이하 포함되었으나 내용 전달에 무리가 없는 경우	2
		문법적 오류가 7개 이상 있고, 내용이 제대로 전달되지 않는 경우	1
총점 (12점)			

예시 답안 1

My role model is my father. He keeps a positive attitude although he works long hours.
He faced difficulties when he started his own business. He not only worked late nights but also studied more to improve his skills. In addition, he always supported our family. Like him, I will work hard and never give up.

나의 롤 모델은 아버지입니다. 아버지는 오랜 시간 일하셔도 항상 긍정적인 태도를 유지하십니다.
그는 자신의 사업을 시작했을 때 어려움에 직면하셨습니다. 아버지는 늦은 밤까지 일하셨을 뿐만 아니라, 기술을 향상시키기 위해 더 많은 공부도 하셨습니다. 또한, 아버지는 항상 우리 가족을 지원해 주셨습니다. 아버지처럼 저도 열심히 일하고 절대 포기하지 않을 것입니다.

예시 답안 2

My role model is Serena Williams. She became a champion tennis player although she had many challenges growing up.
She had difficulties when she entered the professional tennis world as a young girl. She not only trained hard but also stayed focused to win many titles. In addition, she inspires others by showing confidence. Like her, I will work hard and stay focused on my goals.

나의 롤 모델은 Serena Williams입니다. 그녀는 어린 시절 많은 어려움이 있었음에도 불구하고 챔피언 테니스 선수가 되었습니다.
그녀는 어린 소녀로서 프로 테니스 세계에 진입할 때 어려움을 겪었습니다. 그녀는 열심히 훈련했을 뿐만 아니라 많은 타이틀을 따기 위해 집중력을 유지했습니다. 또한, 그녀는 자신감을 보여줌으로써 다른 사람들에게 영감을 줍니다. 그녀처럼 저도 열심히 일하고 제 목표에 집중할 것입니다.

논술형 수행평가 8회

평가 기준			배점
내용 (6점)	**<내용> 채점 조건** ① 고치고 싶은 나의 나쁜 습관　② 그 습관으로 인한 문제점　③ 그 습관을 고칠 방법 (2가지 이상)　④ 기대되는 결과		
	내용 조건 (3점)	<내용 조건> 중 4가지 모두 만족한 경우	3
		<내용 조건> 중 3가지를 만족한 경우	2
		<내용 조건> 중 2가지를 만족한 경우	1
	문장 개수 (3점)	6문장 이상 작성한 경우	3
		5문장 이상 작성한 경우	2
		4문장 이하로 작성한 경우	1
언어 형식 (6점)	**<언어 형식> 채점 조건** ① 비교급+than　② The 비교급 ~, the 비교급　③ 명사절 접속사 that (보어)		
	언어 형식 사용 (3점)	제시된 <언어 형식 조건> 3가지를 목적에 맞게 사용한 경우	3
		제시된 <언어 형식 조건> 3가지 중 2가지를 목적에 맞게 사용한 경우	2
		제시된 <언어 형식 조건> 3가지 중 1가지를 목적에 맞게 사용한 경우	1
	정확한 언어 사용 (3점)	문법적 오류가 3개 이하인 경우	3
		문법적 오류가 4개 이상 6개 이하 포함되었으나 내용 전달에 무리가 없는 경우	2
		문법적 오류가 7개 이상 있고, 내용이 제대로 전달되지 않는 경우	1
총점 (12점)			

예시 답안 1

I spend more time on my phone than I should. The problem is that I waste a lot of time and forget about my schoolwork.
To correct this habit, I will use the following methods. First, I will set a time limit for phone use each day.
Second, I will turn off my phone while I'm studying. The less time I spend on my phone, the more time I can use on other things.
By changing this habit, I hope to become more focused than before.

나는 휴대 전화를 사용하는 데 너무 많은 시간을 보낸다. 문제는 내가 많은 시간을 낭비하고 학교 공부를 잊어버린다는 것이다.
이 습관을 고치기 위해, 나는 다음과 같은 방법을 사용할 것이다. 먼저, 나는 매일 휴대 전화 사용 시간을 제한할 것이다.
두 번째로, 공부할 때는 휴대 전화를 꺼둘 것이다. 내가 휴대 전화에 쓰는 시간을 더 줄일수록, 내가 다른 것에 사용할 수 있는 시간이 더 많아질 것이다.
이 습관을 바꿈으로써, 나는 이전보다 더 집중할 수 있기를 바란다.

예시 답안 2

I stay up later than I should. The problem is that I feel tired during the day and can't concentrate in school.
To correct this habit, I will use the following methods. First, I will go to bed earlier and avoid using my phone at night.
Second, I will set an alarm to sleep on time. The more sleep I get, the more focused I will be.
By changing this habit, I hope to feel more energetic than before.

나는 너무 늦게까지 깨어 있는 습관이 있다. 문제는 낮에 피곤함을 느끼고 학교에서 집중할 수 없다는 것이다.
이 습관을 고치기 위해, 나는 다음과 같은 방법을 사용할 것이다. 먼저, 나는 더 일찍 잠자리에 들고 밤에는 휴대 전화를 사용하지 않을 것이다.
두 번째로, 제때 잠자리에 들기 위해 알람을 맞출 것이다. 내가 잠을 더 많이 잘수록 더 집중력이 높아질 것이다.
이 습관을 바꿈으로써, 나는 이전보다 더 활기차게 느끼기를 바란다.

 ## 논술형 수행평가 9회

평가 기준			배점
내용 (6점)	**내용 조건** (3점)	<내용 조건> 중 4가지 모두 만족한 경우	3
		<내용 조건> 중 3가지를 만족한 경우	2
		<내용 조건> 중 2가지를 만족한 경우	1
	문장 개수 (3점)	5문장 이상 작성한 경우	3
		4문장 이상 작성한 경우	2
		3문장 이하로 작성한 경우	1

<내용> 채점 조건
환경 보호 실천 방안 (4가지 이상)

평가 기준			배점
언어 형식 (6점)	**언어 형식 사용** (3점)	제시된 <언어 형식 조건> 3가지를 목적에 맞게 사용한 경우	3
		제시된 <언어 형식 조건> 3가지 중 2가지를 목적에 맞게 사용한 경우	2
		제시된 <언어 형식 조건> 3가지 중 1가지를 목적에 맞게 사용한 경우	1
	정확한 언어 사용 (3점)	문법적 오류가 3개 이하인 경우	3
		문법적 오류가 4개 이상 6개 이하 포함되었으나 내용 전달에 무리가 없는 경우	2
		문법적 오류가 7개 이상 있고, 내용이 제대로 전달되지 않는 경우	1
총점 (12점)			

<언어 형식> 채점 조건
① 부사절을 이끄는 접속사　② 간접의문문　③ 관계대명사

예시 답안 1

It's very important to protect our environment. Here are some actions I will take to help the environment.
First, I will stop using plastic bags that harm the environment. I will also try to reduce the amount of food waste that I create.
Another way to help is by donating old clothes instead of throwing them away.
I wonder how I can make my family more eco-friendly. I plan to help them use reusable products more often when we go shopping.
I believe that every small effort can protect our planet.

환경을 보호하는 것은 매우 중요합니다. 다음은 환경을 돕기 위해 제가 실천할 몇 가지 방법들입니다.
먼저, 환경을 해치는 비닐봉지 사용을 중단할 것입니다. 또한, 제가 만들어 내는 음식물 쓰레기의 양을 줄이려고 노력할 것입니다.
또 다른 방법은 버리지 않고 헌 옷을 기부하는 것입니다.
저는 제 가족을 어떻게 더 환경친화적으로 만들 수 있을지 궁금합니다. 저는 쇼핑하러 갈 때 그들이 재사용 가능한 제품을 더 자주 사용하도록 도울 계획입니다.
작은 노력 하나하나가 우리 지구를 보호할 수 있다고 믿습니다.

예시 답안 2

It's very important to protect our environment. Here are some actions I will take to help the environment.
First, I will use reusable containers that can be washed and used again. I will also try to reduce the amount of wet tissues that I use. Another way to help is by using paper straws.
I wonder how I can reduce waste at school. I plan to reuse old notebooks when they still have blank pages.
I believe that every small effort can protect our planet.

환경을 보호하는 것은 매우 중요합니다. 다음은 환경을 돕기 위해 제가 실천할 몇 가지 방법들입니다.
먼저, 다시 사용할 수 있는 용기를 사용하려고 합니다. 또한, 제가 사용하는 물티슈의 양을 줄이려고 노력할 것입니다.
또 다른 방법은 종이 빨대를 사용하는 것입니다.
저는 학교에서 어떻게 쓰레기를 줄일 수 있을지 궁금합니다. 저는 오래된 공책에 아직 빈 페이지들이 있을 때 재사용할 계획입니다.
작은 노력 하나하나가 우리 지구를 보호할 수 있다고 믿습니다.

논술형 수행평가 10회

평가 기준			배점
내용 (6점)	**<내용> 채점 조건** ① 방문 날짜, 이름, 위치 ② 간단한 소개 ③ 좋아하는 이유 (3가지 이상)		
	내용 조건 (3점)	<내용 조건> 중 3가지 모두 만족한 경우	3
		<내용 조건> 중 2가지를 만족한 경우	2
		<내용 조건> 중 1가지를 만족한 경우	1
	문장 개수 (3점)	6문장 이상 작성한 경우	3
		5문장 이상 작성한 경우	2
		4문장 이하로 작성한 경우	1
언어 형식 (6점)	**<언어 형식> 채점 조건** ① not only A but also B ② 주격 관계대명사 ③ 목적격 관계대명사		
	언어 형식 사용 (3점)	제시된 <언어 형식 조건> 3가지를 목적에 맞게 사용한 경우	3
		제시된 <언어 형식 조건> 3가지 중 2가지를 목적에 맞게 사용한 경우	2
		제시된 <언어 형식 조건> 3가지 중 1가지를 목적에 맞게 사용한 경우	1
	정확한 언어 사용 (3점)	문법적 오류가 3개 이하인 경우	3
		문법적 오류가 4개 이상 6개 이하 포함되었으나 내용 전달에 무리가 없는 경우	2
		문법적 오류가 7개 이상 있고, 내용이 제대로 전달되지 않는 경우	1
총점 (12점)			

예시 답안 1

Date of visit: June 20
My favorite restaurant is Sushi World. It is located in Daegu. It's a place that serves different types of sushi.
I like it for three reasons: First, the sushi that they prepare is not only fresh but also beautifully presented. Second, the fish that they use is high-quality. Third, the service is friendly and quick. You can enjoy a wonderful time here with your friends or family.
I highly recommend it!
#sushilovers #Daegueats #freshanddelicious

방문 날짜: 6월 20일
제가 가장 좋아하는 식당은 Sushi World입니다. 그것은 대구에 위치해 있습니다. 그곳은 다양한 종류의 초밥을 제공하는 곳입니다.
제가 그곳을 좋아하는 이유는 세 가지입니다: 첫째, 그곳에서 준비하는 초밥은 신선할 뿐만 아니라 보기 좋게 담아냅니다. 둘째, 그곳에서 사용하는 생선은 고품질입니다. 셋째, 서비스가 친절하고 빠릅니다. 여러분은 여기서 친구나 가족과 함께 멋진 시간을 보낼 수 있습니다. 강력히 추천합니다!

예시 답안 2

Date of visit: September 17
My favorite restaurant is Pizza Heaven. It is located in Seoul. It's a place that serves many types of pizza.
I like it for three reasons: First, the pizza that they make is not only crispy but also delicious. Second, the drinks that they provide come in large sizes. Third, the atmosphere is cozy and relaxing. You can enjoy a wonderful time here with your friends or family.
I highly recommend it!
#pizzalovers #Seouleats #cozydining

방문 날짜: 9월 17일
제가 가장 좋아하는 식당은 Pizza Heaven입니다. 그것은 서울에 위치해 있습니다. 그곳은 여러 종류의 피자를 제공하는 곳입니다.
제가 그곳을 좋아하는 이유는 세 가지입니다: 첫째, 그곳에서 만드는 피자는 바삭할 뿐만 아니라 맛있습니다. 둘째, 제공되는 음료는 사이즈가 큽니다. 셋째, 분위기가 아늑하고 편안합니다. 여러분은 여기서 친구나 가족과 함께 멋진 시간을 보낼 수 있습니다. 강력히 추천합니다!

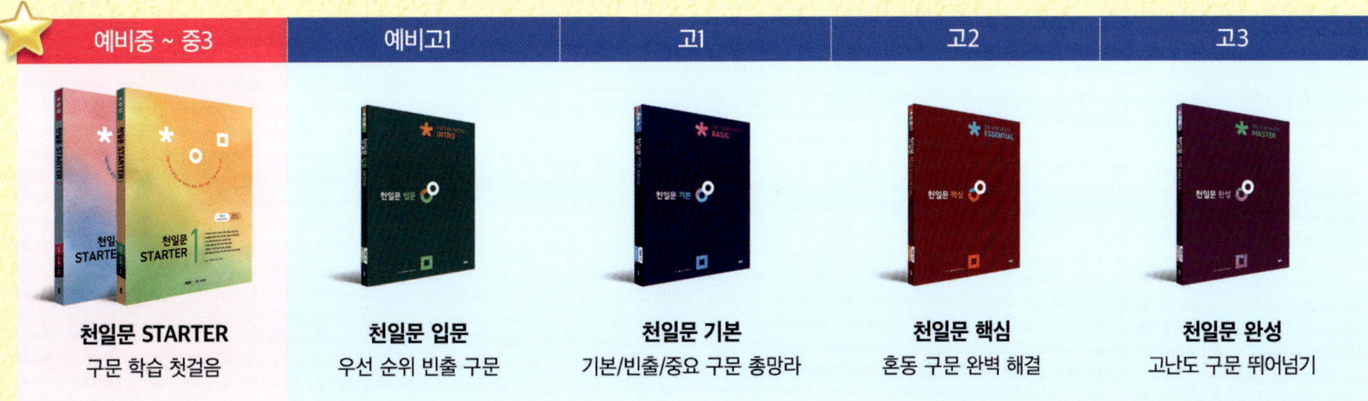

천일문 STARTER

중등 영어 구문·문법 학습의 시작

1. 중등 눈높이에 맞춘 권당 약 500문장 + 내용 구성
2. 개념부터 적용까지 체계적 학습
3. 천일문 완벽 해설집 「천일비급」 부록
4. 철저한 복습을 위한 워크북 포함

구문 대장 천일문, 중등도 천일문만 믿어!

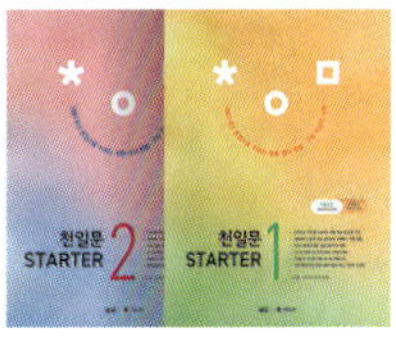

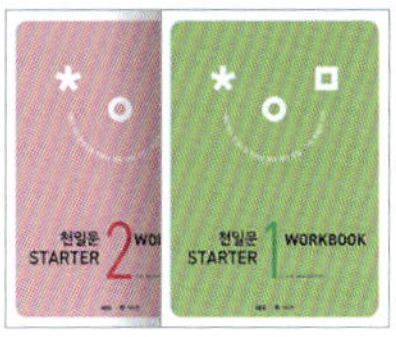

중등부터 고등까지, 천일문과 함께!

예비중 ~ 중3	예비고1	고1	고2	고3
천일문 STARTER	천일문 입문	천일문 기본	천일문 핵심	천일문 완성
구문 학습 첫걸음	우선 순위 빈출 구문	기본/빈출/중요 구문 총망라	혼동 구문 완벽 해결	고난도 구문 뛰어넘기

쎄듀북닷컴(www.cedubook.com)에서 부가 자료를 무료로 다운로드할 수 있습니다.

CEDU쎄듀

더 빨리, 더 많이,
더 오래 남는 어휘

나만의 스마트 단어장 P보카 on 쎄듀런

내게 맞춰 암기하니까, 외워질 수밖에!

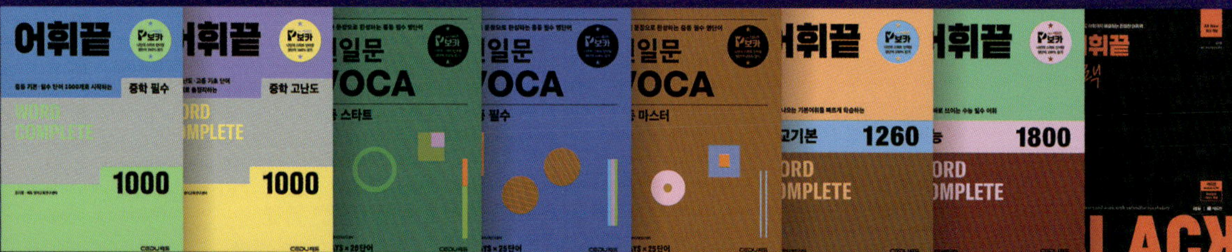

1 '나'에게 딱! 맞는 암기&문제모드만 골라서 학습!

5가지 암기모드

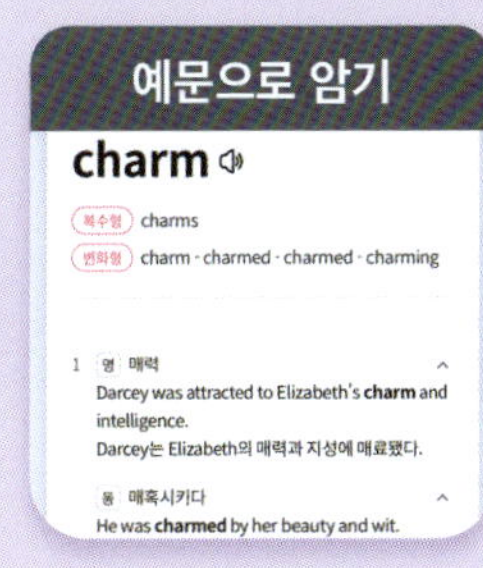

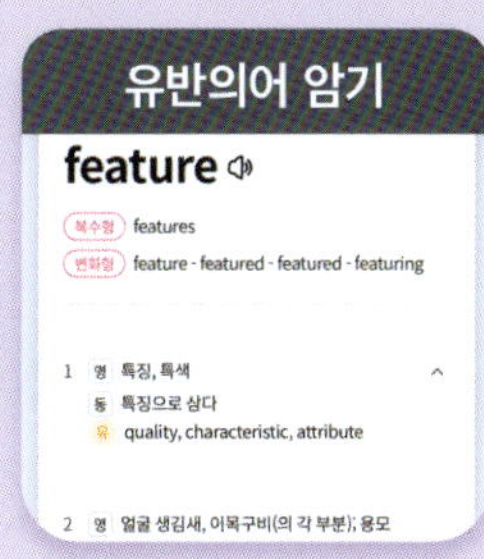

8가지 문제모드

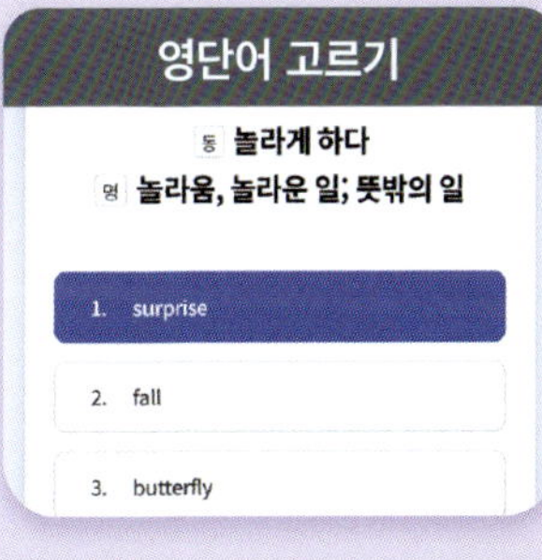

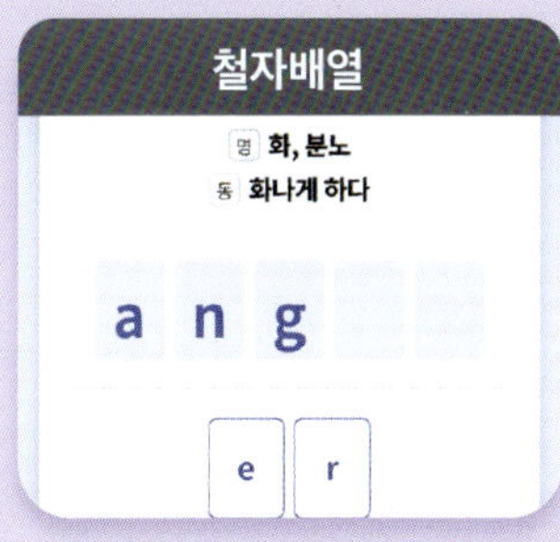

 암기모드를 선택하면, 최적의 문제 모드를 자동 추천!

2 자동 생성 단어장! 단어장만 복습하는 다양한 액티비티!

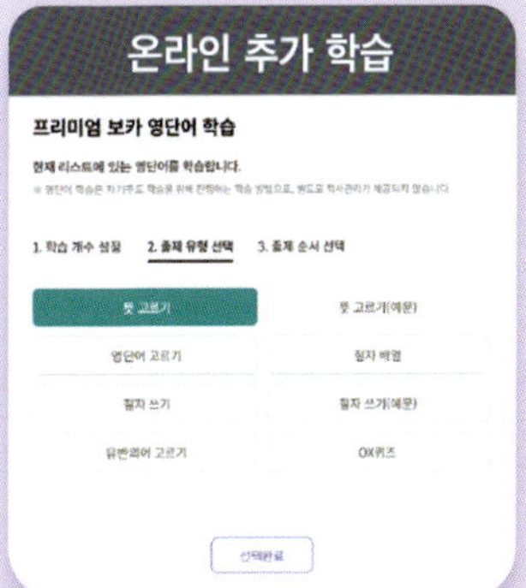

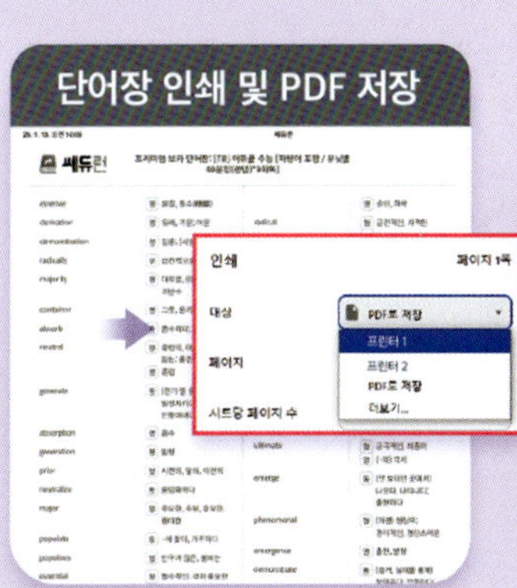

문법 응용력을 높여주는

GRAMMAR Q

✦ Grammar is Understanding ✦

01
교과서
완벽 해부와 반영

02
내신 관리
집중 학습

03
서술형 만점
모의 시험

04
예습+복습
무료 부가자료

쎄듀북닷컴(www.cedubook.com)에서 부가 자료를 무료로 다운로드할 수 있습니다.

CEDU쎄듀

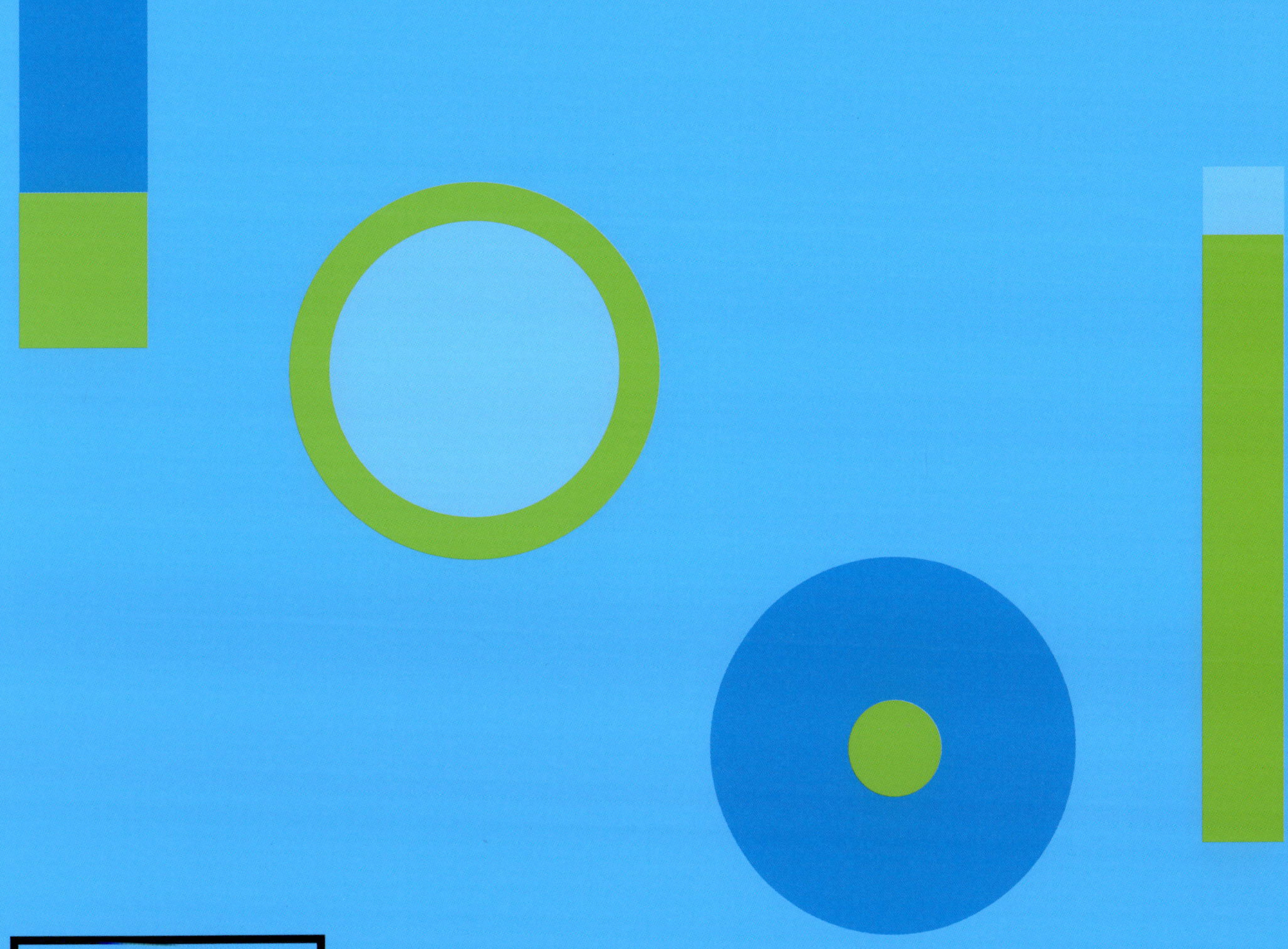

천일문

WORKBOOK

LEVEL 2

중등

WRiTiNG

CEDU 쎄듀

2 LEVEL

천일문

WORKBOOK

중등

WRiTiNG

Unit 01

SVC(2형식)/SVOO(4형식)

배열 영작

[1-2] 우리말과 일치하도록 주어진 단어를 올바르게 배열하세요.

1

네 방은 오늘 매우 지저분해 보인다.
(messy / your room / very / looks)

→ _______________________________________

　　today.

2

그 셔츠는 부드럽고 편하게 느껴진다.
(the shirt / comfortable / feels / and / soft)

→ _______________________________________

　　_______________________________________ .

보기에서 골라 영작

[3-5] 우리말과 일치하도록 〈보기〉에서 알맞은 말을 골라 주어진 단어와 함께 문장을 완성하세요.

〈보기〉 smell	send	buy

3

나의 삼촌은 나에게 간식으로 초콜릿을 좀 사 주셨다.
(some chocolate)

→ My uncle ______________ ______________

　　______________ ______________ as a snack.

4

선생님은 학생들에게 이메일로 수업자료를 보내주셨다.
(class materials, students)

→ The teacher ______________ ______________

　　______________ ______________ by email.

5

지금 우유에서 약간 시큼한 냄새가 난다.
(a bit, sour)

→ The milk ______________ ______________

　　______________ ______________ now.

주어진 단어로 영작

[6-8] 우리말과 일치하도록 주어진 단어와 알맞은 전치사를 사용하여 문장을 완성하세요.

6

나는 부모님께 그들의 기념일에 저녁 식사를 만들어 드릴 것이다.
(a dinner, make, will, my parents)

→ _______________________________________

　　_______________________ on their anniversary.

7

나의 형이 나에게 몇 가지 유익한 조언을 해주었다.
(my brother, useful advice, give, some)

→ _______________________________________

　　_______________________________________

8

가이드는 관광객들에게 관광 일정을 말해주었다.
(the tourists, the guide, the tour schedule, tell)

→ _______________________________________

　　_______________________________________

기출: 조건 영작

9 다음 대화를 읽고 〈조건〉에 맞게 우리말을 영작하세요.

A: Do you exercise often?
B: Almost every day. My brother is a trainer, so he helps me a lot.
A: Cool! How does he help you?
B: <u>그는 나에게 다양한 운동을 가르쳐 줘.</u>

〈조건〉
• 5 단어로 쓸 것
• 주어진 단어를 사용할 것

→ _______________________________________

　　(exercises, different, teach)

---

messy 지저분한　comfortable 편안한　class material 수업자료　a bit 약간　anniversary 기념일　useful 유용한, 도움이 되는　advice 조언, 충고　guide 가이드
trainer (스포츠에서) 트레이너

Unit 02 + SVOC (5형식)

정답 및 해설 p.28

배열 영작

[1-3] 우리말과 일치하도록 주어진 단어를 올바르게 배열하세요.

1

나는 항상 내 손톱을 짧게 유지한다.
(short / I / my nails / keep)

→ _______________________________________

　　all the time.

2

그 코치는 선수들이 매일 연습하게 했다.
(the players / the coach / practice / made)

→ _______________________________________

_______________________________ every day.

3

팬들은 가수가 또 다른 노래를 부르길 원했다.
(wanted / sing / the fans / to / the singer)

→ _______________________________________

_______________________________ another song.

주어진 단어로 영작

[4-8] 우리말과 일치하도록 주어진 단어를 사용하여 문장을 완성하세요.

4

그들은 Tommy를 팀의 주장으로 만들었다.
(make, of the team, the captain)

→ _______________________________________

____

5

그녀는 다른 방에서 전화가 울리는 것을 들었다.
(ring, the phone, hear)

→ _______________________________________

_______________________________ in the other room.

6

선생님은 학생들이 시험이 끝난 후 교실을 나가도록 하셨다.
(leave, let, the students, the teacher)

→ _______________________________________

_______________________________ after the test.

7

그는 아이들에게 복도에서 뛰지 말라고 말했다.
(run, the kids, tell)

→ _______________________________________

_______________________________ in the hallway.

8

그 박물관은 사람들이 사진을 찍도록 허락하지 않는다.
(people, allow, take photos, the museum)

→ _______________________________________

____

기출: 조건 영작

9 우리말과 일치하도록 〈조건〉에 맞게 문장을 완성하세요.

(1)

〈조건〉
• the mouse, the cat, chase를 사용할 것

나는 고양이가 쥐를 쫓는 것을 보았다.

→ _______________________________________

(2)

〈조건〉
• the children, toys, clean up,
　Mr. Clark를 사용할 것

Clark 선생님은 그 아이들이 그들의 장난감을 치우도록 하셨다.

→ _______________________________________

____

---

nail 손톱 all the time 항상 coach (스포츠 팀의) 코치 captain (스포츠 팀의) 주장 hallway 복도 chase 뒤쫓다 clean up ～을 치우다

Unit 01 

현재, 과거, 미래 & 진행형

O— 배열 영작

[1-3] 우리말과 일치하도록 주어진 단어를 올바르게 배열하세요.

1

> Paul은 지금 낮잠을 자고 있다.
> (a nap / is / taking / Paul)

→ ___________________________ now.

2

> 우리는 역에서 버스를 기다리고 있었다.
> (were / the bus / we / waiting for)

→ ___________________________
  at the station.

3

> 미용사가 남자 아이의 머리를 자르고 있다.
> (the hairdresser / the boy's hair / cutting / is)

→ ___________________________ .

O— 빈칸 완성

[4-6] 우리말과 일치하도록 주어진 단어를 사용하여 빈칸에 알맞은 말을 쓰세요.

4

> 나는 내년에 외국에서 공부할 것이다.
> (abroad, study)

→ I ___________________________
  next year.

5

> 그는 일주일에 한 번 체육관에서 운동한다.
> (the gym, exercise, at)

→ He ___________________________
  ___________________________ once a week.

6

> 나의 언니는 지난달에 새로운 일을 구했다.
> (a new job, get)

→ My sister ___________________________
  ___________________________ last month.

O— 주어진 단어로 영작

[7-9] 우리말과 일치하도록 주어진 단어를 사용하여 문장을 완성하세요.

7

> 그들은 요리 대회에서 1등을 했다.
> (win, the first prize)

→ ___________________________
  in the cooking contest.

8

> 그 소녀들은 쇼핑몰에서 새 옷을 사고 있다.
> (shop, the girls, for new clothes)

→ ___________________________
  ___________________________ at the mall.

9

> 너는 이번 토요일에 울타리를 페인트칠할 거니?
> (paint, going, the fence)

→ ___________________________
  ___________________________ this Saturday?

기출: 조건 영작

10 다음 글을 읽고 〈조건〉에 맞게 우리말을 영작하세요.

> Last night, Dad was preparing for dinner.
> (1) 나는 그를 돕기 위해 식탁을 차리고 있었다.
> Suddenly, the power went out. The lights
> came back after an hour. (2) On that day,
> 나는 전기에 감사함을 느꼈다.

〈조건〉
• 주어진 단어를 사용하되 필요시 형태를 바꿀 것

(1) ___________________________
  to help him. (the table, set)

(2) On that day, ___________________________
  ___________________________ . (thankful for, feel, electricity)

nap 낮잠 hairdresser 미용사 abroad 해외에(서) win (상을) 타다 first prize 일등 fence 울타리 go out (불·전기가) 나가다, 꺼지다 set the table 식탁을 차리다
thankful for ~에 감사하는 electricity 전기

Unit 02

현재완료의 개념과 형태

빈칸 완성

[1-4] 주어진 단어를 사용하여 현재완료 문장을 완성하세요.

1 I ______________ ______________ my new
phone. (break)

2 She ______________ just ______________ from
her trip. (return)

3 ______________ you ever ______________ this
restaurant before? (visit)

4 The teacher ______________ ______________
a speech for an hour. (give)

주어진 단어로 영작

**[5-8] 우리말과 일치하도록 주어진 단어를 사용하여 현재완료
문장을 완성하세요.**

5
> 나는 유명한 배우를 한 번 만난 적이 있다.
> (meet, a famous actor)

→ ______________________________________

______________________________ once.

6
> 그들은 결혼한 지 20년이 되었다.
> (married, be)

→ ______________________________________

______________________________ for twenty years.

7
> 그녀는 작년부터 패스트푸드를 먹지 않고 있다.
> (fast food, eat)

→ ______________________________________

______________________________ since last year.

8
> Ian은 그의 가방 싸는 것을 이미 끝냈니?
> (bag, finish, packing)

→ ______________________________________

______________________________ already?

어법 오류 수정

**[9-11] 다음 각 문장의 밑줄 친 부분을 어법상 바르게 고쳐
쓰세요.**

9 I have <u>ride</u> a horse before.

→ ______________________

10 The children <u>has</u> lived in this city for ten years.

→ ______________________

11 My dad <u>has bought</u> the car five years ago.

→ ______________________

기출: 조건 영작

12 우리말과 일치하도록 〈조건〉에 맞게 문장을 완성하세요.

> 〈조건〉
> • 주어진 단어를 사용할 것
> • 현재완료 문장으로 나타낼 것

(1) Ryan과 나는 그 박물관을 방문한 적이 여러 번 있다.
　　(visit, that museum, and)

→ ______________________________________

______________________________ a few times.

(2) 나는 네 메시지를 받지 못했다.
　　(message, receive)

→ ______________________________________

____

give a speech 연설하다　married 결혼한　pack (짐을) 싸다　message 메시지　receive 받다

Unit 03

현재완료의 주요 의미

정답 및 해설 p.28

배열 영작

[1-3] 우리말과 일치하도록 주어진 단어를 올바르게 배열하세요.

1
> 그녀는 그녀의 이메일 비밀번호를 여러 번 잊었다.
> (her / forgotten / she / password / has / email)

→ _______________________________________
  several times.

2
> 나는 스쿠버 다이빙을 한 번도 해본 적이 없다.
> (done / I / scuba diving / never / have)

→ _______________________________________
  _______________________________________.

3
> 우리는 지난주부터 삼촌의 집에서 머물렀다.
> (have / last week / at our uncle's house / stayed / we / since)

→ _______________________________________
  _______________________________________.

한 문장으로 영작

[4-5] 다음 두 문장을 현재완료를 사용하여 한 문장으로 바꿔 쓸 때 빈칸에 알맞은 말을 쓰세요.

4
> I started practicing yoga a year ago.
> I still practice it.

→ I _______________________________________
  for a year.

5
> My mom went to the U.S. for work.
> She is not here now.

→ My mom _______________________________________
  _______________________________________ for work.

주어진 단어로 영작

[6-8] 우리말과 일치하도록 주어진 단어를 사용하여 현재완료 문장을 완성하세요.

6
> Peter는 이미 잠자리에 들었다.
> (go to bed, already)

→ _______________________________________
  ____

7
> 너는 전에 멕시코 음식을 먹어본 적이 있니?
> (Mexican food, try, ever)

→ _______________________________________
  _______________________________ before?

8
> 우리 팀은 마지막 순간에 막 한 골을 넣었다.
> (team, score, just, a goal)

→ _______________________________________
  _______________________ in the final minute.

기출: 조건 영작

9 우리말과 일치하도록 〈조건〉에 맞게 문장을 완성하세요.

> 〈조건〉
> • 주어진 단어를 사용할 것
> • 현재완료 문장으로 나타낼 것

(1) 나는 내가 가장 좋아하는 펜을 잃어버렸다.
  (lose, favorite pen)

→ _______________________________________
  ____

(2) 내 여동생은 이 안경을 2년 동안 써 왔다.
  (sister, these glasses, two years, wear)

→ _______________________________________
  ____

---

password 비밀번호 several 몇몇의, 여럿의 scuba diving 스쿠버 다이빙 Mexican 멕시코(인)의 score 득점을 올리다; 득점 final 마지막의

can/may/will

○― 배열 영작

[1-4] 우리말과 일치하도록 주어진 단어를 올바르게 배열하세요.

1
> Jay는 그가 가장 좋아하는 시를 외울 수 있다.
> (favorite poem / memorize / Jay / his / can)

→ ____

____ .

2
> 당신의 책을 일주일 동안 빌려주시겠어요?
> (me / book / could / lend / your / you)

→ ____

________________________________ for a week?

3
> 나는 공항에서 내 여권을 찾을 수 없었다.
> (find / able / passport / wasn't / I / my / to)

→ ____

________________________ at the airport.

4
> 박물관에서는 플래시를 켜고 사진을 찍어서는 안 된다.
> (take / with flash / may / you / not / photos)

→ ____

________________________ in the museum.

○― 보기에서 골라 영작

**[5-8] 우리말과 일치하도록 〈보기〉에서 알맞은 말을 골라
주어진 단어를 사용하여 문장을 완성하세요.
(단, 한 번씩만 쓸 것)**

> 〈보기〉
> can't   may not   would   be able to

5
> 그들은 곧 그들의 새 아파트로 이사할 수 있을 것이다.
> (move into, will)

→ They ________________________________

________________________ their new apartment soon.

6
> 너는 영수증 없이는 이것을 반품할 수 없다.
> (return, this)

→ ____

without a receipt.

7
> 제게 피자 한 조각을 더 주시겠어요?
> (to me, give, of pizza, another piece)

→ ____

____

8
> 그 옷가게는 일요일에는 문을 열지 않을지도 모른다.
> (open, the clothing store, be)

→ ____

________________________________ on Sundays.

기출: 조건 영작

9   우리말과 일치하도록 〈조건〉에 맞게 문장을 완성하세요.

> 손님들은 오후 3시 이후 언제든지 체크인 해도 됩니다.

> 〈조건〉
> • 6 단어로 쓸 것
> • check in, guests, any time을 사용할 것

→ ____

________________________________ after 3 p.m.

---

poem (한 편의) 시 memorize 외우다 passport 여권 flash (카메라) 플래시 move into ~로 이사하다 receipt 영수증 check in 체크인 하다, 숙박 수속을 밟다

Unit 02+

must/have to/should

정답 및 해설 p.29

배열 영작

[1-4] 우리말과 일치하도록 주어진 단어를 올바르게 배열하세요.

1
모든 방문객들은 안내 데스크에서 서명을 하고 들어가야 한다. (sign in / visitors / must / all)

→ _______________________________

_______________________ at the front desk.

2
안전상의 이유로 모든 사람들은 여기서 안전모를 써야 한다.
(to / a helmet / everyone / wear / has)

→ _______________________________

_______________________ here for safety reasons.

3
너는 네 모든 돈을 한꺼번에 다 쓰지 말아야 한다.
(not / you / your money / should / all / spend)

→ _______________________________

_______________________ at once.

4
그녀는 내일 비행기를 타려면 일찍 일어나야 할 것이다.
(have / wake up / early / she / will / to)

→ _______________________________

_______________________ , for her flight tomorrow.

주어진 단어로 영작

[5-8] 우리말과 일치하도록 주어진 단어를 사용하여 문장을 완성하세요. (필요시 단어를 추가할 것)

5
Jason은 긴 여행 후에 매우 피곤할 것임이 틀림없다.
(tired, be, very)

→ _______________________________

after a long trip.

6
너는 나를 기다릴 필요 없어. 나중에 따라갈게.
(wait for)

→ _______________________________

_______________________ I'll catch up later.

7
아기는 오후에 낮잠을 자야 한다.
(take, the baby, a nap, have)

→ _______________________________

_______________________ in the afternoon.

8
학생은 선생님께 무례하게 굴지 말아야 한다.
(to the teachers, should, be, students, rude)

→ _______________________________

____

기출: 보기에서 골라 영작

9
우리말과 일치하도록 〈보기〉에서 알맞은 단어를 골라 have to를 사용하여 문장을 완성하세요.

〈보기〉
memorize   practice

Jenny는 연극을 위해 그녀의 대사를 연습해야 하지만, 오늘밤까지 모든 대사를 외울 필요는 없다.

→ Jenny _______________________________

her lines for the play, but she _______________

all of them by tonight.

sign in 서명하고 들어가다 front desk 안내 데스크 safety 안전 reason 이유 at once 한꺼번에 flight 항공편 catch up 따라잡다 line 대사; 선, 줄

Unit 03

정답 및 해설 p.29

had better/would like to/used to

배열 영작

[1-4] 우리말과 일치하도록 주어진 단어를 올바르게 배열하세요.

1
너는 코트를 입는 게 좋겠어. 밖은 매우 추워.
(had / a coat / you / wear / better)

→ _______________________.
It's very cold outside.

2
Eddy는 가수가 되기 전에 댄서였다.
(to / a dancer / be / Eddy / used)

→ _______________________
before he became a singer.

3
나는 시내에 있는 새로 생긴 빵집을 방문해 보고 싶다.
(like / the new bakery / visit / would / I / to)

→ _______________________
_______________________ downtown.

4
우리는 이 버스를 놓치지 않는 게 좋겠어.
다음 버스는 30분 후에 와.
(miss / not / we / had / bus / this / better)

→ _______________________.
The next one comes in 30 minutes.

주어진 단어로 영작

[5-8] 우리말과 일치하도록 had better, would like to, used to 중 하나를 골라 주어진 단어를 사용하여 문장을 완성하세요.

5
우리는 오늘 해변에서 선크림을 바르는 게 좋겠다.
(wear, sunscreen)

→ _______________________
_______________________ at the beach today.

6
나중에 피자 먹으러 가시겠어요?
(a pizza, for, go out)

→ _______________________
_______________________ later?

7
Tina는 사물함의 열쇠를 다시는 잃어버리지 않는 것이 좋겠다.
(the locker, the keys, to, lose)

→ _______________________
_______________________ again.

8
나의 할머니는 나에게 그녀의 어린 시절에 대한 이야기를 해주시곤 했다.
(stories, to me, my grandma, tell)

→ _______________________
_______________________ about her childhood.

기출: 조건 영작

9 다음 대화를 읽고 〈조건〉에 맞게 우리말을 영작하세요.

A: What's the matter?
B: I'm feeling stressed. I have to prepare for an English speaking test this Friday, but I also have to go to the band practice.
A: Hmm, 너는 두 가지 중에 선택하는 것이 좋겠어.

〈조건〉
• 7 단어로 쓸 것
• the two, choose, between을 사용할 것

→ Hmm, _______________________
_______________________.

downtown 중심가, 번화가 sunscreen 자외선 차단제 locker 사물함 childhood 어린 시절 stressed 스트레스를 받는 band (가수를 중심으로 한) 밴드

[1-3] 우리말과 일치하도록 주어진 단어를 올바르게 배열하세요.

1
그녀는 무대 위에서 인기 가수처럼 보인다.
(looks / a pop star / she / like)

→ ________________________________

________________________________ on the stage.

2
너는 전주에 가 본 적이 있니?
(to / have / Jeonju / ever / you / been)

→ ________________________________

________________________________ ?

3
미나는 나에게 그녀의 새 휴대 전화를 보여 주었다.
(cell phone / showed / her / me / new / Mina)

→ ________________________________

________________________________ .

[4-7] 우리말과 일치하도록 주어진 단어를 사용하여 빈칸에 알맞은 말을 쓰세요. (필요시 단어를 추가하거나 형태를 바꿀 것)

4
내 우산을 잠깐 들어줄래?
(hold, can, umbrella)

→ __________ __________ __________

__________ __________ for a minute?

5
너는 내 카메라를 다음 주에 돌려줘도 돼.
(return, may, camera)

→ __________ __________ __________

__________ __________ next week.

6
나는 오늘 아침 일찍 일어나야 했다.
(have to, early, wake up)

→ __________ __________ __________

__________ __________ __________

this morning.

7
너는 표를 구매할 필요가 없어. 나에게 두 장이 있거든.
(a ticket, buy, have to)

→ You __________ __________

__________ __________ __________

__________ . I have two.

[8-10] 우리말과 일치하도록 주어진 단어를 사용하여 문장을 완성하세요. (필요시 단어를 추가하거나 형태를 바꿀 것)

8
사람들은 그 선수를 영웅이라고 불렀다.
(call, a hero, people, the player)

→ ________________________________

____

9
폭설이 나의 신발을 젖게 만들었다.
(wet, the heavy snow, shoes, make)

→ ________________________________

____

10
나는 이번 겨울 방학에 유럽으로 여행을 갈 것이다.
(going, this winter vacation, travel, to Europe)

→ ________________________________

____

[11-14] 우리말과 일치하도록 주어진 단어를 사용하여 단어 수에 맞게 문장을 완성하세요.

11

나는 나의 사촌이 내 컴퓨터를 사용하도록 허락했다.
(cousin, computer, use, let / 7 단어)

→ _______________________________________

12

나는 그가 빠르게 헤엄치는 것을 보았다.
(watch, swim, fast / 5 단어)

→ _______________________________________

13

아빠는 내가 캠핑에 가도록 허락하셨다.
(allow, go camping, Dad / 6 단어)

→ _______________________________________

14

그녀는 우리에게 방을 나가라고 명령했다.
(order, the room, leave / 7 단어)

→ _______________________________________

[15-18] 다음 두 문장을 〈보기〉와 같이 현재완료를 사용하여 한 문장으로 바꿔 쓰세요.

〈보기〉
• Mark arrived in Korea in 2020.
• He still lives here.
→ <u>Mark has lived in Korea</u> since 2020.

15

• I lost my ring.
• So I don't have it now.

→ _______________________________________

16

• Tony went to Japan.
• So he's not here right now.

→ _______________________________________

17

• Seho started to study Chinese in 2022.
• He still studies it.

→ _______________________________________
since 2022.

18

• Jessie started to attend the world history class five months ago.
• She still does.

→ _______________________________________
_______________________________ for five months.

고난도

19 다음은 어제 유나에게 생일 선물을 준 사람과 그 선물을 나타내는 표입니다. 표의 내용과 일치하도록 주어진 단어를 사용하여 문장을 완성하세요.
(단, 전치사 to와 for 중 하나를 반드시 사용할 것)

Yuna's Birthday Present List	
Dad	gloves
Mom	a muffler
Grandmother	chicken and fish
Sister	a yellow cap
Best Friend	a movie

(1) Yuna's dad _______________________________
her. (give)

(2) Yuna's mom _______________________________
her. (make)

(3) Yuna's grandmother _______________________
_______________________________ her. (cook)

(4) Yuna's sister _____________________________
_______________________________ her. (buy)

(5) Yuna's best friend ________________________
_______________________________ her. (show)

[20-23] 다음 각 문장에서 어법상 **틀린** 부분을 찾아 바르게
고쳐 쓰세요.

20 A year had 12 months.

_______________ → _______________

21 The hot chocolate tasted very sweetly.

_______________ → _______________

22 The accident has happened three days ago.

_______________ → _______________

23 You have to not pay for your meal.
I already paid for it.

_______________ → _______________

24 대화의 흐름이 자연스럽도록 각 빈칸에 들어갈 말을
〈조건〉에 맞게 영작하세요.

Sumi: Mom, can I have more rice?
Mom: (1) Yes, but _______________.
　　　　You'll have an upset stomach if you
　　　　don't eat slowly.
Sumi: Okay. I'll eat it slowly.
Mom: (2) _______________?
Sumi: Sure! I love ice cream.

〈조건〉
• 주어진 단어를 사용할 것
• 주어, 동사를 포함한 문장으로 쓸 것

(1) Yes, but _______________

_______________.

(better, too fast, eat)

(2) _______________

_______________?

(have, some, for dessert, like, would,
ice cream, to)

[25-26] 다음 대화의 내용과 일치하도록 주어진 단어를 사용
하여 현재완료 시제로 문장을 완성하세요.

25

A: Are you busy these days, Eric?
B: Yes, I am. I'm working on the science
　　project. I started it two weeks ago.
A: When will you finish it?
B: I don't know. I have to work on it a few
　　more weeks.

→ Eric _______________ _______________

_______________ _______________ _______________

_______________ two weeks.

(work on, for)

26

A: Sera plays the violin very well.
B: I agree with you. She started to take
　　violin lessons last summer vacation. And
　　she still takes lessons every weekend.

→ Sera _______________ _______________

_______________ _______________ _______________

last summer vacation. (take)

Unit 01

수동태의 기본 이해

정답 및 해설 p.30

배열 영작

[1-3] 우리말과 일치하도록 주어진 단어를 올바르게 배열하세요.

1 우리 가족 여행은 나에 의해 계획되었다.
(me / planned / family trip / by / was / our)

→ ____________________________________

____________________________________ .

2 지도는 여행 정보 센터에서 직원에 의해 제공된다.
(are / the staff / provided / maps / by)

→ ____________________________________

at the tour information center.

3 학교 댄스파티의 초대장이 내일 발송될 것이다.
(the school's dance party / sent out /
the invitation / will / to / be)

→ ____________________________________

____________________________________ tomorrow.

문장 전환

[4-6] 다음 문장을 수동태로 바꿔 쓰세요.

4 The teacher checks our homework every day.

→ ____________________________________

____________________________________ every day.

5 Our soccer team won the gold medal this year.

→ ____________________________________

____________________________________ this year.

6 The volunteers will clean the city's park.

→ ____________________________________

____

주어진 단어로 영작

[7-9] 우리말과 일치하도록 주어진 단어를 사용하여 문장을 완성하세요.

7 학교 버스는 Johnson 씨에 의해 운행된다.
(drive, the school bus, Mr. Johnson)

→ ____________________________________

____

8 새로운 노래들이 다음 주에 공개될 것이다.
(release, the new songs)

→ ____________________________________

____________________________________ next week.

9 그 코미디 영화는 많은 관객에 의해 시청되었다.
(a large audience, the comedy movie,
watch)

→ ____________________________________

____

기출·조건 영작

10 다음 대화를 읽고 〈조건〉에 맞게 우리말을 영작하세요.

A: Have you heard this song?
B: Yes, I have! 그 노래는 내가 가장 좋아하는
음악가인 Taylor에 의해 쓰였어.
A: Really? I didn't know that!
B: The melodies are so beautiful.

〈조건〉
• 주어진 단어를 사용할 것
• 8 단어로 쓸 것

→ ____________________________________

____________________________________ , Taylor.

(musician, favorite, the song, write)

---

provide 제공하다, 주다 send out 발송하다 invitation 초대장, 초대 release 공개하다 audience 관객 melody 멜로디, 선율 musician 뮤지션, 음악가

Unit 02 수동태의 여러 가지 형태

정답 및 해설 p.30

배열 영작

[1-4] 우리말과 일치하도록 주어진 단어를 올바르게 배열하세요.

1

> 그 식물들은 주말동안 물이 주어지지 않았다.
> (watered / not / the plants / were)

→ ________________________________

   during the weekend.

2

> 그 울타리는 언제 페인트칠되었니?
> (painted / was / when / the fence)

→ ________________________________?

3

> 규칙은 모든 사람들에 의해 따라져야 한다.
> (followed / must / everyone / by / the rules / be)

→ ________________________________.

4

> 이 영화는 아이들에 의해 관람되면 안 된다.
> (by / watched / movie / not / be / kids / should / this)

→ ________________________________

   ________________________________.

문장 전환

[5-7] 다음 문장의 밑줄 친 부분을 주어로 하는 수동태 문장을 완성하세요.

5 My best friend told me the secret.

→ ________________________________

   by my best friend.

6 The teacher showed us the answers.

→ ________________________________

   ________________________ by the teacher.

7 Ms. Miller cooked the guests breakfast.

→ ________________________________

   ________________________ by Ms. Miller.

주어진 단어로 영작

[8-10] 우리말과 일치하도록 주어진 단어를 사용하여 문장을 완성하세요.

8

> 걱정하지 마. 네 실수는 곧 잊혀질 거야.
> (forget, will, mistake)

→ Don't worry. ________________________

   ________________________ soon.

9

> 그 콘서트는 어제 왜 취소되었니?
> (the concert, why, cancel)

→ ________________________________

   ________________________ yesterday?

10

> 내 남동생은 반려동물 훈련에 관심이 있다.
> (interested, brother, pet training)

→ ________________________________

   ____

기출: 조건 영작

11 우리말과 일치하도록 〈조건〉에 맞게 문장을 완성하세요.

> 이 치즈는 농장에서 신선한 우유로 만들어진다.

> 〈조건〉
> • make를 사용하여 수동태로 쓸 것
> • fresh milk, this cheese를 사용할 것

→ ________________________________

   ________________________ on the farm.

water ~에 물을 주다 follow (충고 등을) 따르다 rule 규칙 secret 비밀 guest 손님 mistake 실수 cancel 취소하다 training 훈련

Unit 01

to부정사의 명사적 쓰임

[1-4] 우리말과 일치하도록 주어진 단어를 올바르게 배열하세요.

1
그녀는 토론 동아리에 가입하기로 선택했다.
(the debate club / join / chose / to / she)

→ ________________________________ .

2
새로운 장소를 탐험하는 것은 흥미진진하다.
(explore / it / to / is / a new place / exciting)

→ ________________________________

________________________________ .

3
낯선 사람과는 이야기하지 않는 게 현명하다.
(talk / not / wise / to strangers / is / it / to)

→ ________________________________

________________________________ .

4
우리는 수학여행을 어디로 가는지 아직 모른다.
(don't / where / for the school trip / to / know / go / we)

→ ________________________________

________________________________ yet.

[5-6] 우리말과 일치하도록 주어진 단어를 사용하여 빈칸에 알맞은 말을 쓰세요.

5
밤에 공포 영화를 보는 것은 무섭다.
(watch, it, scary)

→ ____________ ____________ ____________

____________ ____________ horror movies

at night.

6
Karl은 올해 대회에 참가하지 않기로 결정했다.
(participate in, decide)

→ Karl ____________ ____________

____________ ____________ ____________

the contest this year.

[7-8] 우리말과 일치하도록 주어진 단어와 to부정사를 사용하여 문장을 완성하세요.

7
이 앱을 사용하는 방법을 설명해줄 수 있니?
(explain, use, can, this app)

→ ________________________________

8
나는 그 행사에 무엇을 입어야 할지 모르겠다.
(for the event, know, wear)

→ ________________________________

____

9 우리말과 일치하도록 〈조건〉에 맞게 문장을 완성하세요.

〈조건〉
· 가주어 It으로 시작할 것
· an old habit, break, easy를 사용할 것
· 9 단어로 쓸 것

오래된 습관을 고치는 것은 쉽지 않다.

→ ________________________________

____

---

debate 토론 explore 탐험하다 stranger 낯선 사람 participate in ~에 참가하다 explain 설명하다 app(= application) 앱, 애플리케이션 break a habit 습관을 고치다

Unit 02
to부정사의 형용사적 쓰임

정답 및 해설 p.31

배열 영작

[1-4] 우리말과 일치하도록 주어진 단어를 올바르게 배열하세요.

1
> 나는 다음 주에 봐야 할 어휘 시험이 있다.
> (take / I / a vocabulary test / have / to)

→ _________________________________

_________________________ next week.

2
> Mark는 공항에 그를 데려다 줄 사람이 필요하다.
> (him / to / someone / needs / take / Mark)

→ _________________________________

_________________________ to the airport.

3
> 우리 고양이는 가지고 놀 장난감이 많이 있다.
> (toys / cat / our / with / has / play / many / to)

→ _________________________________

_________________________________ .

4
> 그녀는 이번 주말에 할 무언가 재밌는 것을 찾고 있다.
> (to / looking for / something / she / is / fun / do)

→ _________________________________

_________________________ this weekend.

주어진 단어로 영작

[5-8] 우리말과 일치하도록 주어진 단어를 사용하여 문장을 완성하세요.

5
> 장거리 비행에서 읽을 책을 추천해줄 수 있니?
> (a book, read, recommend, can)

→ _________________________________

_________________________ on the long flight?

6
> Daniel은 여행 동안 머무를 호텔을 예약했다.
> (a hotel, stay, book)

→ _________________________________

_________________________ during the trip.

7
> 나는 그녀에게 사실을 말할 기회가 없었어.
> (a chance, tell, have)

→ _________________________________

_________________________ her the truth.

8
> Jessica는 잠을 잘 새로운 침대를 샀다.
> (sleep, a new bed, buy)

→ _________________________________

____

기출: 조건 영작

9 우리말과 일치하도록 〈조건〉에 맞게 영작하세요.

> 〈조건〉
> • to부정사를 사용할 것
> • 주어진 단어를 사용할 것

(1)
> 나는 채소들을 자를 칼 한 자루가 필요하다.
> (cut, a knife, the vegetables)

→ _________________________________

____

(2)
> 그는 그의 감정에 대해 이야기할 사람이 필요하다.
> (talk, someone)

→ _________________________________

_________________________ about his feelings.

---

vocabulary 어휘 take (사람을) 데리고 가다[데려다 주다] look for ~을 찾다 recommend 추천하다 book 예약하다 feelings (복수형) 감정, 마음

Unit 03

to부정사의 부사적 쓰임

정답 및 해설 p.31

[1-4] 우리말과 일치하도록 주어진 단어를 올바르게 배열하세요.

1 나의 가족은 환경을 보호하기 위해 플라스틱을 더 적게 쓰려고 노력한다.
(the environment / protect / to)

→ My family tries to use less plastic __________

__________________________ .

2 이 영어 소설은 읽기 쉽다. (read / easy / to / is)

→ This English novel __________________

__________________ .

3 그는 그의 건강을 개선하기 위해 헬스장에 등록했다.
(health / to / his / improve)

→ He signed up for a gym __________

__________________ .

4 그녀는 그녀의 오랜 친구로부터 소식을 듣게 되어 기뻤다. (old friend / from / was / to / her / pleased / hear)

→ She __________________

__________________ .

[5-9] 우리말과 일치하도록 주어진 단어를 사용하여 문장을 완성하세요.

5 나는 제시간에 일어나기 위해 알람을 맞출 것이다.
(will, wake up, set an alarm)

→ I __________________

__________________ on time.

6 이 옷은 여름에 입기에 시원하다.
(wear, be, cool, these clothes)

→ __________________

__________________ in summer.

7 나는 수학 시험에서 낮은 점수를 받아서 실망했다.
(disappointed, be, a low score, get)

→ __________________

__________________ on the math test.

8 그는 더 나은 음악가가 되기 위해 매일 연습했다.
(a better musician, practice, every day, become)

→ He __________________

__________________ .

9 우리는 우리가 가장 좋아하는 작가를 만나게 되어 설렜다.
(excited, be, favorite author, meet)

→ __________________

__________________ .

10 다음 주어진 문장과 같은 의미가 되도록 to부정사를 사용하여 한 문장으로 쓰세요.

John visited the library because he wanted to research marine life for his science homework.

→ John visited the library __________

__________________ for his science homework.

---

environment 환경 improve 개선하다, 향상시키다 sign up (for) (~을) 신청하다, 등록하다 disappointed 실망한 author 작가 research 조사하다, 연구하다 marine life 해양 생물

Unit 04 

정답 및 해설 p.31

to부정사를 포함한 주요 구문

○━ 배열 영작

[1-3] 우리말과 일치하도록 주어진 단어를 올바르게 배열하세요.

1
> 그녀는 너무 긴장돼서 무대에서 공연할 수 없었다.
> (perform / too / to / nervous)

→ She was _______________________________

_________________________________ on stage.

2
> 나는 오늘 너무 바빠서 점심을 먹을 수 없었다.
> (to / lunch / too / have / busy)

→ I was _______________________________

_________________________________ today.

3
> Paul은 1등을 할 만큼 충분히 빨리 달렸다.
> (first place / to / fast / win / enough)

→ Paul ran _____________________________

_________________________________ .

○━ 주어진 단어로 영작

[4-5] 우리말과 일치하도록 주어진 단어와 to부정사를 사용하여 문장을 완성하세요.

4
> 그는 너무 화가 나서 차분히 얘기할 수 없었다.
> (talk, be, calmly, angry)

→ _______________________________

____

5
> 나의 누나는 차를 운전하기에 충분히 나이가 있다.
> (enough, drive, sister, a car, old, be)

→ _______________________________

____

○━ 문장 전환

[6-8] 주어진 문장과 같은 의미가 되도록 빈칸에 알맞은 말을 쓰세요.

6
> The girl was too shocked to say a word.

→ The girl was ___________ ___________

___________ ___________ ___________

___________ a word.

7
> He is strong enough to carry the heavy box.

→ He is ___________ ___________

___________ ___________ ___________

___________ the heavy box.

8
> I was so sick that I couldn't attend the meeting yesterday.

→ I was ___________ ___________

___________ ___________ the meeting

yesterday.

○━ 기출: 주어진 단어로 영작

9 우리말과 일치하도록 주어진 단어를 사용하여 단어 수에 맞게 쓰세요.

> A: How was the movie last night?
> B: Honestly, 영화 보는 동안 난 너무 졸려서 깨어 있을 수 없었어. (stay, awake, sleepy)
> A: Really? Was the movie that boring?
> B: No, I think I was just tired.

→ Honestly, _____________________________

_________________________ during the movie. (7 단어)

---

perform 공연하다 first place 1위, 우승 shocked 충격 받은 say a word 말하다 attend 참석하다 honestly 솔직히 awake 깨어 있는

Unit 01

명사로 쓰이는 동명사

[1-4] 우리말과 일치하도록 주어진 단어를 올바르게 배열하세요.

1
> 추리소설을 읽는 것은 나의 취미 중 하나이다.
> (is / reading / novels / mystery)

→ ________________________________

    one of my hobbies.

2
> 안전벨트를 착용하지 않는 것은 위험하다.
> (a seatbelt / dangerous / not / is / wearing)

→ ________________________________

________________________________ .

3
> 그의 직업은 새로운 웹사이트를 디자인하는 것이다.
> (is / a new website / his / designing / job)

→ ________________________________

________________________________ .

4
> Cathy는 그녀의 블로그를 새로운 게시물로 계속 업데이트한다.
> (with / updating / keeps / blog / Cathy / new posts / her)

→ ________________________________

________________________________ .

[5-8] 우리말과 일치하도록 주어진 단어를 사용하여 문장을 완성하세요. (필요시 형태를 바꿀 것)

5
> 그는 토요일까지 그의 방을 청소하는 것을 미뤘다.
> (clean, put off, room)

→ ________________________________

________________________________ until Saturday.

6
> 이야기를 쓰는 것은 여러분의 창의력을 키우는 데 도움이 됩니다.
> (stories, writing, to build, help)

→ ________________________________

________________________________ your creativity.

7
> 나는 내년 유럽 여행을 위해 돈을 모으기 시작했다.
> (save, begin, a trip, money, for)

→ ________________________________

________________________________ to Europe next year.

8
> 우리는 식당에 예약했던 것을 잊어버렸다.
> (a reservation, make, forget)

→ ________________________________

________________________________ at the restaurant.

9 다음 대화를 읽고 〈조건〉에 맞게 우리말을 영작하세요.

> A: I'm struggling with this puzzle. It's really difficult.
> B: 한 번에 한 구역에만 집중하려고 노력해 봐.
>   It will be easier that way.

〈조건〉
- 6 단어로 쓸 것
- try, one section, focus on을 사용할 것

→ ________________________________

________________________________ at a time.

---

mystery novel 추리소설 update 업데이트하다 post 게시물; 우편 reservation 예약 struggle with ~을 해결하려고 애쓰다 section 구역 focus on ~에 집중하다
at a time 한 번에

Unit 02

자주 쓰이는 동명사 표현

[1-4] 우리말과 일치하도록 주어진 단어를 올바르게 배열하세요.

1
> 내 여동생은 풍경화를 그리는 것을 잘한다.
> (landscapes / good / painting / at / is)

→ My sister ______________________________

______________________________ .

2
> 그는 아침 일찍 그의 친구들과 함께 하이킹하러 갔다.
> (friends / hiking / with / went / his)

→ He ______________________________

______________________ early in the morning.

3
> 주말 동안 내 반려견들을 돌봐줘서 고마워.
> (you / pet dogs / my / thank / taking care of / for)

→ ______________________________

______________________ over the weekend.

4
> 나는 연극부에 가입함으로써 많은 새로운 친구들을 사귀었다.
> (joining / many / made / the drama club / by / new friends)

→ I ______________________________

______________________________ .

[5-8] 우리말과 일치하도록 주어진 단어를 사용하여 문장을 완성하세요. (필요시 형태를 바꿀 것)

5
> 나의 조부모님은 우리를 곧 보기를 기대하신다.
> (see, forward, grandparents, look)

→ ______________________________

______________________________ soon.

6
> 그 제빵사는 매일 케이크를 장식하는 데 오랜 시간을 보낸다.
> (hours, cakes, decorate, spend, the baker)

→ ______________________________

______________________________ every day.

7
> 나는 불을 끄지 않고 방을 나왔다.
> (the lights, the room, turn off, without, leave)

→ ______________________________

____

8
> 그녀는 사람들의 이름을 기억하는 데 어려움을 겪는다.
> (trouble, people's names, have, remember)

→ ______________________________

____

9 다음 글을 읽고 〈조건〉에 맞게 우리말을 영작하세요.

> Billy and I first met in the school band. We both enjoy talking about different music genres. I play the guitar, and <u>그는 노래하는 것에 관심이 있다.</u> We have the same goal. We both want to become musicians in the future.

〈조건〉
• 5 단어로 쓸 것
• sing, interested를 사용할 것

→ I play the guitar, and ______________________

______________________________ .

---

landscape 풍경 drama 연극; (텔레비전 등의) 드라마, 극 hours (복수형) 오랜 시간 decorate 장식하다 baker 제빵사 genre 장르

Unit 03  분사

정답 및 해설 p.31

○── 배열 영작

[1-5] 우리말과 일치하도록 주어진 단어를 올바르게 배열하세요. (필요시 형태를 바꿀 것)

1
> 나는 내 실수에 대해 당황스러움을 느꼈다.
> (felt / mistake / I / about / embarrass / my)

→ _______________________________

_______________________________.

2
> 그들은 공원에서 잃어버린 개를 찾았다.
> (miss / dog / found / they / the)

→ _______________________________

_______________________ in the park.

3
> 그 실험의 결과는 놀라웠다.
> (the experiment / surprise / the result / of / was)

→ _______________________________

_______________________________.

4
> 내 친구에 의해 쓰여진 편지가 오늘 도착했다.
> (write / today / friend / by / arrived / my / the letter)

→ _______________________________

_______________________________.

5
> 그의 실망스러운 행동은 그의 부모님을 화나게 만들었다.
> (his / made / upset / behavior / disappoint / his / parents)

→ _______________________________

_______________________________.

○── 주어진 단어로 영작

[6-8] 우리말과 일치하도록 주어진 단어를 사용하여 문장을 완성하세요. (필요시 형태를 바꿀 것)

6
> 그녀의 연설은 아주 감동적이었다.
> (touch, speech, very, be)

→ _______________________________

7
> 그 선생님은 학생들의 창의력에 놀랐다.
> (the teacher, creativity, by, the students', amaze, be)

→ _______________________________

____

8
> 그는 해변 근처에 지어진 집으로 이사했다.
> (the beach, the house, near, move to, build)

→ _______________________________

____

기출: 대화문 완성

9 우리말과 일치하도록 주어진 단어를 사용하여 다음의 대화를 완성하세요.

> A: (1) <u>너 짜증나 보인다.</u> What's the problem?
> B: (2) <u>옆집의 시끄러운 음악이 정말 짜증나.</u>
> A: I can hear it too.
> B: Yeah, it's hard to focus on anything!

(1) _______________________________

(annoy, seem)

(2) _______________________________

____

(annoy, next door, be, the loud music, really)

---

experiment 실험 result 결과 behavior 행동 speech 연설 focus on ~에 집중하다 annoy 짜증나게 하다 seem ~처럼 보이다, ~인 것 같다 loud 시끄러운, (소리가) 큰

[1-4] 우리말과 일치하도록 주어진 단어를 올바르게 배열하세요.

1

> 놀이공원에서 노는 것은 아주 재미있다.
> (the amusement park / at / fun / is / playing / very)

→ ________________________________

________________________________.

2

> 미나는 그녀의 숙제를 하기 위해 일찍 집에 왔다.
> (homework / to / came / do / home / early / her)

→ Mina ________________________________

________________________________.

3

> 시청에 어떻게 가는지 저에게 알려주시겠어요?
> (how / get / City Hall / to / me / to / tell)

→ Can you ________________________________

________________________________?

4

> Ann은 주스 한 병을 사는 데 오천 원을 썼다.
> (a bottle of / spent / juice / five / buying / thousand / won)

→ Ann ________________________________

________________________________.

[5-7] 우리말과 일치하도록 주어진 단어를 사용하여 빈칸에 알맞은 말을 쓰세요. (필요시 단어를 추가하거나 형태를 바꿀 것)

5

> 그 탁자는 나무로 만들어진다. (make)

→ The table ____________ ____________

____________ wood.

6

> 진수는 오늘 오후에 집안일을 하느라 바빴다.
> (do, busy, housework)

→ Jinsu ____________ ____________

____________ this

afternoon.

7

> 내일까지 제 택배가 배달될 수 있을까요?
> (package, deliver)

→ Can ____________ ____________

____________ ____________ by

tomorrow?

[8-11] 우리말과 일치하도록 주어진 단어와 to부정사를 사용하여 문장을 완성하세요.

8

> Joe와 나는 서로에게 솔직하기로 약속했다.
> (promise, with, honest, be, each other)

→ Joe and I ________________________________

________________________________.

9

> 공원에는 앉을 벤치가 하나 있다. (a bench, there, sit)

→ ________________________________

in the park.

10

> 그녀는 나에게 그 책을 어디서 사야하는지 물었다.
> (ask, buy, the book, me, to)

→ She ________________________________.

11

> 그 방은 모든 손님들을 수용할 만큼 충분히 크다.
> (enough, all the guests, big, hold)

→ The room ________________________________

________________________________.

[12-16] 다음 문장이 능동태면 수동태로, 수동태면 능동태로 바꿔 쓰세요.

12 My father turned off the TV an hour ago.

→ ______________________________

______________________ an hour ago.

13 My writing skills will be improved by this book.

→ ______________________________

______________________________.

14 The invitation was not delivered by the mailman yesterday.

→ ______________________________

______________________ yesterday.

15 Do the students speak English during the class?

→ ______________________________

during the class?

16 He gave his sons some money.

→ Some money ______________________

______________________________.

[17-18] 우리말과 일치하도록 주어진 단어와 가주어 It을 사용하여 문장을 완성하세요.

17

그 시를 이해하는 것은 어렵다.
(the poem, understand, hard)

→ ______________________________

18

패스트푸드를 너무 자주 먹는 것은 좋지 않다.
(eat, good, very often, fast food)

→ ______________________________

____

[19-20] 다음 두 문장을 〈보기〉와 같이 분사를 사용하여 한 문장으로 연결해 쓰세요.

〈보기〉
Dad gave me a bicycle.
It was made in Italy.
→ Dad gave me a bicycle made in Italy.

19

Susan is staying at the hotel.
It is located downtown.

→ ______________________________

____

20

Look at the old lady.
She is watering the flowers.

→ ______________________________

고난도

[21-23] 주어진 문장과 같은 의미가 되도록 괄호 안의 지시대로 문장을 바꿔 쓰세요.

21

My father was so tired that he couldn't pick me up after school.
(「too ~ to부정사」 구문을 사용할 것)

→ ______________________________

____

22

Jisu studied so hard that she could pass the exam. (「enough + to부정사」 구문을 사용할 것)

→ ______________________________

23

Nick is too sleepy to concentrate on the class. (「so ~ that」 구문을 사용할 것)

→ ______________________________

____

[24-27] 다음 각 문장에서 어법상 **틀린** 부분을 찾아 바르게 고쳐 쓰세요.

24 I don't mind visit the museum again next week.

_________________ → _________________

25 This letter was sent for me by my grandfather.

_________________ → _________________

26 You should be careful to not make the same mistakes.

_________________ → _________________

27 Mom forgot to buy milk yesterday. She bought one more today.

_________________ → _________________

고난도

[28-31] 빈칸에 들어갈 알맞은 말을 〈보기〉에서 골라 분사 형태로 바꿔 쓰세요. (단, 한 번씩만 사용할 것)

〈보기〉
excite   touch   shock   interest

28 Dongmin is _____________ in science. He reads a lot of science books. Becoming a scientist is his dream.

29 In the morning, I saw many ambulances on the road. There was a big accident! It was very _____________ to me.

30 I'm waiting for this Friday. My father and I will go camping. I'm really _____________ about it.

31 I saw a movie last weekend with my family. I cried during the movie because it was very _____________.

32 지난주 학교 축제를 맞아 학생들이 했던 일에 관한 표를 보고, 수동태를 사용하여 각 문장을 완성하세요.

The School Festival	
Minhee	welcome the visitors
Suji	hold a quiz show
Dongho	sell food and soft drinks
Nami	conduct the school orchestra

(1) _____________________________ by Minhee.

(2) _____________________________ by Suji.

(3) _____________________________ by Dongho.

(4) _____________________________ by Nami.

고난도

33 다음 글을 읽고 ⓐ~ⓔ 중 어법상 **틀린** 세 개를 찾아 그 기호를 쓰고, 바르게 고쳐 쓰세요.

> Yena's family moved to Daegu three years ago. They ⓐ were invited to her relatives' house, so they will visit Seoul next month.
> Yena considered meeting her old friends there. She ⓑ remembered to have a good time with them in elementary school. She called them and decided ⓒ to spend one day having fun together. Yena was ⓓ excited seeing them again. Yena and her friends will visit a popular restaurant. It ⓔ is known to its Korean barbecue.

_________ → _______________________

_________ → _______________________

_________ → _______________________

Unit 01 + 대명사

[1-3] 우리말과 일치하도록 주어진 단어를 올바르게 배열하세요.

1

제가 차를 준비하는 동안 편하게 있으세요.
(home / at / make / yourself)

→ Please ________________________

________________ while I prepare some tea.

2

몇몇 사람들은 커피를 좋아하고, 다른 몇몇은 차를 선호한다.
(coffee / others / prefer / like / people / some / tea)

→ ____________________________,

and ________________________.

3

나의 엄마는 세 가지 요리를 만드셨다. 하나는 수프, 또 다른 하나는 샐러드, 나머지 하나는 파스타였다.
(the other / pasta / was / salad / soup / was / another / one / was)

→ My mom made three dishes. ____________

________,________________

and ________________.

[4-7] 우리말과 일치하도록 주어진 단어를 사용하여 문장을 완성하세요. (필요시 단어를 추가하거나 형태를 바꿀 것)

4

나는 가장 친한 친구 두 명이 있다. 한 명은 서울에 살고, 다른 한 명은 부산에 산다.
(live, in Busan, in Seoul)

→ I have two best friends.

________________, and

________________.

5

시험의 모든 문제가 어려웠다.
(on the exam, difficult, question, be, every)

→ ________________________

____

6

각 집은 다른 색으로 칠해져 있다.
(be painted, the houses, of)

→ ________________________

in a different color.

7

Smith 씨 부부는 직접 그 집을 꾸몄다.
(the house, decorate, Mr. and Ms. Smith)

→ ________________________

____

8 우리말과 일치하도록 〈조건〉에 맞게 문장을 완성하세요.

〈조건〉
• (1)은 4 단어, (2)는 6 단어로 쓸 것
• 주어진 단어를 사용하되 필요시 형태를 바꿀 것

(1)

지수는 '오늘 날이 정말 좋구나!'라고 속으로 생각했다. (think, Jisu, to)

→ ____________________________,

"What a nice day!"

(2)

각 나라는 고유한 전통을 가지고 있다.
(have, its own traditions, country)

→ ________________________

____

prefer 더 좋아하다, 선호하다 dish 요리 exam 시험 decorate 꾸미다, 장식하다 tradition 전통

Unit 02⁺ 형용사와 부사

정답 및 해설 p.33

배열 영작

[1-3] 우리말과 일치하도록 주어진 단어를 올바르게 배열하세요.

1
> 우리는 호숫가에서 평화로운 저녁을 즐겼다.
> (evening / we / a / enjoyed / peaceful)

→ ____________________________________

   by the lake.

2
> 우리는 학교 포스터를 디자인할 창의적인 누군가를
> 찾고 있다.
> (creative / are / we / someone / looking for)

→ ____________________________________

____________________ to design the school poster.

3
> 많은 학생들은 Brown 선생님의 수업이 도움이 된다는
> 것을 알게 되었다.
> (Mr. Brown's lesson / found / many / helpful
> / students)

→ ____________________________________

____________________________________.

주어진 단어로 영작

[4-5] 우리말과 일치하도록 주어진 단어를 사용하여 문장을
완성하세요.

4
> 나는 때때로 주말에 미술관을 방문한다.
> (art galleries, visit)

→ ____________________________________

   on weekends.

5
> 엄마는 퇴근 후 보통 피곤해하신다.
> (after work, tired, Mom, be)

→ ____________________________________

보기에서 골라 영작

[6-8] 우리말과 일치하도록 〈보기〉에서 알맞은 말을 골라 주어진
단어를 사용하여 문장을 완성하세요.
(단, 한 번씩만 쓸 것)

> 〈보기〉 much   few   little

6
> 어젯밤에는 비가 거의 안 왔다.
> (be, rain, there, last night)

→ ____________________________________

____

7
> 우리는 그 행사에 대한 정보가 많이 없다.
> (information, have, don't)

→ ____________________________________

____________________________ about the event.

8
> 과학 박람회에 학생들이 거의 참석하지 않았다.
> (the science fair, students, attend)

→ ____________________________________

기출: 도표 영작

9 Sam과 Hailey의 잠자리 습관을 나타내는 표를 보고,
〈보기〉에서 알맞은 말을 골라 문장을 완성하세요.

	Sam	Hailey
(1) be in bed before 10 p.m.	every night	never
(2) read a book before bed	three times a week	once a week

> 〈보기〉 hardly   always

(1) Sam ____________________________________

(2) Hailey ____________________________________.

peaceful 평화로운 creative 창의적인 lesson 수업 gallery 미술관 fair 박람회 be in bed 잠자리에 들다

Unit 01

원급, 비교급, 최상급

배열 영작

[1-3] 우리말과 일치하도록 주어진 단어를 올바르게 배열하세요. (필요시 형태를 바꿀 것)

1
> Jane은 그녀의 언니만큼 똑똑하지는 않다.
> (as / is / her older sister / as / smart / not)

→ Jane ___________________________

___________________________ .

2
> 이 소설책은 저 잡지보다 더 두껍다.
> (that magazine / is / than / thick / this novel)

→ ___________________________

___________________________ .

3
> 오늘이 일 년 중 가장 더운 날이다.
> (of / today / hot / is / the year / day / the)

→ ___________________________

___________________________ .

주어진 단어로 영작

[4-7] 우리말과 일치하도록 주어진 단어를 사용하여 문장을 완성하세요.

4
> 호수의 물은 얼음만큼 차갑다.
> (ice, cold, as, be)

→ The lake water ___________________________

___________________________ .

5
> 이번 수학 시험은 지난번보다 훨씬 더 쉬웠다.
> (a lot, the last one, easy, be)

→ This math exam ___________________________

___________________________ .

6
> Nick은 그의 친구들보다 더 빨리 경주를 완주했다.
> (friends, quickly, the race, finish)

→ Nick ___________________________

___________________________ .

7
> 그녀는 합창단에서 가장 아름다운 목소리를 갖고 있다.
> (in, have, voice, the choir, beautiful)

→ She ___________________________

___________________________ .

어법 오류 수정

8 다음 각 문장의 밑줄 친 부분을 어법상 바르게 고쳐 쓰세요.

(1) He enjoys fishing <u>as many as</u> his dad does.

→ ___________________________

(2) The cheetah is one of <u>the fastest animal</u> on land.

→ ___________________________

기출: 도표 영작

9 다음 표를 보고 〈조건〉에 맞게 문장을 완성하세요.

	Seoul	Tokyo	Taipei
Today's Temperature	-10℃	3℃	13℃

〈조건〉
- (1)은 Tokyo, (2)는 Taipei의 날씨에 대해 쓸 것
- 주어진 단어를 사용할 것

(1) ___________________________
Seoul today. (cold, as)

(2) ___________________________
Seoul today. (than, warm, much)

---

magazine 잡지 throw 던지다 choir 합창단 cheetah 치타 on land 육지에서 temperature 기온, 온도

Unit 02 원급, 비교급을 이용한 표현

정답 및 해설 p.33

빈칸 완성

[1-5] 우리말과 일치하도록 주어진 단어를 사용하여 빈칸에 알맞은 말을 쓰세요. (필요시 형태를 바꿀 것)

1
> 네 숙제를 가능한 한 빨리 끝내라.
> (soon, as, possible)

→ Finish your homework _______________ _______________ _______________ _______________.

2
> 나의 누나는 새로운 직장 때문에 점점 더 바빠졌다.
> (and, busy)

→ My sister became _______________ _______________ _______________ with her new job.

3
> 네가 더 일찍 시작할수록, 너는 더 빨리 끝낼 수 있을 것이다. (early, soon)

→ _______________ _______________ you start, _______________ _______________ you'll finish.

4
> 이 도시의 교통 체증은 매일 아침 점점 더 악화되고 있다. (bad, and)

→ The traffic jam in this city is getting _______________ _______________ _______________ every morning.

5
> 그 호텔은 옆에 있는 건물보다 네 배만큼 더 높다. (tall, four times)

→ The hotel is _______________ _______________ _______________ the building next to it.

배열 영작

[6-8] 우리말과 일치하도록 주어진 단어를 올바르게 배열하세요.

6
> 그의 새집은 예전 집보다 세 배 더 넓다.
> (as / his new house / three times / as / wide / is / his old one)

→ _______________
_______________.

7
> 그 도시는 점점 더 혼잡해지고 있다.
> (crowded / is / more / and / getting / the city / more)

→ _______________
_______________.

8
> 네가 더 열심히 노력할수록, 너는 더 많이 성취할 수 있을 것이다.
> (work / you / will / more / harder / the / the / you / achieve)

→ _______________,
_______________.

기출: 조건 영작

9 다음 대화를 읽고 〈조건〉에 맞게 우리말을 영작하세요.

> A: Did you go to the new shopping mall?
> B: Yes, it's huge!
>   그것은 중심가에 있는 것보다 두 배만큼 더 커.
> A: Oh, really? I should check it out.

> 〈조건〉
> • as ~ as 표현을 사용할 것
> • large, the one을 사용해 쓸 것

→ It _______________
_______________ downtown.

---

traffic jam 교통 체증[정체] wide 넓은 crowded 혼잡한, 붐비는 achieve 성취하다, 달성하다 huge 큰, 거대한 check A out A를 확인하다 downtown 중심가에

Unit 01

and, but, or의 쓰임

○ 배열 영작

[1-3] 우리말과 일치하도록 주어진 단어를 올바르게 배열하세요.

1
선크림을 사용해라, 그렇지 않으면 너는 햇볕에 그을릴지도 모른다.
(get sunburned / you / sunscreen / use / might / or)

→ ________________________________,

________________________________.

2
내 부모님과 친구들 둘 다 내 결정을 지지한다.
(my parents / support / my friends / and / both / my decision)

→ ________________________________

________________________________.

3
그는 새로운 휴대 전화를 사거나 오래된 휴대 전화를 수리할 것이다.
(or / he / fix / a new phone / either / will / buy / the old one)

→ ________________________________

________________________________.

○ 주어진 단어로 영작

[4-8] 우리말과 일치하도록 주어진 단어를 사용하여 문장을 완성하세요. (필요시 단어를 추가하거나 형태를 바꿀 것)

4
목표를 세워라, 그러면 너는 네 꿈을 성취할 수 있을 것이다.
(your dreams, achieve, your goals, set, will)

→ ________________________________

____

5
Joshua와 Mary 둘 다 파티에 올 예정이다.
(be going to, to the party, come, both)

→ ________________________________

____

6
식전 음식으로 샐러드 또는 수프가 제공될 것이다.
(be served, the salad, the soup, will, either)

→ ________________________________

________________________ for the appetizer.

7
그 스웨터와 재킷 둘 다 나에게 잘 맞지 않는다.
(nor, the jacket, the sweater, fit)

→ ________________________________

________________________ well.

8
케이크뿐만 아니라 쿠키도 맛있었다.
(be, as well as, the cookies, the cake, tasty)

→ ________________________________

____

기출: 문장 전환

9 주어진 문장과 같은 의미의 문장이 되도록 〈조건〉에 맞게 바꿔 쓰세요.

My sister as well as I enjoys cooking.

〈조건〉
· not only ~ but also ...를 사용할 것
· 9 단어로 쓸 것

→ ________________________________

____

sunburned 햇볕에 그을린, 햇볕에 심하게 탄 support 지지하다, 지원하다 decision 결정 appetizer 식전 음식 fit (옷 등이) ~에게 맞다

Unit 02+ 부사절을 이끄는 접속사

○ 배열 영작

[1-2] 우리말과 일치하도록 주어진 단어를 올바르게 배열하세요.

1
나는 버스를 기다리는 동안 오래된 친구를 만났다.
(waiting for / was / the bus / while / I)

→ ________________________________
________________________, I met an old friend.

2
선생님이 지시사항을 전달한 후 학생들은 그들의
프로젝트에 착수하기 시작했다.
(the teacher / the instructions / gave / after)

→ The students started working on their
projects ________________________________
________________________________.

○ 보기에서 골라 영작

**[3-5] 우리말과 일치하도록 〈보기〉에서 알맞은 접속사를 골라
주어진 단어와 함께 문장을 완성하세요. (필요시 단어를
추가하거나 형태를 바꿀 것)**

〈보기〉
although   because   until

3
그는 교통 혼잡 시간을 피하고 싶어서 일찍 떠났다.
(the rush hour, to avoid, wanted)

→ He left early ________________________________
________________________________.

4
Zoe는 그녀의 숙제를 끝낼 때까지 잠자리에 들지 않을
것이다. (homework, finish)

→ Zoe won't go to bed ________________________________
________________________________.

5
비록 그녀는 고양이에 알레르기가 있지만, 고양이
한 마리를 입양했다.
(cats, be, allergic to)

→ ________________________________,
she adopted one.

○ 한 문장으로 영작

6
주어진 두 문장을 so ~ that ...을 사용하여 한 문장으로
바꿔 쓰세요.

(1)
The hot chocolate was very hot.
I burned my tongue.

→ ________________________________
____

(2)
The road was very icy.
My mom drove the car carefully.

→ ________________________________
____

○ 기출: 조건 영작

7 우리말과 일치하도록 〈조건〉에 맞게 문장을 완성하세요.

만약 당신이 표가 없으시다면, 당신은 입장할 수
없습니다.

〈조건〉
• 주어진 접속사로 시작할 것
• (1), (2) 모두 a ticket, have, enter를 사용할 것

(1) ________________________________
________________________________ (if)

(2) ________________________________
________________________________ (unless)

---

instruction 지시(사항) work on 착수하다 rush hour (출퇴근) 혼잡 시간대 allergic to ~에 대해 알레르기가 있는 tongue 혀 icy 얼음에 뒤덮인

Unit 03

명사절을 이끄는 접속사

배열 영작

[1-4] 우리말과 일치하도록 주어진 단어를 올바르게 배열하세요.

1
> 내가 문을 잠갔는지 기억이 나지 않는다.
> (the door / remember / if / locked / don't / I / I)

→ ________________________________ .

2
> 나는 모두가 서로를 존중해야 한다고 생각한다.
> (should / I / each other / that / everyone / respect / think)

→ ________________________________
________________________________ .

3
> 그녀가 작품에 많은 노력을 들인 것은 분명하다.
> (that / clear / effort / it / a lot of / put / is / she)

→ ________________________________
________________________________ into her work.

4
> 나는 누가 창문을 열어 두었는지 모른다.
> (left / the window / have / I / who / no idea / open)

→ ________________________________
________________________________ .

주어진 단어로 영작

[5-9] 우리말과 일치하도록 주어진 단어를 사용하여 문장을 완성하세요. (필요시 단어를 추가할 것)

5
> 나는 Harry가 내 사과를 받아줄 지 모르겠다.
> (apology, accept, will)

→ I'm not sure ________________________________
________________________________ .

6
> 그는 나에게 오늘 공항에 언제 도착할 지 말해 주지 않았다.
> (at, would arrive, the airport)

→ He didn't tell me ________________________________
________________________________ today.

7
> 너는 몇 분 전에 네 안경을 어디에 놓았는지 기억하니?
> (glasses, remember, put)

→ Do you ________________________________
________________________________ a few minutes ago?

8
> 네가 왜 회의에 나타나지 않았는지 설명해줄 수 있니?
> (didn't, the meeting, show up, explain, to)

→ Can you ________________________________
________________________________ ?

9
> 그는 아빠의 조언이 매우 도움이 되었다는 것을 깨달았다.
> (very, his dad's, realized, helpful, was, advice)

→ ________________________________
________________________________ .

기출: 한 문장으로 영작

10 주어진 두 문장을 〈보기〉와 같이 한 문장으로 바꿔 쓰세요.

> 〈보기〉
> I wonder. + How does the machine work?
> → I wonder how the machine works.

> I don't know. + Why did he cancel the plan?

→ ________________________________
____

respect 존중하다; 존경하다   put effort into ~에 노력을 기울이다   apology 사과, 사죄   accept 받아들이다   show up (예정된 곳에) 나타나다

Chapter 10 관계대명사

who, which, that

배열 영작

[1-4] 우리말과 일치하도록 주어진 단어를 올바르게 배열하세요.

1 그녀는 나의 생명을 구해주신 의사 선생님이다.
(saved / who / my / the doctor / life)

→ She is ___________________

___________________ .

2 우리는 투어를 이끌어준 가이드에게 감사의 인사를 전했다.
(led / the guide / the tour / who)

→ We thanked ___________________

___________________ .

3 그는 내게 신상품인 그의 스마트폰을 보여주었다.
(that / his / brand new / is / smartphone)

→ He showed me ___________________

___________________ .

4 상을 수상한 그 영화는 내일 개봉할 예정이다.
(the award / won / which / the movie)

→ ___________________

___________________ will release tomorrow.

주어진 단어로 영작

[5-8] 우리말과 일치하도록 주어진 단어와 관계대명사를 사용하여 문장을 완성하세요. (단, that은 제외)

5 그녀는 초록색 눈을 가진 고양이 한 마리를 키운다.
(green eyes, a cat, have, raise)

→ ___________________

____

6 그 가게를 운영하는 매니저는 친절하다.
(the manager, friendly, run, be, the store)

→ ___________________

____

7 Hazel은 그녀에게 완벽하게 맞는 드레스를 발견했다.
(a dress, fit, find)

→ ___________________

___________________ perfectly.

8 관광객들은 두 도시를 연결하는 그 다리를 방문했다.
(connect, the bridge, visit, the two cities, tourists)

→ ___________________

____

기출 : 한 문장으로 영작

9 주어진 두 문장을 관계대명사를 사용하여 한 문장으로 바꿔 쓰세요. (단, that은 제외)

(1) The reporter interviewed the boy.
He won the competition.

→ ___________________

____

(2) The lamp is broken.
It lights the room.

→ ___________________

____

brand new 완전히 새것의, 신상품의 award 상 release 출시하다 run 운영하다 connect 연결하다 competition 대회; 경쟁 broken 고장 난; 깨진 light 밝히다; 빛

Unit 02

who(m), which, that

배열 영작

[1-2] 우리말과 일치하도록 주어진 단어를 올바르게 배열하세요.

1

> 그는 내가 가장 좋아하는 가수 겸 작곡가이다.
> (like / whom / the singer-songwriter / I)

→ He is ___________________________

___________________________ the most.

2

> 너는 내가 어제 추천해준 영화를 봤니?
> (which / recommended / yesterday / I /
> the movie)

→ Did you watch ___________________

___________________________ ?

한 문장으로 영작

[3-4] 주어진 두 문장을 〈보기〉와 같이 관계대명사를 사용하여 한 문장으로 바꿔 쓰세요. (단, that은 제외)

> 〈보기〉
> I lost the book.
> Justin lent it last week.
> → I lost the book which Justin lent last
>   week.

3

> Alice is the student.
> We elected her as school president.

→ Alice is ___________________________

___________________________ .

4

> The shoes finally arrived today.
> I ordered them online.

→ ___________________________

___________________________ finally arrived today.

주어진 단어로 영작

[5-7] 우리말과 일치하도록 주어진 단어와 관계대명사를 사용하여 문장을 완성하세요. (단, that은 제외)

5

> 나는 어제 네가 말했던 사람을 만났어.
> (mentioned, the person, yesterday, meet)

→ ___________________________

____

6

> 그녀가 파티를 위해 구워 온 케이크는 초콜릿 맛이었다.
> (baked, the cake, for the party, be)

→ ___________________________

___________________________ chocolate-flavored.

7

> 나의 형은 그가 더 이상 사용하지 않는 자전거를 팔았다.
> (the bike, use, sell, anymore, brother)

→ ___________________________

____

기출: 한 문장으로 영작

8 다음 두 문장을 〈조건〉에 맞게 한 문장으로 바꿔 쓰세요.

> I apologized to the girl.
> I accidentally pushed her.

> 〈조건〉
> • 9 단어로 쓸 것
> • 관계대명사를 사용할 것

→ ___________________________

____

---

singer-songwriter 가수 겸 작곡가 elect 선출하다 school president 학생회장 mention 말하다, 언급하다 chocolate-flavored 초콜릿 맛이 나는 apologize 사과하다 accidentally 실수로

Unit 03

whose, what

정답 및 해설 p.34

◯━ 배열 영작

[1-4] 우리말과 일치하도록 주어진 단어를 올바르게 배열하세요.

1
> 음식이 훌륭한 그 식당은 항상 붐빈다.
> (food / the restaurant / excellent / is / whose)

→ ________________________________

________________________ is always crowded.

2
> 공연이 환상적이었던 그 뮤지션은 내년에 서울을 다시 방문할 것이다.
> (performance / fantastic / the musician / whose / was)

→ ________________________________

________________ will visit Seoul again next year.

3
> Gia가 말한 것은 모두를 놀라게 했다.
> (Gia / said / what / everyone / surprised)

→ ____________________________ .

4
> 나는 부모님이 나를 위해 해주신 것에 감사드린다.
> (I / for me / did / appreciate / my parents / what)

→ ________________________________

____________________________ .

◯━ 주어진 단어로 영작

[5-8] 우리말과 일치하도록 주어진 단어와 관계대명사 whose 또는 what을 사용하여 문장을 완성하세요.

5
> 그녀가 요리해주는 것은 항상 맛있다.
> (delicious, cooks, always, tastes)

→ ________________________________

6
> 장난감이 부서진 그 아이는 울기 시작했다.
> (broken, the child, was, toy)

→ ________________________________

________________________ started crying.

7
> 나는 생일이 내일인 친구에게 전화를 걸었다.
> (tomorrow, birthday, the friend, be)

→ I called ________________________

________________________________ .

8
> 이 요리는 제가 주문한 것이 아니에요. 저는 파스타를 주문했어요.
> (ordered, this dish, be)

→ ________________________________

________________________ I ordered pasta.

◯ 기출: 조건 영작

9 우리말과 일치하도록 〈조건〉에 맞게 문장을 완성하세요.

> 자원봉사자들은 집이 파손된 사람들을 도왔다.

> 〈조건〉
> • 8 단어로 쓸 것
> • 관계대명사를 사용할 것
> • houses, be damaged, volunteers, help, the people을 사용할 것

→ ________________________________

---

performance 공연 fantastic 환상적인 appreciate 고마워하다 damage 손상을 주다, 훼손하다

[1-3] 우리말과 일치하도록 주어진 단어를 올바르게 배열하세요.

1

> Jason은 여름 방학 동안 할 재미있는 무언가를 찾고 있다.
> (something / looking for / Jason / fun / is)

→ _______________________________________
to do during the summer vacation.

2

> 비록 날씨가 추웠지만, 나는 공원에서 산책을 했다.
> (the weather / although / cold / was)

→ _______________________________________,
I took a walk in the park.

3

> 나는 그가 많이 아프다는 것을 믿을 수 없었다.
> (I / sick / that / believe / very / he / couldn't / was)

→ _______________________________________
_______________________________________ .

[4-6] 우리말과 일치하도록 주어진 단어를 사용하여 빈칸에 알맞은 말을 쓰세요. (필요시 단어를 추가하거나 형태를 바꿀 것)

4

> 그 여자는 우리가 가장 좋아하는 가수이다.
> (like, whom, the singer)

→ The woman is ___________ ___________
___________ ___________ ___________
the most.

5

> 내 남동생은 바퀴가 네 개인 자전거를 탄다.
> (four wheels, which, a bike, have)

→ My little brother rides ___________
___________ ___________ ___________
___________ ___________ .

6

> 너는 길에서 춤을 췄던 그 소년을 기억하니?
> (dance, who, on, the boy, the street)

→ Do you remember ___________
___________ ___________ ___________
___________ ___________ ?

[7-10] 우리말과 일치하도록 주어진 단어를 사용하여 문장을 완성하세요. (필요시 단어를 추가하거나 형태를 바꿀 것)

7

> 나는 누나가 두 명 있다. 한 명은 여기에 살고, 나머지 한 명은 외국에 산다.
> (here, abroad, lives, and)

→ I have two sisters. ___________
___________ ___________

8

> 모든 사람은 각자 다른 의견들을 가지고 있다.
> (every, have, opinions, person, different)

→ ___________________________________
____

9

> 영화 동아리는 우리 학교에서 가장 인기 있는 동아리 중 하나이다.
> (club, popular)

→ The movie club is ___________________
___________________________ in our school.

10

> 이 책이 너무 재미있어서 나는 그것을 두 번 읽었다.
> (read, that, interesting, twice)

→ This book was ___________________
___________________________ .

[11-14] 주어진 단어를 사용하여 각 대화를 완성하세요.

11
A: Who is older, Jackson or Brian?
B: Jackson is _______________ Brian.
  They are twins. (old, as)

12
A: How often do you keep a diary?
B: I _______________.
  (my diary, always)

13
A: How often is Jessie absent from school?
B: She _______________.
  (hardly)

14
A: Where do you want to sit?
B: Let's sit on that sofa. It looks _______________
  _______________ the chair.
  (comfortable, a lot)
A: Okay.

[15-18] 주어진 두 문장을 〈보기〉와 같이 한 문장으로 바꿔 쓰세요.

〈보기〉
Do you know?
Why is Matt really happy now?
→ Do you know why Matt is really happy now?

15
Can you tell me?
Does Sam like ice cream?

→ _______________

____

16
Please tell me.
What time is it in Washington now?

→ _______________

____

17
Do you think?
What is she talking about?

→ _______________

____

18
Can you show me?
How did you make these delicious cookies?

→ _______________

____

19 다음 표를 보고 〈보기〉의 단어와 비교 표현을 사용하여 문장을 완성하세요.

	Starting Year	Members	Fans
Group A	2023	4	3,000
Group B	2020	7	6,000
Group C	2018	7	100,000

〈보기〉 large   early   popular

(1) Group A didn't start _______________
  _______________ Group B.

(2) The number of members in Group B is
  ____
  the number of members in Group C.

(3) Group C is _______________
  _______________ of the three.

20 My mom put too many sugar in her coffee.

_______________ → _______________

21 I can introduce me to foreigners in English.

_______________ → _______________

22 Tim loves both playing baseball and watch baseball games.

_______________ → _______________

23 The movie whom we saw yesterday was interesting.

_______________ → _______________

24 I told my parents about the woman who I helped her after school.

_______________ → _______________

25 I will let you know if I will receive a reply from him tomorrow.

_______________ → _______________

26 Minho went to bed late because of he had too much homework.

_______________ → _______________

27 Do you know the boy whom is walking with a dog?

_______________ → _______________

[28-30] 우리말과 일치하도록 각 〈조건〉에 맞게 문장을 완성하세요.

28

〈조건〉
- 관계대명사를 쓸 것
- 다음 문장을 활용할 것
  The girl's dream is to be a pianist.

꿈이 피아니스트인 그 여자아이는 매일 피아노를 연습한다.

→ The girl _______________________

____________ practices the piano every day.

29

〈조건〉
- 관계대명사를 쓸 것
- 다음 문장을 활용할 것
  I planned to visit the Art Gallery.

내가 방문하려고 계획했던 그 미술관은 내가 그곳에 도착했을 때 닫혀 있었다.

→ The Art Gallery _________________

____

was closed when I got there.

30

〈조건〉
- 관계대명사를 생략할 것
- 다음 문장을 활용할 것
  Sophia wanted to eat Bibimbap.

비빔밥은 Sophia가 먹고 싶어 했던 전통 한국 음식이다.

→ Bibimbap is a traditional Korean food

______________________________ .

[31-33] 주어진 문장과 같은 의미가 되도록 빈칸에 알맞은 말을 쓰세요.

31
> Because the furniture was so heavy, we couldn't lift it.

→ The furniture was ____________

____________ ____________ we

____________ ____________ it.

32
> Nancy is good at cooking as well as drawing.

→ Nancy is good at ____________

____________ ____________ ____________

____________ ____________.

33
> The restaurant is famous for low prices. It's also famous for its great taste.

→ The restaurant is famous for ____________

____________ ____________ ____________

____________ ____________.

34 다음 글을 읽고 각 밑줄 친 부분을 〈조건〉에 맞게 바꿔 쓰세요.

> I'll introduce the book, *The Little Prince*. (1) This is a story about a little boy. The writer met him in a desert. The boy is the Little Prince. (2) He told a story about a rose. He loved it a lot. He also told about the fox which changed because of his love. The boy and the fox became friends.
>
> 〈조건〉
> 관계대명사를 사용하여 두 문장을 한 문장으로 바꿀 것

(1) This is a story about a little boy ____________

____________________________________.

(2) He told a story about a rose ____________

____________________________________.

35 다음 글을 읽고 주어진 단어를 사용하여 문맥에 맞게 각 빈칸에 알맞은 말을 쓰세요.

> My name is Amy. I have a twin sister. Her name is Tracy. We are both good at dancing. My friends like us and want to hang out with us.
>
> However, the situation changed after the school dance contest. My sister won the contest, and she got (1) ____________ ____________________________. After that, all my friends think Tracy (2) ____________ ____________________________ I do.
>
> I want to dance (3) ____________________ ____________________ Tracy. I practice dancing hard these days. I think (4) ____________ ____________, ____________________________.

(1) ____________________________________
(popular, more, and)

(2) ____________________________________
(well, dance, than)

(3) ____________________________________
(well, as)

(4) ____________________________________,

____________________________________.
(dance, much, can, the, practice, well)

쎄듀 초·중등 커리큘럼

초등 (예비초 / 초1 / 초2 / 초3 / 초4 / 초5 / 초6)

구문
- 천일문 365 일력 |초1-3| 교육부 지정 초등 필수 영어 문장
- 개정 초등 천일문 SENTENCE 1 / 2 / 3 — 1001개 통문장 암기로 완성하는 초등 영어의 기초

문법
- 왓츠 Grammar — Start (초등 기초 영문법) / Plus (초등 영문법 마무리)

독해
- 왓츠 리딩 30 40 / 50 / 60 / 70 / 80 / 90 / 100 — 쉽고 재미있게 완성되는 영어 독해력

어휘
- 개정 초등 천일문 VOCA&STORY — 한 권으로 끝내는 초등 필수 영단어 1000개
- 패턴으로 말하는 초등 필수 영단어 1 / 2 — 문장 패턴으로 완성하는 초등 필수 영단어

ELT
- Oh! My PHONICS 1 / 2 / 3 / 4 — 유·초등학생을 위한 첫 영어 파닉스
- Oh! My SPEAKING 1 / 2 / 3 / 4 / 5 / 6 — 핵심 문장 패턴으로 더욱 쉬운 영어 말하기
- Oh! My GRAMMAR 1 / 2 / 3 — 쓰기로 완성하는 첫 초등 영문법

중등 (예비중 / 중1 / 중2 / 중3)

구문
- 천일문 STARTER 1 / 2 — 중등 필수 구문 & 문법 총정리

문법
- 천일문 중등 GRAMMAR LEVEL 1 / 2 / 3 — 예문 중심 문법 기본서
- GRAMMAR Q Starter 1, 2 / Intermediate 1, 2 / Advanced 1, 2 — 학기별 문법 기본서
- 잘 풀리는 영문법 1 / 2 / 3 — 문제 중심 문법 적용서
- GRAMMAR PIC 1 / 2 / 3 / 4 — 이해가 쉬운 도식화된 문법서
- 1센치 영문법 — 1권으로 핵심 문법 정리

문법+어법
- 개정 미리 수능 영어 문법·어법 1, 2 *첫단추 BASIC 개정 — 중학생을 위한 수능 문법·어법 입문

문법+쓰기
- EGU 영단어&품사 / 문장 형식 / 동사 써먹기 / 문법 써먹기 / 구문 써먹기 — 서술형 기초 세우기와 문법 다지기

쓰기
- 개정 천일문 중등 WRITING LEVEL 1 / 2 / 3 *거침없이 Writing 개정 — 중등 교과서 내신 기출 서술형
- 중학 영어 쓰작 1 / 2 / 3 — 중등 교과서 패턴 드릴 서술형

어휘
- 개정 천일문 VOCA 중등 스타트 / 필수 / 마스터 — 2800개 중등 3개년 필수 어휘
- 개정 어휘끝 중학 필수편 — 중학 필수어휘 1000개
- 개정 어휘끝 중학 마스터편 — 고난도 중학어휘 +고등기초 어휘 1000개

독해
- ReadingGraphy LEVEL 1 / 2 / 3 / 4 / 신간 5 / 신간 6 — 중·고등 필수 구문까지 잡는 흥미로운 소재 독해
- Reading Relay Starter 1, 2 / Challenger 1, 2 / Master 1, 2 — 타교과 연계 배경 지식 독해
- READING Q Starter 1, 2 / Intermediate 1, 2 / Advanced 1, 2 — 예측/추론/요약 사고력 독해

독해전략
- 리딩 플랫폼 1 / 2 / 3 — 논픽션 지문 독해

독해유형
- Reading 16 LEVEL 1 / 2 / 3 — 수능 유형 맛보기 + 내신 대비
- 개정 미리 수능 영어 기초 독해 / 유형 독해 *첫단추 BASIC 개정 — 중학생을 위한 수능 독해 입문

듣기
- Listening Q 유형편 / 1 / 2 / 3 — 유형별 듣기 전략 및 실전 대비
- 쎄듀 빠르게 중학영어듣기 모의고사 1 / 2 / 3 — 교육청 듣기평가 대비